Success in
INVEST

FOURTH EDITION

Success Studybooks

Accounting and Costing
Accounting and Costing: Problems and Projects
Book-keeping and Accounts
British History 1760–1914
British History since 1914
Business Calculations
Chemistry
Commerce
Commerce: West African Edition
Communication
Economic Geography
Economics
Economics: West African Edition
Electronics
Elements of Banking
European History 1815–1941
Geography: Human and Regional
Geography: Physical and Mapwork
Information Processing
Insurance
Investment
Law
Management: Personnel
Nutrition
Office Practice
Organic Chemistry
Physics
Principles of Accounting
Principles of Accounting: Answer Book
Principles of Catering
Statistics
Twentieth Century World Affairs
World History since 1945

Success in
INVESTMENT
FOURTH EDITION

R. G. Winfield, BSc (Econ), FCIB
Director of Banking Studies
City of London Polytechnic

and

S. J. Curry, MA
Principal Lecturer in Finance and Investment
Birmingham Polytechnic

Typeset in 9/11 pt Times by
Wearside Tradespools, Fulwell, Sunderland.
Printed in England by Clays Ltd, St Ives plc.

British Library Cataloguing in Publication Data
Winfield, R. G. (Roderick George)
  Success in investment.–4th. ed.–(Success study books).
  1. Great Britain. Investment
  I. Title II. Curry, S. J. (Stephen James) III. Series
  332.60941

ISBN 0–7195–4966–3

Contents

Foreword to fourth edition

Books on investment tend to fall into two categories. The first are the 'lightweights' – chattily readable but limited in scope; the second are the 'heavies' – theoretical, full of mathematical formulae and mainly for the specialist. In *Success in Investment* we have tried to arrive at a midpoint between the two, combining readability with instruction in a book designed to be of maximum practical help to its readers.

Investment is a wide subject touching many areas of business activity. We have therefore had to be selective and to concentrate on main topics that are relevant. We visualize three types of reader: first, the person who has money to invest and wants information on the investment scene today and the different kinds of investment that are available; second, the professional person, not an investment expert, who needs to be informed enough to give sound general advice to clients; third, the student working for professional qualifications.

In this book we aim to provide a comprehensive treatment of investment, integrating theory and practice, bearing in mind the changes of recent years. In the 1950s and 60s there was an important shift in the preference of investors from fixed-interest securities to equities, and new forms of investment, particularly those based on insurance, became popular. In the 1970s, investors increasingly became aware of the problems of inflation and sought other forms of investment: index-linking and floating interest rates were introduced and competition for investment funds was intensified. Alternative forms of investment in real assets, such as stamps, furniture, and wine, also flourished. The 1980s began with a period of recession, but with a falling rate of inflation and the privatization of certain public utilities there was a renewed interest in gilts and equities, with share indices reaching new highs not only in the UK but worldwide, before crashing dramatically on 'Black Monday' – 19 October 1987. By the early 1990s in the UK share prices had recovered, but there was the problem of an upturn in the rate of inflation.

Although the day-to-day workings of the financial world fluctuate continually, basic structures and principles do not. In this book we keep these structures and principles in full focus, but it is frequently necessary to quote specific examples and readers must be on their guard about changes in interest rates, taxation, Government policy and legislation. For this new edition, the text has been thoroughly revised and updated to take into account recent developments in the world of investment, such as the major changes to the broking/dealing system – the so-called 'Big Bang' – which took place in October 1986, the Social Security Act 1986, the Financial Services Act 1986, the Building Societies Act 1986, the Banking Act 1987, and the Finance Act 1990, including the introduction of independent personal taxation. Most tables and statistics have also been brought up to date. It is essential for students of investment to keep abreast of changes by reading the financial columns of the press as well as specialist periodicals such as the *Investors Chronicle* and *Money Management*.

Success in investment depends on being aware of the opportunities available at a given time, and taking full advantage of them. There is no royal road to getting rich quickly, but anyone who understands the main principles and knows the pitfalls and risks is well on the way to making the most of whatever resources are available.

Students on business or professional courses will find the text covers syllabus requirements of The Chartered Institute of Bankers Banking Diploma paper 'Investment' and The Securities Industry Examination papers 'Investment analysis' and 'Private client investment advice and management', and the questions in the book are mainly taken from past examinations set for these, indicated by 'CIB' and 'SIE' respectively. (These have been revised and updated where necessary. As from 1991, the Stage 2 Diplomas – Banking, International Banking and Trustee – were replaced by the Associateship Examinations, which comprise four compulsory core papers and a selection of option papers, of which candidates have to complete four successfully before being eligible for election to Associate status.) It also covers investment and finance aspects of the examinations for the Institute of Chartered Accountants, the Chartered Institute of Management Accountants, the Chartered Association of Certified Accountants, the Chartered Insurance Institute, the Institute of Chartered Secretaries and Administrators, the Society of Investment Analysts, the Business & Technician Education Council National and Higher National Certificates and Diplomas, and degrees in accountancy and business studies.

R.G.W. and S.J.C.

Acknowledgements

In writing the four editions of this book we have been helped by many people, especially those who appraised and criticized it at different stages. We are grateful to Peter Roots, author of the original *Success in Investment*. For this fourth edition we are particularly grateful for help from Brian Watson, formerly of Midland Bank Trust Company, Robin Dix of SIB, Mark Brown of UBS Phillips & Drew, and the staff of the Stock Exchange Investor Research and Education Unit. Our thanks also go to our colleagues at the Polytechnics of Birmingham and City of London. Needless to say, errors of commission and omission remain entirely ours.

Our thanks go to our wives – Linda Curry, who typed the manuscript, and Margaret Winfield – and to editors Janice Brown and Bob Davenport for their unstinting patience and support.

Finally thanks to friends at Birmingham Squash Rackets Club who helped one of the authors release the frustrations of apparently endless revisions of the text!

R.G.W. and S.J.C.

The authors and publishers wish to thank the following for permission to reproduce the material indicated, and other sources which are acknowledged in individual source lines within the text:

BAA plc   Fig 12.2
Barclays de Zoete Wedd Securities Ltd   Figs 4.1, 4.2 and 5.1; Tables 6.1 and 6.5
British Aerospace plc   Fig 7.2
The Chartered Institute of Bankers for questions at the ends of units
Datastream International   Fig 10.3; Table 8.1
Extel Financial Ltd   Fig 9.3
Financial Times   Figs 8.1, 8.2, 8.3, 8.5 and 10.5; Tables 6.4, 10.2, 10.3, 11.1, 13.1, 18.2, 19.2, 19.4 and 19.5
Healey and Baker Research Services   Fig 20.1
Hertzog Hollander Phillips & Co.   Fig 20.3
The Controller, HMSO   Figs 1.1 and 20.1; Tables 1.1, 1.2, 1.3, 1.4, 4.1 and 16.1

International Stock Exchange, London   Figs 14.3 and 14.4; Tables 5.1, 7.1
   and 11.2
Investment Research, Cambridge   Figs 9.6 and 9.7
Macmillan Press Ltd   Tables 6.2 and 6.3
Merrill Lynch Europe Ltd   cover photograph
Midland Montagu Research   Fig 6.1
Money Management   Tables 16.3 and 18.3
NatWest Stockbrokers   Figs 9.4 and 10.3
Planned Savings   Table 17.2
The Securities Association for questions at the ends of units taken from the
   'Private client investment advice and management' exam papers of the
   Securities Industry Examination

1 Investors and investment

1.1 What is investment?

The Multinational Motor Company puts money into developing a new small car. Gushing Oil Incorporated spends millions of pounds in North Sea oil exploration. The Government decides it must step up its road building programme. At the same time Smith is buying Perfect Paints International ordinary shares, Jones is subscribing for Government gilt-edged securities, while Sykes opts for additional life assurance as the means of saving some of his increased salary.

What all these actions have in common is that they are all forms of investment. Each involves the sacrifice of something now for the prospect of something later. This means that individually, as a company, or as a country we forgo the consumption of goods today in order to achieve greater consumption in the future. The essence of investment is *time*, and also *risk*. The sacrifice takes place first and is unavoidable; the returns come later – if at all – and their magnitude is uncertain. (There is an apocryphal story of two German brothers during the latter days of the Weimar Republic. One was honest and sober; the other wayward and drunken. The former put his savings into bonds which were wiped out by inflation; the latter made a million on his 'empties'.)

With some types of investment, such as Government securities, the time aspect predominates, because future returns are absolutely certain in money terms (or as certain as anything can be). With others, such as options or warrants – which are sometimes not much more than a gamble on the price of the shares going up or down – the element of risk is dominant. Often both time and risk are important, as with ordinary shares, for instance.

1.2 The investment process

It is useful to distinguish between investment in 'real' things, such as buildings, plant and machinery, and houses or hospitals, and various types of 'paper' investment. This distinction is not made in any pejorative sense; it does not imply that 'paper' investment is any less valuable to the community.

In a highly industrialized economy, such as that of the United Kingdom, most industrial investment is undertaken by large-scale public and private business enterprises, but a significant proportion of the savings necessary to finance such investment comes from private persons. For example, if a company wished to undertake an expansion programme, it could use its own savings (retained earnings and depreciation allowances) to finance the programme, but it might also raise funds from the general public by offering securities, like shares or debentures. Anyone buying this kind of offering would be acquiring a *financial asset*. In effect, the financial asset would be a claim on the future income from the underlying *real assets* financed by these savings. New financial investment is frequently a prerequisite for 'real' investment in the economy.

More often than not nowadays, a *financial intermediary* intervenes between the ultimate saver and the ultimate borrower. For example, by buying a life assurance policy Sykes acquired a financial asset. He will pay the premiums to the life assurance company, which in turn might invest the proceeds in financial assets issued by companies and the Government. There may even be another link in the chain if the life assurance company invests in a unit trust or an investment trust.

Risk cannot be eliminated from business ventures, but financial claims can be packaged to cater for the different time and risk preferences of investors. For this reason companies and Governments rarely issue only one type of security. For example, those investors who desire low risk might choose a company's fixed-interest stock or preference shares, while those who are ready to accept a stronger element of risk might go for the ordinary shares. Thus different classes of financial asset appeal to different types of investor, even though they are all ultimately claims on the same real assets. Moreover, once 'real' investment is undertaken, it is difficult or impossible to 'undo' by withdrawing resources. But financial assets, if negotiable, provide a means by which the original investor can recover the use of his or her capital, while the original funds remain 'locked' in the project.

Most, but not all, personal investment is of the 'financial' type, the most obvious exception being the owner-occupied house. This is the biggest investment for most people, and in recent years probably the most profitable. But even here 'financial' investment plays a part. The outlay involved in house purchase is greater than most people can supply from past or current savings, so a large part of the required funds is usually provided by a mortgage. The building society provides one of the best examples of a financial intermediary at work. It creates short-term financial liabilities, by borrowing usually at relatively short notice, and acquires long-term financial assets by lending for periods of up to 25 years, or occasionally more. The short-term financial assets of one set of households (the lenders) are matched by the long-term financial liabilities of another set (the borrowers). Short-term lending finances long-term 'real' investment. The building society is willing to finance the borrower on terms that would not be acceptable to the original lender. It can do this only because of its ability to vary its borrowing and lending rates and because it holds sufficient *liquid assets* (assets which are in cash form, or which can be quickly turned into cash) to meet sudden withdrawals.

To sum up, saving inevitably implies investment, either direct 'real' investment or the *net acquisition of financial assets* (or the reduction in financial liabilities). Even a saver who, however unwisely, merely accumulates money in a current account at the bank, or keeps it under the proverbial mattress, is undertaking a form of financial investment. Incidentally, money should not be confused with *wealth*. Savings add to wealth, wealth being the net total of a person's assets and liabilities – real or financial. Sometimes money is used as a synonym for wealth, as in the famous aphorism that money, like muck, is no good unless well spread. Money, or cash, correctly understood, is merely the most liquid of financial assets, and only one component of overall wealth.

1.3 Who are the savers and borrowers?

Domestic savings in advanced industrialized societies come from:

(a) the *personal sector* (households and unincorporated businesses);
(b) the retained profits and depreciation allowances of *companies* in the private sector;
(c) the current surpluses of central *government*, local authorities, and the public corporations.

The net savers and investors are shown in Table 1.1.

Table 1.1 Financial surplus/deficit of different sectors of the UK economy, 1989

	Gross savings (£m)	Net savings (net acquisition of financial assets) (£m)
Personal sector	17 122	−9 519
Public sector	18 238	+7 592
Financial companies and institutions	21 871	+7 110
Industrial and commercial companies	34 417	−23 371
Overseas sector	—	+20 850
Balancing item		−2 662
		0

Source: *Economic Trends*, May 1990.

In this table, the items under *gross savings* are calculated before any deduction for depreciation, stock appreciation, and additions to reserves. The term *net acquisition of financial assets* equals savings less 'real' investment in fixed assets and physical working capital; for the overseas sector it equals the balance of payments current account surplus or deficit but with the sign reversed.

The term 'net acquisition of financial assets' represents the financial surplus, or deficit if negative, of a sector. It shows the extent to which a sector acquires financial assets in excess of financial liabilities during the year. A negative figure indicates that financial liabilities have been issued in excess of financial assets acquired.

Figure 1.1 and Table 1.1 illustrate the changing pattern of savings flows in

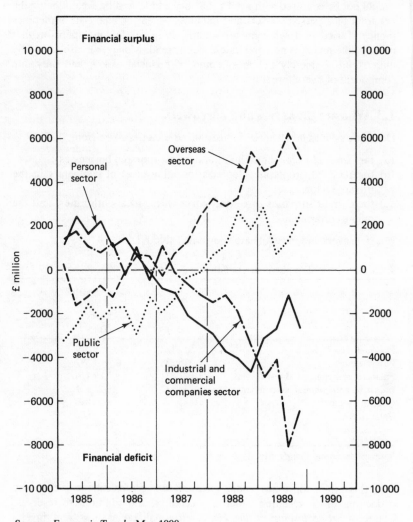

Source: *Economic Trends*, May 1990

Fig. 1.1   Sector financial surplus/deficit

the UK economy in the second half of the 1980s. The savings of the personal sector have declined in both gross and net terms. Gross savings have declined from £22.8 billion in 1985 to £17.1 billion in 1989, largely due to increasing levels of personal borrowing. At the 'net' level, the personal sector has traditionally run a financial surplus since the 1950s; but, due to heavy fixed investment, primarily in residential property, the sector moved into financial deficit in 1986.

Industrial and commercial companies' gross savings increased slightly – from £32.5 billion in 1984 to £34.4 billion in 1989 – but a faster growth in fixed investment resulted in this sector also moving into financial deficit in 1987.

Traditionally, the main deficit sector had been the public sector. The public sector – consisting of central and local government and the public corporations – was a particularly heavy borrower during the 1970s. From 1970 to 1979 the public-sector borrowing requirement (PSBR) averaged 6 per cent of gross domestic product, with a peak of $10\frac{1}{4}$ per cent in 1975–6. The Conservative Government came to power in 1979 committed to reducing the PSBR. By a combination of controlling the growth of public expenditure and privatizing certain public utilities, the Conservative Government managed to achieve a public-sector financial surplus in 1988 – the first time since 1969.

The financial companies and institutions sector was in financial surplus from 1985 to 1989. This primarily reflected the investment strategies of insurance companies and pension funds being orientated more towards financial assets, such as ordinary shares and Government securities, rather than 'real' assets such as property.

The overseas sector was transformed from a deficit sector in 1984–6 to a major surplus sector in 1989. This reflected the deterioration in the UK balance of payments current account. As a result, the UK became a substantial borrower from overseas.

Strictly speaking, the sector surpluses and deficits should sum to zero, because for every borrower there must be a counterpart lender. However, because of errors in compiling data, it is necessary to insert a 'balancing item' in order to achieve such a result. The size of the balancing item – £2.66 billion in 1989 – is indicative of the statistical inaccuracies in collecting data!

1.4 The role of the Stock Exchange

The Stock Exchange, or capital market, is an institution where quoted investments (*stocks and shares*) may be exchanged between buyers and sellers. The term 'stocks and shares' is nowadays rather anachronistic, but is still fixed in the popular imagination. *Stocks* are generally thought of as referring to fixed-interest capital in units of £100 and quoted at so much per cent, while the term *shares* is used for dividend-paying capital, either ordinary or preferred. But the distinction is not a precise one. 'Stock' can be quoted in units of any amount, and it can embrace dividend-paying capital; unlike share capital, stock transfers can take place in fractions of a unit.

Before the Companies Act 1948, many companies preferred ordinary stock units to ordinary shares because until that time all shares had to have distinctive numbers, a requirement which meant an enormous amount of work in the preparation of deeds of transfer and share certificates. So it was easier to issue, say, a 25p stock unit rather than a 25p share. Nevertheless the word 'shares' was frequently used for shares and ordinary stock alike, since for all practical purposes they were, and are, one and the same.

Because the word 'stock' encompasses both ordinary share capital and loan capital, it is nowadays used as a generic term for all securities. (The evidence of any property right is generally termed a *security*, although the word is often clearly inappropriate in its strictest sense. Broadly, it is a legal representation of the right to receive prospective future benefits under stated conditions, and it is in this sense that the words 'stocks' and 'securities' will be used interchangeably throughout this book.) The Stock Exchange provides a market in a wide range of traded securities, generally of medium- to long-term maturities, issued by companies, Governments, and public organizations, both domestic and overseas.

Traditionally the Stock Exchange is thought of as both a primary and secondary market. (A *primary market* is where new funds are raised by the issue of new securities; a *secondary market* is where trade takes place in already-issued securities.) The two markets are closely related, in that the willingness of investors to subscribe to new issues in the primary market is crucially dependent on their ability to dispose of such securities, if necessary, in the secondary market, before the final maturity date. Some securities, such as ordinary shares or undated Government securities, have no guaranteed maturity date.

Strictly speaking, however, the Stock Exchange is only a secondary market, as securities are initially sold first of all to institutions or individuals, who are then free to resell them through the Exchange, provided that the Stock Exchange Council has signified its approval. The new-issue market is thus separate from the Stock Exchange dealing system.

The fund-raising operations of the public sector are largely dictated by fiscal policy – by the extent of the budget deficit or surplus – and not by the cost of funds. But in company fund-raising, the cost, or at least the likelihood of an issue being fully subscribed, should be more influential. This again illustrates the connection between the secondary market and the new-issue market, for the cost of raising new funds is determined by the current yields of existing securities being traded in the stock market. In theory, through the forces of demand and supply, the stock market is constantly reassessing the prospects of companies, so that at any time those securities offer a fair return for the risk involved. If the prospects of a company deteriorate, the value of its debt and equity will fall, so that at the lower price the securities offer the same return (or even an increased return if more risk is now involved) on the lower expected earnings. The converse applies if prospects improve.

So the efficiency with which the Stock Exchange discharges its role as an allocator of capital depends, among other things, on how well securities are valued in the secondary market. If they are fairly valued, and capital is in short supply, only the companies with the best investment prospects will be willing to raise funds on the high yields that have to be paid. But this view has to be qualified. Firstly, most corporate investment is undertaken from retained earnings, and these may not be properly costed. Secondly, the efficiency of the allocatory function depends on the degree of foresight of investors in the market. The stock market prides itself on being a barometer of the future rather than a thermometer of the present, but, in the absence of other information, investors perhaps tend to base the valuation of companies excessively on recent past performance.

Views on how successfully the Stock Exchange fulfils its allocatory function differ widely, partly because the Stock Exchange is seen as the symbol of capitalism. For example, the economist Walter Bagehot in the nineteenth century opposed any changes, saying 'we must not let in daylight upon magic'. Even greater praise came in F. E. Armstrong's book on the Stock Exchange: 'The Stock Exchange as an institution has been evolved by time and perfected by experience . . . It is the Citadel of Capital, the Temple of Values. It is the axle on which the whole financial structure of the Capitalistic System turns. It is the Bazaar of human effort and endeavour, the Mart where man's courage, ingenuity and labour are marketed.'

Lord Keynes was less impressed: 'Speculators may do no harm as bubbles on a steady stream of enterprise. But the position is serious when enterprise becomes the bubble on a whirlpool of speculation. When the capital development of a country becomes a by-product of the activities of a casino, the job is likely to be ill done.'

Keynes was writing in the mid-1930s, but his views have been echoed in more recent times. The establishment in 1977 of the Wilson Committee to review the functioning of the financial institutions was partly in response to these criticisms. The Exchange's secondary role has appeared to predominate over the primary one in most recent years, at least as far as industry and commerce are concerned.

The market capitalization of the ordinary shares of companies fluctuates a great deal, as instanced by the fall in share prices worldwide in October 1987, but some generalizations can nevertheless be made about the size of the market. The market value of shares on the UK Stock Exchange is far below that of the New York and Tokyo Exchanges, but much larger than that of any other country. Moreover, it is generally much easier to trade in UK ordinary shares and Government securities than in the equivalent stocks in most other countries.

Historically, the Stock Exchange in the UK has not been a major source of finance for UK companies: companies have preferred to rely primarily on internal funds. Even as recently as 1972–82, industrial and commercial companies raised less than 5 per cent of their total funds from UK capital issues. Table 1.2 shows a greater reliance on this source in recent years, due to a strong stock market. Debentures became more popular when interest rates were on a downward trend, but much larger sums were raised through bank borrowing.

Table 1.2 Sources of capital funds of industrial and commercial companies (£m)

| | Total from all sources | UK capital issues | | % from UK capital issues |
		Ordinary shares	Debentures and preference shares	
1985	46 185	3 522	816	9.4
1986	48 737	5 608	490	12.5
1987	71 415	13 338	534	19.4
1988	84 440	4 817	1 207	7.1
1989	89 468	2 594	2 980	6.2

Source: *Financial Statistics*, May 1990.

It may seem strange that, during most of the 1970s, companies that needed to use external finance went primarily to the banks, while the public sector relied on capital issues. But the reasoning is quite straightforward. Companies were unwilling to commit themselves to high nominal long-term rates of interest; they preferred to rely on bank overdrafts or medium-term loans with floating interest rates. In contrast, the Government was not commercially restricted in its issuing of debt.

Until the late 1980s, the new-issue market had been essentially one for public-sector rather than corporate fund-raising. Government financing has nearly always been an important element in the life of the Stock Exchange. Even in the years shortly before the First World War, only about a tenth of 'real' investment in the United Kingdom was financed by new issues on the Stock Exchange. UK Government securities amounted to 70 per cent of the nominal value of all securities quoted on the Exchange in 1853 but had shrunk to only 9 per cent by 1914. Then followed the heavy Government borrowing necessary to finance the two world wars, and the depressed conditions of the 1920s and 1930s discouraged the creation of company securities. After 1945, however, the number of quoted industrial companies increased rapidly, and inflation (together with retention of earnings) has boosted their market values, while diminishing those of long-term Government securities.

The mechanics of the Stock Exchange's operations are discussed in chapters 12 to 15.

1.5 Classification of investments

As already indicated in section 1.2 there are a variety of ways by which one can categorize investments, as follows.

1.5.1 Real and financial investment

This book is primarily concerned with financial investments, such as bank and building society accounts, National Savings, Government securities, shares, unit trusts, life assurance, and pensions. But in addition to these 'paper' claims, we also consider 'real' investments, where the investor has ownership of a physical, tangible asset. The primary example of the latter is *owner-occupied house property*. This is without doubt the form of growth investment owned by the largest number of individuals.

Almost everyone realizes that owning the house you live in is one of the best investments you can make. When the mortgage is at last paid off, most home-owners have an asset which has appreciated substantially over the purchase price. And the amount of interest paid, although considerable, has almost certainly been less than the rent payable for the occupation of similar property owned by someone else. The payment of mortgage instalments instead of rent will have given you a real opportunity to acquire something worthwhile to pass on to your children. (The ownership of *property for letting* is an area where few individuals are investors, although this is a regular and common area of investment for institutions.)

Another type of investment is the personal *chattel*, although it is the choice of relatively few investors. Everyone has personal possessions, of course, but the vast majority are acquired for use and consumption or as a hobby, rather than for investment. But precious stones, antiques, postage stamps, and many other specialized fields of collecting can be profitable as investments.

1.5.2 Risk in investment
Investments may be classified according to the degree of risk involved. Risk avoidance is an important topic in itself and may be regarded as one of the underlying themes not only of this book but of any serious approach to investment. There are two kinds of risk:

(a) that capital may be lost in part or altogether or, even if not lost, that short-term fluctuations in value may seriously affect the investor; and
(b) that income may not be paid when due, or may at least be unreliable. A threat to the income can be regarded as endangering the capital too, for if a business has difficulty in paying interest or dividends this is often the result of losses which are, in effect, forced reductions of capital.

Unfortunately, there are difficulties in categorizing investments in this way. The main reason is that within a cateogry – loan stocks, for example – one could buy a range of securities extending from the fairly safe to the downright speculative. Even British Government securities have their attendant risks. The so-called 'undated' stocks such as $3\frac{1}{2}$% War Loan are absolutely safe as regards interest but must be regarded as risk investments so far as capital is concerned, because there is no prospect whatsoever of repayment and the future price of the stock cannot be forecast. Even the dated securities – the index-linked issues excepted – carry risks, because the stated repayment date may be much more remote than the investor's own investment time-horizon.

1.5.3 Term of investment
Investments available to the investor encompass a spectrum from the very short-term to the very long-term. 'Cash' investments are ones which are

instantly accessible without penalty – the best-known examples are 'instant-access' building society accounts and interest-bearing current accounts with banks. National Savings provide products, such as Savings Certificates, for investors who wish to invest for around five years. Investments for twenty years or more would include life assurance, pension plans, and owner-occupied property. Some Government securities, and virtually all ordinary shares, are indefinite investments.

1.5.4 Investment, speculation, and gambling

It is very difficult to distinguish precisely between these three kinds of activity. Certainly they have all been employed at various times in the stock market. Time and risk are two criteria that are sometimes used to differentiate them.

Investment was historically interpreted by trustees as medium- to long-term and low-risk, usually restricted to Government securities. Where equities were concerned, these were to be those of leading, or '*blue-chip*', companies, bought for their future dividends. *Speculation* is generally considered to be more short-term, involving greater risk and based on anticipating market movements rather than judging the long-term fundamentals of a particular investment. Yet the distinction is not quite clear-cut, as many long-term

'Ready? Here it is—I wish for riches beyond my wildest dreams with no encumbering socialist guilt feelings.'

investors consider timing to be an important part of investment strategy; and risk may be worth accepting, providing it is accompanied by the expectation of commensurate reward.

Gambling is considered to involve the shortest waiting period, and the greatest risk, often involving an all-or-nothing outcome. But here, too, the dividing line is sometimes difficult to draw. Betting on the Football League Championship, or backing a horse ante-post, can involve a long wait before the outcome is known. Though risks are usually greater, they are frequently more explicit or calculable than in speculation, as in roulette or poker; and buying shares 'on the margin' or share options also involves the possibility of losing everything. Holding shares for the duration of a Stock Exchange fortnightly account might be termed speculation, but to bet on the course of the stock market over the same period with a bookmaker is considered by the Inland Revenue to be gambling.

1.5.5 Fixed-income and variable-income investments

Investments are often divided into *fixed-income* and *variable-income* investments. Most investments come into one of these two categories; for instance:

Fixed-income investments	Variable-income investments
Gilt-edged securities	Building society shares
Company loan stocks	Equities
Preference shares	Unit trusts

There are such important differences between the securities within these groups, however, that such a division is sometimes a hindrance to understanding. Preference shares, for example, generally produce a fixed income but the security itself fundamentally has more in common with ordinary shares, since preference shares are part of the share capital and are not a loan. Most unit trusts consist of holdings of ordinary shares but, because there is a spread of investment – with the intention of eliminating severe fluctuations in prices – unit trust income tends to be more stable than that from the typical ordinary share.

Another objection to classifying investments in this way is that it ignores those investments which produce no income as such. Obviously in the long run all investments must offer some prospect of a return, but the following investments all fall into a third group:

National Savings Premium Bonds
Chattels (for example, stamp collections, coins, Oriental carpets)
Owner-occupied property
Options (these are covered fully in chapter 11)

National Savings Premium Bonds are well known to offer not interest but prizes. The prize fund is based on a notional sum which would otherwise be available for interest, but the random distribution of the prizes, both large and small, makes the Premium Bond a very speculative investment – if indeed it really is an investment at all. Chattels purchased as investments –

that is, to produce a gain – must be distinguished from those acquired for the enjoyment they give the collector. Owner-occupied property has proved to be an excellent investment in its own right. Options produce no income as such and their attractiveness as investments is wholly dependent on performance of the underlying investment.

1.5.6 Quoted and unquoted investments

Another approach is to consider the division of investments into those which are *quoted* investments and those which are *unquoted*. This separation is not without problems. Firstly, a 'quotation' may be an official one, determined by market forces, on the Stock Exchange. Or it may be determined by the fund manager, as in the case of unit trusts or unit-linked life assurance. In both of these cases the 'quote' will usually be published in the quality press. Secondly, many types of investment can be in both categories: ordinary shares, loan stocks, and warrants, for example. These are all company securities, and investment in unquoted companies – in particular in their equity capital – must always be subject to special considerations. Most investors avoid securities of unquoted companies if only because, since there is no market in them, their disposal may present problems. Examples of quoted and unquoted investments which are explained later in this book include:

Quoted	Quoted or unquoted	Unquoted
British	All company securities:	Bank and building
Government	Ordinary shares	society accounts
securities	Preference shares	National Savings
	Loan issues	
	Warrants	
	Unit trusts	
	Life assurance	

Some unquoted investments, such as certain building society shares or certain bank deposits, are 'cash' investments in that they can be redeemed for the full capital sum invested, with little or no penalty for encashment.

1.5.7 Direct and indirect investments

Direct investments represent investments in a particular organization – Government, bank, building society, company, and so on. Indirect investments are essentially 'investments in investments'. They are particularly useful to the smaller investor, who would be unwise to put money into the more speculative direct investments such as ordinary shares. It is usually uneconomic to invest less than about £2000 in any one security, and it is generally thought that an investor's capital should be spread among at least fifteen securities. There should also be a sensible spread between industries: it is not much use allocating funds between fifteen different engineering firms, because many of the problems experienced by one company in that industry will adversely affect its competitors also. This spreading of investment, or *diversification*, is possible for the small investor only through one of the available vehicles for indirect investment.

The number of these has increased considerably during the post-war years, corresponding with the decline of the direct private investor and the rise of the institutions. The oldest member of the group is the investment trust company. *Investment trusts*, as they are commonly called, are limited companies with capital structures not unlike those of other companies. They differ from the trading company, however, in that their assets consist of the shares of other companies. Thus a purchase of the ordinary shares in an investment trust is an indirect investment in perhaps as many as several hundred other companies.

Unit trusts are not companies but trusts, with objects similar to those of the investment trust – they invest widely and their managers aim generally to produce a total return (both income and capital gain) which is at least better than average. The prices of units reflect the value of the underlying collection of investments, whereas the prices of investment trusts are determined by market factors.

A most important type of indirect investment is in insurance or, more properly, *life assurance*. Life assurance is a contract whereby the insurance company agrees to pay a certain amount if the insured person dies during the course of the contract. The premiums for the cheapest form of life assurance – *term assurance* – are payable for only a limited number of years and payment of the sum assured is made only if death occurs during that period. In such a case there is no savings or investment element.

With an *endowment insurance policy*, however, premiums are payable for a limited period or until earlier death, whereupon the sun assured – which may be with or without bonuses – becomes payable. Such a policy combines both insurance and savings elements. Another kind of policy may be linked to a specific fund such as a unit trust or an internal fund.

Today the most widespread form of indirect investment is the *pension scheme*. The pension fund managers are now the biggest of all the institutional investors and exercise enormous market influence. Quite apart from the State schemes – the flat-rate pension and the earnings-related scheme – many employers, both in the private and in the public sector, now offer their employees attractive pension plans. In addition, following the Social Security Act 1986, both employees and self-employed persons can now make provision independently by means of personal pension plans.

1.5.8 *Size and range of investments*
Figure 1.2 and Table 1.3 show the relative importance of various kinds of investment.

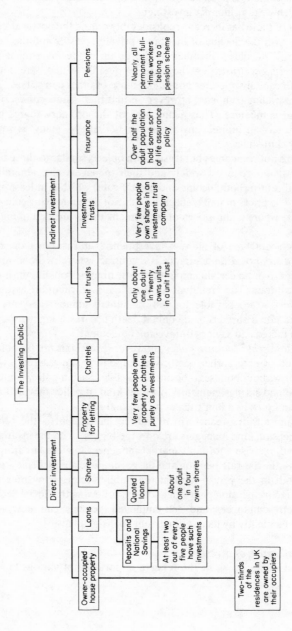

Fig. 1.2   The range of available investments

Table 1.3 Balance sheet of the personal sector (basically households) as at 31 December 1988

	£ billion	% of total assets
Bank accounts	96	4
Building society accounts	149	7
National Savings	37	2
British Government securities	30	1
UK ordinary shares	126	6
Unit trusts	17	1
Life assurance and pension funds	384	17
Others	82	4
Total financial assets	921	42
UK residential property	964	44
Agricultural land and buildings	35	1
Other real assets	130	6
Total real assets	1129	
Non-marketable tenancy rights	153	7
Total assets	2203	100
Total financial liabilities	340	
Net wealth	1863	

Source: *Financial Statistics*, February 1990 (all figures rounded).

Table 1.3 clearly illustrates the predominant influence of residential property, life assurance, and pensions in the wealth portfolios of households. Together they account for nearly two-thirds of the value of financial and real assets.

1.6 Personal and institutional investors

Personal-sector savings that are not required for housebuilding (and real investment by unincorporated businesses) are lent to the Government or companies through the Stock Exchange. But this lending is usually indirect, via intermediaries such as insurance companies and pension funds, rather than directly into securities. In recent years, private individuals have been increasing their total investments but simultaneously reducing their direct investments in the stock market, as Tables 1.4 and 1.5 demonstrate.

Table 1.5 shows that there has been a continuing trend away from personal towards institutional ownership of ordinary shares. Between 1963 and 1989 the proportion of ordinary shares in UK listed companies held directly by individuals fell by two-thirds – from almost 60 per cent to under 20 per cent. At the same time the proportion held by the major institutional investors more than doubled – from 28 per cent to 63 per cent. However, the statistical data should be treated with some circumspection: it is often nothing more

Table 1.4 Personal sector: acquisition and sale of financial assets (£m)

	UK company securities	Overseas securities	Inflows to life assurance and pension funds
1985	−5 680	+933	+18 973
1986	−4 147	+1 111	+19 798
1987	−1 896	+1 663	+20 335
1988	−9 179	+1 117	+21 242
1989	−12 622	+1 645	+28 535

Source: *Financial Statistics*, May 1990.

Table 1.5 Percentage of total market value of UK listed equities held by different groups

31 December	1963	1973	1979*	1989
Pension funds	7.0	12.2	22.5	29
Insurance companies	10.6	16.2	20.5	25
Investment trusts and financial companies	9.0	9.8	8.5	3
Unit trusts	1.2	3.4	3.0	6
Total institutions	27.8	41.6	54.5	63
Persons	58.7	42.0	29.5	18
Charities	2.6	4.4	2.5	2
Industrial and commercial companies	4.8	4.3	4.0	4
Government	1.6	2.5	4.0	5
Overseas	4.4	5.2	5.0	8
Total per cent*	100.0	100.0	100.0	100.0

*Subject to rounding differences. All 1989 figures rounded.
Source: Figures for 1963 and 1973 are from the Diamond Commission, and those for 1979 and 1989 are estimates by UBS Phillips & Drew.

then sophisticated guesswork, and subject to drastic revision in later years. For example, while *Financial Statistics* shows the personal sector as a net seller of £12.6 billion of UK company securities in 1989 (Table 1.4), UBS Phillips & Drew estimated that this sector's percentage holding remained unchanged between 1988 and 1989.

For our purposes, an *institution*, in the broadest sense, is a body which takes funds from individuals and corporate organizations for the purpose of profitable investment. It invests as a principal (that is, in its own name), mainly in the stock market, using professional management and operating within the constraints provided by its own articles or trust deed and by tax and legal considerations. A full list would include charities, the Church Commissioners, trade unions, the Public Trustee, and others; but for most purposes, as in this book, the term *institutional investor* is used to refer to the insurance companies, the pension funds (private, public, and local authority), unit trusts, investment trusts, and financial companies such as merchant banks.

The personal sector was a net disposer of company securities every year from 1955 to 1989. Similar long-term developments, although not so advanced, have been experienced in the USA. The demise of the 'small investor' has prompted one wag to comment that nowadays the term means a fund manager under five feet six!

But why should so many people prefer to hold a claim on a financial institution rather than one directly on the Government or a company? The main reasons are as follows:

(a) Indirect investment may be the most tax-efficient way to invest. Until 1984, new life assurance policies received a tax subsidy. In the case of approved pension schemes, the whole of the contributions are an allowable charge against taxable income up to specified limits. A £100 gross premium costs a 40 per cent taxpayer only a net £60. It is much more difficult for anyone to achieve equivalent returns by direct investment in the stock market, especially when in the case of pension schemes the investment income can be accumulated gross within the fund.

(b) Institutional investors can provide a widely diversified portfolio (i.e. collection of investments) for a relatively small outlay. This may be a broad spread of ordinary shares or, in the case of life assurance and pension funds, it may extend to gilt-edged stocks and property. Thus the small investor is far less exposed to risk than if his or her eggs were in one or two baskets – for even the most highly regarded companies have been known to go into liquidation. Modern financial theory suggests that diversification should be one of the prime objectives of the investor.

(c) The public is increasingly aware of the need for professional management. This in part reflects increased advertising and promotional activities – initially by unit trust groups; more recently by the life assurance companies. But professional management does not – or should not – imply an ability to make exceptionally high profits year after year. It means providing the highest return for the level of risk the investor is willing to undertake, having regard to his or her personal circumstances and tax position.

(d) Estate duty, capital transfer tax, and inheritance tax have to a limited extent forced personal holdings on the market to meet these liabilities, and frequently these holdings, if substantial, are sold directly to institutions.

(e) Finally, some small investors have been made to feel unwanted by the generally poorer dealing and information service they receive in comparison with institutional clients. Brokers' charges on small deals can be prohibitively expensive.

In an attempt to reverse the process of increasing institutional ownership of equities, the then Chancellor of the Exchequer announced in his 1986 Budget statement the introduction of the *Personal Equity Plan* (PEP). In

1990/91 an individual, resident in the United Kingdom, is permitted to invest up to £6000 per year in such a scheme. PEPs are discussed in chapter 16.

Further inducements to direct personal share ownership are employee share-ownership schemes (ESOPS) and employee share-option schemes.

Largely as a result of the Government privatization issues, the number of share-owning adults in the UK rose from under 3 million in 1979 to around 11 million in 1990. But this was 'share widening' rather than 'share deepening' – the number of personal shareholders rose, but their percentage of the total market continued to fall. In fact, a survey by the Stock Exchange in 1990 showed that 60 per cent of personal shareholders held shares in only one company; only 14 per cent held shares in four or more companies.

The concentration of shareholdings with institutional investors is perceived to have a number of negative effects. These include the following:

1.6.1 Stock market efficiency

The minimum size of deal which interests the large institutional fund may preclude investment in small companies. There is a feeling that this raises the *de facto* minimum-size requirements of the new-issue market. Even worse is the position of unquoted companies, largely precluded from institutional backing.

Institutional activity makes a significant contribution to stock market turnover, and gives financial institutions considerable impact on security prices. There is a very high correlation between their net acquisitions of equities and movements in the market indices, suggesting that they are either following or making the market. They have frequently been criticized for their 'herd-like' attitude to investment – all trying to buy or sell at the same time; no one wishing to take an opposite view and be the odd man out. Such behaviour was perhaps responsible for the volatility of the market in October 1987; this instability made rational capital allocation difficult, if not impossible. It was foreseen by Keynes, who wrote:

> It is the long-term investor, he who most promotes the public interest, who will in practice come in for most criticism, wherever investment funds are managed by committees or boards or banks. For it is in the essence of his behaviour that he should be eccentric, unconventional and rash in the eyes of average opinion. If he is successful, that will only confirm the general belief in his rashness; and if, in the short run, he is unsuccessful, which is very likely, he will not receive much mercy. Worldly wisdom teaches that it is better for reputation to fail conventionally than to succeed unconventionally.

1.6.2 Shareholder democracy

Traditionally shareholders have not interfered in company management – there has been a 'divorce of ownership from control'. This has been a consequence of the wide dispersion of shareholdings and the general ignorance and apathy of many investors. But institutional investors collectively now hold majority, or at least strategic, stakes in many companies. Their decisions are crucial in take-over bids. They are frequently invited, along with broker/dealers, to meet top management. They have become the 'élite' investors. This is a situation the Stock Exchange has attempted to resist, because it challenges one of its fundamental tenets, that all investors are equal – the *Take-over Code* (see section 13.3), for instance, was introduced in part to prevent differential offers being made to different classes of shareholder. Nevertheless a feeling remains that the small shareholder may be effectively disfranchised by a body which has tremendous collective power but no real accountability to its own investors.

1.6.3 Company management

Some people believe that the institutions should be more forthright and interventionist towards companies, rather than worrying about treading on the toes of the small investor. The United Kingdom is sometimes compared unfavourably in terms of economic performance with other industrialized countries, and one possible explanation lies in the differences in financial structure. In Germany, in particular, the banks have a strong say in company organization, and it may be that something similar is required in the UK, to disturb sleepy and inefficient management. The institutional investors have always resisted such a role, preferring to sell shares that performed badly rather than trying to intervene directly in the company. They have justified this policy on several grounds:

(a) lack of necessary expertise in management consultancy;
(b) fear that news of intervention would further depress the share price;
(c) fear of nationalization if they were seen to be too powerful;
(d) acquisition of 'inside' knowledge would preclude further share dealing;
(e) fear of adverse publicity if involved in redundancies, factory closures, and so forth;
(f) a belief that their first duty was to their own investors.

To date, the institutional investors' main involvement with companies, through their investment protection committees and the Institutional Shareholders Committee, has been in regard to safeguarding shareholders' interests in respect of directors' pay, share option schemes, and management buyouts. But institutions are increasingly becoming 'locked in' to their large shareholdings, which are often too large to be disposed of through normal market channels. Intervention may eventually be the only answer.

1.6.4 Take-overs and mergers

In the last 30 years the United Kingdom has had a higher level of merger activity than virtually any other major industrialized country. Some mergers have turned out to be successful; most were disappointing. The economic rationale for many of them was mystifying, yet they had largely been supported by the institutions. This was because fund managers, judged on short-term results, were willing to accept offers which were a significant improvement on the previous share price, thus at once improving the performance of, and rationalizing, their portfolios. In the long run, however, many of these businesses might have provided greater earnings and dividends if they had remained independent. So a great deal of economic reorganization may have been simply a consequence of the 'short-termism' of City institutions.

Companies may have been deterred from long-term investment by the fear that any temporary depression of earnings or dividends, as a result of such investment, might adversely affect their share price and thereby invite a take-over bid. Again, contrast can be made with the Continental habit of supplying long-term support, provided that the fundamentals of the company are satisfactory.

Institutional dominance certainly seems a mixed blessing. It has undoubtedly helped the Government finance any borrowing requirement. But it appears to conflict with the current interest in stimulating new entrepreneurial businesses, and there may well be continuing moves in the future to remove the fiscal advantages accorded these institutions and those that invest through them.

1.7 Success in investment

Success in most things is relative, and this is true in the field of investment. Success in investment means earning the highest possible return within the constraints imposed by the investor's personal circumstances – age, family needs, liquidity requirements, tax position, and acceptability of risk. If possible, performance should be measured against alternative investments, or combinations of investments, available to the investor within those constraints. Genuine success also means winning the battle against inflation – against the fall in the real value of savings and capital.

The investor should be aware of, but not daunted by, the fact that investment markets – the stock market in particular – are largely dominated by professional investors. As a consequence, grossly undervalued investments are rarely easy to come by. Moreover, he or she should beware of books subtitled *How I Made a Million* and statements such as 'You can have a high return with no risk.' In reasonably efficient markets, risk and return go together like bread and butter – in the words of Milton Friedman, 'There is no such thing as a free lunch.'

Success involves planning – clearly establishing one's objectives and constraints. Investments should be looked at in terms of what they contribute to the overall portfolio, rather than their merits in isolation. Institutional investment will probably play some part, and performance tables are available to give some guidance. But personal direct investment should not be overlooked particularly in the obvious area of home-ownership, and one's own knowledge, skills, hobbies, and acquaintances can also be put to

'Money can't buy them happiness.'

advantage. Remember the words of the Elizabethan philosopher Francis Bacon:

> If a man look sharply and attentively, he shall see fortune; for though she be blind, yet she is not invisible.

1.8 Questions

1. What are the differences, if any, between 'investment', 'speculation', and 'gambling'?

2. (a) 'From the end of World War II until quite recently there has been a steady fall in personal share ownership.' What reasons are usually given for this trend?

   (b) (i) In the last ten years a number of developments have contributed to an increase in the number of private shareholders. What are these developments?

   (ii) List any factors which have or could have the effect of reversing this trend towards wider share ownership?

(CIB 5/89)

2 Advice and protection

Whether investing directly or indirectly, most investors require some form of advice. In fact, certain investors may prefer to allow their investment adviser full discretion to manage their portfolios. However, most investors are naturally cautious regarding the honesty, competence, and independence of persons to whom they entrust their money. There have been a number of well-publicized scandals in recent years, such as Barlow Clowes, where investors have lost their life-savings through no fault of their own. Fortunately, these cases of fraud and maladministration are unlikely to be as common in the future, because of the Financial Services Act 1986. This Act requires all persons involved in investment business to be 'authorized', and imposes upon them an overriding obligation to give 'best advice'.

2.1 The Financial Services Act 1986

This Act is the most comprehensive attempt ever made in the United Kingdom to regulate investment business. Its guiding principle is self-regulation within a statutory framework.

2.1.1 Scope of the Act

The scope of the Act is very wide and covers investment businesses which deal in or arrange deals in investments, which manage investments, or which give investment advice. Excluded from the last group are financial journalists, where the primary purpose of the newspaper is not to give investment advice, and anyone who gives general advice about classes of investment, as opposed to particular investments – including the authors of this book!

The definition of 'investments' in the Act includes

(a) shares and debentures of a company;
(b) Government, local authority, and other public authority securities;
(c) warrants, options, and similar rights;
(d) depository receipts;
(e) units in unit trusts;
(f) financial and commodity futures contracts;
(g) 'contracts for differences' (these are akin to gambling, usually on the movement of indices);

(h) long-term insurance contracts (excluding those, like 'term' policies, whose sole purpose is protection);

(i) rights to, and interests in, investments falling within any of the above categories. This allows a wide range of investments, including single-premium insurance policies, personal pensions, and friendly-society policies.

The Act does not cover selling or advising on 'general' insurance (such as car or house contents insurance), direct investment in 'real' assets (such as houses and chattels), or deposit or share accounts with banks and building societies.

2.1.2 Authorization and exemption

In order to carry on investment business, a firm or individual must be 'authorized' or 'exempted' from authorization. There are four main methods of authorization, as illustrated in fig. 2.1.

Ultimate power lies with the Secretary of State for Trade and Industry. But he has delegated his power under the Act to a 'designated agency': the

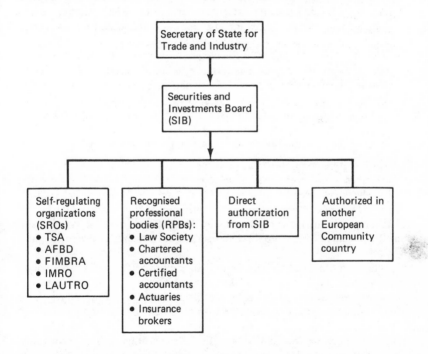

Fig. 2.1   The regulatory framework for investments

Securities and Investments Board, known as SIB. SIB can authorize investment businesses but in turn prefers to delegate responsibility to the *self-
regulating organizations*, known as the SROs.

(a) Self-regulating organizations   At present there are five SROs, and each
is required to impose on its members business rules regarded as 'adequate' by
SIB:

- *The Securities Association* (TSA) covers members of the Stock Exchange,
  and international bond and share dealers.
- *The Association of Futures Brokers and Dealers* (AFBD) has member
  firms engaged in broking and dealing in futures and options, mainly
  through the London Derivatives Exchange, the London Metal Exchange,
  and the London Futures and Options Exchange.

(TSA and AFBD are to merge as the Securities and Futures Authority in
1991.)

- *The Financial Intermediaries, Managers and Brokers Regulatory Association* (FIMBRA) is the largest in terms of numbers of members, but they
  are typically small-scale investment managers and advisers, often acting as
  independent intermediaries for insurance and unit trust products. FIM-
  BRA also covers the few securities dealers outside the Stock Exchange.
- *The Investment Management Regulatory Organisation* (IMRO) has members who are investment managers, including managers and trustees of
  unit trusts, and in-house pension fund managers, such as merchant banks.
  IMRO is mainly concerned with regulating fund management.
- *The Life Assurance and Unit Trust Regulatory Organisation* (LAUTRO) is
  concerned with the retail marketing of unit trusts, life-assurance-linked
  investments, friendly-society policies, and personal pensions.

An investment business can be a member of more than one SRO if it
undertakes a range of investment activities. A major bank, for example,
might be a member of all five SROs through its ownership of a Stock
Exchange member firm, through membership of the London Derivatives
Exchange, through owning life assurance and unit trust businesses, and
finally through ownership of independent investment management subsidiaries.

Where an organization belongs to two or more SROs, SIB can designate
one of them as the *'lead regulator'*. Its function is to deal with apparent
conflicts between one SRO's rules and those of another. (The lead regulator
for banks, incidentally, is not an SRO but the Bank of England.)

(b) Recognized professional bodies   Professional firms such as accountants
and solicitors offer investment advice to their clients as part of their wider
business activities. Under the Act, a *recognized professional body* (RPB) can
authorize its members by means of the issue of an *investment business
certificate*, which can be granted only to persons whose main business is the

practice of the profession rather than investment business; otherwise they must be authorized independently.

(c) **Direct authorization** Direct authorization by SIB is not common, although SIB is empowered to authorize individuals or firms who do not wish to belong to an SRO, or are perhaps in dispute with one. In addition, it should be mentioned that insurance companies regulated under the Insurance Companies Act 1982 and friendly societies governed by the Friendly Societies Act 1974 are deemed to be authorized persons in relation to their fund management and therefore do not need to become members of IMRO. But the marketing and promotion of their policies falls within the scope of the Financial Services Act 1986, and so most have become members of LAUTRO.

(d) **Overseas persons** Nationals of another European Community member country are automatically authorized for the purpose of the Act, provided that they have no permanent place of business in the UK and are authorized in their own country to carry on investment business under a system that imposes authorization standards at least equivalent to those required under the Act. The same applies to any person who is authorized in another member country under a harmonized regime to allow the products in question – say, unit trusts – to be sold throughout the Community, regardless of the member country of origin.

(e) **Exemption** The Act does recognize certain 'persons' as exempt from the prohibition on carrying on investment business without being authorized. These include

- the Bank of England;
- Lloyds (for insurance business only);
- appointed representatives (that is, self-employed representatives of a single company);
- listed money-market institutions (that is, essentially banks and building societies, for deposit and share accounts);
- recognized investment exchanges;
- recognized clearing houses.

(f) **Recognized investment exchanges and clearing houses** Persons running a market or exchange in 'investments' defined earlier need to be 'authorized', unless the market or exchange obtains exemption by becoming recognized by SIB, which approves certain markets or exchanges as *recognized investment exchanges* (RIEs), in the same way in which it recognizes the SROs. SIB must be satisfied that the exchange has adequate rules and procedures to ensure the orderly conduct of business and provide proper protection to investors, and that it has adequate financial resources to perform its functions.

Recognition provides advantages to member firms of that RIE. A good example is the Stock Exchange. This is an RIE and is officially known as the International Stock Exchange of the United Kingdom and the Republic of Ireland Ltd. Member firms cannot obviate the need to become members of TSA – the relevant SRO – but recognition of the Exchange considerably simplifies the requirements members must fulfil when dealing with clients. Other exchanges recognized by SIB include the Baltic Exchange, the International Petroleum Exchange, the London Futures and Options Exchange, the London Metal Exchange, the London Derivatives Exchange, the National Association of Security Dealers Automatic Quotations System in the USA, and the Sydney Futures Exchange in Australia.

Overseas exchanges require recognition from the Department of Trade and Industry. The last two RIEs listed above are examples of such recognition.

Similar provisions apply to clearing houses, both domestic and overseas. A *recognized clearing house* (RCH), such as Talisman for the Stock Exchange (see section 15.8), is an exempted person in respect of anything done by it in its capacity as a 'person' providing clearing services.

2.1.3 Penalties under the Act

(a) **Breach of authorization requirements**   Any person convicted of carrying on investment business in the UK without being authorized, or without being exempted from authorization, is liable to imprisonment for up to two years, or a fine, or both. Any investment agreement entered into with an unauthorized person may be unenforceable in law. Furthermore, the investor is entitled to recover any money paid, and to compensation for any loss sustained through having handed it over.

(b) **Misleading statements and practices**   Any person who makes a statement, promise, or forecast which is misleading, false, deceptive, or simply reckless is committing a criminal offence with a penalty of imprisonment for up to seven years, or a fine, or both. Inclusion of the term 'reckless' indicates that an offence need not involve any element of dishonesty and so covers sales 'hype' which lacks any reasonable basis in fact. In addition, the same penalty applies to any act which creates a false or misleading impression as to the market in, or price of, any investment. This is to prevent market 'rigging'.

2.1.4 Compensation scheme

The *Investors Compensation Scheme* (ICS) was established as an independent company by SIB. ICS can make payments to certain investors who have lost money as the result of the default of an authorized investment business. The investor can claim 100 per cent of any loss up to £30 000, and 90 per cent of any further amount between £30 000 and £50 000. Thus the maximum cover is £48 000. At present, however, the fund is limited to £100 million per year. Furthermore, the ICS does not cover insurance-based investments, which are backed by the Policyholders' Protection Act 1975, nor members of RPBs, who are covered by their own schemes. Banks and building societies also have their own statutory protection schemes for deposits held with them.

2.2 Rules for conduct of business

SIB lays down three tiers of rules and guidelines:

(a) *Principles* There are ten broad 'commandments' which outline the basic requirements for investment firms, such as 'high standards of integrity and fair dealing' and 'to act with skill, care and diligence'.
(b) *Designated ('core') rules* These expand on the ten principles and are legally enforceable.
(c) *Detailed guidance* These are a mixture of rules (which are legally enforceable) and codes of conduct (which are not). This third tier is drawn up by the SROs themselves. SIB is responsible for ensuring that this guidance is 'adequate'.

The designated rules and detailed guidance include the following:

2.2.1 Categories of customer
Investment firms are required to recommend investments which are of a type and size appropriate to the client, having regard to the facts known about the client.

SIB rules permit different types of investor to be treated differently. The SROs can frame their own interpretations.

The TSA rules distinguish between four main types of investor: the market professionals, business customers, expert investors, and private customers. The degree of protection provided is in inverse relation to the expertise and knowledge of the investor.

(a) Market professionals This category includes principally broker/dealers, including market-makers, in the Stock Exchange and those operating outside the Stock Exchange. Under TSA 'conduct of business' rules, market professionals normally receive no protection. They are deemed to be capable of 'looking after themselves' in any transaction in any investment. The same applies to countries, central banks, and other national monetary authorities in respect of the markets in debt and money-market investments only.

(b) Business customers According to the TSA rulebook, these are mostly companies. Additionally, a person who would otherwise be a market professional is treated as a business customer in respect of discretionary management only – that is, dealing on his or her behalf without specific permission for each deal.

(c) Expert investors 'Expert' status is granted if the investor fulfils one of two conditions, according to the TSA rulebook. Firstly, if a person may reasonably be taken to fully understand the risks of a particular type of investment and to be capable of forming an adequate assessment of the merits and personal suitability of any recommendations by the firm, then he or she may be treated as an expert investor in that type of investment. The second route to expert status is via employment: an individual with substantial responsibility for dealing in or managing investments or corporate finance work in an authorized business or money-market institution may be regarded as an expert investor in all investments.

Expert investors are grouped with business customers in terms of degree of protection.

(d) Private customers Private customers are all individual customers except for those who are expert investors and those acting on behalf of market professionals or business customers, but with the addition of any small companies which do not qualify as business customers. It is for this type of customer that the Financial Services Act was primarily intended, and for whom it provides the greatest protection.

To summarize:

- market professionals – no protection except in the case of discretionary management;
- business customers (including 'expert investors') – limited protection;
- private customers – most protection.

In addition, there are two types of customer – 'execution-only' and 'discretionary management' – who cut across the four categories already outlined.

According to the TSA rulebook, the status of 'execution-only' customer is not a permanent classification, rather it is assessed on a transaction-by-transaction basis. Just because the first or a subsequent transaction was done in this way, an investment firm cannot automatically treat all its business with a customer in this way. The customer might otherwise be a private customer or a business customer; or, if this transaction is the first and last deal, the customer may have no other categorization. Essentially, 'execution-only' means that the customer requires no advisory service but initiates the deal, and the only protection provided is the execution of the deal at the best price obtainable. The onus is very much on an investment firm to demonstrate why a customer should be regarded as 'execution-only' and be denied the full protection of a private customer.

Discretionary management also cuts across established customer categorizations. Discretionary customers, including market professionals, are given extra protection (otherwise the preserve of private customers) when they give an investment firm discretion to buy and sell on their behalf without prior approval for each deal.

If the client is a private customer, the firm must inquire into his or her financial circumstances, in order to ascertain the suitability of investments and the ability of the client to meet any liabilities. Private customers in particular must be warned of any investments which are particularly risky.

2.2.2 Written customer agreement letters

Private and discretionary customers are normally required to complete and return a full customer agreement letter before a stockbroker or other adviser can deal on their behalf. Exempted from this requirement are exclusively indirect investments such as unit trusts, life assurance, and pensions. Business and expert investors, not operating on a discretionary basis, may be offered a less detailed 'terms of business' letter. Customer agreements are not mandatory for dealing with market professionals or 'execution-only' customers.

The purpose of the written customer agreement letter is to ensure that the client is absolutely clear as to his or her relationship with the investment firm. All customer agreement letters must include the following information:

(a) basic details about the investment business;
(b) the type of services offered;
(c) if the services include recommending purchases of single-premium life policies or unit trusts, a warning that the purchases cannot be cancelled, other than by mutual agreement;
(d) a statement as to whether the client agrees to receive unsolicited calls from the investment firm;
(e) a warning that, if the ordinary client agrees to accept unsolicited calls, he or she forfeits the right to treat any agreement entered into in consequence of such a call as unenforceable;
(f) the basic method and frequency of payment by the client to the firm, and a statement as to whether the firm will earn any commissions other than from the client (from unit trust managers, for example) and whether these will be passed on to the client.

Full customer agreement letters, required by private and discretionary customers, must also contain:

(g) the client's investment objectives (such as income, or growth, or a mixture);
(h) restrictions or guidelines as to types of investment;
(i) particular exchanges or markets which the client wishes excluded;
(j) a warning of the risky nature of any particular investments, such as futures and options, and whether further funds may be called upon;
(k) whether certain investments are not readily realizable;
(l) arrangements for receiving instructions from and reporting to the client;
(m) arrangements for holding money or investments on behalf of the client;
(n) in the case of managed portfolios, the initial composition and the periods of account for which statements are to be provided;
(o) agreements for discretionary portfolio management must include furth-

er items – in particular, the firm must obtain specific permission to invest money in its own funds, or in investments which the firm is involved in, and special permission to 'gear up' the portfolio by borrowing or investing in items for which only a margin needs to be paid;

(p) arrangements for terminating the contract.

2.2.3 Best advice

Investment businesses must recommend the best type of investment for the client, having regard to his or her other investments and personal and financial circumstances. A key concept is that of *polarization*. Investment firms have become polarized – they must be either totally independent or a tied agent for a particular company. No 'half-way house' is permitted, although some banks have made their branches tied and their investment management subsidiaries independent. An ironic consequence of the Financial Services Act 1986 has been that the range of products available in the branches of banks and building societies has reduced, as almost all of them now only offer unit trusts, life assurance, and pensions of one particular company.

The Act does not give a precise definition of best advice, but, in general terms,

(a) statements of fact must be true;

(b) disadvantages must be disclosed;

(c) criticisms of rival products must be fair.

An independent intermediary must recommend what he or she reckons to be the best product for the client available throughout the market. In practice this is an almost impossible task, given the thousands of products available and the difficulty of forecasting future performance. Company representatives, on the other hand, only have to recommend what is thought to be the best product sold by their company. If, however, no suitable product is available then the client must be advised to go to an independent agent. The same applies to 'appointed representatives', where one company sells only the products of one other company.

Investors should always ascertain whether an adviser is independent or a tied agent. Most banks and building societies have tied themselves to a particular life assurance company, and argue that loss of choice is compensated for by the competitive terms secured for their customers. Independent advice is still available from some of their independent subsidiaries for wealthier clients, and also from accountants and solicitors, as well as stockbrokers.

2.2.4 Best execution

A stockbroker must obtain the best price available for a client when dealing in securities. This is discussed in more detail in chapter 14.

2.2.5 Disclosure of commission

As a result of the Financial Services Act 1986, there has been pressure to provide investors with fuller information so as to ensure that they receive 'best advice'. This has resulted in considerable controversy over commissions paid, particularly with regard to life assurance. One area of particular dispute has been the question of a 'level playing field' for both independent intermediaries and tied agents. Independent advisers have felt that harsher disclosure requirements are being applied to them than to tied agents. The SIB view has been that this distinction is justifiable, as independent advisers are agents of the client, while company representatives are agents of the company. The compromise that has been reached is a system of 'soft' disclosure. Commission rates paid to independent advisers have to be disclosed to customers. However, the commission need not be shown in cash terms, but rather as a percentage of the premiums, and the disclosure will not be made at the point of sale but in a letter sent to the customer by the insurance company within fourteen days of receiving an application form. However, the customer has the right to ask for the figures in cash terms. In the case of tied agents, the customer will receive only a statement of the extent to which premiums are absorbed by general charges and expenses. These points are discussed in more detail in section 17.10.

2.2.6 Advertisements and illustrations of benefits

The Financial Services Act 1986 introduced much stricter controls on the contents of advertisements, including financial 'tip sheets'. Any risks involved must be clearly spelt out – in what are known as 'wealth warnings'! Particular restrictions apply to the use of past performance as an indicator of future performance. In the case of 'with-profits' life assurance and pensions, all life assurance companies have to provide illustrations of future benefits on a standardized basis laid down by SIB and LAUTRO. As all the elements in the calculation – investment returns, expenses, mortality, etc. – are determined on the same basis, all life companies show the same illustrative figures for the same type of contract. This is to indicate that individual past performance cannot be relied upon to repeat itself in the future, but the standardized figures provide little guidance to the investor or to the independent intermediary required to give best advice.

In the case of unit trusts and unit-linked life assurance and pensions, the rules do allow past performance figures to be quoted, but not for unfairly selective time-periods. Typically, five-year figures are required.

Advertisements for unit trusts, life assurance, or pensions which require the investor to send money rather than write in for more information are required to give details of charges. Life assurance companies also have to provide details of surrender values in the early years, based on present performance and charges.

2.2.7 'Cold-calling' and 'cooling-off'

Unsolicited calls (or 'cold-calling') are defined as personal visits or conversations made without the investor's express invitation – for example, doorstep selling, personal encounters in the street, or a telephone call to a person's home or place of work. If the investor has not agreed to accept such calls, in a customer agreement letter, they must be restricted to the subject of unit trusts, life assurance policies, or personal pensions. These are allowed presumably because traditionally they have been 'sold' rather than 'bought'! However, the investor has a fourteen-day 'cooling-off' period to reconsider and cancel any contract entered into. Furthermore, if the contract is for other than unit trusts, life assurance or personal pensions, it may be unenforceable. However, as mentioned in section 2.2.2, investors who have agreed to accept such calls retain the right to a 'cooling-off' period only for regular-premium life assurance.

In the case of 'cold-calling', the 'conduct of business' rules do require that personal visits are not made at unsocial hours and that the potential clients must always be asked if they wish the interview to proceed. Also, selling under the guise of market research ('sugging') is not permitted.

2.2.8 Protection of funds
Money belonging to a client must be kept in a bank account separate from that of the investment business, as a safeguard against insolvency.

2.3 Sources of advice

The investor cannot necessarily expect to be protected from all advice that proves to be bad, or from his or her own ignorance or stupidity. There is no remedy for losses incurred through following bad advice, if that advice was given in good faith. Anyone can be wrong, and there is no comeback as long as the opinion expressed is honesty and genuinely held, and the person giving advice is not exceeding the scope of his or her professional expertise. This is why an investor should become familiar with the range and use of the various types of investment, and be aware of the current investment climate, so that the advice received can be evaluated and assessed.

Advice on investment matters is plentiful. There are as many people prepared to advise on investment as there are people prepared to advise the Government on its policies. Investment is a popular hobby, and where hobbies are concerned expense is rarely a major factor. So many people, having a few shares, and having had one success, come to believe that they have a flair for investment that can be developed to make fortunes for themselves and for all their friends and acquaintances. When questioned about their less-successful purchases, they maintain a discreet silence.

The investor should beware of such amateurs. However convincing the take-over story based on 'inside' knowledge seems, however much the friend employed by a large company claims to know about its current progress, and however much the man on the train has made out of a particular share, the potential investor should either ignore what they say or at least evaluate it carefully. The tale about the take-over may be true, but it may merely be a rumour. Few people in large companies can see the whole picture of their company's activities. And a large profit on a purchase may mean only that the top price has been reached rather than that further appreciation is indicated.

2.3.1 The bank manager

Many investors look to their bank manager for their general financial and investment advice. Usually this is as good a source as any, since bank managers see a good deal of the financial world in their day-to-day dealings with a wide range of customers and business associates. They are not, however, specially trained in investment matters. Bank managers vary considerably in their knowledge of investments, and many of them have investment portfolios of their own which compel them to keep abreast of market trends and thinking. Many others, however, do not have the 'feel' of investments and are not able to give advice other than of a very general kind.

It is desirable that bank managers should become more investment-orientated. Certainly they must know what rival organizations such as the National Savings Bank and the building societies are currently offering depositors. They should be familiar with the returns available on the National Savings investments and their suitability for customers in different tax situations. They will be mindful of their customers' needs for life assurance, and in particular the many advantages of unit trusts and insurance bonds. But investors should be aware that bank managers' advice is unlikely ever to be wholly disinterested. Bankers like having deposit accounts; and it is only natural for them to prefer their own bank's unit trust and insurance subsidiaries to those of their rivals, even if the track record does not always justify that preference!

Because most banks are now tied to a particular insurance company, they are restricted to their own tied products, unless the investor has sufficient capital to justify a referral to their independent investment management subsidiary.

By training, bank managers are not experts in investment and, while they may be able to give general advice, they generally steer clear of giving specific advice on marketable securities. Banks will ask Stock Exchange broker/dealers for advice on portfolio construction and individual investments if their customers wish. In some cases these broker/dealers will be subsidiaries of the bank.

2.3.2 Stockbroker/dealers

The best available advice on the purchase of equities probably comes from stockbroker/dealers with experienced and able teams of analysts at their disposal. Only the largest firms can afford large research departments, and generally these are the firms least willing to take on the small client. They do most of their business with the large institutions such as the insurance companies, merchant banks, and pension funds, where the size of the individual orders produces commission for the broker/dealers large enough to justify intensive research on a limited number of companies.

Nevertheless, the smaller investor should have no difficulty in finding a broker/dealer. The Investor Research and Education Unit at the Stock Exchange publishes a directory of firms that wish to take on private clients. In fact, personal investors have more choice than ever – from low-cost 'no frills' telephone dealing services to sophisticated discretionary fund management. There are plenty of traditional smaller firms striving to attract clients. Some smaller firms have amalgamated in order to spread research and administrative costs; examples include the National Investment Group and Allied Provincial.

The amount of research and analysis done by smaller firms will be less than that done by the big firms, because of the nature of their business. But firms willing to accept the smaller investor can offer a personal service to their clients which many big firms, with their demanding institutional clients, cannot. As with all professions, the quality of the service one obtains depends on the ability of the particular person with whom one deals. Investment advice can usually be evaluated only in the medium term, so, when dealing with a new broker/dealer, it may be necessary to take certain things on trust until sufficient time has gone by to be able to assess the advice given.

In addition to the above, there are 'no advice', execution-only dealing services, such as Sharelink – a subsidiary of British Telecom and stockbrokers Albert E. Sharpe in Birmingham. A similar scheme, called Marketline, is operated by brokers Henry Cooke Lumsden. Others, such as Barclayshare, provide dealing services at low cost but also offer extras like regular valuations, advice, and bulletins. These are discussed in more detail in section 15.4.

2.3.3 Other informed sources

Many investors rely on their solicitors, accountants, and insurance brokers for investment advice. The reservations made as to advice given by bank managers apply broadly here too. People whose principal activity is not directly related to investment can hardly be expected to be aware of all the latest developments in that area and to be fully in touch with market trends and opinion.

Accountants and solicitors authorized by the professional bodies are required to give independent investment advice. Insurance brokers will usually be tied. Many so-called investment advisers, or 'consultants', are really insurance brokers masquerading under another name. Solicitors can retain commission earned only if the client gives permission, while accountants must inform the client of the amount of commission earned. In practice, both solicitors and accountants sometimes reduce their fee by the amount of commission earned.

Unfortunately, the number of independent professional investment advisers – members of FIMBRA – whose services are available to the small investor is shrinking. The cost of all services is continually rising, and small investors cannot pay for expensive advice. What they need is a good supply of general information that they can apply to their own circumstances. The number of newspapers and journals recognizing this is increasing, and some are listed in appendix 1 at the end of this book.

All-round financial services, including tax planning and borrowing of all kinds, are frequently required as well as investment advice. The number of companies setting out to supply this need is rising, although they still include only a few recognized institutions. There is a need not only for more advisers but also for a greater awareness among the public of how necessary these services are.

2.4 Professional management

There is probably no other activity where the expert is so often wrong as in the field of investment. If the investment is absolutely strightforward – putting funds on deposit or into some form of life assurance, for instance – the matter is relatively simple, but there are no foolproof ways of making money out of risk investments like ordinary shares. The personal investor may therefore consider appointing professional managers to look after his or her investments, and possibly even a full discretionary management service. The competent manager will give any recommendations only in the context of an investor's overall strategy, and that always means considerable attention being paid to the need to diversify interests.

We shall consider the services given by stockbroker/dealers, merchant banks, clearing banks, and others.

2.4.1 Stockbroker/dealers

Some stockbroker/dealers offer a service to clients which goes beyond the mere giving of advice. They are prepared to take over the management of portfolios, dealing with them at their discretion. The size of portfolio which will be taken on varies with the firm, but sums less than £25 000 will usually be invested in unit trusts. Some broker/dealers make a charge for this service, but others make no charge over and above their commissions. The risk of a 'free' service is that the broker deals excessively, to generate commission. This is known as *'churning'*, and is forbidden under the Financial Services Act 1986 and TSA 'conduct of business' rules. These define 'churning' as the generating of commission by recommending transactions to customers, or carrying them out, with unnecessary frequency, or dealing in excessive size. The onus is on the firm to justify the transactions it carries out, particularly in relation to discretionary portfolios.

As the standard of advice varies throughout the range of firms offering portfolio management, it is impossible to generalize on the quality of this type of service.

2.4.2 Merchant banks

Merchant banks offer investment management services to personal clients and institutions. They all have a minimum size of portfolio which they will take on. Most merchant banks are not interested in portfolios of less than £100 000 for direct management. Smaller sums will tend to go into unit trusts. Charges vary around 1 per cent. Merchant banks usually require full discretionary powers in their portfolio management, and the funds are largely, if not exclusively, invested in equities.

Merchant banks manage very substantial sums, and they all have their own analytical departments. In addition, by using many firms of broker/dealers for their business, they receive the output of most of the research departments of the large stockbroking/dealing firms. Their management services should therefore produce better results than those of other institutions with smaller business and consequently less resources. The only way in which it is possible to judge performance overall is to compare the records of unit trusts managed by merchant banks against those managed by other institutions, but the ownership of the unit trusts concerned, and therefore the institutions responsible for investment, changes from time to time and strict comparison is difficult.

2.4.3 Clearing banks

The investment portfolio management services offered by the clearing banks are generally in a lower key than those offered by merchant banks. Their analytical departments are smaller than those of the merchant banks, and their expertise depends largely on their assessment and modification of the advice and recommendations received from the stockbroker/dealers allocated to each client's portfolio. Usually the investment management service is operated by the executor and trustee departments of the banks concerned. It forms part of a financial service offered by those departments principally to the bank's general customers who require independent advice. It covers estate planning, personal tax advice, executorship, and family trust administration as well as private portfolio management. The banks also have a measure of institutional business, such as pension fund trusteeship and custodian services.

The minimum portfolio requirements for the investment management services of clearing banks range from £25 000 to £50 000. Charges are around 0.75 per cent, with minimum fees of at least £200 per annum. Generally speaking, the service is geared more to the individual circumstances of the customer than those of the other institutions. The banks will recommend investments other than Stock Exchange securities if they feel that these are best suited to the customer's requirements, whereas the services offered by other institutions are primarily for the management of Stock Exchange portfolios. For this type of service, knowledge of the whole of the customer's circumstances is necessary.

The investment policy pursued by the banks is less active than that of many of the other portfolio management institutions, with the emphasis on the purchase and regular review of holdings suitable for the investor's requirements in the medium to long term. Maximizing of capital growth and comparison of performance against recognized indices take a secondary place to portfolio planning and maintenance. The service offered, therefore, is similar to the portfolio management which a private investor might do himself or herself. For this reason, the banks tend to attract those people who do not have the time or inclination to look after their own portfolios, rather than those knowledgeable investors who are looking to an institution for superior investment expertise.

The unit trusts run by the clearing banks, with a few exceptions, show unspectacular performances, with appearances in either the top or bottom of the performance tables being rare. Given the attitude of the clearing banks to investment policy generally, this is hardly surprising. In fairness, however, it should be borne in mind that medium-term performance is not achieved by spectacular success in one short period followed by spectacular failure in another. Trusts with the best long-term performance are not always in the 'top twenty' over short periods.

2.4.4 Other management services
Other firms providing advisory or discretionary management services are investment advisers, accountants, solicitors, and fund management groups. Accountants have only recently moved into this area, and the larger firms are restricted by being precluded from investing in corporate clients' shares. Fund managers normally look for a minimum of at least £100 000 for individual management.

2.5 Questions

1. (a) A financial adviser selling life assurance and unit trusts must be a member of:

   A LAUTRO only.
   B FIMBRA only.
   C either FIMBRA or LAUTRO.
   D both FIMBRA and LAUTRO.

   (b) Under the Financial Services Act 1986 virtually all public securities trading must take place on a Recognized Investment Exchange (RIE).
   State:

   Either the *full* name under which the Stock Exchange operates as a RIE;
   Or   the name of *one* other RIE recognized by the Securities and Investments Board or the Department of Trade and Industry.

   (c) The self-regulating organization which is responsible for Stock Exchange member firms and their employees and which reports to the

Securities and Investments Board under the Financial Services Act 1986 is:

A TSA.
B FIMBRA.
C IMRO.
D LAUTRO.

(d) In the context of the Financial Services Act 1986, give one example of a 'Recognized Professional Body'.

2. (a) What is the fundamental purpose of the Financial Services 1986 and what machinery is in force to give effect to this purpose?
   (b) Explain *three* of the rules relating to the conduct of business which have to be adhered to by investment practitioners under the Financial Services Act.

(CIB 10/88)

3. (a) Name the self-regulating organizations (SROs) approved by the Securities and Investments Board under the Financial Services Act 1986.
   (b) Most major bank groups belong to several, if not all, of the SROs. Explain why this is so and relate your answer in particular to *two* of the SROs.
   (c) What is the special regulatory mechanism employed in cases where an institution belongs to two or more SROs?

(CIB 5/89)

4. Mrs A is a widow aged 67. She receives pensions totalling £14 000 per annum. She has a portfolio of ordinary shares in UK quoted companies and British Government stocks. This is currently valued at £120 000 and produces a gross annual income of approximately £5000. The investments were inherited from her father, who died in 1980, and the only changes which have taken place since then have been the result of take-over bids, rights issues, or scrip issues. She also has bank deposit and building society accounts amounting to £15 000. Mrs A manages quite well on her income, but she is rather worried about her investments. She feels they should be reviewed. She also finds the paperwork is getting too much for her.

Describe the portfolio management services offered by the clearing banks and explain whether this type of service would be suitable for Mrs A.

(CIB 9/83)

3 Taxes

3.1 The tax environment

One of the most important influences, where investment matters are concerned, is the incidence of taxation, since tax reliefs and liabilities influence investment decisions made in respect of most portfolios. Only those investors exempt from taxation – charities and pension funds – and those below the tax thresholds do not have to take taxation into account. Every investor needs to know his or her marginal rate of income tax – that is, the rate of tax payable on any increase in income – in order to be able to compare the net-of-tax returns from different investments and to be able to calculate total net income.

The impact of changes in taxation on investment decisions has been dramatic in recent years. Most notable has been the reduction in the highest rate of income tax. At one time the highest rate of income tax on investment income was 98 per cent! The figure in 1990/91 is 40 per cent. High marginal rates of income tax led wealthy investors to seek capital gains, which were taxed much more leniently, at the expense of income. Nowadays the difference in the taxation of income and capital (known as fiscal bias) is much less pronounced. While the highest marginal rate of income tax has been reduced, the rate for capital gains tax has actually increased in recent times for wealthy individuals. Instead of the long-established fixed rate of 30 per cent, individuals, in 1990/91, pay tax on capital gains at their marginal income tax rate, 25 per cent or 40 per cent. The compensating factor has been an allowance for the effect of inflation, such that assets currently liable are assessed for capital gains tax only on gains made from April 1982 to the present day.

The most profound change to the personal taxation system for many years took place in April 1990. Since then, married couples are automatically assessed as two individuals, instead of jointly, for the purposes of income tax and capital gains tax. This change has led to many couples reallocating investments between partners in order to take optimum advantage of the new tax regime. This is discussed in more detail later in this chapter.

In the first part of this chapter we examine the broad principles of income tax, capital gains tax, and inheritance tax, which are the three taxes which directly affect personal investors. The rates and allowances will obviously change to some extent every year, so the figures quoted are illustrative only. Up-to-date figures can be obtained from an investor's local tax office, or from one of the many guides published each year. Particularly good are the *Lloyds Bank Tax Guide*, the *Which? Tax Saving Guide*, and, for more detail, the *Tolley's Tax Guide* or the *Allied Dunbar Tax Guide*.

3.2 Income tax

3.2.1 Background

Income tax in the United Kingdom is based on income received between 6 April in one year and 5 April in the following year. What counts as 'income' can change from time to time. For example, in recent years Chancellors have declared that 'gains' made on offshore 'roll-up' funds (see section 16.13) and the gain in value due to accrued interest on fixed-interest securities are taxable income, not genuine capital gains. The distinction between income and capital gain can therefore be seen to be somewhat arbitrary. Loss of Government revenue through tax avoidance brought about the above changes. Similarly, anyone making capital gains on a very regular basis risks being classed as a 'trader' by the Inland Revenue, and therefore subject to income tax.

Further confusion sometimes arises because 'income' is not always taxed on the basis of the current year. For instance, where interest is paid 'gross' to an investor, the interest is normally taxed on a 'preceding-year' basis. This means that the tax bill for one tax year depends on the interest received in the previous tax year. To further complicate matters in such cases, the opening and closing two years are taxed on a 'current-year' basis!

Certain types of investment income will be received 'gross' of tax, as above, and others 'net'. Some investments are completely tax-free, such as National Savings Certificates and Personal Equity Plans. Investors should be clear about the distinction between those investments which pay income 'gross' and those that are 'tax-free'. In the former case, the liability still remains with the investor to pay the tax if liable. Other 'income' exempt from income tax includes gifts or presents received, inheritances, prize winnings, and money borrowed.

An investor needs to determine his or her total income for the tax year. This requires the addition of earnings, pensions, and investment income relevant to that tax year. Income received 'net' needs to be grossed-up for basic-rate tax. This means multiplying the 'net' figure by 100 divided by 100 minus the basic rate of income tax. For 1990/91, this means multiplying by $\frac{100}{75}$. The purpose of doing this calculation is to determine whether the investor is eligible for a tax rebate, or is liable to pay additional tax on the investment income if it falls within the higher-rate tax band. 'Tax-free' investments should not be included in the calculation.

All the income aggregated together is known as the *gross* income. From this figure, the investor is entitled to deduct *outgoings*, such as gross mortgage interest (on the first £30 000 of the mortgage), pension payments, and investments in the Business Expansion Scheme. The balance figure is known as *total* income. From this figure, the investor can then deduct *allowances* to arrive at the *taxable* income on which income tax is charged.

3.2.2 Rates and allowances

The tax bands and principal allowances for 1990/91 are shown in Table 3.1 and discussed in subsequent sections.

The income tax rates of 25 per cent or 40 per cent are applied to income after deducting the relevant outgoings and allowances. For example, imagine that Rita Hale is an architect earning £29 000 per annum, from which pension contributions of 6 per cent are deducted by her employer. She is 38 years of age, single, and lives in her own property subject to an endowment mortgage of £35 000, paying interest of 10½ per cent per annum. Two years ago she inherited £80 000 on the death of her mother and, following this inheritance, started investing in stocks and shares. Her well-diversified portfolio – 25 per cent gilt-edged securities and 75 per cent equities – is expected to produce £2100 income net of basic-rate tax in the 1990/91 tax year. Her tax liability for 1990/91 would be determined as follows:

		£
Earnings		29 000
Investment income grossed-up (£2100 × $\frac{100}{75}$)		2 800
Gross income		31 800
less Outgoings:		
Gross mortgage interest (£30 000* × 10½%)		3 150
Pension contributions (£29 000 × 6%)		1 740
Total income		26 910
less Personal allowance		3 005
Taxable income		23 905
	£	
Tax at 25% on £20 700	5 175	
Tax at 40% on £3 205	1 282	
	6 457	

Total income after tax = £25 343 (i.e. £31 800−£6 457)

* £30 000 limit, not whole £35 000.

The £700 tax has already been paid at source on the investment income, and the earnings are taxed under PAYE. (The investment income paid net has to be grossed-up for basic-rate tax, and the mortgage interest has to be taken 'gross' even when paid 'net' under MIRAS (see section 20.5), because of the need to establish precisely any higher-rate tax liability.)

3.2.3 Independent taxation

From the date that income tax was introduced in 1799 until April 1990, a

Table 3.1 Tax bands and principal allowances for 1990/91

	Rate	Band
Basic-rate band	25%	0–£20 700
Higher-rate band	40%	£20 701+

	£	Extra allowance above standard rates
Personal allowance	3 005	
Married couple's allowance	1 720	
Additional personal allowance	1 720	
Age allowance		
Age 65–74		
Personal	3 670	665
Married couple's	2 145	425
Age 75+		
Personal	3 820	815
Married couple's	2 185	465
Income limit	12 300	
Widow's bereavement allowance	1 720	
Blind person's allowance	1 080	

husband was legally responsible for his wife's tax affairs. Even if she opted for separate taxation, her investment income was still aggregated with her husband's for tax purposes. Since April 1990, however, a wife's income, from no matter what source, is automatically taxed as her own, and can therefore, if so wished, be kept private from her husband. A wife is required to complete a separate tax return.

Both partners receive a personal allowance, with higher allowances for persons aged 65–74 and 75 and over. The husband also receives a *married couple's allowance*, currently worth £1720 (1990/91). Where one partner is aged between 65 and 74, or 75+, the respective figures for the married couple's allowance for 1990/91 are £2145 and £2185. The age of the elder spouse determines the level of the married couple's allowance, but the personal allowances are determined by their individual ages.

The main beneficiaries from these income tax changes are couples where the wife does not work but has investment income. Previously, the wife's personal allowance could be used only for earned income. Under the new system, the wife can receive investment income up to the personal allowance entirely free of tax. Where investments were previously in the husband's name or in joint names, it is now more tax-efficient for such couples to transfer investments into the wife's name until the investment income of the wife is equal to her personal allowance. For instance, exchanging sufficient investments to provide a non-taxpaying wife with £3005 investment income will save a couple £751 if they are 25 per cent taxpayers and £1202 if they pay tax at 40 per cent (1990/91). In such circumstances, the appropriate investments for the wife are ones which pay income gross, or where tax can be reclaimed.

Where assets held in joint names are to be split in some proportion other than 50 : 50, it is necessary to sign a *Notice of declaration of beneficial interest in joint property and income*, stating the relevant proportions.

A wife's State pension is taxed as her own, irrespective of which partner paid the contributions, whereas previously a wife could use her allowance only if she personally had made the contributions.

Only the married couple's allowance is transferable between partners. If the husband has little or no income, his wife can use the married couple's allowance.

3.2.4 Age allowance clawback

Age allowance replaces the personal and married couple's allowances for persons aged 65 or over, and an increased age allowance applies to persons aged 75 or over. However, for persons with 'total' (before allowances) income above the 'income limit' of £12 300 (1990/91) there is a 'clawback' of £1 of the age allowance for every additional £2 of total income above £12 300.

Under independent taxation, married couples each have an income limit before they are subject to the age allowance clawback. The extent to which the *married couple's allowance* is clawed back is determined by the husband's income, not that of the wife, even if the allowance has been given on her age, as the elder spouse. Where the husband's income exceeds the income limit, the excess is first applied to reducing his own personal age allowance and then to clawing back the married man's allowance.

The benefit of the extra allowance therefore disappears altogether at the following levels:

	Age	£
Personal allowance	65–74	13 630
	75+	13 930
Married couple's allowance	65–74	14 480
	75+	14 860

At and above these levels of 'total' income, persons effectively receive the standard personal and married couple's allowances, irrespective of age. This is known as the 'age allowance trap'. The clawback of the additional allowances between £12 300 and these higher income limits produces an effective high marginal rate of tax within the relevant income band. For example, assume an investor, aged 65 or above, currently has total income in excess of £12 300 but below the upper limits listed above. Two pounds of extra earned or investment income results in the loss of £1 of the age allowance. Taxable income – the difference between total income and allowances – thus increases by £3. Twenty-five per cent tax levied on £3 is 75p. Therefore the effective rate of tax on the marginal income is $\frac{75p}{£2.00} \times 100 = 37\frac{1}{2}$ per cent. Of course, once income exceeds the upper income limits the marginal rate drops back to the basic rate of 25 per cent, until taxable income exceeds £20 700.

3.2.5 Mortgage interest tax relief

Mortgage interest tax relief, on the first £30 000 of a qualifying mortgage, is allocated to the person in whose name the mortgage is registered, or split equally if the mortgage is in joint names. It can be advantageous under the new system to reallocate the mortgage interest relief between partners. The exact split required must be notified to the Inland Revenue, using a special form called the '*Allocation of interest election*'. If a couple pay mortgage interest 'net' under MIRAS, and they are basic-rate taxpayers or non-taxpayers, such an election is unnecessary. However, a couple with a non-MIRAS loan, where interest is paid gross, would lose out from an equal split if one spouse is a taxpayer and the other is a non-taxpayer and some mortgage relief is allocated to the latter.

Other beneficial examples of an election, even under MIRAS, would include where one spouse is subject to higher-rate tax and the other is not. Here the tax relief on the interest should be claimed by the higher-rate taxpayer only. Another example would be where one partner is above the lower income limit for age allowance clawback but the other partner is not – the mortgage interest tax relief should be allocated to the higher-income spouse if it results in an increase in their total allowances.

3.2.6 Additional personal allowance

The *additional personal allowance* is given to parents who are single, divorced, or widowed, provided that they are caring for the child or children. It supplements the single person's allowance, and is equal to the married couple's allowance. Only one allowance is available per parent, irrespective of the number of children.

3.2.7 Widow's bereavement allowance

In the year of bereavement, a widow can claim an additional allowance, known as the '*widow's bereavement allowance*'. This can be claimed in the following year as well, unless she has remarried before the start of that tax year.

3.2.8 Blind person's allowance

This is an allowance, in addition to other allowances, for blind persons.

3.2.9 Children's income

Children's income is normally aggregated with their parents' income, until marriage or the age of eighteen, whichever is the earlier. This is obviously to prevent tax avoidance as a result of parents artificially routing income through a minor's name. This means that, if a minor acquires income from investments provided by a parent, the child's marginal tax rate will be the same as that of the parent. However, from 1991/92, if the income is not in excess of £100, the income is taxed as the child's, independently of that of the parent. If it is in excess of £100, the whole of the income is aggregated with that of the parent.

If the child receives gifts from a non-parent (including close relatives such as grandparents) or earnings from a part-time job, the child is entitled to his or her own personal allowance, and can therefore receive tax-free income up to this limit.

3.3 Capital gains tax

3.3.1 Background
Capital gains tax (CGT) applies to realized 'real' gains made on 'chargeable' assets since 31 March 1982 or the date of acquisition, whichever is the later.

The term 'realized' means that CGT is a tax payable on the gain which has accrued by the time of the 'disposal' of an asset. 'Disposal' usually means that an asset is sold, but it can also include giving away, exchanging, or even losing an asset. 'Real' gains are gains remaining after stripping away the effect of inflation, as measured by changes in the Retail Prices Index (RPI). Any gains accrued before April 1982 are entirely exempt from capital gains tax.

3.3.2 Tax rate
Capital gains tax is levied on individuals and married couples at their marginal rate of income tax – that is, 25 per cent or 40 per cent (1990/91). Capital gains realized in the tax year are added to other income in order to determine the tax liability.

Small investors are unlikely to pay capital gains tax because of the indexation for inflation, and because an initial amount per person (£5000 in 1990/91) is exempted from tax. Since independent taxation, a husband and wife each have an annual exemption of £5000, and each child is entitled to his or her own exemption, irrespective of the original source of the capital.

Realized losses can be set off against realized gains in any tax year, and any unused losses can be carried forward indefinitely to reduce future gains. But the whole or part of the annual exemption not used in a particular year is lost, since it cannot be carried forward.

3.3.3 Exempted investors and assets
Certain types of transfer, investor, and asset are completely exempt from CGT, irrespective of the size of the gain. These include:

(a) Transfers between a husband and wife.
(b) Transfers on death. CGT applies only to lifetime disposals of assets, not to those bequeathed. Persons inheriting assets under a will or intestacy acquire them at their value on the date of death. However, there may be a liability to inheritance tax (see section 3.4).
(c) Certain types of investor, including charities, pension funds, friendly societies, local authorities, and persons not 'ordinarily resident' in the UK.
(d) Principal place of private residence. The CGT exemption for owner-

occupied property extends to grounds not exceeding one acre, or such larger area as is appropriate to the size and character of the house.

(e) All forms of National Savings, such as National Savings Certificates, and bank and building society Save-As-You-Earn.

(f) Gilt-edged securities and 'qualifying' corporate debt. The latter includes all forms of company debentures and loan stocks, other than convertibles, which are issued in sterling by a company with a full Stock Exchange listing, or quoted on the Unlisted Securities Market, and acquired by the investor after 13 March 1984. The exemption also extends to futures and options on these investments. (In the case of qualifying corporate debt, where part or all of the loans becomes irrecoverable, the loss can be used by the investor for capital gains tax purposes, provided the debt was held on, or issued after, 15 March 1989.)

(g) Proceeds of a life assurance or friendly-society policy.

(h) Personal Equity Plans.

(i) Shares in a Business Expansion Scheme on first disposal, if held for five years.

(j) 'Wasting' chattels. These are personal possessions with an investment value which have a predictable life of 50 years or less. They include wine, yachts, racehorses, and racing pigeons.

(k) Private motor cars, including vintage and veteran cars.

(l) 'Small-value' chattels – individual items, such as books, antiques, or jewellery, disposed of with a value of £6000 or less.

(m) British money, including gold sovereigns dated after 1836 and Britannia coins.

(n) Foreign currency for personal use.

(o) Betting winnings – including betting on the movement of share indices.

(p) Decorations for bravery, unless purchased.

(q) Gifts to charities and national heritage bodies such as the National Trust.

Because the above are exempt from capital gains tax, in order to preserve symmetry, any losses realized on them cannot be set off against gains made elsewhere (with the exception of (f)).

As mentioned earlier in the chapter, certain gains may be subject to income tax rather than capital gains tax. This is the case with gains made on 'deep-discounted' bonds, single-premium life assurance, offshore 'roll-up' funds, and the interest which 'accrues' between payment dates on gilt-edged and most other interest-bearing securities.

Persons and assets not exempted from capital gains tax are known respectively as *'chargeable' persons* and *'chargeable' assets*.

3.3.4 Indexation
As mentioned earlier, capital gains tax is applied to realized 'real' gains made by chargeable persons on chargeable assets between acquisition and disposal

dates but no earlier than 31 March 1982. Dealing expenses can be added to the acquisition cost and deducted from the disposal value.

Imagine that Alan Evans bought shares for £1000, including dealing expenses in 1970. The market value of the same shares at 31 March 1982 was £10 000. Alan sold all of the shares on 21 April 1990 for £21 000, after deducting expenses. What would be his capital gains tax liability, if any, assuming his other taxable income in 1990/91 was £15 000 and he realized no other gains or losses? As he owned the asset before 31 March 1982, he can take as the base price either the original price, or the value on that date, whichever is the greater. In this case he obviously benefits from the use of the much higher 1982 value of £10 000. This figure can be inflated in line with movements in the RPI from 31 March 1982 to 31 March 1990. The respective RPI figures for these two dates are 79.4 and 125.1 (31 January 1987 = 100.0).

$$\text{Revaluation of 31 March 1982 value} = £10\,000 \times \frac{125.1}{79.4}$$

$$= £10\,000 \times 1.576$$

$$= £15\,760$$

$$\text{Chargeable gain} = £21\,000 - £15\,760$$

$$= £5\,240$$

$$\text{Annual exemption} = \underline{£5\,000}$$

$$\therefore \quad \text{Taxable gain} = £5\,240 - £5\,000 = £240$$

The addition of £240 to other income of £15 000 gives a total taxable income of £15 240, which is below the higher-rate tax band. Therefore the whole of the taxable gain of £240 is subject to tax at 25 per cent, which gives a CGT figure of £60. This is very small relative to the actual gain of £20 000 made on the shares.

Of course, if the assets had been acquired after 31 March 1982, then the actual acquisition date would have replaced 31 March 1982 as the base date for indexation.

Two specific rules are designed to prevent anomalies involving assets held before 1 April 1982. Firstly, if the gain or loss would be smaller using the actual acquisition price rather than the 31 March 1982 value as the base value for indexation from that date, then the original acquisition price is used. Secondly, if there is a gain after indexation when using one figure but a loss when using the other, then the gain is said to be within the 'neutral' zone and there is no chargeable gain and no allowable loss. In order to abide by these two rules, investors need to have maintained records going back perhaps many years. As an alternative – certainly for those whose filing is not their strong point – the Inland Revenue allows investors to make an irrevocable election to have all of their assets acquired before 31 March 1982 treated as if they acquired them at their value on that date.

3.3.5 Matching bargains

Complications can arise in share dealing when shares of the same type and company are bought and sold in varying amounts over a period of time. The problem is to match the purchase with the sale. The procedure used to simplify this problem is to identify shares sold with purchases in the following order of priority:

1. Shares bought on the same day.
2. Shares bought on the previous nine days, on a first-in, first-out basis.
3. Shares acquired from 6 April 1982 and which are not included in the first two categories above. These are all put together in one pool – known as the *'new holding'* – and the purchase price is determined by a weighted average.
4. All shares bought up until 5 April 1982 would normally be averaged in price and form the frozen *'1982 holding'*. The term 'frozen' is used because the average price is fixed, and is not affected by new acquisitions.
5. Shares bought after the date of sale.

3.3.6 'Bed-and-breakfast' deals

These deals are so called because the investor sells shares before 4.30 p.m. one day and buys them back again after 8.30 a.m. the following morning. The purpose of this seemingly irrational behaviour is to realize a capital gain or loss for CGT purposes. A gain of up to £5000 (1990/91) might be established in order to use all or part of the previously unused annual exemption. As a result, the base price is uplifted for determining the gain on any subsequent sale.

The cost of a 'B&B' deal can be quite modest, as the stockbroker may only charge for commission on one deal. The other expenses are the Stock Exchange market-maker's bid-offer spread, $\frac{1}{2}$ per cent stamp duty reserve tax levied on the repurchase price, and possibly two 10p contract (PTM) levies paid to fund the Panel for Take-overs and Mergers (see section 13.3).

The incidence of 'B&B' deals is greatest near the end of the tax year, when investors know what their capital gains tax position is likely to be for the year. In some cases, a loss may be realized in order to keep the 'net chargeable' gain to no more than the amount of the annual exemption. However, because of the size of the annual exemption and the provision for indexation of the cost, 'B&B' deals are not necessary for the majority of small investors.

3.3.7 Chattels

As outlined earlier, 'wasting' chattels, motor cars, coins and currency, and 'small-value' chattels are exempt from CGT. As far as other chattels are concerned, there is a small concession in that if the sale price is in excess of £6000, then the gain is taken to be the lower of either the actual chargeable gain or the sale value minus £6000, multiplied by $\frac{5}{3}$. For example, imagine that a picture was bought for £1000 in December 1972, had an estimated value of £3000 at 31 March 1982, and was sold for £6600 in April 1990. The indexed cost would be £4728, i.e. £3000×$\frac{125.1}{79.4}$ (see section 3.3.4), and the chargeable gain would be £6600−£4728 = £1872. However, on the other basis of assessing the gain, this would be reduced to (£6600−£6000)×$\frac{5}{3}$ = £1000.

A disposal for less than £6000 that results in a chargeable loss is regarded as a sale at £6000.

3.3.8 Business retirement relief
If a person disposes of a business, or of shares in a family company, at the age of 60 or more − or earlier if retiring due to ill health − then the chargeable gain is exempt from CGT up to £125 000 (1990/91), plus relief on half the gains between £125 000 and £500 000. Relief can be claimed if the person disposes of shares in a family company, provided the person has been a full-time director of the company for the previous ten years. A 'family' company is one in which the person has 25 per cent or more of the voting rights, or at least 5 per cent, with him or her and the immediate family having more than 50 per cent. However, the full relief applies only if the person has owned the business or shares for at least ten years. The amount of relief is reduced by 10 per cent for each year less than ten.

3.3.9 Other cases
Special rules apply to life assurance companies and trusts. These are discussed in chapters 17 and 22 respectively. Complications can also arise with rights issues, take-overs, and regular-savings schemes. These are dealt with in the relevant chapters.

3.3.10 Independent taxation
Capital gains tax has been affected, like income tax, by the change to independent taxation in April 1990. Since that date, husbands and wives have been taxed separately for CGT, each receiving the annual exemption. As a result, small investors are even less likely to pay CGT than before. Transfers of assets between a husband and wife are exempt from CGT; the recipient is deemed to acquire the assets at the same acquisition price as originally paid by the spouse.

As with income tax, tax planning for CGT may well indicate that assets should be transferred between spouses in order to minimize the overall tax liability. A case in point might be a husband paying income tax at 40 per cent, and using his full exemption each year, while his wife is a non-taxpayer who does not use her exemption at all. A transfer of some assets to the wife will be tax-efficient. She can use her own annual exemption against gains she realizes, but her personal allowance can be used only on her earned or investment income, not on capital gains.

One rule that remains unchanged is that a married couple can normally have only one principal residence between them exempted from CGT.

3.4 Inheritance tax

3.4.1 Background

Inheritance tax (IHT) was introduced in 1986 to replace capital transfer tax (CTT), which in turn had replaced estate duty in 1974. The term 'inheritance' tax is in fact a misnomer. Like its two predecessors, IHT is a tax on the aggregate amount an individual gives away, rather than the aggregate amount someone inherits. Strictly speaking, it is therefore a form of estate duty. Like the original estate duty, it is sometimes referred to as a 'voluntary' tax, since it usually applies only to gifts made at death, or within seven years of death. Unlike CTT when first introduced, it does not normally tax gifts made during a person's lifetime, except within the last seven years of life.

The scope of IHT is much wider than CGT. It includes all financial assets and property and chattels owned by UK-based individuals, whether in the UK or the rest of the world, and even UK assets of persons domiciled outside of the UK. Unlike with CGT, owner-occupied property is liable to IHT.

Because IHT is levied on the individual, and not jointly in the case of married couples, it was not much affected by the introduction of independent taxation in 1990.

3.4.2 Tax rates

When someone dies, it is necessary for probate purposes to determine the total value of assets he or she bequeathed plus the value of gifts made during the previous seven years less any outstanding liabilities. An estate cannot be distributed to the beneficiaries until '*probate*' (or '*letters of administration*' if there is no will) has been granted. In order to receive this *grant of representation*, an executor must first establish and pay any IHT due. IHT is charged at the rate of 40 per cent (1990/91) on assets in excess of a tax-free threshold of £128 000 (1990/91).

Value of estate, after deducting outstanding liabilities	*Rate*
0–£128 000	0%
£128 001+	40%

Gifts made between three and seven years of death are subject to IHT reduced according to a tapering scale, as shown in Table 3.2.

Table 3.2 The tapering scale for inheritance tax

Years between gift and death	% of full death-rate charge
0–3	100
3–4	80
4–5	60
5–6	40
6–7	20
7+	0

3.4.3 Exemptions
These fall into three categories:

(a) those gifts that are tax-free irrespective of when they are made;
(b) those gifts that are tax-free during a person's lifetime;
(c) those gifts that are tax-free on death.

(a) Gifts tax-free at all times   There is no IHT to pay on gifts between a husband and wife, whether made on death or during their lifetime, provided they are both domiciled in the UK. This means that a husband could bequeath everything to his wife, or vice versa, completely free of IHT. But this would not necessarily be advisable, because it would simply defer the liability until the surviving spouse died, and it would make no use of the £128 000 exemption (1990/91) on the earlier death. In such a circumstance, a widow or widower can alter the terms of the will using a 'deed of family arrangement'. The exempted amount could be passed directly to children, or grandchildren, by varying the terms of the deceased's will, so thereby deferring IHT throughout their lives.

Other tax-free gifts include gifts to UK charities, established political parties, museums, and the National Trust.

(b) Gifts tax-free during lifetime only

- Gifts made out of 'normal' income are exempt from IHT. This means that the gifts must come out of the donor's usual after-tax income, rather than from capital. After paying for the gifts, the donor should have sufficient income remaining to maintain his or her normal standard of living. A typical example would be where someone pays the premiums on a life assurance policy for his or her own life, but on death the policy is to pay out to a particular named beneficiary. Most insurance companies will provide documents and set up a trust for a policy at neglible cost.
- There is a small-gifts exemption which exempts gifts of up to £250 each to any number of different persons in a tax year.
- Gifts to a bride or groom on marriage are exempt within limits – up to £5000 from a parent, £2500 from a grandparent or great-grandparent, and up to £1000 from anyone else.
- Gifts made for the 'maintenance of the family' are exempt. This covers gifts to support a spouse or an ex-spouse, for the maintenance and education of children, and to certain dependent relatives. The last group would include those infirm or elderly and a widowed, separated, or divorced mother or mother-in-law.
- In addition to the above, a person can make tax-free gifts each year using an annual exemption of £3000 (1990/91). This can be carried forward, in whole or part, for one year only. However, it cannot be used in conjunction with the small-gifts exemption – if someone is given more than £250 (1990/91) in a year, and it is not covered by one of the other exemptions, then all of it must be set off against the annual exemption if it is to be free of IHT.

- *Potentially exempt transfers* (PETs) are gifts made during a lifetime that will become exempt from IHT provided that the donor survives seven years after making the gift. PETs include outright gifts to individuals, over and above the exemptions listed above, and gifts to most types of family trust, except for discretionary trusts (see chapter 22). However, to qualify as a PET, the gift must be made *'without reservation'* – the donor must relinquish all rights to receive income or gain from an asset, or to enjoy 'benefits in kind' in any way. For example, if someone gave away their house to a younger member of the family, but continued to live in it rent-free, it would not normally qualify as a PET.

  It is not necessary to inform the Inland Revenue at the time of the gift, unless the gifts are chargeable lifetime transfers (see below) or gifts are substantial in a tax year. If the donor dies within seven years of making the gift, inheritance tax will apply, subject to the annual exemption and the tapering scale. The liability to pay rests with the donee.

For example, if Mrs White had given away £166 000 four and a half years before death, and bequeathed a further £50 000 of net assets, what would be the IHT liability? The taxable transfers are £216 000−£6000−£128 000 = £82 000. The deduction of £6000 represents the annual gifts exemption of £3000 for that year, and the preceding year, assuming it had not otherwise been used. The gifts are dealt with in chronological order – the ones made longest ago are dealt with first. So the £82 000 consists of £32 000 (i.e. £160 000−£128 000) plus £50 000. The tax charge in 1990/91 would be

	£
£32 000×40%×60%	7 680
£50 000×40%	20 000
	27 680

(c) Gifts tax-free on death   There is no IHT liability on lump sums received from most pension schemes. 'Reasonable' funeral expenses are an allowable deduction from the value of the estate.

3.4.4 Chargeable transfers
Gifts which do not fall into any of the above categories – mainly gifts into 'discretionary' trusts or to companies – are called *'chargeable lifetime transfers'*. If the total value of chargeable lifetime transfers made within the last seven years exceeds the tax-free threshold of £128 000 (1990/91), tax becomes due on these 'lifetime' transfers.

The lifetime rate is half the death-scale rate, i.e. 20 per cent. Chargeable lifetime transfers made more than seven years previously are ignored. Only if the seven-year running total exceeds the tax-free limit, £128 000, is tax charged at 20 per cent on the excess. PETs made in the seven years before death become chargeable transfers at the time of death, and the recipients will be liable for the tax. At death, tax becomes due at 40 per cent on the excess of the chargeable transfers in excess of £128 000 (1990/91). This may necessitate paying extra tax on chargeable lifetime transfers made in the most recent years, after allowing for the tapering relief.

3.4.5 Valuation of quoted investments

There are a variety of rules for valuing different types of assets disposed of as chargeable transfers. Among the most common such assets are quoted securities. These are valued as the lower of

(a) the 'quarter-up' method, or
(b) the average of the highest and lowest priced bargains of the day.

The 'quarter-up' method means taking one quarter of the difference between the buying and selling price of a security, and adding it to the Stock Exchange dealer's buying price. For example, if the price quoted was 100–104, meaning that the market-maker was willing to buy at 100p and sell at 104p, the quarter-up method would give a price of 101p. This bid–offer spread, at the official close of business for the day, and details of the bargains during the same day, can be found in the *Stock Exchange Daily Official List* (SEDOL).

This approach is used both for 'fully listed' companies' securities and for those of companies quoted on the Unlisted Securities Market (USM), which is the second tier of Stock Exchange quoted companies. In the case of unquoted securities, the valuation must be negotiated with the Share Valuation Division of the Inland Revenue.

Authorized unit trusts are valued at their bid price – the lower of the two prices quoted – at the close of the relevant day.

3.4.6 Concessions

(a) Loss on sale IHT charges may be reduced if a loss is incurred by an executor on the sale of quoted securities or unit trusts within the twelve months immediately following the death of the donor. The difference between the probate values and the sale proceeds is described as the *loss on sale*, and this amount can be deducted from the total value of the estate on death. IHT is charged on the reduced amount. But any proceeds which are reinvested may not be eligible for this relief.

(b) Quick-succession relief IHT is intended to tax the transfer of assets between generations; it is not intended to penalize families who suffer the misfortune of having deaths in quick succession. In such circumstances there is relief against the second and subsequent liabilities. *Quick-succession relief* is provided to reduce the impact of deaths within five years of each other.

If someone dies within twelve months of receiving a chargeable transfer on which IHT has been paid, a fraction of the first tax liability can be set off against the second. The fraction is calculated as

$$\frac{\text{value of gift at time of first transfer}}{\text{above value} + \text{tax paid on first transfer}}$$

For example, suppose Mrs Coggins inherited £6000, on which £4000 IHT had been paid, and died within twelve months, leaving an estate subject to IHT. The fraction of the previous tax paid which can be taken into account is

$$\frac{£6000}{£10\,000} \times 100\% = 60\%$$

60% × £4000 = £2400, which can be offset against the IHT liability on her estate.

If someone dies between one and five years after receiving a gift, the fraction is reduced by 20 per cent for each complete year since the first transfer.

(c) Interaction with capital gains tax   If the recipient (i.e. the donee) of a chargeable transfer subsequently sells the asset, then the acquisition cost for capital gains tax purposes will be the value at the time of receiving the asset *plus* any inheritance tax paid by the donee. Of course when someone dies there is no CGT to pay, only a potential IHT. But in the case of chargeable lifetime transfers there can be a double taxation in the form of both CGT and IHT. However, gifts on which there may be an immediate charge to IHT – that is, gifts to discretionary trusts and companies – are one of the few examples where 'hold-over relief' is available. This means that, rather than the donor paying the CGT at the time of gift, CGT is deferred until the donee eventually sells the gifted assets, at which point the gain is assessed on the donor's original acquisition price, or on the value at 31 March 1982.

(d) Business property relief   If a person is self-employed, or involved in a small business, business property relief is available to ensure that IHT does not threaten the survival or independence of the business. The relief reduces the value placed on business property bequeathed, or given away within seven years of death. If the business is a company, relief is granted on the value of shares transferred. Holdings of more than 25 per cent of the voting shares are eligible for relief at 50 per cent of the value, provided the shares were owned for two years or more and are not fully listed or dealt in on the USM. Relief is not normally applicable to businesses which consist mainly of dealing in stocks and shares, land and buildings, or other investments.

Similar relief of 50 per cent of the value is available in the form of agricultural property relief if a person has owned agricultural property for at least seven years, or has owned and farmed it for at least two years, provided the owner has vacant possession immediately before transfer or within twelve months.

3.4.7 Conclusion

Inheritance tax is not just a potential problem for the very rich. Because of the non-exemption of owner-occupied property, many ordinary families may, perhaps to their surprise, find themselves subject to it. This liability can be reduced by taking advantage of the complete exemption of most gifts made more than seven years before death. Insurance policies can be taken out to provide cover against any inheritance tax liability arising unexpectedly because of early death. One popular type of policy is 'decreasing-term assurance'. This is cheap because the policy has no value if the policyholder survives the full seven years. The sum assured diminishes over the seven years in line with the outstanding IHT liability.

For a detailed understanding and exploitation of all the tax planning aspects relevant to IHT, an individual requires the services of an experienced professional adviser, such as an accountant or a solicitor, especially if considering the use of trust funds.

Inheritance tax and the independent taxation of income and capital gains since April 1990 are strong grounds for a husband and wife to consider carefully the division of assets between themselves, currently and at any future date. But of course there are wider aspects than simply taxation to take into account.

In conclusion, it is worth remembering that taxation is an important determinant of investment strategy, but it is not the only one. Investors should not be deceived into believing that an investment is appropriate simply because it offers tax-efficiency. Other factors – such as access to capital, penalties for withdrawal of funds, profitability of underlying assets, and of course the degree of risk – all need careful consideration.

3.5 Questions

1. (a) Calculate the net return for a higher rate taxpayer when a building society's net rate is quoted at 6 per cent for basic-rate taxpayers.

   (b) An investor purchased 9000 XYZ Plc shares in January 1986 for £7830. She sold these shares in October 1987 for £9810. The following are the relevant Retail Prices Index figures:

   January 1986 96.25   October 1987 102.9 (January 1987 = 100)

   Calculate the chargeable capital gain. (Ignore the annual tax allowance.)

   (c) When they are disposed of, which of the following investments must be recorded on a UK investor's tax return under the heading 'Chargeable Assets Disposed of'?

   A National Savings Certificates.
   B Life assurance policies.
   C Gilt-edged stocks.
   D Unit trusts.

   (d) For probate and other valuations of shares, the standard source of information is:

   A the *Financial Times*.
   B Extel news cards.
   C the *Stock Exchange Daily Official List*.
   D TOPIC.

(e) Under the inheritance tax legislation, a potentially exempt transfer will become subject to tax if death occurs within which of the following maximum periods?

A 4 years.
B 5 years.
C 6 years.
D 7 years.

2. Alice Williams, a widow aged 63, is concerned about her tax position in the current year. Her net income from part-time employment and her widow's pension, for the year ending 5 April 1991, is likely to be £10 000. Her investment income – on a 'cash received' basis – should be £300 on dated gilts and £1100 on her equity holdings. Building society interest should amount to £300.

   She lives with her daughter in the family home, recently valued at £75 000, which she regards as her main private residence. By the end of April 1990 she expects to have completed the sale of her country cottage. This cost £6000 in 1971. The agreed value of the cottage on 31 March 1982 is £12 500. The net sale proceeds are likely to be about £35 000.

   Estimate Mrs Williams' tax liabilities for 1990/91. (All calculations to the nearest £.)

   (N.B. Relevant RPI figures (January 1987 = 100) are:
   March 1982   79.4   April 1990   125.1.)

   (CIB 10/89)

3. Mr Fred Burley, married with two children, owns his own small family butcher's business, and, at the age of 51, he has decided to retire. This decision has been made due to the fact that the business has stagnated due to competition from the nearby supermarkets, and also because he wishes to pursue his hobby of breeding and racing pigeons, for which he has a national reputation. In furtherance of this activity he has decided to sell his domestic property, which is a house and extensive grounds, and move to a cheaper property. He has decided to sell most of his 300 racing pigeons, which are expected to fetch approximately £100 each, retaining only a few breeding pairs. He reckons the sale of the business and the change of property should release approximately £70 000 for investment. Ultimately he feels he may settle abroad, where he has a number of close friends connected with his hobby.

   Identify what matters need to be considered by Mr Burley in relation to his capital gains and inheritance tax position.

   (SIE 12/88)

4. (a) Outline the ways in which quoted securities can be valued for inheritance tax purposes when sold within twelve months of death.
   (b) Mrs Wood inherits £250 000 on the death of her husband. She dies eighteen months later, bequeathing £350 000. What would be the inheritance tax liability if she had made no gifts during her lifetime?

(c) Discuss the methods by which inheritance tax might be mitigated or avoided.

(SIE 12/87)

4 Cash and non-marketable investments

4.1 Introduction

As outlined in chapter 1, many investments are not quoted on a stock market. In some cases this does matter, because the investor can readily realize them with the original borrower for the full face value. They can be converted into spending power at once, or in a very short time. Hence they are known as 'cash' investments.

Other investments can also be non-marketable but may not be 'cash' investments. Examples include 'term' and 'notice' accounts with banks and building societies. Investors are willing to some extent to sacrifice liquidity in exchange for a higher expected return. However, an investor should beware of 'locking away' all savings in long-term investments which cannot be readily repaid except in exceptional circumstances, such as death, or on prohibitive terms. A general rule of thumb is that 10 per cent of an investor's portfolio, or six months' income, should be maintained in 'cash' investments. However, this is not a hard and fast rule but will vary according to an individual's circumstances.

In this chapter we concentrate on 'direct' investments. Certain indirect non-marketable investments – such as life assurance – are dealt with in later chapters.

4.2 Cash investments

Cash investments are loans made by investors to the Government or to financial institutions and which are repayable on demand or at short notice without risk or penalty to income or capital. A good example is an 'instant-access' account with a bank or building society.

All investors should keep part of their capital in a suitable cash investment, so that money is easily realizable in the event of an emergency. It would be unwise to rely for unexpected cash needs on investments which have to be sold on the Stock Exchange, as it might be necessary to realize them at a time when the market for those particular investments is depressed. Similar reservations apply to most National Savings investments, such as Savings Certificates, for early withdrawal usually means some loss of 'interest'. Most loans to local authorities are not repayable on demand.

The disadvantage of cash investments is that they do not grow – that is to say, the amount of money available can never be greater than the amount originally invested, together with interest earned. Equally, it can never diminish; but, as the value of the money is continually falling as a result of inflation, holders of a cash investment are dependent on their net interest return to maintain the real value of their money. Unless the annual interest received, after allowing for any tax liabilities, is greater than the annual rate of inflation, the investment fails to maintain its value. For this reason the amount held permanently in this type of investment should normally not be greater than the sum required to maintain an adequate emergency reserve.

All temporary investments should be in the form of cash investments. An investor whose capital is provided by savings out of income should make use of a suitable cash investment until sufficient funds have accumulated to make a more permanent investment worthwhile. Any moneys which are known to be needed within a year or so should usually also be placed in this type of investment, so as to avoid loss in the event of market prices being lower at the time the cash is required.

There may also be times when the investor takes a particularly gloomy view about the alternative quoted investments. In such circumstances he or she will doubtless consider keeping a substantial percentage of his or her funds in cash form – or, indeed, may decide to be 100 per cent liquid. For much of the early 1970s most of the cash investments outperformed not only equities and the property market but Government securities too. Over the post-war years, however, equities have been a better investment on the whole, particularly in the period since 1975. (see figs 4.1 and 4.2).

4.3 Bank and building society accounts

In recent years, banks and building societies have become increasingly alike, converging in terms of the range of investment products they have on offer. Indeed, in 1989 Abbey National became the first building society to convert itself into a fully fledged bank. This coming together of banks and building societies was accentuated by the Building Societies Act 1986, which allowed building societies a much greater degree of commercial freedom. However, the controls still remained tighter than those imposed on banks by the Banking Act 1987 – thus the rationale for some building societies considering conversion into banks.

The Building Societies Act 1986 requires that at least 90 per cent of a building society's total commercial assets (that is, total assets less liquid and fixed assets) be in the form of loans for house purchase to individuals which are secured by a first mortgage. Societies are also limited to raising a maximum of 40 per cent of their funds from the wholesale money markets,

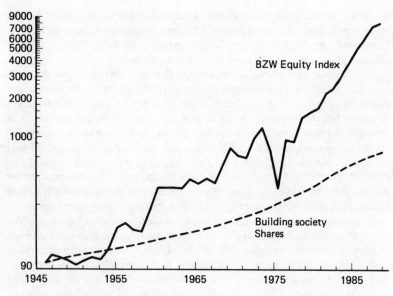

Source: Barclays de Zoete Wedd, 1989

Fig. 4.1   £100 invested in equities and building society shares, with net income reinvested

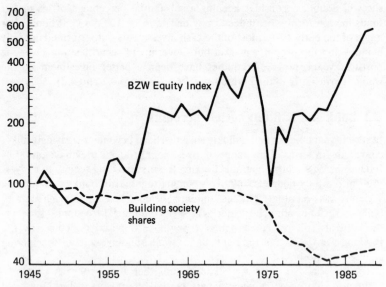

Source: Barclays de Zoete Wedd, 1989

Fig. 4.2   £100 invested in equities and building society shares, with net income reinvested and adjusted for inflation

and they are allowed to invest their liquid funds only in authorized banks and in Government and Government-guaranteed securities. Under the 1986 Act, conversion into a bank requires the approval of both shareholders and mortgagers. In the case of the Abbey National, conversion approval was easily achieved because of the allocation of 'free' shares, resulting from the allocation of ownership of the existing reserves.

Following the Report of a Committee of Inquiry set up after the collapse of a recognized bank (Johnson Matthey Bankers, in 1984), the Banking Act 1987 was introduced. One of the main proposals of the Report was that the previous distinction between recognized banks and licensed deposit-taking institutions should be replaced with a single authorization to take deposits. This change was brought about in the 1987 Act, which introduced a single category of *'authorized institutions'* (AIs), over which the Bank of England has broad supervisory powers. Authorized institutions must have a paid-up capital and reserves of at least £1 million, and those wishing to use the term 'bank' in their name must have capital of at least £5 million. Certain institutions – including the National Savings Bank and the local authorities – are exempted from registering as AIs. Also, building societies are separately controlled under their 1986 Act.

'It just means we address you as sir and madam.'

Both banks and building societies have traditional standard savings accounts – the '*seven-day deposit*', and the basic *ordinary share account* respectively – which can be opened for as little as about £5. The banks' seven-day deposit accounts require seven days' notice, or seven days' loss of interest, for withdrawals. They pay a relatively uncompetitive rate of interest, and their continuing existence is a testimony to small-saver ignorance and inertia.

Building societies also offer '*deposit*' *accounts*, but they represent something rather different from those of banks. They represent the 'creditors' of a building society, and take priority over the 'shareholders', whose funds represent the overwhelming proportion of a building society's liabilities. Deposit accounts of a building society are unattractive to most investors because they offer an even lower rate of interest – usually ¼ to ½ per cent less – than the basic ordinary share account. Share accounts themselves are low-risk investments – since 1945, no ordinary share investor with a building society which is a member of the Building Societies Association has lost any of his or her savings.

Both banks and building societies offer higher-interest accounts, generally known as '*premium*' accounts, which have been the fastest growing accounts in recent years. In order to qualify for the higher rate, the investor must invest either a higher minimum sum or for a longer period, or both, as compared to the standard accounts. Often the minimum sum is £500 or £1000, and higher minimum sums often command even higher rates. '*Term*' accounts involve investing for a minimum period, usually between six months and five years. Early withdrawals are either not permitted or are possible only at penal rates. They normally offer a fixed premium over some basic account or yardstick rate, such as banks' base rate, not a fixed rate of interest. '*Notice*' accounts are similar, except that they require a fixed period of notice, usually between one and six months, rather than a fixed investment period.

Banks and many building societies now offer *high-interest cheque-book* accounts, which are ideal 'cash' investments, although some do stipulate a high minimum amount per cheque, as well as a minimum of around £1000 per account.

Both banks and building societies offer *regular savings,* or *subscription, schemes* whereby the investor agrees to save a regular monthly amount for at least a year or more, with a restricted number of withdrawals, and in return receives a premium rate of interest. The amount to be invested can vary from between around £5 to around £500 per month. Conversely, many premium accounts offer a regular *monthly income* facility which may be particularly attractive to pensioners.

Banks and some building societies also offer fixed-interest accounts which guarantee a *fixed*, rather than variable, rate of interest, for periods usually up to one year. They also provide *offshore* accounts (principally in the Channel Islands), for both residents and non-residents of the UK, and both offer two different tax-free regular savings schemes: SAYE and TESSA.

In *Save-As-You-Earn* (SAYE) schemes, £1 to £20 per month can be invested for five years or more. At the end of five years the capital sum repaid includes a bonus equivalent to 8.3 per cent compound per annum. Alternatively, the capital can be left for a further two years, when the return is equivalent to 8.6 per cent compound for seven years. No interest is paid if the capital is encashed during the first year, and only 6 per cent compound tax-free is paid if the scheme is held between one and five years.

Since January 1991 any investor aged eighteen or over can hold one Tax Exempt Special Savings Account (TESSA) with a bank or building society. Unlike other accounts, TESSAs cannot be jointly owned. A TESSA lasts for five years and, provided that the capital is not withdrawn within the five-year period, any interest earned is entirely tax-free. The rate of interest is determined by the individual bank or building society. If the investor is not satisfied with the rate of interest, the TESSA can be transferred – it is 'portable' – to another bank or building society without loss of tax benefits. Interest credited to the account can be withdrawn net of a basic-rate tax deduction within the five-year period without prejudicing the tax-exempt status of the TESSA. The balance of the gross interest which would normally pay the basic-rate tax liability can be withdrawn at the end of five years, plus the interest earned on it.

Any withdrawal of capital or of interest in excess of the net interest results in the loss of the tax advantages. All interest previously credited is taxed at that point, at the prevailing basic rate of tax. But if the investor dies within the five-year period, the investment can be paid into the deceased's estate with no tax deduction.

Up to a total of £9000 per person can be invested over five years, on the basis of either

(a) regular savings of up to £150 per month, or
(b) a lump sum at the start of each year, subject to a maximum of

Year 1	£3000
2	£1800
3	£1800
4	£1800
5	£600

After five years, any further interest arising is subject to tax in the usual way.

TESSA accounts are an attractive supplement or alternative to other tax-free interest-bearing regular-saving schemes, such as bank or building society SAYE and National Savings Yearly Plan.

4.4 Composite rate tax

Until 6 April 1991, *composite rate tax* (CRT) was deducted at source from bank, building society, and other types of deposit investments. The recipient of the interest was credited with having paid basic-rate tax, even though CRT was at a lower rate – 22 per cent (1990/91). Non-taxpayers could not reclaim CRT, but the higher-rate taxpayer was still liable for higher-rate tax on the grossed-up return. For example, assume that an investment paid $7\frac{1}{2}$ per cent, net of CRT. The grossed-up return, or 'gross equivalent', with basic-rate tax at 25 per cent, was 10 per cent (i.e. $7\frac{1}{2}\% \times \frac{100}{75}$). The net returns would have been as follows:

Non-taxpayer	$7\frac{1}{2}\%$
Basic-rate taxpayer	$7\frac{1}{2}\%$
Higher-rate (40%) taxpayer	6% (i.e. 10% $(1-0.4)$)

The rate for CRT was a weighted average of the zero rate paid by non-taxpayers and the basic-rate element paid by basic and higher-rate taxpayers, as determined by the Inland Revenue.

CRT was beneficial for basic-rate taxpayers because the tax credited was greater than the tax actually paid. This advantage was clearly at the expense of non-taxpayers, who should have avoided such investments as far as possible.

CRT applied only to personal investors: other investors and certain investments were excluded, including

(a) deposits held on behalf of pension funds, friendly societies, registered charities, companies, clubs, and societies;
(b) deposits held for persons 'not ordinarily resident' in the UK;
(c) deposits held offshore;
(d) the National Savings Bank – investors in both the Ordinary and the Investment Account receive interest gross;
(e) time deposits of £50 000 or more.

Until 6 April 1991, the most tax-efficient 'cash' and 'near-cash' investments for non-taxpayers were offshore high-interest cheque-book accounts and the National Savings Bank Investment account. From 1991/92 non-taxpayers have a much wider choice. Apart from the tax-free products such as SAYE and TESSA, tax is deducted at source at the basic rate but is reclaimable. Additionally, there are special arrangements whereby non-taxpayers can be paid gross, on completing the necessary certificate.

4.5 The compounded annual rate (CAR)

Comparison between different investments can sometimes be misleading because of the differing ways in which interest is paid. For example, imagine that investment A pays 8 per cent gross at the end of the year, whereas investment B pays 6 per cent net, payable quarterly. The compounded annual rate (CAR) is equivalent to the annual percentage rate (APR) used in consumer credit. It is a measure of the true annual return earned on an investment, allowing for the reinvestment of interest paid within the year.

The formula is

$$CAR = \left(1 + \frac{r}{n}\right)^n - 1$$

where r is the quoted rate and n is the number of times that interest is paid within a year. So, for investment B,

$$CAR = \left(1 + \frac{0.06}{4}\right)^4 - 1$$

$$= (1.015)^4 - 1$$

$$= 1.0614 - 1$$

$$= 0.0614$$

$$= 6.14\%$$

In cash terms, the quarterly interest payments, allowing for reinvestment, would be 1.50, 1.52, 1.55 and 1.57 per cent, totalling 6.14 per cent.

To complete the comparison it is necessary to gross-up investment B or net-down investment A to put them on an equivalent basis. The grossed-up return or 'gross equivalent' for investment B is $6.14\% \times \frac{100}{75} = 8.19\%$, assuming basic-rate tax is 25 per cent. Thus investment B offers the better return.

4.6 Protection schemes

Both banks and building societies operate statutory protection schemes for investors. Under the Banking Act 1987, the Deposit Protection Scheme guarantees 75 per cent of deposits up to £20 000 with an authorized institution. The building societies' Investor Protection Scheme provides a guarantee of 90 per cent of an individual's total holdings with a particular society, again on investments up to £20 000.

The building societies' protection scheme does not have a permanent fund of money, because past calls for reimbursement have been very few. Losses by building societies as a result of bad debts have historically been very small. In 1985, for example, provisions for mortgage losses for the industry as a whole accounted for only one hundredth of 1 per cent of mortgage assets.

4.7 Finance house accounts

'Finance houses' is the correct name for those institutions – commonly called 'hire-purchase companies' – which provide credit to the general public to assist with the purchase of consumer goods. In contrast to bank lending, which is usually negotiated with established customers at the branch bank, most hire-purchase finance is arranged at the 'point of sale' – the garage, television shop, or furniture store. The growth in the personal loan business of the clearing banks has meant, and will continue to mean, a reduction in the provision of hire-purchase finance to the more creditworthy customer. Hire purchase is a more expensive form of borrowing because it is provided for those less able to raise money and so the risks are correspondingly higher.

Finance houses have, however, been able to expand other sections of their business which have a lower risk potential. Much of their activity now concerns the provision of instalment finance and leasing services to companies and firms to assist them in the purchase of capital equipment.

When lending money to a finance house, an investor should try to find out the exact nature of the major part of its activities, to ensure that an above-average risk is not involved. Generally investors should be wary of houses offering unusually high rates of interest. If such high rates are paid to depositors, funds must be lent at correspondingly higher rates. Borrowers who are prepared to pay above-average rates must represent above-average risks. Nevertheless, the deposit will come within the Deposit Protection Scheme. The average investor probably looks no further for security than the finance houses that are wholly or partly owned by the big banks.

The interest paid by finance houses is subject to income tax, which is deducted at source, at the composite rate until 1991/92. Because of the greater risk, rates are higher than those paid by banks on their deposits. Generally rates are quoted for deposits at one month's, three months', and six months' notice, although arrangements can be made for longer or shorter periods of notice, or for fixed periods at fixed rates. The rates obtainable on agreeing to give three or six months' notice are generally slightly better than the clearing banks' rates and are linked to the Finance Houses Base Rate.

4.8 Local authority deposits

Deposits directly with local authorities can be made for periods varying from overnight to many years. Very-short-term deposits are normally restricted to sums much larger than are likely to be available to the personal investor. 'Temporary' loans are for any period less than one year. They are typically term or notice accounts, and the minimum investment may be £5000 or more. From 1991/92 they are no longer subject to CRT. The rates paid are somewhat lower than those obtainable from finance houses – reflecting the lower level of risk attached to local authorities.

Loans direct to local authorities for periods exceeding one year are usually 'mortgages', because they are charged on the authority's assets and revenues. Such mortgages – otherwise known as 'town-hall' or 'over-the-counter' bonds – are advertised in the press and bought direct without any dealing expenses.

Minimum sums of around £1000 are usually required, to be invested for fixed periods, normally from two to seven years. As they are term investments, loans are normally repayable before maturity only on the death of the lender, although, if the interest rate payable exceeds the current rate, the authority may be happy to repay if some emergency arises, because it could then reborrow elsewhere more cheaply. There is a limited 'unofficial' market in these mortgages, but prices are relatively unfavourable to the vendor. Interest is paid half-yearly, net of tax. Some issues are offered below par, to provide a small element of capital gain as well as interest.

Generally local authority deposits are suitable for the small investor looking for a low-risk investment offering a good yield, where the capital is not needed for the term of the loan. They would be a suitable alternative to a building society term share.

Neither of these investments should be confused with local authority stocks or yearling bonds, which are both Stock Exchange quoted investments.

4.9 National Savings

The National Savings movement is operated by the Department for National Savings in conjunction with the Treasury. Originally intended for small, unsophisticated savers, the attraction of National Savings often varies with Government borrowing needs. In 1990, for example, rates were generally uncompetitive because the Government was repaying rather than issuing new debt. Generally, interest rates on National Savings products are more 'sticky' than those of banks and building societies – they do not respond immediately to changes in interest rates generally in the UK economy. Table 4.1 shows the principal types of investment offered and their relative importance in the National Debt at March 1990.

Table 4.1 Principal National Savings schemes and the value invested*, March 1990

	£m
National Savings Bank Ordinary Account	1561
National Savings Bank Investment Account	8029
Fixed-interest National Savings Certificates	8580
Index-linked National Savings Certificates	4347
National Savings Yearly Plan	767
National Savings Income Bonds	8211
National Savings Capital Bonds	489
National Savings Premium Bonds	2334

* Figures include accrued bonuses.
Source: *Financial Statistics*, May 1990.

National Savings products vary in a number of respects. Fixed-interest and index-linked National Savings Certificates (NSCs), Yearly Plan, and Premium Bonds are completely tax-free, as is the first £70 of interest on the National Savings Bank Ordinary Account. Other interest receivable is paid gross but is subject to tax at the investor's marginal rate. Fixed-interest NSCs, Yearly Plan, and Capital Bonds provide a guaranteed return for five years. Index-linked NSCs provide a guaranteed 'real' return (i.e. over and above inflation) over five years. The returns on other products can vary.

Income Bonds are designed to provide a monthly income, but interest can be withdrawn from the Ordinary and Investment accounts to achieve the same end. Other products, apart from Premium Bonds, are designed to provide capital growth. Savings Certificates, Yearly Plan, and Capital Bonds earn the best returns if held for the full five years.

4.9.1 National Savings Bank Ordinary Account
The National Savings Bank – formerly called the Post Office Savings Bank – was set up in 1861 for the safekeeping of savings and the encouragement of thrift.

A two-tier interest rate applies to the Ordinary Account. The higher rate of 5 per cent is paid for each whole month the account holds £500 or more, provided the account has been open for a full calendar year. Otherwise the rate is 2½ per cent.

An account can be opened with as little as £5. The maximum amount is £10 000, but this figure is merely of academic concern. The £70 of tax-free interest is obtained with £1400 in the account; anything more earns only 5 per cent subject to marginal-rate income tax. Another point to note is that interest is earned only on whole calendar months, so it is more sensible to withdraw sums at the beginning rather than the end of a month. Overall, this account is uncompetitive and of little concern to serious investors.

4.9.2 National Savings Bank Investment Account
The attraction of this account has been that the interest rate is paid gross, not subject to CRT. Until 1991/92, this account was therefore a logical alternative to bank and building society accounts for non-taxpayers, but from April 1991 it lost this competitive advantage in attracting funds from non-taxpayers. Although tax is not deducted at source, basic-rate and higher-rate taxpayers must pay the tax to the Inland Revenue.

One month's notice is required for withdrawals. The minimum deposit is £5 and the maximum holding is £25 000. Money earns interest on a daily basis, and the interest rate changes periodically.

4.9.3 Fixed-interest National Savings Certificates
First issued in 1916 to help finance the First World War, there have been many issues of NSCs with different terms, although only the latest issue can be purchased at any one time. They increase in value by the addition of predetermined sums at regular intervals – the rate increases every anniversary of purchase, but the increment is credited only on the quarter days (i.e. the annual increment is divided into four parts). These capital accretions are free of income tax and capital gains tax. The return increases over a five-year period. For example, the 35th issue offers the returns shown in Table 4.2.

Since nothing is added to the value of a unit until the end of the first year, NSCs should not be used as very-short-term investments. It will also be particularly expensive to encash them during the final year – in the example

Table 4.2 Fixed-interest National Savings Certificates, 35th issue

End of year	Tax-free return added in each complete year	Average return per year from date of purchase
1	6.50%	6.50%
2	7.50%	7.00%
3	9.27%	7.75%
4	10.78%	8.50%
5	13.59%	9.50%

The overall return after five years is 9.50 per cent.

shown in Table 4.2, the rate earned in year five alone is 13.59 per cent tax-free. Clearly, investors who doubt whether they can leave their investments undisturbed for the whole five-year period should think carefully before buying fixed-interest NSCs. Although they are attractive when interest rates generally are falling, the opposite is obviously true when interest rates rise. Then the investor must make a decision as to whether to encash them early.

Each unit costs £25, and a maximum of £1000 (40 units) of the 35th issue may be held in addition to holdings of previous issues. There is also provision for an additional amount of the 35th issue to be bought by reinvestment from earlier issues – these are known as 'Reinvestment Certificates'. The current limit is £10 000. Units can be encashed individually.

Issues which have reached their full five-year terms can be held indefinitely, rather than encashed, and continue to earn interest. This rate of interest – known as the *General Extension Rate* – is the same for all such issues, from the 7th issue onwards. However, in June 1990 the rate was only 5.01 per cent tax-free, and the Department for National Savings admitted that, as part of the Government's public-sector debt repayment policy, it was setting this variable extension rate well below other interest rates. Encashment of all units is possible at a few days' notice.

4.9.4 Index-linked National Savings Certificates
The first index-linked NSCs were the Retirement Issue, restricted to persons of pensionable age and hence known as 'Granny Bonds'. With later issues the age requirement was gradually relaxed, and eventually all age restrictions were abolished.

The 5th issue was introduced in July 1990 and provides guaranteed tax-free increments over five years, in addition to full inflation-proofing. The inflation-proofing starts retrospectively at the end of the first year, and the extra increments are earned monthly from the date of purchase, provided the certificate is held for at least two years. Table 4.3 shows the average rate per year, over and above inflation, from the date of purchase.

The average rate over the full five years is 4.50 per cent compound, on top of the inflation-proofing, but the 'real' rate in year 5 alone is over 15 per cent!

At the time of writing, investors are permitted to hold from £25 to £5000 of

Table 4.3 Index-linked National
Savings Certificates, 5th issue

End of year	Average rate per year
1	0%
2	0.50%
3	1.00%
4	2.00%
5	4.50%

the 5th issue, buying them in multiples of £25. Certificates can be encashed individually.

Past issues continue to be index-linked and earn special bonuses, or they can be switched into 'Reinvestment Certificates'.

4.9.5 National Savings Yearly Plan

Yearly Plan is a regular monthly savings scheme offering a tax-free return, guaranteed up to five years. Investors agree to save a fixed amount of between £20 and £200 per month, in multiples of £5, for one year. At the end of the first year they receive a Yearly Plan certificate, which can be held for a further four years. The guaranteed return over the full five years at the time of writing is 9.50 per cent compound. In effect, Yearly Plan is equivalent to a regular-savings version of fixed-interest NSCs, and the rates for early encashment are similar.

Like NSCs, no increment is added until the end of the first year, when 6 per cent is earned, and the average rate per year increases to 7 per cent for certificates held for less than a further two years, and 8 per cent for certificates held for between two and four years. Increments are accumulated on a monthly basis. Unlike NSCs, the whole certificate must be encashed at any one time. At least fourteen days' notice is required.

There is no restriction on an investor taking out a succession of plans, starting a nearly Yearly Plan each year, or taking out more than one in a particular year, provided that the total monthly subscription does not exceed the prescribed maximum. Interest rates are fixed for the duration of a Plan, but National Savings can vary the rates for new Plans at any time. Plans not redeemed after the full five years are subject to the General Extension Rate.

4.9.6 National Savings Income Bonds

These provide a regular monthly income with no tax deducted at source. They are therefore suitable for non-taxpayers – particularly pensioners – who require a monthly income facility. The rate of interest is variable, but usually slightly above the Investment Account rate. Six weeks' notice is given of any change in the interest rate.

Interest is earned on a daily basis and, after a bond has been held for six weeks, income is paid on the 5th of each month. Investors should note, however, that three months' notice of withdrawal is required, and, if the bond has not been held for a full year at the time of repayment, only half the interest is paid on the whole or part redeemed.

The minimum investment if £2000 and the maximum holding is £25 000, and bonds are bought and redeemed in multiples of £1000.

4.9.7 National Savings Capital Bonds

These were introduced in January 1989 and provide a guaranteed growth investment for five years; but, unlike NSCs, increments are accumulated gross of tax, and the investor must pay the tax liability each year, even when no interest has been received. (The annual statement of value shows how much interest has been added.) They are therefore more suitable to non-taxpayers who do not require income.

At the end of five years a £100 Series 'B' Capital Bond is guaranteed to grow to £184.25. This is equivalent to a compound interest rate of 13 per cent per annum over the five years. As with NSCs, earlier encashment results in a lower return. The annual rate increases from 8.50 per cent over the first year to 18.80 per cent in year 5. No increment is earned on bonds repaid in the first year. Capital Bonds do not continue to earn interest after five years.

Capital Bonds require a minimum investment of £100, and can be bought in multiples of £100, up to £100 000 maximum. As with Income Bonds, three months' notice of withdrawal is required. Part of a bond may be encashed, provided the amount to be repaid and the amount remaining are both at least £100.

4.9.8 National Savings Premium Bonds

Introduced in 1956, Premium Bonds have done valiant service for the

'I very much doubt he'll accept as sufficient security the fact that you might be a delayed Ernie prizewinner.'

National Savings movement, but they are not 'investments' within the usual meaning of the word. No interest is paid, but a bond which has been held for three calendar months following the month in which it was purchased is eligible for inclusion in the regular draw for prizes ranging from £50 to £250 000, tax-free. A sum equivalent to interest of 6.5 per cent is distributed by weekly and monthly prize draws. The prizes are drawn by ERNIE, which is an acronym for Electronic Random Number Indicator Equipment.

Premium Bonds are denominated in £1 units, and sold in multiples of £10. For adults the minimum purchase is £100, although a lower limit of £10 is available for children. The maximum is £10 000. Eight days' notice is required for repayment.

Given 'statistically average luck' a person holding £1000 worth of bonds may expect to win a prize every year. Of course it is possible for someone with the maximum holding to win nothing in a year, but the odds against this happening are 55 000 to 1! Nevertheless Premium Bonds are a gamble and should not form more than a small proportion, if any, of an investor's portfolio.

4.10 Summary

In this chapter we have reviewed a wide range of investments provided principally by banks, building societies, and the Department for National Savings. These satisfy a requirement by some investors for investments which are low-risk and low-expense, provide a 'reasonable' return, and are easily understood. Some also satisfy the need for liquidity. However, none of these investments is likely to provide spectacular returns, and only index-linked NSCs provide a guaranteed return protected against inflation.

Although this type of investment may appeal to the uninitiated, the investor does require a basic understanding of tax in order to choose the appropriate schemes. Also, changes in interest rates in the economy affect the relative attractiveness of the different investments.

Often these types of investment are chosen by persons with modest sums to invest. All, apart from SAYE and TESSA, are available to young children, although in the case of Premium Bonds these must be bought for them by parents, guardians, or grandparents. Generally money can be invested in the names of children under the age of seven, but withdrawals and encashments are not allowed until the child reaches that age, except in special circumstances. From April 1991, investing on behalf of young children has become much simpler because of the abolition of CRT and the £100 threshold before a minor's investment income is aggregated with a parent's for tax purposes.

4.11 Questions

1. (a) An investment promises interest of 5 per cent in the first year, 6 per cent in the second, 7 per cent in the third, and $8\frac{1}{2}$ per cent for the fourth and final year. Interest is credited to the saver's account once each year over the four-year period.

Calculate:

Either the growth in value of £1000 invested for four years;

Or   the compound average annual interest rate over the four-year period (to one decimal place).

(b) Which of the following investments is most tax-efficient for a non-taxpayer?

A Fixed-interest National Savings Certificates.
B National Savings Bank Investment Account.
C National Savings Yearly Plan.
D National Savings Bank Ordinary Account.

(c) Which of the following investments currently provides the highest income return for the personal investor paying tax at the basic rate?

A National Savings Income Bonds.
B National Savings Bank Investment Account.
C Bank or building society SAYE.
D National Savings Capital Bond.

(d) What is the minimum investment in National Savings Certificates?

(e) Which of the following arguments for Premium Bonds as an investment is both correct and relevant for the higher-rate taxpayer?

A The prize fund is subject to tax at the composite rate but the actual prizes are free of tax.
B The chance of winning a prize increases with the size of the holding.
C The prize fund is based on interest at a rate somewhat lower than that available on conventional National Savings Certificates.
D The prize fund is maintained at a level equivalent to the tax-free return on National Savings Income Bonds.

(f) Bank A pays interest on a certain account at 5.75 per cent net, payable annually, while Bank B's rate is 5.5 per cent p.a. net, payable quarterly. Calculate the compounded annual return for Bank B to show which interest rate is the more attractive.

2. 'Every investor should keep part of his capital in a suitable cash investment.' Discuss.

3. (a) Fixed-interest National Savings Certificates have a number of unique features. Describe the characteristics of this form of investment and mention briefly any advantages and disadvantages for different types of investor.

(b) State briefly the advantages and disadvantages of index-linked National Savings Certificates as an investment.   (CIB 4/82)

4. Describe the various forms of investment offered by banks and building societies and indicate their advantages and disadvantages for different types of investor.

5 Gilts and related securities

5.1 The gilt-edged securities market

The term 'gilt-edged' is generally recognized as meaning effectively 'risk-free' or, to be more precise, backed by the UK Government. Market professionals tend to use the term 'gilts' as shorthand for 'British Government securities'. Indeed, an official Stock Exchange brochure declared that 'gilt-edged is just a nickname for Government Stocks. Certificates issued by the Bank of England (on Government's behalf) to stockholders are not, and never have been, edged with gilt!' Sometimes the term 'gilts' is used to describe a wider range of securities, to include all forms of public-sector or quasi-public-sector debt, including that of local authorities, public boards, and Irish and Commonwealth Governments. In this book we refer to this broader class as 'gilts *and related securities*'. British Government securities are free of default risk, since they are explicitly guaranteed by the UK Government.

Traditionally, gilts have formed a major part of the National Debt and have been used to finance budget deficits of the UK Government. The gilt-edged market expanded particularly rapidly during the First and Second World Wars, and also in the 1945–51 period, when gilts were issued to pay for the nationalization of industries such as coal, railways, steel, and gas.

During the 1980s there was a dramatic reversal in the expansion of the gilt-edged market. This was as a consequence of the Government operating a financial surplus, and also generating funds from privatization issues. In his 1990 Budget statement, the Chancellor announced that £25 billion of National Debt had been repaid in the previous three years. Indeed, it was possible to predict the complete elimination of the gilt-edged market in the early part of the twenty-first century, on current trends.

One novel element in the policy of public-sector debt repayment (PSDR) has been the introduction of *'reverse auctions'*. With specified stocks, the Bank of England invites holders to sell all or part of their holdings back to the Government. The successful applicants are those whose asking price is at or below the highest price deemed acceptable to the Bank of England. Successful applicants receive their asking price, rather than the maximum figure acceptable to the Bank.

Another consequence of the contraction of the gilt-edged market has been the reintroduction of *consolidation*. In 1989 the Bank of England offered to convert 9¾% Conversion Stock 2006 into 9% Treasury Loan 2008 on favourable terms. This was seen as an attempt by the Bank to restructure the gilts market into fewer but larger individual issues, thus preserving liquidity at a time of market contractions. The nominal value of stocks ranges from £56 million of Treasury 3% (1966 or after) to £3.75 billion of Treasury 8¾% 1997.

Conversion 3½% (1961 or after) is gradually being redeemed by means of a *sinking fund*. The object of a sinking fund is for the borrower to set aside a regular amount each year so that redemption can take place gradually over the life of the stock. This stock is being redeemed by means of purchases in the open market.

When the Government needs to issue new gilts to replace expiring ones, it may do so in a number of different ways. The most substantial issues are advertised by prospectus. The price of a new stock is determined by reference to a similar stock already in issue but the terms are generally marginally better, to induce investors to subscribe for the issue.

Establishing the right price is usually relatively easy, because of the substantial volume and range of securities already available, with redemption dates stretching from a few months until well into the next century. The main problem lies in the volatility of the market. A relatively small change in the economic environment can suddenly make the issue extremely attractive or, conversely, can ruin its prospects.

Issues are rarely taken up in full, so the bulk of the issue is frequently taken up by the Bank of England Issue Department and other Government departments. The stock is then sold to investors *on tap* over a period at prices that reflect market conditions and official policy. Such stocks are known as *tap stocks*. One or more 'taps' may be available at any one time. Gilt-edged issues are sometimes made direct to banks. Because such 'directed loans' are an instrument of monetary policy, banks do not lightly refuse to subscribe to them, though they are not legally bound to do so.

A trend in new issues has been to issue stock payable by instalments, the final instalment being the largest. For instance, on 16 August 1984 £950 million 10½% Treasury Convertible 1992 was issued at a tender price of 95.25 – that is £95.25 per £100 nominal value of stock. (By convention, the £ sign is omitted.) £30 per £100 nominal was paid on application, with £30 and £35.25 paid in the two following months.

Since 1979, many fixed-interest issues have been made *by tender*. Investors are invited to bid at or above a minimum specified price. A 'striking' price is fixed, at which the whole of the issue is fully subscribed. In the case of undersubscription, the minimum price applies. A *tender* differs from an *auction*; in the case of the latter, investors (if successful) pay the actual price they submitted. In order to avoid the risk with auctions of making mispriced bids, personal investors (unlike institutions) can apply on the basis of a 'non-competitive bid price', which is the average bid price of all the institutional bids. Small bids are guaranteed stock on this basis.

5.2 Categories of British Government securities

Stocks can be categorized according to their term to maturity, or to whether they are denominated in money (as is normally the case), or in terms of purchasing power.

The Stock Exchange and the *Financial Times* differ in respect of their categorizations according to remaining life. The Stock Exchange divides stocks into 'shorts' (0–7 years), 'mediums' (7–15 years), 'others' (over 15 years), and index-linked. The *Financial Times* has 'shorts' (0–5 years), 'mediums' (5–15 years), 'longs' (over 15 years), undated, and index-linked. There are six major undated stocks, sometimes known as 'one-way option' stocks, because their redemption is at the option of the Government, not the investor. They are sometimes incorrectly referred to as 'irredeemable' stocks. This overstates the fact that, because of their low rates of interest,

Table 5.1 Nominal and market value of gilts, fixed interest and related securities at 30 September 1989

	No. of securities	Nominal value £m	Market value £m
Public sector: UK			
Short (0–7)	45	49 582.5	49 151.8
Medium (7–15)	31	41 211.0	41 993.1
Others (over 15)	24	23 163.7	21 235.8
Index-linked	13	12 651.7	15 005.2
Subtotal British funds	113	126 608.9	127 385.9
Public sector: Republic of Ireland			
Short (0–7)	39	7 046.7	6 851.4
Medium (7–15)	18	2 887.8	2 909.0
Others (over 15)	10	1 300.2	1 320.6
Subtotal Irish Government	67	11 234.7	11 081.0
Corporation and county stocks: UK	93	651.5	403.4
Public boards etc.: UK	38	136.4	90.8
Public sector: overseas			
Commonwealth and provincial securities	13	6.5	3.1
Commonwealth corp stocks	2	4.0	3.7
Foreign stocks, bonds, etc.			
Sterling	137	3 752.0	3 921.5
Foreign currency	11	88.2	32.8
Subtotal foreign stocks, bonds	148	3 840.2	3 954.3
Corporation stocks: foreign	16	1.5	0.7
Total public sector	490	142 483.7	142 922.9

Source: The International Stock Exchange, London (1989)

they are unlikely to be redeemed in the foreseeable future. All of them are in fact redeemable.

In September 1988 there were 125 British Government stocks, with a nominal and market value of approximately £141 billion. The pace of contraction can be illustrated by the fact that by September 1989 there were 113 stocks with a nominal value of £127 billion (see Table 5.1).

A problem of categorization can arise because some stocks have two dates after the name: Exchequer 3% Gas 1990–95, for instance. In 1989 this had a life of between one and six years. Should it therefore be regarded in the *Financial Times* as a 'short' or a 'medium'? The answer lies in the *coupon* – the nominal interest rate. Three per cent was well below prevailing interest rates in 1989, and consequently the stock sold at a discount to its par value of 100. On 1 November 1989 the price was $76\frac{1}{2}$. The Government could therefore be expected to redeem this stock as late as possible – in 1995 – and therefore during 1989 it was classified in the *Financial Times* as a medium-dated security.

It should be emphasized that the maturity categorizations of stock are of no real significance to the personal investor. The taxation treatment and dealing expenses are in no way affected by the fact that a stock is a 'short', 'medium', 'other', or 'index-linked' according to the Stock Exchange. The names of individual stocks – for example, Exchequer, Treasury, Funding, etc. – are of no significance other than for identification purposes. For example, Exchequer 3% Gas does not depend on the fortunes of the gas industry. Note also that all gilts are quoted as a percentage of nominal value and fractions of £1 – for example, $112\frac{1}{32}$, $96\frac{5}{16}$.

5.3 Index-linked securities

As shown in Table 5.1, in September 1989 there were thirteen index-linked British Government stocks. These were first introduced in 1981 and were initially restricted to pension funds. Their attraction is illustrated in fig. 5.1, which shows that conventional gilts have failed to keep pace with inflation since the 1930s, even when gross interest was reinvested. In maturity dates, index-linked stocks range from 1992 to 2024. All of them guarantee to maintain the purchasing power of income and capital over the life of the stock. Interest payments are revised in line with changes in the Retail Prices Index, while the capital repayment on redemption reflects changes in the RPI since the issue date.

Index-linked gilts and index-linked National Savings Certificates provide the two direct means by which an investor can obtain guaranteed protection from inflation. The gilts are more flexible, because they are available to anyone, including corporate investors; they have no minimum and maximum holding limits; and they provide a much wider range of maturity periods. On the other hand, whereas NSCs are entirely tax-free, the interest received on gilts is taxable. Brokerage expenses are incurred with purchases and sales of gilts, whereas NSCs are free of dealing expenses. Gilts are also more risky

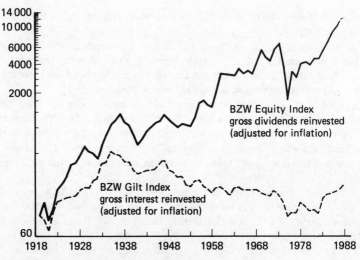

Source: Barclays de Zoete Wedd, Equity–Gilt Study, 1989

Fig. 5.1   Inflation-adjusted performance of gilts and ordinary shares, 1918–88

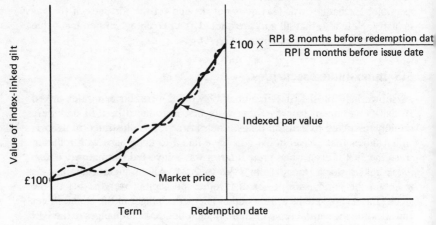

Fig. 5.2   Market price of index-linked gilts

than NSCs, because the price of an index-linked gilt can fluctuate independently of the indexation factor, particularly if there is a long time until redemption (see fig. 5.2). The indexation process is also slightly different. In the case of gilts, the relevant RPI figure is that ruling eight months previously, in respect of both interest and capital redemption.

5.4 The importance of dates

The investor can sell gilt-edged securities through the Stock Exchange at any time. Why, then, are the dates of any significance?

Let us consider the case of three stocks at prices quoted in late 1989:

		Price
3% Treasury	1992	$84\frac{1}{2}$
$3\frac{1}{2}$% Funding	1999–2004	$56\frac{1}{4}$
$3\frac{1}{2}$% War Loan	1952 or after	$36\frac{13}{16}$

All three stocks had similar coupons, but their prices were very different. The Treasury stock redeemable in 1992 was considerably more expensive than the others because of the close proximity of the latest possible redemption date. $3\frac{1}{2}$% Funding is not redeemable until 2004; its price was therefore markedly lower. War Loan, considered by investors as unlikely ever to be redeemed, languished at less than 37. The first two stocks thus have differing support from the latest possible redemption dates. This *pull to maturity* is a very important factor in determining the prices of gilt-edged securities.

The exact redemption dates of securities can be found in the *Stock Exchange Official Year Book*. For example, $3\frac{1}{2}$% Funding Stock 1999–2004 is redeemable at any time between 14 July 1999 and 14 July 2004 by drawings (that is, holders, chosen by ballot, are paid the full redemption price) or otherwise.

5.5 Risk and volatility

The purchase and holding of gilts can involve risks that are not associated with investments such as National Savings Certificates. Subject to due notice, National Savings Certificates can be redeemed and the investor can transfer them to a better-yielding investment if the opportunity arises. Marketable securities are more flexible in that there are no periods of notice required, or explicit penalties of loss of interest, but the prices of marketable securities adjust to reflect changes in interest rates. This can be advantageous when interest rates fall, because at such times securities with a fixed rate of interest become more valuable. But the opposite applies when interest rates generally are rising. Thus gilts provide no guarantee of capital repayment unless they are held until the redemption dates.

The risk to capital is most obvious in the case of the undated stocks. Because there is no pull to maturity, such stocks have no fundamental price support at all and currently sell at large discounts to their nominal values, and at a fraction of the market prices which prevailed in the early post-war period. Generally, the longer dated a stock, the more volatile the price performance. Consider as an example the price range of two stocks in late 1989:

	Prices (1989)		Difference as a
	Low	High	% of low
13½% Exchequer 1992	103¹³⁄₁₆	109¾	5.72
13½% Treasury 2004–2008	123⅝	134⅝	8.90

Of the two, the fluctuations in the longer-dated stock were the wider.

Another general feature of price behaviour concerns the coupon – the nominal rate of interest. Given the same dates, the lower-coupon stocks are usually the more volatile:

	Prices (1989)		Difference as a
	Low	High	% of low
12% Treasury 1995	102¹⁷⁄₃₂	108¹¹⁄₁₆	6.00
3% Exchequer Gas 1990–95	72	79⅞	10.94

Volatility is thus an important factor in decision-making. The prices of the longer-dated index-linked stocks can be particularly volatile.

One means by which an investor can reduce the capital risk of holding longer-dated gilts is by purchasing *convertible* issues. For example, Treasury 10½% Convertible 1992 was issued in August 1984 and offered holders the option of converting into a long-dated stock, Conversion 9¼% 2003. Conversion was at the holder's option in each May and November between 7 November 1985 and 7 November 1987 into £98, £96, £94, £92, £90 respectively of £100 nominal Conversion 9¼% 2003. If interest rates had fallen during the conversion period, investors could have switched into the long-dated stock at a predetermined price. In fact, interest rates did not make the switch attractive, so holders of the 1992 stock let the option lapse.

5.6 Interest payments

British Government securities normally pay interest half-yearly (see the calculations in section 5.7), and net of basic-rate tax. Non-taxpayers can reclaim the tax deducted at source, and higher-rate taxpayers have an additional tax liability. Two notable exceptions are 2½% Consols and 3½% War Loan. The former pays interest quarterly, and the latter normally pays it gross. There are four other cases where interest is paid gross:

(a) stocks purchased directly through the National Savings Stock Register (formerly the Post Office) rather than through the Bank of England register which is used by stockbrokers;

(b) where the gross interest payable is not more than £2.50 per half-year;

(c) certain stocks purchased by non-residents; these are known as FOTRA stocks ('Free of Tax to Residents Abroad') and application must be made to the Inspector of Foreign Dividends – they are identified in the *Financial Times* by the symbol #.

(d) charities and pension funds, on application, can receive interest gross.

It should be made clear that, if an individual does receive interest gross, he or she is still liable to pay the tax.

All paying agents, including the Bank of England, close their transfer books for interest and dividend purposes a few weeks before payment is due. The ex-dividend (ex div or xd) date for gilts is about five weeks before the interest-payment date. On or after this date, the seller will be entitled to the next payment and the buyer will not receive his first interest for a further six months.

The *Stock Exchange Official Year Book* gives details of interest-payment dates of all stocks, as does the *Financial Times* in Mondays' issues. The *FT* also gives details every Monday of the last time when stocks went ex-dividend.

Certain gilts can also be bought or sold *specially ex-dividend*. This means that, for a further period of up to 21 days before the normal xd date, the stocks can be dealt in at the buyer's or seller's request on this basis. There are three exceptions to this rule:

(a) short-dated stocks,
(b) 3½% War Loan,
(c) any stocks bought on the National Savings Stock Register.

This facility was attractive to those investors who were more interested in capital appreciation than in highly taxed income, but this was effectively stopped in 1985 when rules were introduced on 'dividend-stripping' (or 'bond-washing') – see section 5.7.

5.7 Accrued income

'*Accrued interest*' is the interest that builds up in the price of a stock between interest dates (see fig. 5.3). All gilt-edged stock prices are quoted '*clean*',

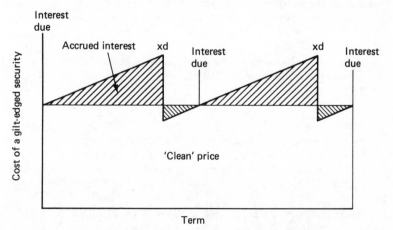

Fig. 5.3 Accrued interest between interest payments

which means that gross accrued interest is separated out of the price of a stock and must be added or subtracted to arrive at the total purchase price. If the price is quoted *cum [with] dividend*, interest for the period from the last interest date to the settlement date (normally the business day after purchase) is added to the purchase price. Thus the total price of £10 000 nominal of Exchequer 15% 1997 purchased on 16 November 1989 at 120 was calculated as follows:

	£
£10 000 nominal at 120	12 000.00
Accrued interest for 21 days (from 27 October to 17 November, since interest on this stock is payable on 27 April and 27 October), i.e. $\frac{21}{182} \times 7\frac{1}{2}\% \times £10\,000$	86.54
	12 086.54

(Actual half-years may vary from 181 to 184 days.)

If the purchase price is *ex [without] dividend*, gross interest to the next payment date is deducted from the price. Thus the price of £10 000 nominal of Exchequer 12% 2013–1017 purchased on 16 November 1989 at 121 xd was:

	£
£10 000 nominal at 121	12 100.00
Accrued interest for 25 days (from 17 November to 12 December, since interest on this stock is payable on 12 June and 12 December), i.e. $\frac{25}{183} \times 6\% \times £10\,000$	−81.97
	12 018.03

The 1985 Finance Act introduced the Accrued Income Scheme, which was designed to prevent higher-rate taxpayers selling stocks cum-div shortly before the stock was due to go ex-div, and thereby capitalizing interest payments in the sale price – so called 'dividend-stripping'. Capital gains on gilts are tax-free. However, under the Accrued Income Scheme, accrued interest is taxed at the seller's marginal rate of income tax – only gains calculated on the 'clean' price are tax-free. The buyer will be subject to income tax on the balance of the interest payment at the interest date. For example, assume an investor sells £10 000 nominal of Conversion 9% 2011 on 16 November 1989 at 97:

	£
£10 000 nominal at 97	9 700.00
Accrued interest for 128 days (from 12 July to 17 November, since interest on this stock is paid on 12 January and 12 July), i.e. $\frac{128}{184} \times 4\frac{1}{2}\% \times £10\,000$	313.04
	10 013.04

If the gilt had originally been acquired by the seller at a price below 97, the capital gain would be tax-free. However, the seller pays tax on £313.04. If the seller pays tax at a marginal rate of 40 per cent, the tax is £125.22. On 12 January 1990 the buyer of the £10 000 nominal receives an interest payment equivalent to £450 gross. But £313.04 has already borne tax in the hands of the seller; so the buyer is liable to tax only on the balance of £136.96.

The rules against tax avoidance outlined above apply to most transactions in interest-bearing securities. The only securities excepted are Treasury and local authority bills and certificates of deposit. In addition, no charge arises on an individual who holds no more than £5000 nominal of relevant securities or if the investor is the personal representative of a decreased person, or a trust for the disabled, or is non-resident.

5.8 Dealing in gilts

Gilts can be purchased or sold in two main ways:

(a) through a stockbroker/dealer – either directly or indirectly through an agent like a bank;
(b) through the larger post offices as agents for the Stock and Bonds Office (the National Savings Stock Register).

When bought or sold through a broker/dealer, gilts are dealt with for immediate or *cash* settlement – actually the next business day after the transaction. The only dealing expenses are the broker/dealer's commission on the *consideration* (that is, the cost of the purchase). Although in share dealings it is not possible to deal in fractions of shares, in gilt-edged dealings one can deal to the nearest penny. This is especially useful to people who wish to invest a specific amount. Commission rates are at the discretion of the broker.

Thus the cost of buying a nominal £5912.37 amount of 2½% Consols at 27 (including cost of accrued interest) is worked out as follows:

	£
Consideration: 5912.37×£0.27	1596.34
Broker's commission at 1% on consideration	15.96
	1612.30

Most brokers have a minimum commission in excess of £15.96, which would raise the total cost. Purchasing through an agent like a bank may involve an additional handling charge.

It is also possible to invest a fixed sum in gilts. Thus (ignoring expenses) £5000 invested in 2½% Consols at 27 would purchase a nominal value calculated as follows:

$$\frac{£5000}{0.27} = £18\,518.52$$

5.9 The National Savings Stock Register

Most British Government stocks can be purchased and sold through larger post offices, which act as agents for the Stock and Bonds Office at Blackpool. Commission charges are much lower than those of stockbroker/dealers for small bargains. On purchases, the minimum charge is £1, and this increases by 50p for every £125 consideration (or part thereof) over £250. For sales, the scale is the same, except that small sales are charged 10p for every £10 or part thereof. Thus the purchase of £1596.34 market value of 2½% Consols would involve commission of £6.50. This is approximately 0.4 per cent.

For non-taxpayers, the National Savings Stock Register has the advantage that interest is paid gross. Also, unlike the Bank of England register, it is possible for children to have stock registered in their own name. Gilts bought on the NSSR cannot be sold through a broker, and vice versa, unless the stock has previously been transferred to the appropriate register. The annual transfer limit from the Bank of England register to the NSSR is £5000 nominal of any particular stock in a calendar year. There is no limit to transfers in the opposite direction, and there is no charge for transfers.

The disadvantages of buying and selling through the Post Office can be briefly summarized:

(a) Purchases are limited to £10 000 market value of any one stock in any one day; there is no limit on sales.
(b) Transactions are normally effected on the day following receipt of the order, but no guarantee can be given as to when dealing will take place.
(c) No advice is available.
(d) 'Limit' orders are not possible.
(e) Dealings are not possible in the full range of British funds, although many of them are available in this way.

Using the National Savings Stock Register is cheap for very small transactions. For larger transactions it may well be worth paying a higher commission in the knowledge that the transaction can be effected immediately and settled on the following day.

5.10 Registered and bearer stocks

Most holdings of gilt-edged stocks are in *registered* form – that is:

(a) the issuing body or its registrars (the Bank of England in the case of gilts) keeps a register in which are recorded the names and addresses of holders together with the amount of stock held;
(b) the holder receives a certificate proving his or her title to his holding;
(c) transfer is generally in accordance with the Stock Transfer Act 1963 – the seller alone is required to execute a stock transfer form.

On the other hand, a considerable number of British Government stocks – for example, 3½% War Loan – have a small part of the issue in *bearer* form – that is, payable to the individual who has possession of the stock, without formal transfer. Interest on most of these is payable on application free of tax to residents abroad.

5.11 Local authority quoted stocks

After British Government stocks and a few others that are guaranteed by the British Government, British corporation and county stocks are the most secure investments available. Many stocks are issued by British local authorities, and are a charge on the income of those authorities. There are dated and undated stocks, including a few genuinely irredeemable stocks (stocks which by their terms of issue can never be redeemed). Some pay their interest quarterly and others half-yearly, and interest rates and redemption dates vary widely. A great many authorities issue such stocks, from Aberdeen and Barking to Warwickshire and York.

5.11.1 Availability
The main problem connected with investing in local authority stocks is that of availability, which contrasts sharply with the very free market in British Government stocks. It can be seen from Table 5.1 that their total market value is less than ½ per cent of that of British Government securities. Many issues are comparatively small and by their nature tend to be held by the institutions and so rarely come on the market. The larger issues are made by the bigger corporations; generally speaking, the larger the issue the freer – the more liquid – the market. The most liquid market in this sector is in the stocks of the now abolished Greater London Council, some of which carry the earlier names of Corporation of London and London County Council.

The yields obtainable on local authority stocks are rather higher than those obtainable on equivalent British Government stocks, because of the slightly greater risk and the poorer marketability.

5.11.2 Taxation
Local authority quoted investments are exempt from capital gains tax. This also applies to the stocks of public boards, Commonwealth and foreign Government stocks, and miscellaneous issues discussed later – provided that the stock

(a) is public sector or corporate debt,
(b) is expressed in pounds sterling,
(c) is not convertible into another currency,
(d) was issued or acquired after 13 March 1984.

All such investments are 'qualifying corporate bonds' for CGT purposes.

5.12 Yearling Bonds

Many of the larger local authorities issue negotiable 'yearling' bonds – so called because most of them are repaid after one year. These are usually issued in weekly batches; the names of the issuing authorities, together with the amounts issued, the interest rate, and the issue prices, are announced every Tuesday morning.

An investor interested in a particular week's issue will in the preceding week ask his or her bank manager or stockbroker/dealer to see that his or her name is entered on the placing list. While the rate of interest cannot be predicted, it is possible to make a fairly close estimate based on the previous week's rate and the trend in interest rates. An applicant can, if desired, instruct his or her agent as to the minimum interest rate that is acceptable. Dealings start in the newly issued bonds on Wednesdays, in minimum denominations of £1000. Over the years interest rates have fluctuated sharply, from as low as 5 per cent in early 1972 to over 17 per cent in the autumn of 1980.

The *Stock Exchange Daily Official List* contains details of such short-dated bonds. The names of the borrowing authorities are not published in the *List*, but can be found in its sister publication, the *Stock Exchange Weekly Official Intelligence*.

5.13 Public boards

Another sector of the public authority loan market is that consisting of public boards such as the port authorities and the Agricultural Mortgage Corporation PLC. Some of these resemble local authority stocks in so far as security is concerned, but there are others in which the investor should not place as much confidence. A prospective investor in this market should always ascertain the exact terms of a stock and the nature of the security, so that it may be properly compared with other loans. Most of the water boards, previously an important part of this sector, were 'privatized' in late 1989.

5.14 Commonwealth stocks

A few stocks quoted on the Stock Exchange are issued in London by Governments and local authorities of Commonwealth countries. Although the political risks attaching to stocks issued by foreign authorities are well known, the realities of the situation were not brought home to holders of Commonwealth stocks until Rhodesia's Unilateral Declaration of Independence in 1965. It was not until 1980 that settlement terms for investors were agreed. Even in 1989, certain investors have not *assented* to the new terms.

The confidence placed in certain Commonwealth Governments causes their stocks to be quoted at prices comparable with those of United Kingdom local authority stocks. The doubtful stability of a few Governments results in their stocks being quoted to give yields very much above those available on gilts. In comparing Commonwealth and United Kingdom stocks, the investor should weigh up the political risks to the best of his or her ability and assess the yields obtainable accordingly. But, as Table 5.1 indicates, Commonwealth stocks are now a tiny market.

It should be realized that Commonwealth stocks do not carry the guarantee of the British Government. Commonwealth Government stocks can be exempted from capital gains tax, provided that they are denominated in pounds sterling.

Commonwealth stocks are free of all United Kingdom taxes to residents abroad.

5.15 Irish Government stocks

Table 5.1 includes the public-sector debt of the Irish Government, because Irish Government securities are dealt in primarily through the Dublin unit of the International Stock Exchange of the United Kingdom and the Republic of Ireland. They are not attractive to UK investors because of their poorer marketability, and the fact that they are expressed in Irish pounds ('punts') means that they are not exempt from capital gains tax for UK investors.

5.16 Foreign Governments' bonds

Some foreign Government stocks and bond issues are quoted on the Stock Exchange in the United Kingdom. Those denominated in sterling are known as 'bulldog bonds'. Generalization is impossible: apart from the variety of terms and borrowers involved, political factors play an important part in price movements, and many issues are purely speculative.

In the past, some foreign Governments have defaulted on their liabilities to bondholders and often, after such a default, proposals have been put forward for schemes under which some form of payment might be made. Thus it is now frequently possible to find two types of the same issue, namely *assented* and *unassented bonds*. Assented bonds are sometimes described as being *enfaced*, because the revised terms are set out on the face of the certificate. The Hungarian 7½% Sterling Bond issue of 1924 is one such issue: new terms were assented to in 1968, the interest rate being reduced to 4½ per cent as part of the agreement.

The foreign bond market is one for the specialist, and the private investor is usually advised to stay in markets that are less complicated and speculative.

5.17 Miscellaneous fixed-interest stocks

Some fixed-interest investments do not fall into any well-defined category.

A few stocks are issued in the United Kingdom by the International Bank for Reconstruction and Development (better known as the World Bank). Their prices compare with corporation stocks and the better-quality Commonwealth loans.

Other important issues include those of the Inter-American Development Bank and the British institutions' 3i plc and its subsidiary companies.

5.18 Questions

1. (a) Which of the following is *not* true of 2½% Consolidated Stock (Consols)?

    A It is the only gilt-edged stock that pays interest quarterly.
    B It is sometimes used as a proxy for interest rates generally.
    C It requires Parliamentary approval for its redemption.
    D It is the only gilt-edged stock that always pays interest gross.

   (b) What is the unique feature of 3½% War Loan?

   (c) Index-linked gilts are indexed as to:

    A interest only.
    B capital only.
    C interest and capital.
    D interest and capital with a bonus at maturity.

   (d) State *two* differences between index-linked National Savings Certificates and index-linked gilts.

   (e) The correct term for 'yearling bonds' is:

    A town-hall floating stocks.
    B town-hall bonds.
    C local authority short-dated stocks.
    D local authority negotiable bonds.

2. Compare and contrast the tender and auction methods of issuing new gilt-edged stock. How important are these methods today?

                                                                (CIB 5/90)

3. What are the main features of the accrued income (interest) scheme?

                                                                (SIE 1/87)

4. Explain and discuss the consequences and implications for investment and investors of the UK Government maintaining a persistent public-sector debt repayment (PSDR) policy.

                                                                (SIE 12/89)

6 Gilt yields

6.1 What is yield?

All fixed-interest quoted securities bear a nominal rate of interest – the *coupon* – which relates to the rate of interest on £100 nominal of the stock, even though the stock may have been issued at 98 per cent or 101 per cent and irrespective of whether the current market price is lower or higher. The two vital considerations when buying fixed-interest securities are:

(a) the amount of income which the investment will produce or *yield* in relation to the market price;
(b) the period of time before the issue will be redeemed (if indeed it is likely to be redeemed at all).

In the case of irredeemable stocks, the yield consists only of interest; but, where the stocks are dated, the capital appreciation (or depreciation) to the maturity date must also be taken into account. The investor's tax position is

BANX

also of the utmost importance. The basis of yield calculations is the price at the date of purchase, together with the total costs of purchase (the consideration plus all dealing costs); but for simplicity's sake we shall ignore dealing costs in this chapter. In considering the various kinds of yield – there is no one simple definition – we will take the following as our first example:

£100 8% Treasury Stock 2002–2006
Interest payable on 5 April and 5 October
Purchased on 3 November 1989 at 83½

6.2 Interest yield

The *interest yield* – otherwise known as the *flat yield* or *running yield* – is given by the following expression:

$$\text{Interest yield} = \frac{\text{nominal rate} \times £100}{\text{'clean' price}}$$

Hence, for the stock above,

$$\text{interest yield} = \frac{8\% \times £100}{£83.50} = 9.58\%$$

The 'clean' price means the price separate from 'accrued interest'. As shown in section 5.7, accrued interest is calculated from the last dividend date to settlement day, which in the case of gilt-edged securities is the next business day after the bargain is transacted. So, in this particular example, accrued interest is interest from 5 October to 6 November (6 November settlement because 3 November was a Friday), which is:

$$\frac{32 \text{ days}}{182 \text{ days}} \times £4 = £0.70$$

This sum is charged for separately.

Since February 1986 all gilt prices have been quoted 'clean' but, in the case of corporate fixed-interest securities, the accrued interest has to be deducted from the quoted price in order to arrive at the clean price.

The figure of 9.58 per cent is the *gross interest yield* of the Government stock. To arrive at the *net interest yield*, the investor's marginal rate of tax is deducted. Thus, for a 25 per cent taxpayer,

$$\text{net interest yield} = 9.58\% \times (100\% - 25\%)$$
$$= 7.19\%$$

and, for a 40 per cent taxpayer,

$$\text{net interest yield} = 9.58\% \times (100\% - 40\%)$$
$$= 5.75\%$$

6.3 Gross redemption yield

This yield takes into account the capital gain (or loss) if the security is assumed to be held to the date of redemption. Calculating the redemption yield is more complex, because it consists of two elements:

(a) the interest yield;
(b) the capital gain or loss if the stock is held to maturity.

Interest is usually paid half-yearly, but the capital gain (or loss) occurs only at the end of the period. Therefore, in calculating the yield, compound interest must be taken into account. This involves a rather complex formula. Resort to the formula is rarely necessary, however, because bond yield tables and specialist lists are readily available (see Table 6.1). The following approximate expression is sometimes used, but, because it ignores the compound-interest factor, it is not really accurate enough for an informed investment decision:

$$\text{redemption yield} = \text{interest yield} + (\text{or} -) \frac{\text{gain (or loss) to maturity}}{\text{period to maturity}}$$

Where the maturity period is quite short and the gain or loss is quite small, this gives a reasonable approximation. But as the maturity period lengthens, or the gain or loss to maturity is increased, this formula becomes less reliable. As an example, consider again 8% Treasury Stock 2002–2006, redeemable at the latest on 5 October 2006. The interest yield was 9.58 per cent. What was the redemption yield in late 1989?

$$\text{Interest yield} = \underline{\ 9.58\%}$$

$$\text{Average gain to maturity} = \frac{(100-83.5)}{17} = \underline{\ 0.97\%}$$

$$\text{Redemption yield} = 10.55\%$$

6.4 Net present value and yield

In fact the true redemption yield for the above stock in late 1989 was 10.06 per cent – a significant difference. To calculate a true redemption yield can be quite laborious (even with a calculator), but an appreciation of the principles involved is necessary.

Clearly, what the investor can expect from an investment of £83.50 in £100 of 8% stock is

	£
34 half-yearly interest payments of £4	136
1 final payment on redemption	100
	236

Table 6.1 Extract from Gilts Daily Price List for 10 December 1990

Amount of loan £m	STOCK	Issue date	Redemption date	Foot notes	PRICE in 32nds	Accrued Interest days	gross	Flat yield	Gross Redemption yield	1/32 variation p	Net yields at various tax rates			% Chg on week	Volatility	Next xd date
											10%:0	25%:0	35%:0			
LIFE OF 5 - 15 YEARS																
89	Exch 9.00 2002	3/87	19/11/2002	h	89~17	22	.542	10.052	10.567	2.0	9.595	8.140	6.955	1.533	6.88	12/ 4
1360	Treas 13.75 00/03	2/79	25/ 7/2003		116~09cd	139	5.236	11.825	10.955	1.9	9.719	7.859	6.999	1.209	5.37	19/12
1000	Treas 10.00 2003	1/86	8/ 9/2003		96~02	94	2.575	10.410	10.571	1.9	9.541	7.999	6.900	1.516	6.81	30/ 1
703	Treas 10.00 2003A	11/90	8/ 9/2003		96~02	23	.630	10.410	10.572	1.9	9.542	7.999	6.901	1.547	6.94	30/ 1
1620	Treas 11.50 01/04	5/79	19/ 3/2004		104~05	83	2.615	11.041	10.821	2.0	9.703	8.023	7.000	1.517	5.89	11/ 2
443	Fund 3.50 99/04	7/54	14/ 7/2004		54~16xd	-34	-.326	6.422	9.547	2.5	9.029	8.258	6.686	1.543	9.36	7/ 6
1362	Conv 9.50 2004	10/84	25/10/2004		92~22	47	1.223	10.249	10.512	1.8	9.508	8.006	6.887	1.583	7.27	19/ 3
2992	Conv 9.50 2005	4/85	18/ 4/2005		92~23	54	1.405	10.246	10.491	1.8	9.487	7.985	6.873	1.579	7.37	12/ 3
2200	Treas 12.50 03/05	11/78	21/11/2005		112~29	20	.685	11.071	10.645	1.6	9.500	7.778	6.832	1.584	6.68	15/ 4

Note: In the fifth column, the symbol ~ is simply the decimal point – it indicates that fractional amounts of £ have been converted to the nearest p.
Source: Barclays de Zoete Wedd Bond Research

Now, each of the successive payments of interest is really less valuable than the previous one. If £1 is invested at 10 per cent per year, it will grow in value to £1.33 after three years:

	£
Initial investment	1.00
Interest 1st year	0.10
	1.10
Interest 2nd year	0.11
	1.21
Interest 3rd year	0.12
	1.33

so £1 receivable in three years' time will have a lower present value than £1 receivable now.

The future value of £1 is given by the formula

value after n years $= (1+r)^n$

where r is the annual rate of interest. Thus

£1 invested for 3 years at 10% $= (1+0.10)^3 = £1.33$

The present value of £1 receivable in n years' time is found by inverting the formula:

$$\text{present value} = \frac{1}{(1+r)^n}$$

Thus the present value of £1 receivable in three years when the interest rate is 10 per cent is

$$\frac{1}{(1+0.10)^3} = £0.75$$

To calculate the true redemption yield, we would have to make no less than 35 different calculations using the semi-annual interest rate of 5 per cent. Fortunately tables are available, such as Table 6.2. Applying the figures from Table 6.2 to our example, the present value of £100 receivable in seventeen years (i.e. after 34 half-year periods for a semi-annual interest rate of 5 per cent) is

£100×0.1904 = £19.04

From Table 6.3, the present value of £4.00 per half-year for seventeen years is

£4×16.193 = £64.77

The total present value, £19.04+£64.77 = £83.81, is actually slightly more than the original 'clean' price of £83.50. This implies that the annualized yield

Table 6.2 Present value factors to determine the present value of single payment received *n* years from the present

Years	1%	2%	3%	4%	5%	6%	7%	8%	9%	10%	11%	12%	13%	14%	15%	16%	17%	18%	19%	20%	Years
1	9901	9804	9709	9615	9524	9434	9346	9259	9174	9091	9009	8929	8850	8772	8696	8621	8547	8475	8403	8333	1
2	9803	9612	9426	9246	9070	8900	8734	8573	8417	8264	8116	7972	7831	7695	7561	7432	7305	7182	7062	6944	2
3	9706	9423	9151	8890	8638	8396	8163	7938	7722	7513	7312	7118	6931	6750	6575	6407	6244	6086	5934	5787	3
4	9610	9238	8885	8548	8227	7921	7629	7350	7084	6830	6587	6355	6133	5921	5718	5523	5337	5158	4987	4823	4
5	9515	9057	8626	8219	7835	7473	7130	6806	6499	6209	5935	5674	5428	5194	4972	4761	4561	4371	4190	4019	5
6	9420	8880	8375	7903	7462	7050	6663	6302	5963	5645	5346	5066	4803	4556	4323	4104	3898	3704	3521	3349	6
7	9327	8706	8131	7599	7107	6651	6227	5835	5470	5132	4817	4523	4251	3996	3759	3538	3332	3139	2959	2791	7
8	9235	8535	7894	7307	6768	6274	5820	5403	5019	4665	4339	4039	3762	3506	3269	3050	2848	2660	2487	2326	8
9	9143	8368	7664	7026	6446	5919	5439	5002	4604	4241	3909	3606	3329	3075	2843	2630	2434	2255	2090	1938	9
10	9053	8203	7441	6756	6139	5584	5083	4632	4224	3855	3522	3220	2946	2697	2472	2267	2080	1911	1756	1615	10
11	8963	8043	7224	6496	5847	5268	4751	4289	3875	3505	3173	2875	2607	2366	2149	1954	1778	1619	1476	1346	11
12	8874	7885	7014	6246	5568	4970	4440	3971	3555	3186	2858	2567	2307	2076	1869	1685	1520	1372	1240	1122	12
13	8787	7730	6810	6006	5303	4688	4150	3677	3262	2897	2575	2292	2042	1821	1625	1452	1299	1163	1042	0935	13
14	8700	7579	6611	5775	5051	4423	3878	3405	2992	2633	2320	2046	1807	1597	1413	1252	1110	0985	0876	0779	14
15	8613	7430	6419	5553	4810	4173	3624	3152	2745	2394	2090	1827	1599	1401	1229	1079	0949	0835	0736	0649	15
16	8528	7284	6232	5339	4581	3936	3387	2919	2519	2176	1883	1631	1415	1229	1069	0930	0811	0708	0618	0541	16
17	8444	7142	6050	5134	4363	3714	3166	2703	2311	1978	1696	1456	1252	1078	0929	0802	0693	0600	0520	0451	17
18	8360	7002	5874	4936	4155	3503	2959	2502	2120	1799	1528	1300	1108	0946	0808	0691	0592	0508	0437	0376	18
19	8277	6864	5703	4746	3957	3305	2765	2317	1945	1635	1377	1161	0981	0829	0703	0596	0506	0431	0367	0313	19
20	8195	6730	5537	4564	3769	3118	2584	2145	1784	1486	1240	1037	0868	0728	0611	0514	0433	0365	0308	0261	20
21	8114	6598	5375	4388	3589	2942	2415	1987	1637	1351	1117	0926	0768	0638	0531	0443	0370	0309	0259	0217	21
22	8034	6468	5219	4220	3418	2775	2257	1839	1502	1228	1007	0826	0680	0560	0462	0382	0316	0262	0218	0181	22
23	7954	6342	5067	4057	3256	2618	2109	1703	1378	1117	0907	0738	0601	0491	0402	0329	0270	0222	0183	0151	23
24	7876	6217	4919	3901	3101	2470	1971	1577	1264	1015	0817	0659	0532	0431	0349	0284	0231	0188	0154	0126	24
25	7798	6095	4776	3751	2953	2330	1842	1460	1160	0923	0736	0588	0471	0378	0304	0245	0197	0160	0129	0105	25
26	7720	5976	4637	3607	2812	2198	1722	1352	1064	0839	0663	0525	0417	0331	0264	0211	0169	0135	0109	0087	26
27	7644	5859	4502	3468	2678	2074	1609	1252	0976	0763	0597	0469	0369	0291	0230	0182	0144	0115	0091	0073	27
28	7568	5744	4371	3335	2551	1956	1504	1159	0895	0693	0538	0419	0326	0255	0200	0157	0123	0097	0077	0061	28
29	7493	5631	4243	3207	2429	1846	1406	1073	0822	0630	0485	0374	0289	0224	0174	0135	0105	0082	0064	0051	29
30	7419	5521	4120	3083	2314	1741	1314	0994	0754	0573	0437	0334	0256	0196	0151	0116	0090	0070	0054	0042	30
31	7346	5412	4000	2965	2204	1643	1228	0920	0691	0521	0394	0298	0226	0172	0131	0100	0077	0059	0046	0035	31
32	7273	5306	3883	2851	2099	1550	1147	0852	0634	0474	0355	0266	0200	0151	0114	0087	0066	0050	0038	0029	32
33	7201	5202	3770	2741	1999	1462	1072	0789	0582	0431	0319	0238	0177	0132	0099	0075	0056	0042	0032	0024	33
34	7130	5100	3660	2636	1904	1379	1002	0730	0534	0391	0288	0212	0157	0116	0086	0064	0048	0036	0027	0020	34
35	7059	5000	3554	2534	1813	1301	0937	0676	0490	0356	0259	0189	0139	0102	0075	0055	0041	0030	0023	0017	35
36	6989	4902	3450	2437	1727	1227	0875	0626	0449	0323	0234	0169	0123	0089	0065	0048	0035	0026	0019	0014	36
37	6920	4806	3350	2343	1644	1158	0818	0580	0412	0294	0210	0151	0109	0078	0057	0041	0030	0022	0016	0012	37
38	6852	4712	3252	2253	1566	1092	0765	0537	0378	0267	0190	0135	0096	0069	0049	0036	0026	0019	0013	0010	38
39	6784	4619	3158	2166	1491	1031	0715	0497	0347	0243	0171	0120	0085	0060	0043	0031	0022	0016	0011	0008	39
40	6717	4529	3066	2083	1420	0972	0668	0460	0318	0221	0154	0107	0075	0053	0037	0026	0019	0013	0010	0007	40
41	6650	4440	2976	2003	1353	0917	0624	0426	0292	0201	0139	0096	0067	0046	0032	0023	0016	0011	0008	0006	41
42	6584	4353	2890	1926	1288	0865	0583	0395	0268	0183	0125	0086	0059	0041	0028	0020	0014	0010	0007	0005	42
43	6519	4268	2805	1852	1227	0816	0545	0365	0246	0166	0112	0076	0052	0036	0025	0017	0012	0008	0006	0004	43
44	6454	4184	2724	1780	1169	0770	0509	0338	0226	0151	0101	0068	0046	0031	0021	0015	0010	0007	0005	0003	44
45	6391	4102	2644	1712	1113	0727	0476	0313	0207	0137	0091	0061	0041	0027	0019	0013	0009	0006	0004	0003	45
46	6327	4022	2567	1646	1060	0685	0445	0290	0190	0125	0082	0054	0036	0024	0016	0011	0008	0005	0003	0002	46
47	6265	3943	2493	1583	1009	0647	0416	0269	0174	0113	0074	0049	0032	0021	0014	0010	0006	0004	0003	0002	47
48	6203	3865	2420	1522	0961	0610	0389	0249	0160	0103	0067	0043	0028	0019	0012	0008	0005	0004	0002	0002	48
49	6141	3790	2350	1463	0916	0575	0363	0230	0147	0094	0060	0039	0025	0016	0011	0007	0005	0003	0002	0001	49
50	6080	3715	2281	1407	0872	0543	0339	0213	0134	0085	0054	0035	0022	0014	0009	0006	0004	0003	0002	0001	50

with a constant discount of x % per year

Years 0 to:	1%	2%	3%	4%	5%	6%	7%	8%	9%	10%	11%	12%	13%	14%	15%	16%	17%	18%	19%	20%	Years 0 to:
1	0.990	0.980	0.971	0.962	0.952	0.943	0.935	0.926	0.917	0.909	0.901	0.893	0.885	0.877	0.870	0.862	0.855	0.847	0.840	0.833	1
2	1.970	1.942	1.913	1.886	1.859	1.833	1.808	1.783	1.759	1.736	1.713	1.690	1.668	1.647	1.626	1.605	1.585	1.566	1.547	1.528	2
3	2.941	2.884	2.829	2.775	2.723	2.673	2.624	2.577	2.531	2.487	2.444	2.402	2.361	2.322	2.283	2.246	2.210	2.174	2.140	2.106	3
4	3.902	3.808	3.717	3.630	3.546	3.465	3.387	3.312	3.240	3.170	3.102	3.037	2.974	2.914	2.855	2.798	2.743	2.690	2.639	2.589	4
5	4.853	4.713	4.580	4.452	4.329	4.212	4.100	3.993	3.890	3.791	3.696	3.605	3.517	3.433	3.352	3.274	3.199	3.127	3.058	2.991	5
6	5.795	5.601	5.417	5.242	5.076	4.917	4.767	4.623	4.486	4.355	4.231	4.111	3.998	3.889	3.784	3.685	3.589	3.498	3.410	3.326	6
7	6.728	6.472	6.230	6.002	5.786	5.582	5.389	5.206	5.033	4.868	4.712	4.564	4.423	4.288	4.160	4.039	3.922	3.812	3.706	3.605	7
8	7.652	7.325	7.020	6.733	6.463	6.210	5.971	5.747	5.535	5.335	5.146	4.968	4.799	4.639	4.487	4.344	4.207	4.078	3.954	3.837	8
9	8.566	8.162	7.786	7.435	7.108	6.802	6.515	6.247	5.995	5.759	5.537	5.328	5.132	4.946	4.772	4.607	4.451	4.303	4.163	4.031	9
10	9.471	8.983	8.530	8.111	7.722	7.360	7.024	6.710	6.418	6.145	5.889	5.650	5.426	5.216	5.019	4.833	4.659	4.494	4.339	4.192	10
11	10.368	9.787	9.253	8.760	8.306	7.887	7.499	7.139	6.805	6.495	6.207	5.938	5.687	5.453	5.234	5.029	4.836	4.656	4.486	4.327	11
12	11.255	10.575	9.954	9.385	8.863	8.384	7.943	7.536	7.161	6.814	6.492	6.194	5.918	5.660	5.421	5.197	4.988	4.793	4.611	4.439	12
13	12.134	11.348	10.635	9.986	9.394	8.853	8.358	7.904	7.487	7.103	6.750	6.424	6.122	5.842	5.583	5.342	5.118	4.910	4.715	4.533	13
14	13.004	12.106	11.296	10.563	9.899	9.295	8.745	8.244	7.786	7.367	6.982	6.628	6.302	6.002	5.724	5.468	5.229	5.008	4.802	4.611	14
15	13.865	12.849	11.938	11.118	10.380	9.712	9.108	8.559	8.061	7.606	7.191	6.811	6.462	6.142	5.847	5.575	5.324	5.092	4.876	4.675	15
16	14.718	13.578	12.561	11.652	10.838	10.106	9.447	8.851	8.313	7.824	7.379	6.974	6.604	6.265	5.954	5.668	5.405	5.162	4.938	4.730	16
17	15.562	14.292	13.166	12.166	11.274	10.477	9.763	9.122	8.544	8.022	7.549	7.120	6.729	6.373	6.047	5.749	5.475	5.222	4.990	4.775	17
18	16.398	14.992	13.754	12.659	11.690	10.828	10.059	9.372	8.756	8.201	7.702	7.250	6.840	6.467	6.128	5.818	5.534	5.273	5.033	4.812	18
19	17.226	15.678	14.324	13.134	12.085	11.158	10.336	9.604	8.950	8.365	7.839	7.366	6.938	6.550	6.198	5.877	5.584	5.316	5.070	4.843	19
20	18.046	16.351	14.877	13.590	12.462	11.470	10.594	9.818	9.129	8.514	7.963	7.469	7.025	6.623	6.259	5.929	5.628	5.353	5.101	4.870	20
21	18.857	17.011	15.415	14.029	12.821	11.764	10.836	10.017	9.292	8.649	8.075	7.562	7.102	6.687	6.312	5.973	5.665	5.384	5.127	4.891	21
22	19.660	17.658	15.937	14.451	13.163	12.042	11.061	10.201	9.442	8.772	8.176	7.645	7.170	6.743	6.359	6.011	5.696	5.410	5.149	4.909	22
23	20.456	18.292	16.444	14.857	13.489	12.303	11.272	10.371	9.580	8.883	8.266	7.718	7.230	6.792	6.399	6.044	5.723	5.432	5.167	4.925	23
24	21.243	18.914	16.936	15.247	13.799	12.550	11.469	10.529	9.707	8.985	8.348	7.784	7.283	6.835	6.434	6.073	5.746	5.451	5.182	4.937	24
25	22.023	19.523	17.413	15.622	14.094	12.783	11.654	10.675	9.823	9.077	8.422	7.843	7.330	6.873	6.464	6.097	5.766	5.467	5.195	4.948	25
26	22.795	20.121	17.877	15.983	14.375	13.003	11.826	10.810	9.929	9.161	8.488	7.896	7.372	6.906	6.491	6.118	5.783	5.480	5.206	4.956	26
27	23.560	20.707	18.327	16.330	14.643	13.211	11.987	10.935	10.027	9.237	8.548	7.943	7.409	6.935	6.514	6.136	5.798	5.492	5.215	4.964	27
28	24.316	21.281	18.764	16.663	14.898	13.406	12.137	11.051	10.116	9.307	8.602	7.984	7.441	6.961	6.534	6.152	5.810	5.502	5.223	4.970	28
29	25.066	21.844	19.188	16.984	15.141	13.591	12.278	11.158	10.198	9.370	8.650	8.022	7.470	6.983	6.551	6.166	5.820	5.510	5.229	4.975	29
30	25.808	22.396	19.600	17.292	15.372	13.765	12.409	11.258	10.274	9.427	8.694	8.055	7.496	7.003	6.566	6.177	5.829	5.517	5.235	4.979	30
31	26.542	22.938	20.000	17.588	15.593	13.929	12.532	11.350	10.343	9.479	8.733	8.085	7.518	7.020	6.579	6.187	5.837	5.523	5.239	4.982	31
32	27.270	23.468	20.389	17.874	15.803	14.084	12.647	11.435	10.406	9.526	8.769	8.112	7.538	7.035	6.591	6.196	5.844	5.528	5.243	4.985	32
33	27.990	23.989	20.766	18.148	16.003	14.230	12.754	11.514	10.464	9.569	8.801	8.135	7.556	7.048	6.600	6.203	5.849	5.532	5.246	4.988	33
34	28.703	24.499	21.132	18.411	16.193	14.368	12.854	11.587	10.518	9.609	8.829	8.157	7.572	7.060	6.609	6.210	5.854	5.536	5.249	4.990	34
35	29.409	24.999	21.487	18.665	16.374	14.498	12.948	11.655	10.567	9.644	8.855	8.176	7.586	7.070	6.617	6.215	5.858	5.539	5.251	4.992	35
36	30.108	25.489	21.832	18.908	16.547	14.621	13.035	11.717	10.612	9.677	8.879	8.192	7.598	7.079	6.623	6.220	5.862	5.541	5.253	4.993	36
37	30.800	25.969	22.167	19.143	16.711	14.737	13.117	11.775	10.653	9.706	8.900	8.208	7.609	7.087	6.629	6.224	5.865	5.545	5.255	4.994	37
38	31.485	26.441	22.492	19.368	16.868	14.846	13.193	11.829	10.691	9.733	8.919	8.221	7.618	7.094	6.634	6.228	5.867	5.545	5.256	4.995	38
39	32.163	26.903	22.808	19.584	17.017	14.949	13.265	11.879	10.726	9.757	8.936	8.233	7.627	7.100	6.638	6.231	5.869	5.547	5.257	4.996	39
40	32.835	27.355	23.115	19.793	17.159	15.046	13.332	11.925	10.757	9.779	8.951	8.244	7.634	7.105	6.642	6.233	5.871	5.548	5.258	4.997	40
41	33.500	27.799	23.412	19.993	17.294	15.138	13.394	11.967	10.787	9.799	8.965	8.253	7.641	7.110	6.645	6.236	5.873	5.549	5.259	4.997	41
42	34.158	28.235	23.701	20.186	17.423	15.225	13.452	12.007	10.813	9.817	8.977	8.262	7.647	7.114	6.648	6.238	5.874	5.550	5.260	4.998	42
43	34.810	28.662	23.982	20.371	17.546	15.306	13.507	12.043	10.838	9.834	8.989	8.270	7.652	7.117	6.650	6.239	5.875	5.551	5.260	4.998	43
44	35.455	29.080	24.254	20.549	17.663	15.383	13.558	12.077	10.861	9.849	8.999	8.276	7.657	7.120	6.652	6.241	5.876	5.552	5.261	4.999	44
45	36.095	29.490	24.519	20.720	17.774	15.456	13.606	12.108	10.881	9.863	9.008	8.283	7.661	7.123	6.654	6.242	5.877	5.552	5.261	4.999	45
46	36.727	29.892	24.775	20.885	17.880	15.524	13.650	12.137	10.900	9.875	9.016	8.288	7.664	7.126	6.656	6.243	5.878	5.553	5.261	4.999	46
47	37.354	30.287	25.025	21.043	17.981	15.589	13.692	12.164	10.918	9.887	9.024	8.293	7.668	7.128	6.657	6.244	5.879	5.553	5.262	4.999	47
48	37.974	30.673	25.267	21.195	18.077	15.650	13.730	12.189	10.934	9.897	9.030	8.297	7.671	7.130	6.659	6.245	5.879	5.554	5.262	4.999	48
49	38.588	31.052	25.502	21.341	18.169	15.708	13.767	12.212	10.948	9.906	9.036	8.301	7.673	7.131	6.660	6.246	5.880	5.554	5.262	4.999	49
50	39.196	31.424	25.730	21.482	18.256	15.762	13.801	12.233	10.962	9.915	9.042	8.304	7.675	7.133	6.661	6.246	5.880	5.554	5.262	4.999	50

Source: J. Murdoch and J. A. Barnes, *Statistical Tables* (Macmillan) 2nd edn

is slightly more than 10 per cent. Further calculations show it to be 10.06 per cent – appreciably less than indicated by the approximate method and a very material difference to an investor in a sensitive market where modest price changes can signal a change of policy. The annual redemption yields quoted in the *Financial Times* are obtained by simply multiplying the semi-annual yield by two, rather than by using the compounded annual rate.

The gross redemption yield is thus made up of two elements:

	First year
Interest yield	9.58%
Gain to redemption	0.48%
	10.06%

As the stock's price is pulled towards par as it approaches the redemption date, its interest yield will reduce. Thus, in order to provide a constant redemption yield each year, capital growth must increase both absolutely and as a percentage of the market price.

6.5 Net redemption yield

The interest bears tax at the investor's marginal rate, while the gain is entirely free of capital gains tax. Clearly, therefore, the gross redemption yield has little meaning for anyone but the non-taxpayer. To ascertain the actual yield, tax must be deducted from the interest yield at the appropriate rate for basic-rate and higher-rate taxpayers:

	25% taxpayer	*40% taxpayer*
Interest yield (gross)	9.58	9.58
less Income tax	2.39	3.83
	7.19	5.75
Gain to redemption	0.48	0.48
Net redemption yield	7.67	6.23

Thus the higher-rate taxpayer is 1.44 percentage points worse off than the basic-rate taxpayer.

The difference in the net redemption yields is greater for stocks selling close to par, and greater still for those selling at a substantial premium to par. In the latter case the gross redemption yield is less than the gross interest yield, because of the element of capital loss. The capital loss in such circumstances cannot be offset against the taxable income. For example, take Treasury 15½% 1998, selling for 125⅝ on 3 November 1989. The gross interest and redemption yields were respectively 12.34 per cent and 10.92 per cent. The capital loss percentage points per year were thus $10.92 - 12.34 = -1.42$ per cent.

	25% taxpayer	40% taxpayer
Interest yield (gross)	12.34	12.34
less Income tax	3.08	4.94
	9.26	7.40
Loss to redemption	−1.42	−1.42
Net redemption yield	7.84	5.98

Here the higher-rate taxpayer is 1.86 percentage points worse off than the basic-rate taxpayer.

Contrast that with Exchequer 2½% 1990, which at the same time, selling for 92$\frac{9}{16}$ xd, had gross interest and redemption yields of 2.70 per cent and 10.04 per cent respectively:

	25% taxpayer	40% taxpayer
Interest yield (gross)	2.70	2.70
less Income tax	0.67	1.08
	2.03	1.62
Gain to redemption	7.34	7.34
(10.04%−2.70%)		
Net redemption yield	9.37	8.96

Here the difference is only 0.41 percentage points. Low-coupon short-dated stocks are therefore particularly attractive to higher-rate taxpayers. Consequently they sell on lower gross redemption yields than higher-coupon stocks of the same maturity. However, because income tax rates have been reduced in recent years – particularly the top rate – the impact is now less marked than previously.

This method of calculating the net redemption yield is again only an approximation. For a more accurate calculation, reference needs to be made to a gilts price list such as Table 6.1. (Curiously, at the time of writing, the BZW gilts list does not show the net redemption yields for an investor paying a marginal 40 per cent income tax rate and 0 per cent capital gains tax on gilts. The middle figure in the net yields refers to a basic-rate taxpayer who is exempt from capital gains tax. Most companies will be liable to corporation tax at 35 per cent on both their income and their capital gains.)

6.6 Grossed-up net redemption yield

This yield calculation – otherwise known as the gross equivalent yield – also provides a most useful means of comparison. Not all investments have a redemption element. How, for example, does a low-coupon short-dated Government stock compare with a National Savings Income Bond where the return is all taxable? Although these instances are hardly comparable, such comparisons may have to be made from time to time, and the grossed-up net redemption yield provides the means.

The grossed-up net redemption yield is also useful in deciding whether or not a particular investment is suitable for a certain type of taxpayer. The calculation is simple: the net redemption yield is simply 'grossed-up' at the individual's marginal rate of income tax. Thus, in the case of Exchequer 2½% 1990,

$$\text{a 25\% taxpayer receives } 9.37\% \times \frac{100}{75} = 12.49\% \text{ grossed-up}$$

$$\text{a 40\% taxpayer receives } 8.96\% \times \frac{100}{60} = 14.93\% \text{ grossed-up}$$

Such a stock therefore represents a better investment for the higher-rate taxpayer.

It is not usually necessary to calculate the 'gross-equivalent' yields in order to make choices between stocks – the rankings are the same as for the net redemption yields. (Some years ago, the highest marginal rate of tax on investment income was 98 per cent, and this gave rise to some quite phenomenal grossed-up net redemption yields.)

6.7 Index-linked yields

Table 6.4 shows interest and redemption yields on the range of gilt-edged securities featured in the *Financial Times*. The index-linked gilts appear to have very low yields relative to those of conventional gilts. The reason for this apparent anomaly is that the index-linked yields are 'real' yields – i.e. over and above the rate of inflation. The *FT* does not give the interest yields of the index-linked stocks, but instead shows two sets of gross redemption yields – one based on the assumption of 10 per cent inflation and the other on 5 per cent inflation until redemption. The actual rate in mid 1990 was closer to 10 per cent. Notice that the 5 per cent inflation rate gives a higher real redemption yield in all cases. This is because the indexation adjustment is based on the eight months previous to the interest or redemption dates. The consequence of this lag is that investors benefit when inflation is falling but suffer when inflation is rising.

Stockbroker/dealers such as BZW provide tables such as Table 6.5 to illustrate the inflation rates necessary for investors, in differing tax brackets, to be indifferent between an index-linked gilt and a conventional non-index-linked alternative. The break-even inflation rates represent the minimum required to justify investment in the index-linked stock.

6.8 Yield curves

The normal pattern of return is for yields to increase relative to the length of

Table 6.4 Gilt yields

BRITISH FUNDS

1990 High	Low	Stock	Price £	+ or –	Yield Int.	Red.
		'Shorts' (Lives up to Five Years)				
99 23/32	97 3/32	Treas. 8pc Cv 1990 ‡‡	99 5/8	.....	8.03	–
98 19/32	96 19/32	Treas. 10pcCv 1990	98 19/32	.....	10.14	14.18
96 5/8	93 1/8	Exch 2½pc 1990	96 5/8	.....	2.59	10.99
98 21/32	97 7/16	Treas 11¾pc 1991	98 5/8xd	.....	11.91	14.39
95 5/16	92 7/16	Funding 5¾pc '87–91‡‡	95 5/16	.....	6.03	12.22
93 27/32	89¾	Treas. 3pc 1991	93 9/16	.....	3.21	10.79
96 31/32	94 23/32	Treas 10pc Cv '91 ‡‡	96 31/32xd	.....	10.31	13.20
97 5/16	94 23/32	Exch. 11pc 1991	97 7/32	–1/16	11.31	13.36
93 31/32	90 5/16	Treas. 8pc 1991	93 9/16	–1/16	8.55	13.09
101 1/16	97 11/32	Treas 12¾pc 1992‡‡	99 21/32xd	–1/16	12.79	13.01
96	92¾	Treas 10pc 1992	95 9/16	–1/16	10.46	13.08
92 19/32	89⅛	Treas. 8pc 1992 ‡‡	92 13/32	–1/16	8.66	12.83
97 5/16	93 5/16	Treas 10½pc Cv 1992‡‡	96 3/32	–1/16	10.93	12.87
87 27/32	82 13/16	Treas. 3pc 1992	87¾	.....	3.42	10.02
100 11/16	95 13/16	Exch. 12¼pc '92	98 25/32	–1/16	12.40	12.88
104	98 7/16	Exch 13½pc 1992	101 5/16	–1/16	13.33	12.71
91½	86¾	Treas 8¼pc 1993	91	.....	9.07	12.34
96 7/16	90¾	Treas 10pc 1993‡‡	94 17/32	.....	10.58	12.37
103 3/16	96 7/32	Treas 12½pc 1993‡‡	100 13/32xd	.....	12.44	12.30
86	82	Funding 6pc 1993‡‡	86	.....	6.98	11.33
107 13/32	99¾	Treas 13¾pc 1993‡‡	104	–1/16	13.22	12.21
91	84¾	Treas. 8½pc 1994	89 7/16xd	+1/32	9.50	12.20
111 3/32	102 7/16	Treas 14½pc 1994‡‡	107 9/32	–3/32	13.53	11.98
107 9/16	99¼	Exch 13½pc 1994	103 13/16	–1/16	12.99	12.13
96 13/32	88 31/32	Treas. 10pc Ln. 1994‡‡	93 13/16	–1/16	10.65	11.96
104½	96 7/32	Exch. 12½pc 1994	101 7/32	–3/32	12.35	12.12
92½	85	Treas 9pc 1994‡‡	90 3/32	–1/16	9.99	12.01
		Five to Fifteen Years				
103 15/16	94 17/32	Treas 12pc 1995	100 1/32xd	–1/16	11.99	11.96
80½	73	Exch 3pc Gas 90–95	80½	.....	3.73	7.94
96 31/32	88 1/16	Exch. 10¼pc 1995	93 23/32xd	.....	10.93	11.91
108	97 17/32	Treas 12¾pc 1995‡‡	103 23/32	.....	12.29	11.75
112 11/16	101⅜	Treas. 14pc '96	107 25/32xd	.....	12.99	12.03
92 7/32	82 17/32	Treas. 9pc 1992–96‡‡	88 25/32	.....	10.14	11.75
119 13/32	107 5/32	Treas 15¼pc 1996‡‡	113⅝	–5/32	13.42	11.93
110⅞	99⅛	Exch 13¼pc 1996‡‡	105 13/16	–5/32	12.56	11.88
96 13/32	85½	Conversion 10pc 1996	91 29/32	–3/32	10.88	11.81
112 3/32	98 31/32	Treas 13¼pc 1997‡‡	105⅞xd	–⅛	12.51	11.96
99 3/32	87 7/16	Exch 10½pc 1997	94	–5/32	11.17	11.84
91 3/16	79 5/16	Treas 8¾pc 1997‡‡	86	–5/32	10.17	11.68
121 1/16	106½	Exch 15pc 1997	114 3/32	–1/16	13.15	12.04
95 13/16	83½	Exch. 9¾pc 1998	90 3/16xd	–⅛	10.81	11.76
81¼	70 3/16	Treas 6¾pc 1995–98‡‡	76 5/16	–5/16	8.85	11.35
126 7/16	110¼	Treas. 15½pc '98‡‡	118 3/16	–5/32	13.10	11.94
107 5/16	93¼	Exch. 12pc 1998	100 15/16	–5/32	11.89	11.83
95⅝	82 1/16	Treas 9½pc 1999‡‡	89¼xd	–5/32	10.64	11.53
109 5/16	94 7/16	Exch. 12¼pc 1999	102 5/16	–3/32	11.97	11.82
99⅞	85 15/16	Treas. 10½pc 1999	93½	–⅛	11.23	11.70
98 13/32	84 5/16	Conversion 10¼pc 1999	91 15/16	–5/32	11.15	11.68
89 5/16	75 31/32	Treas. 8½pc Ln 2000‡‡	83 15/32xd	–1/16	10.18	11.43
92 5/16	78 17/32	Conversion 9pc 2000‡‡	86 3/16	–⅛	10.44	11.40
114 13/32	98 5/16	Treas. 13pc 2000	106 13/16xd	–1/16	12.16	11.84
97⅝	82¾	Treas 10pc 2001	90 13/16	–⅛	11.01	11.55
98	85 5/16	Treas. 10pc 2001 "A"	90 13/16	–⅛	10.96	11.54
117	102⅛	Treas. 14pc '98–01	109 11/16	–3/32	12.76	12.05
96 21/32	81⅛	Treas 9¾pc 2002	89 11/32	–⅛	10.91	11.42
90 15/32	81⅛	Treas. 9¾pc 2002 'A'	89 11/32	–⅛	10.91	11.96
96 7/16	84¼	Treas 9¾pc 2002 "B"	89 11/32	–⅛	10.85	11.42
91 27/32	76⅝	Exch. 9pc 2002	84	–1/16	10.71	11.36
119 3/32	102 1/16	Treas. 13¾pc 2000–03	110 25/32xd	–7/32	12.41	11.89
99 7/16	82 13/16	Treas 10pc 2003	91 5/16	–5/32	10.95	11.29
106½	90 3/16	Treas. 11½pc 2001–04	98¾	–¼	11.65	11.70
99¾	83	Treas. 10pc 2004	91½	–7/32	10.93	11.22
56¼	45⅞	Funding 3½pc '99–04	51 5/16xd	–5/16	6.82	10.04
96½	79 13/16	Conversion 9½pc 2004	88¼	–7/32	10.76	11.18

BRITISH FUNDS – Contd

1990 High	Low	Stock	Price £	+ or –	Yield Int.	Red.
		Over Fifteen Years				
96 11/16	79 27/32	Conversion 9½pc 2005	88 5/16	–5/32	10.76	11.14
104½	86 13/32	Exch. 10½pc 2005	95 7/16	–3/16	11.00	11.14
117⅝	98 9/16	Treas. 12½pc 2003–05	107 13/16	–5/32	11.58	11.35
84⅞	69 11/16	Treas. 8pc 2002–06‡‡	77¼	–7/32	10.36	11.05
111⅝	93 21/32	Treas. 11¾pc 2003–07	102 21/32xd	–3/16	11.45	11.36
89 31/32	73 23/32	Treas 8½pc 2007 ‡‡	81⅝xd	–5/32	10.41	10.92
125 13/16	105 11/32	Treas. 13½pc '04–08	115⅜	–5/32	11.70	11.29
94½	77⅜	Treas. 9pc 2008 ‡‡	85⅝	–5/32	10.51	10.83
85 27/32	69 31/32	Treas 8pc 2009	77⅝	–5/32	10.31	10.79
94¾	77¼	Conv 9pc Ln 2011 ‡‡	85⅝xd	–5/32	10.51	10.76
63⅝	50 11/16	Treas. 5½pc 2008–12‡‡	56½	–9/32	9.73	10.65
83	67⅛	Treas. 7¾pc 2012–15‡‡	74⅜xd	–¼	10.42	10.73
122¼	100	Exch. 12pc '13–'17	110 11/16	–5/32	10.84	10.77
		Undated				
41 3/32	33 9/16	Consols 4pc	37 5/32xd	–1/16	10.77	–
36 17/32	29 11/16	War Loan 3½pc‡‡	32 15/16	–1/16	10.63	–
61 15/16	55⅝	Conv. 3½pc '61 Aft	58½	–1/16	5.98	–
32⅜	27⅛	Treas. 3pc '66 Aft	29 3/16	–1/16	10.28	–
25⅞	20 15/16	Consols 2½pc	23⅝xd	–3/32	10.58	–
25½	20¾	Treas. 2½pc	23 13/32	–1/16	10.68	–
		Index–Linked				
		(b)			(1)	(2)
116 27/32	110¾	Tr. 2pc '92‡‡(97.8)	116 13/16	.....	4.76	6.32
108 19/32	103¼	Do. 2 '94(102.9)	108½	–1/16	3.92	4.61
159 13/32	150⅝	Do. 2pc '96(67.9)	159 3/16	–1/16	3.77	4.21
131⅝	123½	Do 2½pc '01(78.3)	129 9/16	–5/16	4.20	4.48
128⅝	119⅞	Do. 2½pc '03(78.8)	126⅜	–⅜	4.20	4.45
131 15/16	122	Do. 2pc '06(69.5)	128½xd	–⅜	4.19	4.38
123 9/16	113 5/16	Do. 2½pc '09(78.8)	119½	–⅜	4.14	4.32
128 7/16	117¾	Do. 2½pc '11(74.6)	124 7/16	–⅜	4.09	4.26
107 1/16	97⅝	Do. 2½pc '13(89.2)	103½	–5/16	4.03	4.19
115¾	105 3/16	Do. 2½pc '16(81.6)	111⅝xd	–5/16	3.97	4.12
119½	102¼	Do. 2½pc '20(83.0)	108 9/16	–5/16	3.92	4.05
95¾	86 1/16	Do. 2½pc '24 ‡‡(97.7)	91⅝xd	–5/16	3.83	3.96

Prospective real redemption rate on projected inflation of (1) 10% and (2) 5%. (b) Figures in parentheses show RPI base for indexing, (ie 8 months prior to issue) and have been adjusted to reflect rebasing of RPI to 100 in January 1987. Conversion factor 3.945. RPI for October 1989: 117.5 and for May 1990: 126.2.

Source: *Financial Times*, 3 July 1990

the period to redemption. This can be clearly shown by a *yield curve*, which plots the yields of a number of dated stocks against years to maturity, at a specific point in time. Figure 6.1, for example, shows that yields at the short end of the market increased considerably between May 1988 and October 1989.

One problem with plotting yield curves is that, for tax reasons, high-coupon stocks tend to sell on higher yields than medium-coupon stocks, which in turn sell on higher yields than low-coupon stocks. This is particularly

Table 6.5 Comparison of index-linked gilt yields with other gilt yields from Gilts Daily Price List for 10 December 1990.

INDEX-LINKED BREAKEVEN INFLATION RATES AT VARIOUS INCOME TAX RATES

Index-Linked Stock	PRICE	Comparison Stock	PRICE	0%	Breakeven inflation rates at Income Tax of 25%	35%
INDEX LINKED 2.0% 1992	126⁻18	TREASURY 10% 1992	98⁻16	8.89	5.41	4.04
INDEX LINKED 2.0% 1994	116⁻14	TREASURY 10.00% 1994	97⁻30	7.27	4.87	3.92
INDEX LINKED 2.0% 1996	170⁻22	CONVERSION 10.00% 1996	96⁻22	7.28	5.03	4.13
INDEX LINKED 2.5% 2001	139⁻30	TREASURY 10.00% 2001	95⁻31	6.62	4.63	3.83
INDEX LINKED 2.5% 2003	135⁻30	TREASURY 10.00% 2003	96⁻02	6.49	4.51	3.72
INDEX LINKED 2.0% 2006	137⁻12	TREASURY 8% 02/06	81⁻08	6.29	4.49	3.78
INDEX LINKED 2.5% 2009	126⁻20	TREASURY 8.00% 2009	81⁻23	6.02	4.37	3.72
INDEX LINKED 2.5% 2011	130⁻26	TREASURY 8.00% 2009	81⁻23	6.03	4.39	3.74
INDEX LINKED 2.5% 2013	108⁻04	TREASURY 8.00% 2009	81⁻23	6.06	4.43	3.79
INDEX LINKED 2.5% 2016	115⁻28	TREASURY 8.00% 2009	81⁻23	6.09	4.48	3.84
INDEX LINKED 2.5% 2020	112⁻00	TREASURY 8.00% 2009	81⁻23	6.13	4.53	3.90
INDEX LINKED 2.5% 2024	93⁻30	TREASURY 8.00% 2009	81⁻23	6.20	4.61	3.99

Index-Linked Stock	PRICE	Comparison Stock	PRICE	Breakeven inflation rates at Income Tax of 40%
INDEX LINKED 2.0% 1992	126⁻18	TREASURY 3.00% 1992	92⁻24XD	2.83
INDEX LINKED 2.0% 1994	116⁻14	FUNDING 6% 1993	91⁻00	4.14
INDEX LINKED 2.0% 1996	170⁻22	TREASURY 6.75% 95/98	82⁻05	4.26
INDEX LINKED 2.5% 2001	139⁻30	FUNDING 3.5% 99/04	54⁻16XD	4.45
INDEX LINKED 2.5% 2003	135⁻30	FUNDING 3.5% 99/04	54⁻16XD	4.42
INDEX LINKED 2.0% 2006	137⁻12	FUNDING 3.5% 99/04	54⁻16XD	4.20
INDEX LINKED 2.5% 2009	126⁻20	TREASURY 8% 02/06	81⁻08	3.65
INDEX LINKED 2.5% 2011	130⁻26	TREASURY 5.5% 08/12	59⁻29	3.82
INDEX LINKED 2.5% 2013	108⁻04	TREASURY 5.5% 08/12	59⁻29	3.87
INDEX LINKED 2.5% 2016	115⁻28	TREASURY 7.75% 12/15	78⁻04	3.47
INDEX LINKED 2.5% 2020	112⁻00	TREASURY 7.75% 12/15	78⁻04	3.54
INDEX LINKED 2.5% 2024	93⁻30	TREASURY 7.75% 12/15	78⁻04	3.62

Source: Barclays de Zoete Wedd Bond Research

noticeable at the short end of the gilt market. Consequently it would be possible to construct three separate yield curves. The yield curves in fig. 6.1 are based on an adjustment process which calculates what the yield curve would be if all stocks were selling at par – in other words, it removes the distorting effects of high and low coupons.

It can be seen that at the end of 1989 the UK had a downward-sloping – or 'inverted' – yield curve. The term 'inverted' refers to the fact that the normal state of affairs is for short-term interest rates to be lower than long-term rates.

There are a variety of theories postulated to explain the shape of the yield curve. One of the most popular – the *'expectations'* theory – states that long-term interest rates reflect the market's expectation of future short-term interest rates. Thus a downward-sloping yield curve implies, according to this theory, that short-term rates are expected to fall in the future.

The *'liquidity preference'* theory states that the yield curve will have an upward bias, because investors prefer the greater certainty of short-term gilts, which are less volatile than long-dated gilts. Table 6.1 shows the

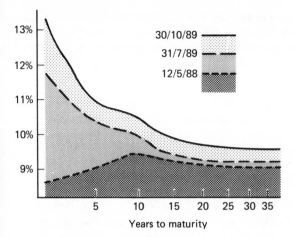

Source: Midland Montague Research

Fig. 6.1   Par yield curves of British Government securities

volatility indices of various medium-dated gilts. The volatility index is a measure of the percentage price change in a gilt resulting from a one percentage point change in its redemption yield. On 13 November 1989 the most short-dated high-coupon gilt had a volatility index of 0.16, while $2\frac{1}{2}\%$ Index-linked 2024 had a volatility index of 20.8 – the highest in the market. As can be seen in Table 6.1, volatility tends to be greater the lower the coupon and the longer the redemption date.

The *'market segmentation'* theory, in contrast, is based on a belief that expected future interest rates have virtually no influence on the shape of the yield curve. According to this theory, borrowers and lenders at the short end of the market are entirely different from those at the long end, and therefore short-term and long-term interest rates are determined by the interplay of separate sets of demand and supply forces. Banks, building societies, and general insurance companies are the predominant investors at the short end; life assurance companies and pension funds at the long end. The Government operating a tight fiscal policy – such as public-sector debt repayment – would have the effect of raising the prices and lowering the yields of medium- and long-dated gilts. A stringent monetary policy, on the other hand, would have the effect of raising short-term interest rates. Because of the differing nature of their liability structures, financial institutions would be reluctant to exploit interest discrepancies between the different segments of the market.

6.9 Gilt-edged switching

6.9.1 Tax switching
Individuals who were higher-rate taxpayers used to find it advantageous to sell a stock cum-dividend and buy again later ex-dividend, or 'specially

ex-dividend'. However, this practice was effectively stopped by the rule on 'dividend-stripping' (or 'bond-washing') introduced in February 1985. Since that date, the seller of a bond has been liable to income tax on the accrued interest (see section 5.7).

6.9.2 Anomaly switching

The yield on a stock is described as an *anomaly* if it is out of line with stocks with similar coupons and redemption dates. The commonest cause of an anomaly is Government sales of 'tap' stocks, which are frequently cheap compared with stocks of a similar maturity, because of the effect of heavy Government sales. This anomaly is usually corrected when the Government raises the tap price, for tactical reasons, or when the tap runs dry. Some gilt-edged stocks with sinking funds, on the other hand, may appear anomalously expensive, either because the fund buys in stock through the market or because of a possibility of redemption at par. The same would apply to stocks bought in through 'reverse' auctions.

Anomalies can be detected by examining relative prices and yields. Some brokers keep price records for pairs of stocks. These show – usually in chart form – how price differences or relative prices of pairs of stocks change over time, but they are really only appropriate for stocks of similar life and coupon. It is probably more useful to look at the redemption yields of two stocks. If, for example, stock A yields $\frac{3}{4}$ per cent more than stock B, and the differential has previously ranged between 0 and $\frac{1}{2}$ per cent, stock A appears to be anomalously cheap.

Alternatively, yield curves can be used – see fig. 6.2. It is then possible

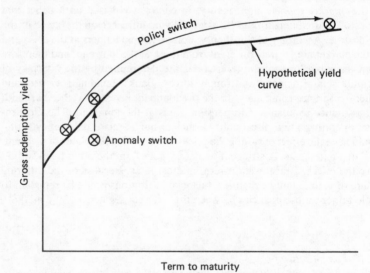

Fig. 6.2   Gilt-edged switching

clearly to identify deviations of actual gross redemption yields for individual stocks from those predicted by the curve. The investor may decide to sell those that appear 'dear' and buy those that appear 'cheap' for his or her particular maturity period – bearing in mind, however, that, when the yield curve is calculated in gross terms, high-coupon stocks (particularly at the short end of the market) always look cheap relative to low-coupon ones because of the differences in tax treatment. The net-of-tax yields should be calculated, or a yield curve be drawn showing yields net of the investor's marginal rate of tax, before a permanent switch is made.

Some stocks appear to have permanently anomalous positions, for reasons other than their size of coupon. This is particularly noticeable with undated stocks, where there are substantial differences in yield despite very similar coupons. For example, $3\frac{1}{2}$% War Loan appears relatively expensive. This is probably because the interest is paid gross, and this appeals to overseas investors who are saved the necessity of applying to the Inspector of Foreign Dividends for exemption from tax. Similarly, $2\frac{1}{2}$% Consols almost invariably appear dear if compared with $2\frac{1}{2}$% Treasury, perhaps because interest on the former is paid quarterly, as against half-yearly for other stocks, but also apparently because the ownerships of the two stocks differ: Consols is held more by private individuals, while Treasury is held more by institutions. $3\frac{1}{2}$% Conversion appears very expensive – the low yield reflects a 'lottery' element in that 1 per cent of the remaining stock is redeemed each year at its full face value.

6.9.3 Policy switching

If a fund having long-term liabilities fixed in money terms invests in long-dated gilts, a change of interest rate will cause the present value of both its assets and its liabilities to move up or down together. But where the liabilities are long-term and the fund invests in short-dated gilts, serious problems could arise if interest rates should fall. This is because there will be an increase in the present value of the future liabilities, but little scope for an increase in the value of the assets already standing near their redemption values. This is known as *income risk*, because the danger of investing short-term is a reduction in income if interest rates fall.

The opposite problem is faced by a financial institution such as a bank, with essentially short-term liabilities. If it invests long-term, and interest rates subsequently rise, the assets then fall in value while the liabilities remain largely unchanged. This is known as *capital risk*. The 'liquidity preference' theory is premised on the belief that more investors are concerned to avoid capital risk rather than income risk.

Clearly, investors should not adopt investment policies that are wildly inappropriate to their liabilities. If they do so, they should have sufficient reserves to cover themselves against the risks. The perfect matching of liabilities and assets is known as *immunization*: it implies that a change in the interest rate has an identical effect on both.

In order to improve profit, a fund may decide to move away from a matched position, but usually the intention is to return to it as soon as an expected profit has been made. The reason for the change is the expectation of a change in overall interest rates, or in the shape of the yield curve. If interest rates are expected to fall, a fund may move longer than its normal 'preferred habitat' in order to achieve greater capital gains from the more volatile longer-dated gilts. Conversely, if interest rates are expected to rise, a fund may move shorter to avoid capital losses. Of course, if these expectations prove ill-founded, the funds face respectively capital risk and income risk as discussed above. Anomaly switches are low-risk/low-return; policy switches are high-risk/high-return.

6.10 Questions

1. (a) The formula for calculating the flat yield of a redeemable British Government stock is:

   A redemption yield % multiplied by par divided by market price.
   B gross interest % multiplied by par divided by market price.
   C market price divided by net interest %.
   D market price divided by gross interest %.

   (b) Which of the following investments offers the highest net return to a basic-rate taxpayer?

   A National Savings Bank Investment Account.
   B National Savings Certificates – current standard issue.
   C National Savings Income Bonds.
   D $2\frac{1}{2}$% Consols at $26\frac{5}{8}$.

   (c) When the coupon of a fixed-interest stock exceeds the gross redemption yield (GRY), the price of the stock will be:

   A below par and the GRY will be below the flat yield.
   B above par and the GRY will be above the flat yield.
   C below par and the GRY will be above the flat yield.
   D above par and the GRY will be below the flat yield.

   (d) A gilt-edged stock has its interest and redemption yields quoted in the *Financial Times* as 3.49 per cent and 6.71 per cent respectively. The gross equivalent yield for an investor who pays 40 per cent income tax is:

   A 8.58 per cent.
   B 8.67 per cent.
   C 8.76 per cent.
   D 8.85 per cent.

(e) If 3½% War Loan stands at 39⅝, what is the real gross yield assuming an inflation rate of 6 per cent?

    A 2.60 per cent.
    B 2.82 per cent.
    C 2.75 per cent.
    D 2.67 per cent.

(f) Index-linked gilts:

    A become most attractive to investors when inflation is thought likely to increase.
    B offer a higher real gross redemption yield the higher the assumed rate of inflation.
    C provide indexation of interest and capital and a bonus at maturity.
    D are all 'low-coupon' and short-dated.

2. (a) In August 1989 Treasury 3% 1992 cost £84¹³⁄₁₆, at which price the gross redemption yield was 9.14 per cent. By means of calculations assess the stock's respective attractiveness for (i) basic-rate and (ii) higher-rate taxpayers.

                                                     (CIB 5/90)

(b) A gilt has a 'flat' yield of 12 per cent and a gross redemption yield of 10 per cent.

    (i) Explain the terms 'flat' and 'gross redemption' yield.
    (ii) Comment on the suitability to a private client of such a stock.

                                                   (SIE 12/88)

3. Calculate the net redemption yield and gross equivalent for

(a) a basic-rate taxpayer
(b) a higher-rate taxpayer

for the following stocks:

		Gross yields (%)	
	Price	Flat	Redemption
Exchequer 3% Gas 1990–95	76½	3.92	9.02
Exchequer 12% 2013–17	108³⁄₃₂xd	11.10	11.03
Treasury 13¼% 1997	104¹³⁄₃₂	12.69	12.22
Funding 3½% 1999–04	50⁷⁄₃₂xd	6.97	10.24
War Loan 3½%	32⁵⁄₁₆	10.83	—

N.B. Assume the year is 1990

4. (a) Explain the expression 'yield curve' as applied to gilt-edged securities.
   (b) Explain fully what is meant by 'gilt-edged switching'.

7 Company securities

The capital of companies in the United Kingdom may be divided into two principal classes: *share capital* and *loan capital*. Each of these may be subdivided into various classes of capital for any particular company. It is unusual for a company of any size to have only one class of capital. Companies must have share capital but they may have various classes of share capital and no loan capital, or a combination of different classes of both share and loan capital.

In simple terms, the owners of the share capital of a company own the company itself, and the holders of loan capital are creditors of the company. Thus the holders of share capital are not creditors and have no security, and the holders of loan capital have no rights in the company beyond the payment of interest on their loans and repayment of the loans in accordance with the terms on which they were issued. The amount which a company may borrow by way of loan capital is laid down in its articles of association.

7.1 Company fixed-interest finance

Loan capital may be secured or unsecured, and companies frequently issue both kinds of stock. Where the loan is secured, the capital is charged on certain assets of the company to which the holders of that capital may look for repayment in the event of the company being wound up. Holders of unsecured loan stock, on the other hand, are entitled to repayment equally with the ordinary creditors of the company. Some creditors may be secured and therefore rank before unsecured loan capital – for example, when a company, wishing to borrow from its bankers, is required to give the bank security for its overdraft. For the protection of its holders, the terms of issue of loan capital usually limit the company's borrowing powers, not only in respect of debts which would take priority over the loan capital, but also in respect of further loan capital which would rank equally.

Another class of loan capital consists of *convertible* loan stocks, which are often (though not necessarily) unsecured. These usually carry a lower coupon than a straightforward loan stock, because they carry the right of conversion into ordinary shares at some future date. They are discussed in chapter 11.

Not all classes of a company's capital need to be quoted on a stock exchange. Thus a company might have only one or two classes of loan capital quoted and the share capital retained within a family, or it might have one or more classes of loan stock issued privately to institutions and not quoted on an exchange while its share capital is quoted.

7.1.1 Debentures and debenture stocks

The definition of a *debenture* is very wide and does not necessarily imply that the security gives any charge over the assets of the borrower. This should stand as a warning to the incautious investor, but as the term is generally used in investment it is taken to imply that some form of security is given. Thus debenture and debenture stocks are usually similar to mortgages, and indeed the word 'mortgage' is commonly used to describe them – 6% First Mortgage Debenture Stock, for instance.

Debentures 'pure and simple' are rarely issued nowadays, and not many are still outstanding. Recent issues of this nature have been in the form of *debenture stocks*. The amount of the debenture is expressed in the form of stock, and transactions on the market are carried out in the same way as for any other type of stock. Whereas Government stocks are transferable in multiples of 1p, debenture stocks may be transferable only in multiples of £1, £5, or even £100, the minimum amount being written into the terms of issue of the stock.

Usually, corporate trustees are appointed for the assets charged as security for debentures and debenture stocks; generally they are banks or insurance companies. A trust deed is drawn up and completed by the company and by the trustee, setting out the terms of the issue, the security charged, the powers of the trustee and the duties of the company in respect of the stock, and the security. The trustee's duty is to act on behalf of the holders of the issue, even though the company pays its fee. It usually has the power to approve any changes in the security and minor amendments to the require-ments of the trust deed in the light of changing circumstances. If the trustee believes that a proposed change may be prejudicial to the interests of the holders of the issue, it may require the company to obtain approval of its proposals from a meeting of debenture-holders.

Debenture stocks are quite commonly secured on certain specific assets of the company, with a floating charge over the rest of the company's assets. It is not strictly necessary for there to be a specific or *fixed charge*, however; and a *floating charge* – a form of security which only a limited company can give – embodies the right to take possession of all of a company's assets as they stand at any particular time.

All secured debt ranks for repayment before unsecured debt in the event of the company being wound up. If the trustees consider that the security of the holders is in danger through the company's actions, they may apply for a receiver to be appointed to liquidate sufficient of the charged assets to repay the capital of the issued stock and any arrears of interest.

7.1.2 Unsecured loan stocks

Unsecured loan stocks, as their name indicates, are stocks representing loans to the company which are not secured or charged on the company's assets. In the event of liquidation they rank after secured loans, equally with general creditors, and before share capital.

Trustees are appointed for unsecured loan stocks in the same way as for debenture stocks, but they of course hold no assets. They watch the interests of stockholders, particularly with regard to restrictions on borrowing, which are usually included in the terms of issue of these stocks. This protects the position of stockholders by limiting the amount of capital and other borrowing ranking both before the stock and also equally with it. A limit on total borrowing of say, twice the share capital is a common provision, but this will exclude short-term borrowing in the normal course of business and inter-group loans.

A few companies (notably the clearing banks) issue *subordinated* loan stocks, repayment of such stocks being subordinated to all other creditors. Such stocks clearly involve a greater risk than the more usual kinds of loan capital and the investor can accordingly obtain a better return.

7.2 Company fixed-interest stocks: investment criteria

The prospective investor in the company fixed-interest market is faced with a bewildering choice if he or she looks at the whole range of available stocks. There are redeemable and irredeemable stocks; debentures, debenture stocks, and unsecured loan stocks; unsecured loan stocks in companies which have no debenture stocks in issue; first-, second-, and even third-mortgage debenture stocks charging the same assets; unsecured loan stocks where charges ranking in priority are not quoted in the market; subordinated loan stocks; and stocks that are only one issue among as many as twenty made by the same company with different terms for interest and repayment.

7.2.1 Common factors

All fixed-interest stocks have certain things in common. They carry a fixed rate of interest – usually payable half-yearly – and the rights attaching to them are ascertainable. All interest is subject to tax and is paid with income tax at basic rate deducted at source by the company and passed over to the Inland Revenue. Interest-bearing company securities are subject to the Accrued Income Scheme (see section 5.7), but, unlike gilts and related securities, prices of company securities are inclusive of accrued interest. Since 2 July 1986, stock without conversion rights purchased after 13 March 1984 is not liable to capital gains tax if the company is quoted on the Stock Exchange. However special rules apply to deep-discounted stocks.

7.2.2 Deep-discounted bonds

These are interest-bearing securities which are issued at a large discount to their normal value, and hence provide the investor with a return composed largely of capital gain. In the extreme case of zero-coupon bonds, the return will be entirely capital gain. (In the USA, zero-coupon bonds are known as 'streaker' bonds, because they are bare of interest!) In the UK, the Government introduced legislation in 1988 to deter the issuing of all such securities.

Where a loan stock is issued at a discount of more than $\frac{1}{2}$ per cent per year over the life of stock, or below 85 per cent of the redemption price, the discount is treated as income accruing over the life of the stock on a compound yield basis. All or part of the gain is taxed as income in the hands of the investor, at the time of disposal or redemption. Thus, a ten-year stock issued at 90 and a 25-year stock issued at 80 in 1989 would both be regarded as deep-discounted bonds. However, if the stocks were sold before redemption, and had appreciated at a faster rate in that period than the redemption yield at issue would have indicated, the 'excess' growth would technically be liable to capital gains tax, but, of course, most corporate debt will be 'qualifying' corporate debt, and therefore exempted from CGT.

These provisions do not apply to index-linked securities in the normal course of events, but in 1989 they were extended to include non-index-linked gilts and related securities.

7.2.3 Yield
Yields on apparently similar stocks may differ. Differences in price, and therefore yield, reflect the market's assessment of the issuing company's standing and of the risk elements in the particular stocks. A high yield in relation to the market in general shows an above-average risk element. Investors wanting a high yield from a redeemable fixed-interest investment will find suitable stocks, but should not be tempted by exceptionally high yields. Risk is discussed in more detail in chapter 9.

Marketability can be a problem with stocks in this sector, and it may not be possible to buy exactly the stock selected. New issues usually command a free market, and most of the stocks of the largest companies can also be bought and sold freely, but comparing Table 7.1 with Table 5.1 shows that the market value of UK corporate loan capital is only about 13 per cent of that of British Government stocks.

The yield structure of a hypothetical company is illustrated in fig. 7.1.

7.2.4 Sinking funds and redemption
The vast majority of stocks issued are redeemable with reference to some future date or dates. Many companies anticipate redemption by setting aside a part of each year's profit in a *sinking fund*.

An equivalent cash amount may be used in various ways:

(a) to purchase the stock itself in the open market – because the company is buying at current market price, there is then no question of preferring some creditors at the expense of others;

(b) to redeem part of the issued stock at par (or as otherwise agreed) on the

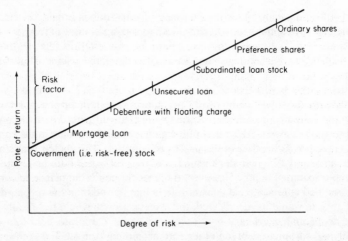

Fig. 7.1   Risk and return: loan capital in relation to Government stocks and share capital

basis of drawings (the stock to be redeemed being determined by ballot);
(c) to purchase other investments which are then held until the company considers it prudent to redeem the stock – perhaps not until the final redemption date.

The existence of a sinking fund improves the marketability and market rating of a stock.

7.3 Preference shares

Preference shares receive a fixed rate of dividend. They do not form part of loan capital and, on a winding-up, they rank ahead of ordinary shares but after loan capital and all other creditors for repayment.

7.3.1 The effect of corporation tax
Preference shares are a *fixed-income* investment but not a *fixed-interest* investment. As they form part of the share capital of a company, the income paid to the investor is dividend and not interest. This may seem an artificial distinction to the average investor, but it is in fact an important one. All loan interest is a charge on company profits, and the cost of loan capital to a company is consequently the interest paid less the corporation tax that would have been payable on that interest.

Preference share dividends are payable out of taxed profits and therefore cost the company more than loan stock interest on the same amount of capital. For a corporate investor, however, preference share dividends are *franked income* for corporation tax, whereas loan stock interest is not.

Franked income is that part of a company's income which is paid to it out of profits that have suffered corporation tax and is thereby exempt from further corporation tax, whereas other investment income is unfranked and therefore liable for corporation tax in the hands of a company investor. Thus, from the tax point of view alone, preference shares are a better investment for companies than loan stocks.

Following the introduction of the imputation system of corporation tax in 1973, the coupons of preference shares were changed from a gross to a net basis at the then prevailing rate of income tax of 30 per cent. Thus a 10 per cent gross preference share became 7 per cent net. This meant that if the basic rate of income tax changed then so did the gross return. For example, at basic-rate income tax of 25 per cent, the gross coupon of our example would become 7 per cent $\div 0.75 = 9.33$ per cent.

7.3.2 Lack of attraction
To the personal investor it is difficult to find anything to commend preference shares as investments, except for a relatively high yield. They have all the disadvantages of British Government fixed-interest undated stocks with none of the advantages. The interest on the Government stock is guaranteed, whereas the dividends on preference shares depend on the availability of company profits. Any capital gains that might be made on them are liable to capital gains tax, whereas gains on Government stocks and stocks of quoted companies are exempt. Furthermore, preference shares possess the same marketability problems as company loan stock.

It is of course possible to buy preference shares whose yield far exceeds that obtainable on any gilt-edged stock. This is again a reflection of risk. Except where tax benefits can accrue, yield is a measure of the market's view of the risk attaching to the particular stock or share. Investors should always be suspicious of a yield which is significantly higher than that obtainable from similar investments.

The loan capital of a company is generally referred to as the *prior charges* of that company. This term indicates that, along with creditors, the holders of that capital have a prior claim on the assets of the company in the event of liquidation. Some prior charges have priority over others. In the share capital of a company, preference shares have priority over other types of share capital, but some preference shares may rank ahead of other preference shares. As with debentures and unsecured loan stocks, an investor should be aware of the nature of the investment that is being purchased.

7.3.3 Types of preference share
Some companies have several issues of preference shares. These may rank either in a certain order or *pari passu* (on an equal basis). They may be classified as first and second preference shares, but the absence of such classification does not guarantee that they rank equally. Often preference shares with different rates of dividend rank *pari passu*. The order of priority usually relates equally to the availability of profits out of which to pay a

dividend and to capital priority on winding-up.

Preference shares may be either *cumulative* or *non-cumulative*. If there are insufficient profits in one year to pay a cumulative preference dividend, that dividend must be paid before any payment is made to the holders of a lower class of capital. Even though a cumulative preference share dividend may be years in arrears, all arrears must be paid off before a dividend is declared on preference shares ranking lower in priority, and on ordinary shares. With non-cumulative preference shares, once a dividend is passed for one year the right to receive it is lost and no arrears are due on resumption of payment. Preference shares are understood to be cumulative unless specifically stated otherwise.

Some companies have preference shares with rights to participate in profits beyond the fixed dividend. These *participating preference shares* vary enormously in their terms, but the investor is fortunate to find one where there is still scope for increases in dividends. Very few, if any, are now available, as there is always an upper limit to the amount of participation, and in the course of time this effectively converts the share to a preference share with a higher fixed dividend than that available when it was first issued. Some participating preference shares are called *preferred ordinary shares*. These generally combine the fixed dividend of a preference share and the voting rights of an ordinary share.

Holders of preference shares, although 'proprietors' of the company through the holding of share capital, usually cannot vote at general meetings of the company. However, such shares usually carry voting rights when the dividend is in arrears. The articles of association of the company or the terms of issue of the shares will give full details of any such rights.

Some preference shares are described as 'redeemable', but care is needed when assessing these. Redemption may either be set for a particular time or be at the option of the company. Following the Companies Act 1981 (now incorporated into the Companies Act 1985), all preference shares are redeemable at the option of the company provided that the interests of creditors are safeguarded. Convertible preference shares normally carry conversion rights, at the investor's option, into the ordinary shares. They are very similar to convertible loan stocks.

7.4 The equity

As far as investment in companies is concerned, the highest risk is carried by the holders of the ordinary share capital. Other things being equal, total returns obtainable on ordinary shares should therefore be higher than those obtainable on prior-charge capital and preference shares. Ordinary shares represent the type of investment that transfers to the investor a part or share of a business enterprise. Ordinary shares are not loans, and their holders have no specific rights against the company. In fact the ordinary shareholders *are* the company, in so far as together they can control the company's activities and future.

Ordinary shares as a whole are usually referred to as *equities*. This accurately describes their significance, as the holders of the ordinary capital of a company usually own between them the equity of that company. Equity in this sense means *that which remains after the rights of creditors and mortgages are cleared*. The equity in a private house, for instance, is the market value less the amount of an outstanding mortgage. The equity in a company is the value of the assets remaining after creditors, debenture and loan stockholders, and preference shareholders have been paid what they are entitled to.

The equity is usually owned by the ordinary shareholders, but this is not invariably so. The equity must be owned by the holders of share capital, but there can be several classes of share capital. For example, some companies have both preferred and deferred ordinary shares. The latter – sometimes known as 'founder's shares' – are entitled to the residual interest in the capital and therefore represent the true equity shares.

The rights of the holders of the equity of a company extend not only to the assets alone but also to the earnings. Thus the profits made by a company after providing for all debts, interest, and taxation are applied to the holders of the share capital according to their rights. With a straightforward capital structure, therefore, the preference shareholders receive their fixed dividend and the balance belongs to the ordinary shareholders. Not all of this balance is normally paid out by way of dividend: what is not distributed is retained by the company and increases the assets attributable to the ordinary capital.

7.4.1 Nominal values

Inexperienced investors might find it confusing that some companies have ordinary shares of £1 each; some have ordinary shares of 25p each (all shares quoted in the *Financial Times* are 25p shares unless otherwise stated); and others have 50p, 5p, or some other value expressed in the title of the shares. From an investment standpoint, such distinctions are largely irrelevant. It makes no difference whatsoever what denomination the shares are quoted in. If a company has net assets of, say, £5 000 000, it cannot have any significance to the investor whether there are 4 000 000 £1 shares issued and £1 000 000 of reserves or 16 000 000 25p shares and £1 000 000 of reserves, except that the quoted price of the nominal £1 shares would be four times that of the 25p shares.

The law of the United Kingdom requires shares of companies to have a nominal, or par, value. This is in contrast to some countries, such as the United States of America and Canada, where shares may have no nominal value and are then described as of '*no par value*'. In the example here, the equity capital could be expressed as £5 000 000 divided into a number of shares of no par value. The reserves of a company belong to the holders of equity equally with the nominal amount of equity capital, and the distinction in the UK is really an artificial one. It may be that in due course shares of no par value will be issued in the UK.

7.4.2 Dividend payments

Dividends on ordinary shares are declared in respect of the company's trading period, usually a year. There are two types of dividend: *interim* and *final*. Interim dividends may be declared by the directors, but final dividends may be paid only on approval by the ordinary shareholders at the annual general meeting of the company, after the end of the company's financial year.

The directors usually declare and pay an interim dividend during the second half of the company's year, and propose a final dividend to be paid the day after the annual meeting. Thus dividends are usually paid at about six-monthly intervals. More often than not the final dividend is at a higher rate than the interim one.

Sometimes companies pay more than two dividends for one year; sometimes only one. Sometimes two interims are paid and no final. The annual general meeting has the power to reduce a final dividend but not to increase it, although the exercise of such power is very rare in quoted companies.

All dividends are paid net of tax, which has to be accounted for by the company as *advance corporation tax* (ACT) – see chapter 8.

Before a dividend payment is made, the register of a company or undertaking must be closed to enable the dividend warrants (that is, cheques plus certificates of deduction of tax) to be prepared. It is clearly impossible for all transfer forms lodged with the registrar up to the day on which a dividend payment is due to be registered and for the transferees to receive the dividend warrants. If transactions took no account of this, dividends would be paid to many one-time holders who had recently sold their shares and who owed these dividends to the purchasers. To restrict these 'wrong' payments to a minimum, bargains during a few weeks before the payment date are executed without regard to the dividend to be paid, which will belong to the vendor. Shares are thus quoted *ex-dividend* during that period (abbreviated to *xd*). A vendor of shares xd keeps the next dividend payment; similarly, a purchaser xd has no right to the next dividend payment. Bargains not specifically marked xd are assumed to be *cum* (with) the next dividend.

Some companies have 'B' shares in existence. These pay a dividend in the form of additional shares ('scrip') instead of cash, but the former tax advantage no longer exists. A 'scrip' dividend is taxed identically to a 'cash' dividend. A higher-rate taxpayer will have to meet the additional tax burden, but there is no tax credit for a non-taxpayer.

Split-level investment trusts have two classes of share capital: income and capital shares. The former are entitled to all the income; the latter to the capital gain. These are discussed in more detail chapter 16.

7.4.3 Non-voting shares

Although frowned on by the Stock Exchange, which prevents further issues of them, some issues of equity shares that have no voting rights are still outstanding. These are usually called 'A' ordinary shares. They were devised to keep the voting control in a company in the hands of a minority while bringing in capital from general investors. Where they still exist, they are usually quoted at lower prices than the voting ordinary shares. This price differential usually becomes significant if the company becomes a take-over target. Acceptance or rejection of the bid will rest with the voting shares.

It is difficult to justify the existence of non-voting ordinary shares: those who carry the risk in a company should be able to control its future together. In recent years several companies have enfranchised these shares, and at the same time given a bonus issue to the previous voting shares to compensate them for the dilution in control.

7.4.4 Redeemable ordinary shares

Since the Companies Act 1981 it has been possible to issue redeemable ordinary shares provided that there is at least some non-redeemable equity. Redeemables have all the rights of ordinary shares – voting rights, dividend rights, etc. They can be redeemed either by a transfer of an equivalent sum from undistributed profits to a specific *capital redemption reserve*, or out of the proceeds of a new issue of shares.

In addition, the Companies Act 1985 gives companies the right to repurchase their standard ordinary shares, provided that this has the shareholders' approval, subject to a maximum percentage of ordinary shares. Guinness and Amstrad are two companies which announced such intentions at times when they declared that their shares were undervalued in the market.

7.5 Legal personality and limited liability

When a company is incorporated, it becomes a distinct legal entity quite separate from its members, even though there may be only two of them and one of these owns 99 per cent of the shares. It follows from this that anyone dealing with the company is not dealing with its members as such. Consequently, the company's rights and duties must be quite distinct from those of its members, although the separation of powers is not as clear-cut where such members are also directors.

From this concept of *separate entity*, that of *limited liability* naturally follows. Since members *per se* are not responsible for the actions of the company, their liability must be limited. Thus anyone purchasing shares in a company will find that the share certificate states the extent, if any, of any remaining liability. Most shares in quoted companies are fully paid, so, no matter whether the investor buys them in the market at above or below the nominal price, the company cannot require him or her to provide further capital. If, however, shares are in partly paid form, there is a real liability. If the company is sound, this is not perhaps a serious matter, but no investor wants to throw good money after bad. Where a company becomes insolvent and has to be wound up, the shareholders receive something only after all the creditors have been satisfied in full. Often, however, they lose everything. If their shares are only partly paid, the liquidator can require them to repay the outstanding amount.

7.5.1 Formation of a company

The Companies Act 1985 provides for the formation of two kinds of company: *public limited companies*, which are specifically defined, and *private companies*, which form the residuary category. A public company is a company limited by shares and

(a) the memorandum of which states that the company is to be a public company;
(b) which is registered as such;
(c) the name of which ends with the words 'public limited company' or 'p.l.c.' (or its Welsh equivalent);
(d) which has no fewer than two members;
(e) which has a minimum issued share capital of £50 000.

Table 7.1 Quoted corporate securities at 30 September 1989

	No. of companies	No. of securities	Nominal value (£m)	Market value (£m)
Company securities				
Loan capital				
UK		982	15 081.9	16 508.8
Irish		11	34.8	39.0
Overseas		31	246.9	864.6
Subtotal		1 024	15 363.6	17 412.4
Preference capital				
UK		1 181	5 778.2	17 809.5
Irish		22	139.6	190.7
Overseas		132	251.6	20 063.7
Subtotal		1 335	6 169.4	38 063.9
Ordinary and deferred				
UK	1 954	1 963	43 641.1	494 046.1
Irish	60	54	841.3	6 809.0
Overseas	534	701	50 930.7	1 324 738.7
Subtotal	2 548	2 718	95 413.1	1 825 593.8
Total company securities	2 548	5 077	116 946.1	1 881 070.1
Junior markets				
Unlisted Securities Market				
Loan capital		8	33.8	21.9
Preference capital		31	147.1	259.3
Ordinary and deferred	443	453	1 121.2	9 948.4
Total USM	443	492	1 302.1	10 229.6
Third Market				
Loan capital	—	—	—	—
Preference capital		1	1.3	3.4
Ordinary and deferred	64	71	129.1	624.9
Total Third Market	64	72	130.4	628.3

Source: The International Stock Exchange, London (1989).

A company is formed after certain important documents – the memorandum of association and the articles of association – have been lodged with the Registrar of Companies. For all companies, a *Certificate of Incorporation* is issued by the Registrar, but a public company requires, in addition, a *Certificate to Commence Business*.

Note that a public company is not necessarily a 'quoted' company. The majority of public companies are not 'quoted' on the Stock Exchange, but only public companies can seek a quotation.

Table 7.1 shows that in September 1989 there were slightly fewer than 2000 UK companies and ordinary shares listed on the Stock Exchange 'Official List' – the main market – plus about another 500 on the junior markets. (The different markets on the Stock Exchange are discussed in chapter 12.)

7.5.2 The memorandum of association
This document contains six clauses:

(a) the name of the company, the last words usually being 'limited' or 'public limited company';
(b) the part of the United Kingdom where the company's registered office is situated (England, for instance, or Scotland);
(c) the objects of the company;
(d) a statement that the liability of the members is limited;
(e) the amount of nominal capital and how it is divided;
(f) a statement signed by the subscribing members that they wish to form a company.

The most important of these clauses is (c), the objects clause. This clause determines what the company can legally do, and is usually drawn extremely widely, so as to allow the company to undertake a range of different operations. Transactions outside the objects are said to be *ultra vires*, but the European Communities Act 1972 provides that, for a person dealing with a company in good faith, the transaction shall be treated as being within the company's capacity even though the objects clause itself would not allow it.

7.5.3 The articles of association
The articles of association contain the *internal* regulations of the company. The Companies Act 1985 contains model articles, known as *Table A*, which many companies adopt unamended; these apply to any company that does not register its own articles.

The principal matters covered by the articles are as follows:

(a) the issue of shares and the rights and obligations of members;
(b) transfer of shares;
(c) alteration of capital;
(d) meetings;
(e) voting and proxies;
(f) directors – their qualifications, powers, and duties;

(g) dividends, reserves, and capitalization of profits;
(h) accounts and audit;
(i) winding-up.

The articles are binding on both the company and its members, but it is unlikely that many members will have any knowledge of a company's articles unless these are brought to their attention in a company announcement or in the press.

Some matters may be dealt with in both the memorandum and the articles. Where the two are in conflict, it is the memorandum which prevails. Either document can be altered on the passing of a special resolution.

7.5.4 Directors

In theory, the control of a company is exercised by the shareholders. They do in fact exercise ultimate control, but Table A – the model set of articles – provides that the business of the company shall be managed by the directors.

Until the passing of the Companies Act 1980, statute law was not specific about the duties of directors, but the courts had recognized two duties: a *fiduciary duty* and a *duty of care*. When representing the company, the directors are said to be agents of the company. Their position in relation to the shareholders is not quite clear. In some circumstances they are agents; in others more akin to trustees. But it is certainly true that in relation to the shareholders the directors occupy a position of trust and so, for example, must inform the members of any contracts involving the company in which they have a personal interest. A company cannot, generally, lend money to its directors, and it is well-established law that where the interests of the company and those of individual shareholders are in conflict the interests of the company shall prevail. The 1980 Act imposed a special duty on directors in requiring them to have regard to the interests of their employees as well as their shareholders.

Every public company must have at least two directors. Directors are elected each calendar year at the annual general meeting and normally retire by rotation every three years and on reaching the age of 70, but in both circumstances they can be re-elected.

7.6 The rights and duties of shareholders

The rights of the ordinary members are necessarily limited by the considerable powers which the directors exercise on their behalf and on behalf of the company itself. Since, in law, a company is a person with its own rights, the directors are bound to regard the company's interests as paramount. Thus, for example, while the shareholders can reduce a proposed dividend they cannot increase it, for this might create insurmountable liquidity problems for the company. The principal rights of ordinary shareholders are:

(a) to receive the annual report and accounts;

(b) to receive notice of the annual general meeting and other meetings of members;
(c) to attend, vote, and speak at meetings;
(d) to appoint a proxy to attend meetings, to request a poll, and to vote on a poll;
(e) to share in the profits of the company – either in the form of dividends or by an increase in the reserves – and the residue on a winding-up;
(f) to subscribe for any new share capital or convertible loan stock in proportion to their existing holdings;
(g) to transfer their shares freely unless restricted in the articles of association.

Legislation since 1967 has imposed an obligation on voting shareholders to notify the company whenever a purchase or sale of their shares affects in any way a substantial interest in that company. The Companies Act 1989 requires any person acquiring a 3 per cent interest in the voting capital, or reducing or increasing such an interest by more than 1 per cent, to notify the company of the details of such transactions within two days. The Companies Act 1985 enables companies to require shareholders to reveal the beneficial interest in holdings over the previous three years. Before 1976, where shares were registered in the name of a nominee, the company had no means of knowing where the real ownership lay. This meant that a company could be facing a gradual take-over by another company without being aware of it, particularly if the use of several different nominee names masked the same beneficial ownership.

7.7 Meetings

There are different kinds of members' meetings and, before looking in turn at the business of each, we shall consider several matters some of which may be common to more than one class of meeting.

7.7.1 The quorum
For the meeting there must be a *quorum* – that is, a specified minimum number of shareholders that must be present before the meeting can be valid. For general (i.e. shareholders') meetings, this number can be set at two.

7.7.2 Resolutions
Matters at meetings are determined by *resolutions* which are voted upon. There are three kinds of resolution. An *ordinary* resolution, not defined by the Companies Act 1985, is sufficient for most purposes including all the routine matters dealt with at an annual general meeting. Other examples of business dealt with in this way include an increase in the authorized or issued share capital; the removal of a director; and the removal of an auditor before the expiry of his or her term of office. Ordinary resolutions are passed by a simple majority of those voting, and require at least fourteen days' notice.

Certain important matters, however, require the passing of a *special* or an *extraordinary* resolution, for both of which a 75 per cent majority of those voting is required. Such resolutions are decided at an extraordinary general meeting.

Special resolutions are required, for instance, for the following:

(a) to alter the objects clause in the memorandum or any of the articles;
(b) to change the name of the company;
(c) to reduce capital (the consent of the court is also required);
(d) to have the company wound up voluntarily;
(e) to sanction a winding-up, whereby the company's property is exchanged for shares in another company.

Twenty-one days' notice is required for a special resolution.

Among the most important matters requiring an extraordinary resolution is the winding-up of a company on the grounds that, by reason of its liabilities, it cannot continue business. The period of notice required is not specified but must be at least fourteen days, which is the period of notice required for an extraordinary general meeting.

7.7.3 Voting and proxies

In order that a member may vote at a meeting at which he or she cannot be present, the Companies Act provides for the appointment of proxies. A *proxy* need not be a member of the company. A proxy cannot vote except on a *poll*, and can speak only to demand a poll. Corporate bodies can appoint a proxy or, alternatively, a *representative* who for the duration of the meeting has all the rights of a member.

Normally voting is by a show of hands. A poll can, however, be demanded either by five or more members or by members representing one-tenth of the voting capital. On a poll, the usual procedure is to allow one vote for each share held. When sending out proxy forms, companies usually suggest the names of directors of the company who will then act as proxies, voting as they see fit unless otherwise instructed (see fig. 7.2).

7.7.4 The annual general meeting

The principal meeting of the shareholders is called the *annual general meeting*. It is laid down that one a.g.m. be held in every calendar year, and that the interval between meetings should not exceed fifteen months. At least twenty-one days' notice must be given.

The usual business transacted at an annual general meeting consists of the following routine matters:

(a) the consideration of the directors' report and accounts;
(b) the declaration of a final dividend;
(c) the election of the directors;
(d) the appointment and remuneration of the auditors.

All such matters are designated *ordinary business*; any other matters are

---

British Aerospace Public Limited Company

Form of Proxy for use at the Annual General Meeting on 10th May, 1988

I/We, the undersigned, (See Note 1 overleaf) being a member/members of British Aerospace Public Limited Company hereby appoint the Chairman of the Meeting or

_____   **140X00000000200X**

IN BLOCK LETTERS (see note 2)

as my/our proxy to vote for me/us and on my/our behalf at the Annual General Meeting of the Company to be held at 3.00 p.m. on 10th May, 1988 and at any adjournment thereof. I/We request my/our proxy to vote in the manner indicated below (see note 3) on the following resolutions:

Routine Business   ORDINARY RESOLUTIONS

		FOR	AGAINST
Resolution 1	To adopt the accounts of the Company for the year ended 31st December, 1987 and the reports of the directors and auditors thereon	☐	☐
Resolution 2	To declare a dividend	☐	☐
Resolution 3	To re-elect the following Directors		
	(a) Sir Raymond Derek Lygo	☐	☐
	(b) Sir Kenneth Durham	☐	☐
	(c) Sydney Gillibrand	☐	☐
	(d) Philip William Wilkinson	☐	☐
	(e) Dudley Graham Eustace	☐	☐
Resolution 4	To re-appoint Peat Marwick McLintock as auditors of the Company	☐	☐
Resolution 5	To authorise the Directors to determine the remuneration of the auditors	☐	☐

Special Business   SPECIAL RESOLUTIONS

		FOR	AGAINST
Resolution 6	To alter the Articles of Association by the adoption of new Article 11 (authority for allotment of equity securities)	☐	☐
Resolution 7	To alter the Articles of Association by the adoption of new Article 125A (provision for stock dividends)	☐	☐

ORDINARY RESOLUTIONS

		FOR	AGAINST
Resolution 8	To increase the maximum fee payable to the Directors	☐	☐
Resolution 9	To amend the Rules of the British Aerospace SAYE Share Option Scheme and the British Aerospace Executive Share Option Scheme	☐	☐

Source: British Aerospace plc

Fig. 7.2   A form of proxy

deemed *special business* (see fig. 7.2).

The annual general meeting is the only regular opportunity for directors and shareholders to meet each other. The power of the individual shareholder is generally very limited, although he or she may be in a position to exercise significant influence, as illustrated by the activities of anti-apartheid shareholders at meetings of companies with South African interests. In many companies, interests are widely spread, so that even a 2 or 3 per cent holding can be influential at a meeting where less than 10 per cent of the shares, and a far smaller proportion of members, are represented. Some substantial public companies, however, are still controlled by the family that formed the business.

Little effective control is exercised over the directors in many companies, and there is increasing support for the view that, as in some other countries, every board should include some non-executive directors, part of whose responsibility would be to look after the interest of the shareholders.

A number of companies have, in recent years, attempted to encourage shareholders to attend the annual general meeting by offering inducements such as a buffet lunch, product samples, or vouchers for use in their retail outlets. Other companies simply provide the shareholders with benefits whether or not they attend meetings. One, for example, offers a 25 per cent discount on dry-cleaning in its retail shops; another, a funeral company, once provided a free burial or cremation for deceased shareholders.

7.7.5 Extraordinary general meetings

All general meetings of shareholders other than the annual meeting are referred to as *extraordinary general meetings*. These can be called by the directors at any time, and shareholders representing one-tenth of the voting capital can require them to convene one. If the directors do not comply with the request, the shareholders themselves can call a meeting and charge the company with the expenses incurred. The period of notice required is not less than fourteen days, unless a special resolution is to be passed, in which case the period is 21 days.

7.7.6 Class meetings

These are meetings held to consider matters which are of special concern to persons other than the ordinary shareholders. Such matters might include a proposal to reduce the level of the preference dividend, or to vary in some way the rights of debenture-holders. At such meetings the parties concerned would be those entitled to vote.

7.7.7 Special business and special notice

All items of business at an annual general meeting, other than the routine matters, and all matters laid before the members at an extraordinary general meeting are termed *special business*.

Certain business requires *special notice* of twenty-eight days. Some such business may be particularly appropriate as items of special business at an annual general meeting – for instance, a resolution to appoint as auditor a person other than the retiring auditor. Other matters requiring special notice would be more appropriate at an extraordinary general meeting, such as resolutions to remove directors or auditors before the expiration of their terms of office. The terms 'special resolution', 'special business', and 'special notice' have no necessary connection with each other.

7.8 Auditors

The role of the auditor has become increasingly important since audit was first made compulsory under the Companies Act 1948. An audit must be carried out by accountants who are approved persons under the Companies Act 1989. Auditors are guided in the presentation of accounts not only by the legal requirements but also by the *Recommendations on Accounting Principles* and the *Statements of Standard Accounting Practice*.

The Recommendations on Accounting Principles were first published in the 1940s and are of persuasive authority only, allowing considerable flexibility in many cases. Many accountants believed that greater uniformity was necessary, and in 1969 an Accounting Standards Committee was set up to attempt to standardize many areas of accounting. Following the recommendations of the Dearing Report, the Accounting Standards Committtee was replaced in 1990 by a more powerful Accounting Standards Board appointed by a newly constituted Financial Reporting Council.

Auditors must comply with the Statements of Standard Accounting Practice or qualify the accounts. If, therefore, the directors of a company decide to depart from a particular standard, the auditors cannot give the usual satisfactory report stating that the accounts have been examined and that they give a 'true and fair' view of the company's position. Qualification used to be tantamount to a statement that all was not well with the company, but in recent years many leading companies have had their accounts qualified because of non-compliance with a particular standard.

The Companies Act 1985 requires that auditors must be reappointed by ordinary resolution at the annual general meeting. If they are to be replaced, 28 days' notice is required. If the auditors resign, they must state whether or not there are circumstances that should be reported to the shareholders and, if so, what these are. The auditors can demand that an extraordinary general meeting be held at which they can state the circumstances surrounding their resignation. This legislation strengthens the position and independence of the auditor.

7.9 The audited accounts

Before the Companies Act 1948, disclosure requirements were not onerous and, while many companies had for several years complied with enlightened accounting practices – for example, in producing consolidated accounts – many others sought merely to comply with the law. Today not only has the law been greatly strengthened but also the widespread, if not wholehearted, compliance with standard accounting practice means that accounts now provide much more information than formerly, which certainly makes the professional investor's task easier. But smaller investors often feel oppressed by the sheer quantity of information. Many companies, therefore, are now trying to present information in ways that are more easily assimilated, and some also prepare a separate report for their staff. Sometimes these take the form of a simplified set of accounts, perhaps illustrated by pie diagrams, charts, and so forth. The Companies Act 1989 allows listed companies to provide investors with a short form of the report and accounts, unless a shareholder expresses a positive request for the fuller version.

The report and accounts must be sent to all shareholders and holders of debenture and loan stocks not less than 21 days before the annual general meeting. A copy must be lodged with the Registrar of Companies not more than seven months after the company's financial year ends. The content of the published accounts is discussed in chapter 9.

7.10 Stock Exchange requirements

The Stock Exchange requires listed companies to provide shareholders, through the audited accounts, with more information than the minimum required by law. The directors are also required to state the reasons for any significant departures from standard accounting practice and to explain any material failure to meet a published forecast. This last requirement is intended to discourage company chairmen from making rash prophecies.

In addition to the audited accounts, listed companies are required by the Stock Exchange to publish preliminary results at the end of their full year and also at the half-year stage. Preliminary results for the full year, reported by newspapers such as the *Financial Times*, provide the earliest formal indication of a group's performance, and are more newsworthy than the report and accounts, which usually follow about a month later. The information required in a preliminary announcement is not extensive, the main items being turnover, profits before and after tax, earnings per share, and dividends paid and proposed. Comparative figures are also required.

7.11 Questions

1. (a) Which of the following is a 'deep discounted' bond?

	Life at issue date	Price, £
A	10 years	96
B	10 years	90
C	5 years	98
D	25 years	89

(b) A company's 'A' shares are usually less valuable than its other ordinary shares because:

A they have no pre-emptive rights.
B they get no votes.
C dividends are deferred.
D they receive no dividend.

(c) Which of the following matters is not an item of ordinary business at a company's annual general meeting?

A Approval of the final dividend.
B Increase of the authorized capital.
C Appointment of auditors.
D Election of directors.

2. In 1988 a major UK public company made a successful take-over offer
   which was funded mainly by a further issue of its own ordinary shares. A
   significant part of the total consideration, however, was in the form of
   Convertible Cumulative Participating Redeemable Preference (CCPRP)
   shares of 20p each. Describe the characteristics of CCPRP shares.

   (CIB 5/90)

3. State ways in which preference shares differ from loan capital.

4. What are the normal rights and obligations of ordinary shareholders in a
   quoted company?

8 Equity yields and ratios

8.1 Risk and return

Ordinary shares – or equities, as they are more commonly known – are the most popular type of security for most investors because they offer the greatest opportunities for above-average returns. As figs 4.1, 4.2, and 5.1 illustrate, equities have performed extremely well when compared with building society and gilt-edged investments over the period 1918–88. According to the BZW Equity–Gilt Study, equities achieved an average nominal return of 11.7 per cent per year and a real rate of return (that is, over and above inflation) of 7.2 per cent compound over the period, assuming gross income was reinvested. To put it into perspective, an investor who invested £100 at the end of 1918 in equities, and continued to reinvest the gross income, would have had a portfolio worth approximately £230 000 at the end of 1988. The value of the equities would have increased 130 times in real terms, and this in turn would have increased a further 17.8 times due to inflation.

In contrast, a gilt-edged portfolio would have increased in real terms over the same period by only 1.1 per cent compound, again assuming gross income was reinvested.

The record of investing in equities in recent years has been even better than the historical average. Between December 1974 and December 1988 the average real return on equities was 15.8 per cent. This almost continuous 'bull' market (that is, 'rising' market) is illustrated in fig. 8.1. Share prices in the UK have risen almost uninterruptedly since January 1975, except for setbacks in 1976 and 1987 – the latter known as 'Black Monday', because of the sudden worldwide fall emanating from the United States. There has never previously been an upward movement of this length or magnitude in the modern history of the stock market. In past bull markets it was rare for share prices to rise for more than three straight years in a row and, until the present run began, share prices had fallen in almost as many years as they had risen. Since the 1920s the usual pattern has been a bull market for between two and seven years, followed by stagnation or downward movement for between two and seven years.

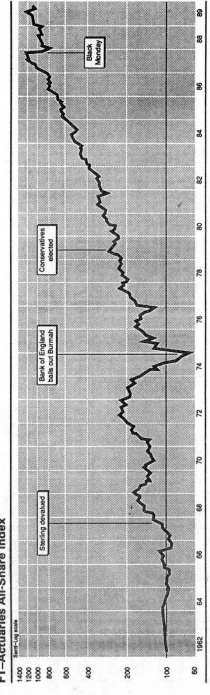

FT–Actuaries All-Share Index

Semi–Log scale

Sterling devalued

Bank of England bails out Burmah

Conservatives elected

Black Monday

Fig. 8.1   UK share prices (FT–Actuaries All-Share Index), 1962–89

Source: *Financial Times–Actuaries*

It must be remembered that share indices are only an average of the performance of a range of equities. Some do very well, as exemplified in recent years by Hanson, Glaxo, BTR, and Sainsbury. Hanson was worth £1.6 million in 1964; by October 1989 its market capitalization had risen to £8.7 billion. On the other hand, some shares have fallen out of favour (see Table 8.1). Some other companies have gone into liquidation, or been rescued by take-over. (Polly Peck crashed spectacularly in late 1990).

Table 8.1 Share price performance: the best and worst, 1980–9

From the whole stock market	% gain	Among stocks in FT-SE 100	% gain	From the whole stock market	% fall
1 Polly Peck Intl	126,590	1 Polly Peck Intl	126,590	1 NSM	93.3
2 Albert Fisher	8,360	2 Glaxo	2,761	2 BOM Holdings	93.1
3 Scottish Ice Rink	5,500	3 Hanson	2,109	3 Blacks Leisure	86.6
4 Helical Bar	4,707	4 BTR	1,403	4 Lasmo Units	85.7
5 Williams Holdings	4,472	5 Sainsburys	1,338	5 Central and S'wood	78.9
6 Hazelwood Foods	4,347	6 Rothmans Intl 'B'	1,308	6 Brown and Jackson	71.0
7 Mountleigh Group	3,927	7 BAT	1,281	7 Benjamin Priest	68.9
8 Priest Marians	3,920	8 Fisons	1,071	8 Charterhall	64.3
9 Southend PR	3,475	9 Ladbroke	998	9 Spong Holding	63.9
10 Baggeridge Brick	3,339	10 Reed International	918	10 Cluff Resources	62.3
11 Blockleys	2,903	11 RMC	913	11 Bestwood	58.3
12 Cantors	2,900	12 Ranks, Hovis	904	12 Kalamazoo	52.7
13 Glaxo	2,761	13 Sun Alliance Group	884	13 Eagle Trust	52.0
14 Rosehaugh	2,575	14 Tarmac	870	14 Chloride Group	48.9
15 BM Group	2,468	15 BOC	852	15 Alpine Group	46.9
16 Friendly Hotels	2,440	16 Maxwell Commun	798	16 Geevor	42.8
17 Capital Gearing Trust	2,400	17 Tesco	767	17 Kalon Group	39.1
18 George Ingham	2,390	18 Cookson Group	713	18 Bridgend Group	32.7
19 First Nat Finance	2,248	19 Smith and Nephew	692	19 Benchmark Group	32.7
20 M&G Group	2,200	20 Unilever	673	20 Brooke Tool	31.7

Note: The third column excludes liquidations
Source: Datastream

Investors can reduce risk by holding a diversified portfolio of shares, and by investing for a reasonable period of time. Risk generally falls with the length of time for which shares are held. According to the BZW Equity–Gilt Study, an investor who was a non-taxpayer would not have lost money in real terms in any 25-year period since 1918, i.e. 1918–43, 1919–44, 1920–45, etc. For shorter periods, the risk of losses generally increases. Table 8.2 shows that from 1945 to 1988 investors who were non-taxpayers lost money in real terms 24 per cent of the time over ten-year periods, 21 per cent of the time over five-year periods, and 42 per cent of the time over one-year periods.

Normally, one would expect the percentages of real losses to decline as the

Table 8.2 Investment periods and returns, 1945–88

Investment period	Periods of real gain	Periods of real loss	Total periods
1 year	25	18	43
5 years	31	8	39
10 years	26	8	34
25 years	19	0	19

investment period increases. However, this rule is not borne out by the figures since 1945. The reason is that the results are distorted by the stock market 'crash' of 1972–4. The negative real returns in 1973 and 1974 were 39 per cent and 58 per cent respectively. The eight ten-year periods which registered negative real returns were all between 1964 and 1982.

For taking these risks, non-taxpayers earned an average real return of 6.2 per cent between 1945 and 1988; top-rate taxpayers earned 1.7 per cent after tax.

8.2 The dividend yield

The calculation of yield on fixed-interest investments is relatively simple, as one is dealing with a fixed-income return. By their very nature, equities do not have a fixed return, however, and no investor can know for certain what rate of dividend will be declared in the future. The *dividend yield* is a historic measure; it looks backward, not forward, since calculations are based on the latest annual dividend rate (unless the company has already indicated what rate of annual dividend will be paid in the current year). The formula is

$$\text{gross dividend yield} = \frac{\text{grossed-up dividend per share}}{\text{market price of share}} \times 100\%$$

Dividends used to be declared as a percentage of the nominal share capital. This figure then had to be expressed as a percentage of the current market price. Nowadays the common practice is simply to declare 'dividends per share'. However, these figures are 'net' – the dividend is declared net of the tax credit which the shareholder receives – so, in order to work out the equivalent gross yield, the net dividend needs to be 'grossed-up' at the basic rate of tax. For example, if the net dividend per share is 3.5p, the quoted price of share AZ Plc is 80p, and the basic rate of income tax is 25 per cent, then

$$\text{gross dividend yield} = \frac{3.5p \times 100/(100-25)}{80p} \times 100\% = 5.83\%$$

The dividend yield is frequently quoted as a measure of the return on an equity, because of its ready availability (in the *Financial Times* for most large companies) and because it is analogous to the interest yield on debt capital. But it takes no account of future trends or variability in dividend – it is a totally static measure. The dividend yield is also very dependent on the company's payout policy. Dividends declared may be only a small proportion of the profits of the company available for the equity shareholders, but the earnings retained are not 'lost' to the shareholders but rather represent deferred income – that is, they provide for the financing of assets to produce greater future profits and dividends. On the other hand, dividends are sometimes in excess of earnings, and the historic yield is misleading if the dividend cannot be maintained.

130   Success in Investment

Percentage

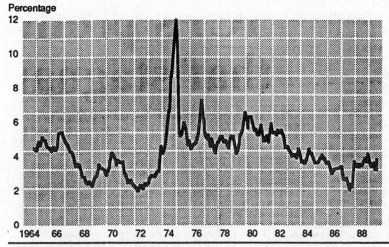

Source: *Financial Times*–Actuaries

Fig. 8.2   FT–Actuaries All-Share Index – dividend yield, 1964–89

As fig. 8.2 illustrates, the average dividend yield of the cross-section of
equities measured by the *FT*–Actuaries All-Share Index (actually a misnomer – it does not include all shares) has fluctuated considerably over 25
years. A general market rule of thumb is that when the Index is yielding over
5 per cent it is reasonably cheap, and when it is yielding under 4 per cent it is
dear. Just before the 'Black Monday' crash in October 1987 the Index was
yielding under 3 per cent, while in late 1974 it was over 13 per cent.

8.3 The earnings yield

The *earnings yield* is frequently regarded as a better measure of the
shareholder's return than the dividend yield, because it is unaffected by the
payout policy. The formula is

$$\text{earnings yield} = \frac{\text{'full' earnings per share}}{\text{market price of share}} \times 100\%$$

The earnings yield measures the potential dividend yield – that is, what the
dividend yield would be if all the profits were distributed. In order to provide
such a comparison, it is necessary to gross-up the earnings.

Assume that AZ Plc has profits of £84 million:

	£m
Profit	84.0
Corporation tax at 35%	29.4
Profit after tax ('nil' earnings)	54.6

'Nil' earnings represent what could be retained in the business if the company paid a 'nil' dividend. But if the company wishes to distribute all of the profits as dividends, the £54.6 million can be distributed as a 'net' dividend, assuming there are no tax complications. The company must pay *advance corporation tax* (ACT) of 25 per cent of the gross dividend, which is equivalent to $\frac{25}{75}$ths of the net dividend. If there are no tax complications, the ACT can be offset against the company's full corporation tax charge, leaving a residual tax known as *mainstream tax*. The investor receives a tax credit for the ACT which the company pays, and so receives grossed-up dividends equal to the net dividends plus the ACT. This produces the following results:

	£m
Maximum 'net' dividend	54.6
ACT = $\frac{25}{75}\times54.6$	18.2
Mainstream CT = 29.4−18.2	11.2

Thus if AZ Plc decided to distribute all of its profits, the figure would be as follows:

	£m	
Profit	84.0	
Mainstream CT	11.2	
Available to pay gross dividend ('full' earnings)	72.8	(86.7% of profits)
ACT	18.2	
'Net' dividend	54.6	

Let us assume there are 500 million ordinary shares in AZ Plc. Full earnings per share are therefore

$$\frac{£72.8 \text{ million}}{500 \text{ million}} = 14.6\text{p}$$

The earnings yield is therefore

$$\frac{14.6\text{p}}{80\text{p}}\times100\% = 18.25\%$$

8.4 Dividend cover and payout ratio

The *dividend cover* represents the number of times a dividend is covered by earnings. The higher the cover, the greater the security of the dividend. A low cover may indicate that a level of dividend cannot be sustained. A figure below 1 means that dividends exceed earnings, and are therefore being paid out of reserves. That situation cannot persist for long. In the case of AZ Plc, dividend cover is

$$\text{dividend cover} = \frac{\text{earnings yield}}{\text{dividend yield}}$$

$$= \frac{18.25\%}{5.83\%}$$

$$= 3.1 \text{ times}$$

The *Financial Times* does not provide the earnings yield for individual shares in its share information pages, but the earnings yield can be readily determined:

$$\text{earnings yield} = \text{dividend yield} \times \text{dividend cover}$$

The *Financial Times* does provide earnings yields for the various share indices. On Monday 13 November 1989, the 500 Share Index had a dividend yield of 4.33 per cent and an earnings yield of 10.24 per cent. No figures for dividend cover are provided for the indices, but these can easily be derived:

$$\text{dividend cover for 500 Index} = \frac{10.24\%}{4.33\%} = 2.36$$

The reciprocal of the dividend cover is the *payout ratio*:

$$\text{payout ratio} = \frac{\text{dividend yield}}{\text{earnings yield}}$$

For the 500 Share Index – a reasonable measure of a cross-section of British industry and commerce – the payout ratio in November 1989 was

$$\frac{4.33\%}{10.24\%} = 0.42$$

8.5 The price/earnings ratio

In the *Financial Times*, and in most other investment publications, the price/earnings (P/E) ratio is used in preference to the earnings yield. Essentially, they are simply two different ways of measuring the same thing.

$$\text{P/E ratio} = \frac{\text{market price of share}}{\text{'net' (or 'nil') earnings per share}}$$

If we ignore the different interpretations of earnings per share, we can see that the P/E ratio is simply the reciprocal of the earnings yield, expressed as a ratio instead of a percentage.

Complications arise because of taxation. For P/E ratio purposes, 'net' or 'nil' earnings are used. These represent earnings not grossed-up for basic-rate tax. If we use the earnings calculated earlier for AZ Plc,

$$\text{'nil' earnings per share} = \frac{\pounds 54.6 \text{ million}}{500 \text{ million}} = 10.92\text{p}$$

$$\text{P/E ratio} = \frac{80\text{p}}{10.92\text{p}} = 7.3$$

The *Financial Times* uses 'net' earnings per share to calculate P/E ratios. 'Net' earnings are defined as '*actual* net dividends plus retentions'. Thus net earnings are based on actual distribution policy, whereas 'nil' and 'full' earnings are based on hypothetical distribution policies. Provided that advance corporation tax can be fully offset against the full corporation tax charge, 'nil' and 'net' earnings are the same figure. For AZ Plc, for example, an actual distribution policy of 0 per cent would provide net dividends of zero and retentions of £54.6 million, equal to 10.92p earnings per share. An actual distribution policy of 100 per cent would produce net dividends of £54.6 million and retentions of zero, again equal to 10.92p earnings per share. Any intermediate dividend policy would also produce 'net' earnings per share of 10.92p.

A problem arises, however, when there is 'unrelieved' ACT. ACT can be offset against the full corporation tax charge to the extent of $\frac{25}{35}$ths, if the rate of ACT is 25 per cent and the full corporation tax rate is 35 per cent. Thus the minimum mainstream tax rate is 10 per cent of taxable profits. However, if the UK corporation tax charge is low, the ACT on dividends paid may exceed $\frac{25}{35}$ths and the excess is said to be 'unrelieved'. This represents an additional tax burden. This might occur, for instance, if a company had high overseas earnings. A double-taxation agreement would prevent the profits from being subject to two separate levies of corporation tax, but the ACT could not be offset against the overseas corporation tax.

'Nil' earnings ignore 'unrelieved' ACT, on the grounds that if a company paid no dividends it would have no unrelieved ACT. 'Net' earnings, on the other hand, treat unrelieved ACT as an additional tax charge to be deducted before arriving at earnings. Consequently 'net' earnings = 'nil' earnings less any unrelieved ACT. Thus 'net' earnings are less than, or equal to, nil earnings. In the extreme case, where all corporation tax was incurred overseas and none of the ACT was relievable, 'net' earnings would be between 75 per cent and 100 per cent of 'nil' earnings. Seventy-five per cent would be the case if the company determined to pay out 100 per cent of profits, despite the unrelieved ACT position. In this case, 25 per cent of the after-tax profits would be paid as unrelieved ACT. However, if the company had a 100 per cent retentions policy, there would be no unrelieved ACT and 'net' would be equivalent to 'nil' earnings. Thus, when a company has a potential unrelieved ACT position, its 'net' earnings figure depends upon its actual distribution policy.

Note that, if a company has 'unrelieved' ACT, the 'full' earnings figure will also be affected, and will no longer be simply the grossed-up 'nil' earnings per share. In these circumstances, 'full' earnings are more correctly defined as the sum of 'nil' earnings plus the maximum amount of recoverable ACT.

The *Financial Times* uses 'net' earnings to calculate P/E ratios, but puts the P/E ratio into parentheses – i.e. ( ) – if the ratio would differ by 10 per cent or more when calculated on a 'nil' basis.

Over a recent 25 years the P/E ratio for the market as a whole has ranged from a high of over 22 in 1968 to a low of 3.7 in December 1974. The long-term average has been around 12 (see fig. 8.3).

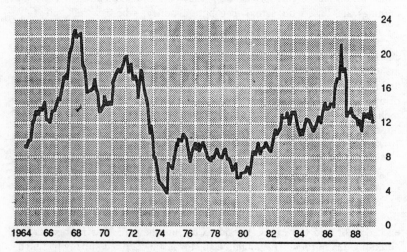

Source: *Financial Times*–Actuaries

Fig. 8.3   FT–*Actuaries 500 Share Index – P/E ratio, 1964–89*

P/E ratios can be used for comparing one share with another. A cursory glance at the financial press reveals an enormous range in P/E ratios, as with dividend yields, and frequently the most sought-after shares have been those with the highest P/E ratios. Figure 8.4 will help to explain this seeming paradox. This diagram illustrates the future earnings and dividend profiles of four companies: W, X, Y, and Z. The earnings and dividends per share of the four companies are expected to grow perpetually at rates of 18, 12, 10, and 0 per cent respectively. Purchase of a share entitles the investor to a future stream of dividends from that share.

The shareholder's total return is composed of two parts: an initial dividend yield, based on the next expected dividend, and a growth factor, representing the expectation of higher future dividends to the long-term investor, and of capital gain (if share prices rise with dividends and earnings) to the investor who decides to sell. On this basis, investors will be prepared to bid up the price of 'growth stocks', causing the dividend yields to fall to relatively low levels.

Referring back to fig. 8.4, if all investors were aware of the expected growth rates and all investors required a total return of 20 per cent, we could

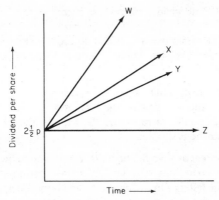

Fig. 8.4   Four companies with different growth rates (all taxes are ignored)

predict the dividend yields of the four shares.

Annual growth rate (%)+Dividend yield (%) = Total return (%)

W	18	2	20
X	12	8	20
Y	10	10	20
Z	0	20	20

By assuming no taxes of any form, we remove the problem of defining dividends and earnings. If each company pays out half of earnings as dividends (all dividends are 2½p), earnings will be twice dividends, and the earnings yield will be twice the dividend yield. We can then derive the P/E ratio and the share price (share price = P/E ratio×earnings per share of 5p):

	Earnings yield (%)	P/E ratio	Share price
W	4	25	£1.25
X	16	6¼	31p
Y	20	5	25p
Z	40	2½	12½p

Thus the P/E ratios range from 2.5 to 25, dividend yields from 2 to 20, and earnings yields from 4 to 40, even though each share offers a return of 20 per cent! Both dividend and earnings yields dramatically understate the shareholder's return with 'super-growth' shares. The dividend yield of Z accurately measures the shareholders' return only because dividends are static. The earnings yield of Y likewise is a good indicator only because the retained earnings are reinvested in the company at the shareholder's rate of return, 20 per cent (that is, one-half of earnings are reinvested at 20 per cent so that total earnings grow at 10 per cent).

This model is highly simplified, but the principles are sound. A glance in the *Financial Times* will show that the sectors with the best growth prospects, such as property, stores, leisure, and electronics, have relatively high P/E ratios and low dividend yields; the reverse is true of textiles, tobacco, and metals.

Thus the main determinants of a P/E ratio are the expected growth rate, the payout ratio, and the shareholders' required rate of return. All other things being equal,

- a higher rate of growth will increase the P/E ratio;
- a higher payout ratio will increase the P/E ratio;
- but an increase in interest rates and the shareholders' required rate of return will lower the P/E ratio.

For the stock market as a whole, high P/E ratios tend to be associated with the 'bull' market conditions of high anticipated earnings and dividends growth, and low or falling rates of interest. The opposite applies in a 'bear' market.

8.6 Reverse yield gap

After the Second World War, insurance companies and pension funds principally invested in gilt-edged securities. Inflation was low, and so were interest rates. Typical interest yields for Treasury bills were ½ per cent and for Consols 2 or 3 per cent, while equities had dividend yields of 4–5 per cent and earnings yields of 12–13 per cent. There seemed little risk of capital loss if one invested in gilts, and in fact prospects of capital appreciation if interest rates were to fall in the recession expected by many, as after the First World War. Equities, on the other hand, were risky: memories were fresh of the liquidations and dividend cuts experienced in the 1930s.

The 'cheap money' policy was abandoned by the Conservative administration of 1951, when Bank Rate was increased to 2½ per cent, having been held at 2 per cent for no less than twelve years. But the change had been apparent before then. War Loan reached its post-war peak of 108 in October 1946. From then on it fell precipitately, to 50 by mid-1961, and to less than half of that in the 1970s.

During the mid-1950s many insurance companies and pension funds diversified into equities, and to a lesser extent into property: the 'cult of the equity' was born. The main reason for this switch was a recognition that inflation and higher interest rates were likely to be persistent features of a full-employment policy. Given the 'demand-pull' type of inflation prevalent in the 1950s, dividend income could be expected to rise with money incomes, and this was particularly attractive to pension funds and insurance companies offering with-profits policies. Equities offered higher yields than gilts, together with a prospect of capital appreciation, whereas gilts had begun to fall in value as interest rates rose. In addition, a diversified portfolio of equities came to be seen as less risky than previously imagined: there seemed little likelihood of a repeat of the slump of the 1930s.

A reorientation of institutional investment policy accordingly took place, mainly by directing the new funds into equities, but also partly by selling substantial amounts of gilts for reinvestment in equities.

By October 1959 the persistent rise in share prices had driven the average dividend yield calculated for major representative companies below the yield on 2½% Consols for the first time since records had been kept. This was the beginning of the so-called *'reverse yield gap'*.

In a competitive market-place, risk must be compensated for by extra return, as outlined in section 8.1. But it should be remembered that the total return on an equity is the sum of the dividend yield plus the expected growth rate in dividends. For the shorter-term investor this equates to income plus capital gain. Since the late 1950s there has existed, a 'reverse yield gap', which is the excess guaranteed return on gilts as compared with equities. Nowadays this is usually measured by the gross redemption yield on a 25-year high-coupon gilt index less the *FT*–Actuaries All-Share Index dividend yield (see fig. 8.5).

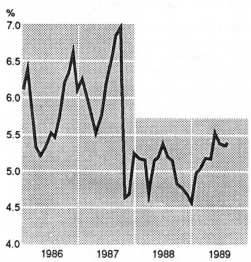

Source: *Financial Times*

Fig. 8.5   Reverse yield gap, 1986–9

The reverse yield gap tends to widen and narrow as inflationary expectations increase and decrease respectively. At any one time it is a measure of the minimum growth in equities' dividends and market values necessary in order to compensate for their shortfall in immediate returns. The wider the reverse yield gap, the greater the attraction of gilts, all other things being equal.

8.7 Questions

1. (a) 'Full' or 'maximum' earnings is the basis for calculating the:

   A earnings yield and dividend cover.
   B price/earnings ratio and dividend cover.
   C earnings yield and price/earnings ratio.
   D price/earnings ratio, dividend cover and earnings yield.

   (b) A company announces that its earnings per share are 'up 27 per cent' and its dividend 'up 20 per cent'. It follows that:

   A return on sales and on capital is improved.
   B dividend cover is improved.
   C the P/E ratio will be higher.
   D the dividend yield will be lower.

   (c) A price/earnings ratio in the *Financial Times* is:

   A the share price divided by the earnings per share.
   B the 'net' earnings per share multiplied by the cover.
   C the share price divided by the dividend per share.
   D the reciprocal of the gross dividend yield.

   (d) The dividend cover is:

   A the earnings yield divided by the gross dividend yield.
   B the share price divided by the net dividend.
   C the reciprocal of the P/E ratio.
   D $\frac{2}{5}$ths of the net dividend.

2. (a) What are the main factors determining differences in dividend yields between shares?

   (SIE 7/89)

   (b) What are the main factors determining differences in price/earnings ratios?

   (SIE 7/88)

3. Raymond Williams has dabbled in stocks and shares for a year or so, with some success, but he has never bothered much, he says, with the 'theoretical side'. He asks you to explain to him the London Share Service pages of the *Financial Times* and points to the entry in Saturday's edition for Courts (Furnishers) Plc.

1988 High/Low		Stock	Price	+ or −	Dividend Net (p)	Cover	Yield Gross	P/E
298	158	Courts 'A' ß	181	+1	4.9	2.1	3.6	17.3

   (a) In the course of the discussion that follows, a number of points arise. Give your answers to the following questions:

   (i) What is the nominal value of Courts' shares?
   (ii) What is the significance of the letter 'A' in the 'Stock' column?

(b) Using the figures given above,

   (i) explain how the *FT* has calculated the gross dividend yield.

  (ii) calculate the gross earnings yield on the shares.

(c) Explain the purpose of the P/E ratio and, in general terms, how the *Financial Times* calculates the P/E ratio.

(d) How does the information differ on a Monday in the *Financial Times*?

(CIB 10/88)

4. The issued capital of ZA Ltd consists of 500 million ordinary shares of 25p each, fully paid. In the last financial year pre-tax profits, all earned in the United Kingdom, were £90 million. Corporation tax was at the rate of 35 per cent, basic-rate tax 25 per cent, and advance corporation tax $\frac{25}{75}$ths. A dividend of 25 per cent net was paid on the ordinary shares. The current share price is 90p. Calculate:

(a) dividend yield;

(b) earnings yield (full basis);

(c) price/earnings ratio (nil basis);

(d) dividend cover.

Show how you arrived at your answers.

9 Share and debt analysis

9.1 Fundamental analysis

The objects of investment analysis are twofold:

(a) to determine the characteristics of an investment – its degree of risk, its yield, its tax position – and its suitability in the portfolios of different types of investor;
(b) to suggest whether the security is cheap or dear relative to other investments, taking into account differences in risk.

With regard to equity investments, the second purpose is usually over-emphasized, and the analyst is seen merely as a purveyor of 'buy' or 'sell' recommendations. In this role, most analysts belong to the mainstream of *fundamentalists*, although there is also a minority group (or 'cult') called the *technicians*.

The fundamentalists tend to look forward. They are concerned with future earnings and dividends, and the risk attached to them. The technicians tend to be backward-looking, as their sole preoccupation is with the action of the market itself, particularly price and volume changes; they believe that past price data hold the key to the future.

9.2 Earnings and dividends

9.2.1 Discounted future dividends

Fundamentalists are strong believers in the *intrinsic* (or 'true') value of a share. This is the present value of the future dividend stream expected from the share, which can be expressed in the following formula:

$$V_0 = \frac{D_1}{(1+r)} + \frac{D_2}{(1+r)^2} + \frac{D_3}{(1+r)^3} + \frac{D_4}{(1+r)^4} + \ldots + \frac{D_n}{(1+r)^n}$$

where V_0 = intrinsic value of the share today, time 0

$D_1, D_2, \ldots, D_n$ = dividends at times $1, 2, \ldots, n$

r = discount rate, the required rate of return on the share

The obvious disadvantage of this approach is its requirement to forecast individual dividends (D_1, D_2, etc.) to time n; as n is in theory infinite, this is obviously impossible. In addition, the discount rate, r, may also change over time. To make this method manageable, one is forced to compromise by assuming that dividends either grow at some constant rate for ever or grow at different rates for specified future time-periods.

To take the simpler case, let us assume that the next expected dividend, D_1, is 10p per share, that dividends are expected to grow at a rate g of 12 per cent a year for ever, and that the required rate of return, r, is 16 per cent. Given these assumptions, the formula becomes

$$V_0 = \frac{D_1}{r-g}$$

$$= \frac{10p}{0.16-0.12}$$

$$= \frac{10p}{0.04}$$

$$= £2.50$$

If the actual share price was, say, £3, the analyst would recommend a 'sell'; if £2 a 'buy'.

Incorporating different growth rates (to correspond, for example, to the life cycle of the product and the company) makes the arithmetic more complicated, but the principle is the same. Dividends are usually forecast, apart from perhaps the immediate term, by predicting earnings and multiplying these by a target *payout ratio* (the proportion of earnings paid out as dividends).

In predicting future earnings, one should beware of simply extrapolating past earnings figures. There is a theory – that of 'higgledy-piggledy growth' – which says that, with a few notable exceptions, there is little correlation between past and future earnings growth. Companies which have done badly in the past may be reorganized or taken over; those that have done well may suffer from a slowdown in market growth or from the inroads made by new competitors.

Analysts place great emphasis on the *quality* of earnings, by which they mean their stability and security. For each major product area, the analyst must pay attention to the nature and prospects of demand for the products or services, the structure and state of competition in the industry, cost conditions and profitability, and the importance of research and development.

One problem is that it may be a long time before the share price reaches its 'true' value, appearing almost permanently under- or overvalued. The 'intrinsic' value may be swamped in the short or medium term by speculative factors, and the fundamentals themselves may have changed before these have been overcome. This approach requires a strong nerve, for frequently the long-term investor is going against the trend, selling when share prices are high and rising, while buying when they are low and falling. In this respect, as Keynes remarked, he may appear 'eccentric' and 'unconventional', and need the support of a long-term contract!

9.2.2 Market yield

Rather than using the formal dividend valuation model outlined in section 9.2.1, many analysts and fund managers prefer to estimate an appropriate *dividend yield* or *price/earnings ratio* for the share. These can then be applied to the 'normalized' dividend and earnings per share respectively.

The three main factors affecting the 'true' prospective P/E ratio are growth expectations, the payout ratio, and the discount rate (incorporating the risk-free rate of interest and a risk premium).

Most analysts who use this approach do so fairly loosely. Generally, they take the average P/E ratio for the sector as a whole and, in an *ad hoc* fashion, add on the odd percentage point or two for above-average growth or payout, and knock off points for excessive risk in the form of greater instability of sales or financial gearing.

Another very straightforward method of using P/E ratios is to establish a 'norm' based on average past levels, either for the share or for the stock market. In a similar way, some analysts calculate P/E ratio relativities (traditional P/E ratio differentials between the share and others in the industry, sector, or stock market as a whole). Significant deviation from this premium or discount would warrant investigation of the fundamentals of the company. The investor should beware, however, of mechanical trading systems, signalling when to buy and sell. P/E ratio differentials cannot remain inviolable, independent of economic changes in demand and supply in the industry and the company.

9.2.3 Leading indicators

A *leading indicator* is an economic variable which changes in advance of ('leads') another economic variable. It may be a causal relationship – changes in one leading to changes in the other – or both may be reacting to a third factor, but with different reaction times.

A number of leading indicators for the economy are regularly published in *Economic Trends*. The money supply and bank advances have featured in several studies, because of both their direct impact on the financial markets and the widespread belief that they affect the economy generally after a time-lag of six to eighteen months. At one time, increases in the money supply were thought to be good for gilts and equities in the short run, because of the expected consequential fall in interest rates. Nowadays, broker/dealers are more concerned about the inflationary effect of such increases and the Government's likely response in the form of tighter credit and higher interest rates.

There is considerable dispute as to whether the money supply is a leading or coincident indicator. In the United Kingdom, most of the evidence supports the latter view. But even if a signficant leading indicator were found, it would probably not remain one for long. If such an indicator became widely recognized among broker/dealers, the market would react to, if not anticipate, changes in its value, thus reducing or eliminating the lead time altogether.

9.2.4 Profit forecasts

Rather than using a formal model to predict the exact level of a share price, a popular method among analysts is simply to compare their personal dividend and earnings estimates for a particular company with those being made by other analysts. The presumption is that the share price is a reflection of consensus opinion. If one analyst's estimates are on the high side compared with market opinion, that analyst will consider the share an attractive investment. He or she expects the announcement of the results to provide a pleasant surprise for the market, and hopes that this will be quickly reflected in the share price itself.

At the aggregate level, movements in corporate profits are correlated closely with the stock market indices – but, unfortunately for analysts, the market appears to lead the disclosure of company profits. Profits are themselves dependent on the level of economic activity. So here again the analyst and fund manager can compare their own forecasts of the business cycle with those of other investors, and take a view on the market. This area has been studied in detail by leading brokers such as UBS Phillips & Drew and Hoare Govett, who regularly report to the financial press after they have briefed their own clients. In addition, a mass of information is published regularly by such authoritative bodies as the National Institute for Economic and Social Research (NIESR), the London Business School, the Bank of England, the Henley Centre for Forecasting, and others.

Any general view of the market can be converted into a view on individual shares by the use of 'beta coefficients'. If one is *bullish* about the market as a whole, one should buy shares with high betas (those which are highly responsive to movements in the market). If one if *bearish*, one should sell, again especially those shares with high betas. Betas are discussed in section 9.2.5.

9.2.5 Risk

An investor in ordinary shares should never forget that he or she is in a risk situation. The degree of risk attached to an individual share depends on the amounts of business and financial risk.

Business risk is largely determined by the type of economic activity in which the company is involved: it is the risk of profit fluctuation due to changes in demand (arising from changes in tastes, new products, competitors' strengths, overall economic activity, and so on) or in supply (due to factors such as new methods of production or varying costs of labour or raw materials). To a certain extent, companies can reduce business risk by means of diversification.

Financial risk is measured by the fluctuations in shareholders' returns and the probability of liquidation, brought about by the use of borrowed funds and especially short-term borrowings. The ratio of borrowed funds to overall capital is called the *gearing ratio*, and the ratio of short-term ('current') assets to liabilities is called the *current ratio*. The more highly geared and the more illiquid the company, the greater the financial risk. It is a 'voluntary' risk, however, in the sense that it could be avoided by having a 'clean' balance sheet – no borrowed funds – but many companies believe that the risk is justified by the enhanced return to the shareholders. As long as the company can earn a higher return on its total assets than the cost of borrowed funds, the shareholders will benefit from the 'surplus' on the debt-financed assets.

To take a simple example, imagine three companies – A, B, and C – identical in every respect except their financial structures, which are as follows:

Company	Total debt Coupon	Amount (£m)	Net worth (£m)	Total capital (£m)
A	—	—	100	100
B	12%	50	50	100
C	12%	75	25	100

Company A is financed entirely by shareholders' funds (net worth), while company C has a book-value capital gearing ratio of 75 per cent. Accordingly A's shareholders are relatively better off in bad times, C's in good times. This is illustrated in Table 9.1, where it is assumed that under very difficult economic conditions a rate of return of only 4 per cent on assets can be expected, that a normal rate of return is 16 per cent, and that under exceptionally favourable circumstances the rate of return can reach 28 per cent. Table 9.1 shows that the volatility of returns for the highly geared company C is much greater than that for B, which in turn is greater than that for A. The *indifference level* is the overall rate of return, equal to the cost of debt capital, where the returns to the shareholder are the same in each company.

The *volatility* of a share is nowadays frequently expressed in terms of its *beta coefficient*. The rate of return on a share (dividend income and capital change expressed as a percentage of the opening market value) for successive periods is plotted on one axis of a graph; the return on a share index – representing the average performance of a large number of shares – is plotted on the other axis (see fig. 9.1). The slope of the line, defined as the beta coefficient, measures the volatility, or riskiness, of the share relative to the market as a whole. Figure 9.1 makes it clear that company A's share price is

Table 9.1 Returns to shareholders in different types of company

	Economic conditions			
	Very poor	Indifference level	Normal	Very good
Rate of return on assets before interest and taxes	4%	12%	16%	28%
Company A				
Earnings before interest and taxes	£4m	£12m	£16m	£28m
Less interest	0	0	0	0
Taxable income	£4m	£12m	£16m	£28m
Corporation tax (say, 50 per cent)	£2m	£6m	£8m	£14m
Attributable to shareholders	£2m	£6m	£8m	£14m
Net return to shareholders	2%	6%	8%	14%
Company B				
Earnings before interest and taxes	£4m	£12m	£16m	£28m
Less interest	£6m	£6m	£6m	£6m
Taxable income	−£2m	£6m	£10m	£22m
Corporation tax (say, 50 per cent)	0	£3m	£5m	£11m
Attributable to shareholders	−£2m	£3m	£5m	£11m
Net return to shareholders	−4%	6%	10%	22%
Company C				
Earnings before interest and taxes	£4m	£12m	£16m	£28m
Less interest	£9m	£9m	£9m	£9m
Taxable income	−£5m	£3m	£7m	£19m
Corporation tax (say, 50 per cent)	0	£1½m	£3½m	£9½m
Attributable to shareholders	−£5m	£1½m	£3½m	£9½m
Net return to shareholders	−20%	6%	14%	38%

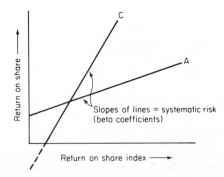

Fig. 9.1   Measuring the beta coefficients of shares

much less volatile than that of company C. A is said to be a *defensive* share
and C an *aggressive* one. The volatility depends on both business and
financial risk, but also on the extent to which the fortunes of the company are
correlated with those of other firms. It is important not only how much the
share price moves up and down but also to what extent it does so together
with, or independently of, the stock market as a whole. The greater the
degree of independence the better so far as risk minimization is concerned,
because risk can then be reduced by holding a combination of shares.
Diversification enables the investor to eliminate 'independent' risk so that
only 'systematic' risk remains, and it is this risk that is measured by the beta
coefficient. In our example, the greater financial gearing of company C
means that its earnings are more volatile than those of companies A and B,
and so also its dividends and share price are likely to be.

In a competitive market, risk must be compensated for by extra return.
High-risk fixed-interest stocks should yield more than low-risk ones, equities
more than stocks and high-risk equities more than low-risk ones. Considerable evidence exists to confirm that the greater the volatility of a share, on
average the higher the return (see fig. 9.2).

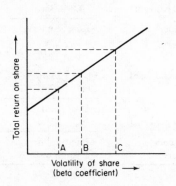

Fig. 9.2   The relationship between risk and return

According to the capital-asset pricing model (CAPM), the equation for the
slope of the line in fig. 9.2 is given by

$$E(r) = R_f + (R_m - R_f)\beta$$

where $E(r)$ = expected total return on a share

R_f = risk-free rate of interest, usually measured by the Treasury
bill rate

R_m = return on the stock market, usually measured by the overall
return on the *FT*–Actuaries All-Share Index

and β = beta coefficient of the share

For example, if $R_f = 10$ per cent, $R_m = 15$ per cent, and $\beta = 1.2$, then the CAPM predicts that the total return on the share should be

$$10\% + (15\% - 10\%)1.2 = 16\%$$

9.3 Asset values

The holders of the equity of a company are entitled to the earnings and assets of that company after prior claims have been discharged. Apart from earnings, therefore, the other tangible factor in assessment of ordinary shares is the value of the assets attributable to the equity. This information is given in the balance sheet of the company and notes to the accounts, but assets should not be assumed to be worth the figures stated there. Briefly, the balance-sheet value of assets attributable to the equity is the nominal value of the equity plus the total reserves. The real value of the assets may be more or less than the balance-sheet figure and be different in different circumstances. For instance, the value of a factory might be very much higher as a going concern than as an empty building on the liquidation of the company. The balance-sheet value of the factory – cost less accumulated depreciation – reflects neither circumstance. Trade investments in the balance sheet may be worth more or less than the figure shown. This sort of situation can arise with many balance-sheet items. In recent years, balance-sheet values of companies have become increasingly arbitrary. Property is revalued, while other assets are usually left at historic cost. Some companies have even included the value of their brand names in the balance sheet. For service-industry companies in particular, such as advertising agencies, there is little relationship between the value of tangible assets and the value placed on the companies' earning power.

In general, asset values are less important than earnings in determining share prices. A company's earnings are available for distribution or for investment in expansion. The value of the assets employed can be realized only on liquidation, although their value may be significant in the event of a take-over bid being made for the company. If earnings on assets employed fall to low levels, the asset value may underpin the market price in the anticipation of another company becoming interested in those assets for use in an amalgamated concern. In other words, assets producing inadequate earnings are meat and drink to the take-over specialist.

9.4 Management

The third important factor in the assessment of the equity of a company is an intangible one: the quality of the management. This will not be found in the company's balance sheet, and analysis of the published results will show it only after a number of years. With the benefit of hindsight it is possible to distinguish those companies where management has been exceptional. These are companies where profits have increased regularly over a long period at a rate greater than that achieved by their competitors.

The quality of a company's management is the most difficult factor to assess and evaluate. It nevertheless has a marked influence on the market price of the equity capital. Whereas asset value and past earnings are a guide to the true value of an equity share, it is the ability of management to recognize changing circumstances, and to amend policy to take account of those changes, which is the principal growth factor in the success of the best companies. Market price reflects the views of investors as to the future potential of a company. Good management is normally taken fully into account in the market price of a share, but this price may adjust dramatically if major management changes are intimated. News of boardroom dissent or the appointment or departure of an influential personality may all have a considerable impact on the share price.

9.5 Interpretation of the annual report and accounts

To the average investor, the annual report and accounts are the major, if not the only, source of primary information for fundamental analysis on a public company. They contain a *profit and loss account*, a *balance sheet*, a *directors' report*, a *statement of accounting policies*, a *source and application of funds statement*, *notes to the accounts*, and the *auditors' report*. In addition, most company chairmen issue an annual statement to shareholders, discussing the company's operations during the year, together with some comments about future prospects and often with a few general economic and political remarks thrown in for good measure. In addition to the annual report and accounts, the Stock Exchange requires that listed companies publish half-yearly financial statements. These interim statements are usually unaudited.

The content of the annual report and accounts is governed by the Companies Act 1985 as amended by the Companies Act 1989, the accounting bodies, and the Stock Exchange. The accounting bodies have attempted to standardize accounting practice by issuing *statements of standard accounting practice* (SSAP). Listed companies in particular are required to follow such standards, violating them only in very exceptional circumstances. They risk the suspension of their quotation if they do not concur, although the Stock Exchange has been reluctant to enforce such a penalty. However, under the Companies Act 1989, powers are given to the Secretary of State for Trade and Industry to call upon a company to rectify its financial statements where they have not been prepared in accordance with accounting standards.

The report and accounts may provide some basis for understanding the business activities and the past financial performance of a company. For listed companies, they must indicate the breakdown of turnover, profitability, and assets for each business and geographical segment. Experienced analysts, however, build up a picture of a company from a variety of sources, such as trade journals and information received from customers, suppliers, and competitors. The 'accounts' are only a starting point. Much of the information contained in the latest set will have been anticipated from other

'Hold everything . . . the chairman's daughter has done a drawing for the cover
of the annual report.'

sources, the 'accounts' thus performing a largely confirmatory role.

Some investors naïvely believe that studying the 'accounts' is all one has to do in order to determine whether or not the shares are 'a good buy'. In fact, the analysis of the report and accounts must be supplemented by a considerable knowledge of the industry, the sector, and even the economy as a whole. Different companies have different accounting practices, despite the attempts at standardization. This is not too important if the latest results are seen as part of a series beginning five or ten years before and stretching for the same period into the future. The analyst looks at how the lastest results fit into that pattern, and how far they may alter it. The greatest influence on the share price rating in the long term is any evidence of a change in the growth rate. But the hardest part of the job is deciding how far any information revealed by the 'accounts' is already discounted in the share price. The purpose, after all, of fundamental analysis is to discover which shares are 'cheap' or 'dear', not which companies are 'good' or 'bad'.

9.5.1 Income statement

Bankers traditionally pay most attention to the balance sheet, because of their interest in security, but equity investors are likely to be far more interested in the *profit and loss account*, an example of which is shown in Table 9.2. This shows the breakdown of sales and profits for a hypothetical company, CW Plc. It is a *consolidated* profit and loss account, since it relates to a group of companies in the United Kingdom – the parent company and its subsidiary and associated companies. More detailed information would be provided in the notes to the accounts.

Table 9.2 Consolidated profit and loss account for CW Plc for the year ended 31 March 19. .

		£m
(a)	Turnover	1625
(b)	Net operating expenses	(1507)
(c)	Operating profit	118
(d)	Share of profits of associated companies	17
(e)	Net interest payable	(35)
(f)	Profit on ordinary activities before taxation	100
(g)	Tax on profits on ordinary activities	(35)
	Profit on ordinary activities after taxation	65
(h)	Minority interests	—
(i)	Profit for the financial year on ordinary activities attributable to shareholders	65
(j)	Extraordinary items	—
	Profit for the financial year	65
(k)	Dividends	35
(l)	Retained profit for the year	30
(m)	Earnings per ordinary share (pence)	30.5

The following relate to items in Table 9.2:

(a) The turnover figure represents external sales only. Sales within the group are ignored.
(b) The Companies Act 1985 requires the disclosure of cost of sales in order to determine operating profit. These include raw materials and consumables, changes in stock and work-in-progress, staff costs (including directors' remuneration), depreciation of fixed assets, plus other external charges such as auditors' fees and hire charges, and exceptional items. These will be shown in a note to the accounts. Exceptional items are usually gains or losses arising from normal business activity but of a large and separately identifiable nature – for example, banks' write-offs of loans to the Third World.
(c) Operating profit is an important measure of company performance. It reflects the earning power of the overall assets of the business, no matter how they are financed, and is unaffected by taxation.
(d) An associated company is one in which the investing company or group is involved in financial and operating policy decisions but does not have sufficient dominance for it to be classified as a subsidiary, according to the Companies Act 1989. This Act defined dominant influence as the holding of a majority of the voting rights, or the right to direct the

operating and financial policies of the subsidiary. In cases which do not satisfy these criteria, a share of the associate's profit or loss, in proportion to the equity interest, is taken into the consolidated profit and loss account.

(e) Other income, not derived from the trading of the company, must be shown separately, and will be set off against any interest payable. In the case of CW Plc, investment income received is £5 million, and interest payable is £40 million.

(f) Profit on ordinary activities before taxation represents the total taxable income from activities, excluding extraordinary items (discussed below).

(g) Taxation is shown here at 35 per cent, but in practice the actual amount is unlikely to be a straight percentage of the profit figure at the prevailing corporation tax rate. A company's liability may in practice be affected by rates of tax paid on overseas income, and by various allowances.

(h) If a company has consolidated interests in subsidiary companies, but does not own 100 per cent of them, there will be a corresponding minority interest because the whole of the subsidiary's profit would have been included in operating profit. The minority interest represents the share of after-tax profits belonging to the outside shareholders in the subsidiary companies.

(i) This represents the after-tax profits belonging to CW Plc shareholders.

(j) Extraordinary items are usually important non-recurring items outside of normal trading activity, such as the gain or loss on the disposal of a business. There is sometimes disagreement as to whether an item should be shown as 'exceptional' or 'extraordinary'. Exceptional items are added or subtracted 'above the line' – that is, before determining the level of taxable profit. Extraordinary items, on the other hand, are added or deducted 'below the line' – the adjustment is made to after-tax profits. The reason for this distinction is to make the trend in operating profit more meaningful. Likewise, extraordinary items are not included in calculations of earnings per share (see below).

(k) Net dividends may consist of both preference and ordinary dividends net of advance corporation tax. In the case of CW Plc, a separate note to the accounts would show that these are £4 million and £31 million respectively.

(l) Retained profits for the year represent the difference between 'profit for the financial year' and dividends. They will be added to the existing reserves in the balance sheet.

(m) Earnings per ordinary share are determined by dividing 'profit for the financial year on ordinary activities attributable to shareholders', less preference dividends – known as 'equity earnings' – by the number of outstanding ordinary shares. In the case of CW Plc, this means dividing £65 million less £4 million by 200 million, producing earnings per share of 30.5p.

9.5.2 *The balance sheet and other items*

One of the requirements of the Companies Act is that a balance sheet be sent out to each shareholder and stockholder annually. Where the company has subsidiaries, a consolidated balance sheet must be submitted *in addition to* the balance sheet of the parent company. (The consolidated profit and loss account normally *displaces* the holding company's account.) As with all balance sheets, that of a company shows the position on the day on which it was drawn up. It therefore gives a picture that is already out of date, but the information contained can nevertheless be of interest to the shareholder and, still more so, to the creditor.

Accounts must contain the specific information required by the Companies Act to be disclosed, and must also show a 'true and fair view' of the state of the company's affairs at the balance-sheet date and of the profit or loss for the accounting period covered. A 'true and fair view' involves an appropriate classification and grouping of the items, and therefore the balance sheet needs to show in summary form the amounts of the share capital, reserves, and liabilities as on the balance-sheet date, and the amounts of the assets representing them, together with sufficient information to indicate the general nature of the items. A 'true and fair view' also implies the consistent application of generally accepted principles.

It is essential to understand that the phrase 'true and fair view' has the technical meaning outlined above, and is not synonymous with 'true worth'. Figures shown in the balance sheet for both fixed and current assets are not the amounts expected to be realized if the company were wound up ('liquidated'). They do not disclose the 'break-up' value of the company's assets, but are based on the assumption that the company will continue as a 'going concern'. Except for possible revaluation of land and buildings, fixed assets are generally shown in the accounts at historical cost less an allowance for depreciation. Current assets, including stocks of finished goods and work-in-progress, are also shown in the balance sheet at cost, unless their net realizable value is estimated to be lower than their cost.

The balance sheet in Table 9.3 is presented in the general format prescribed by the Companies Act 1985, amended by the Companies Act 1989. Again, fuller detail would be found in the notes to the accounts. *Total assets less current liabilities* represents the permanent capital tied up in the business, used to finance longer-term assets and also short-term assets not financed from short-term sources.

The following relate to items in Table 9.3:

(a) *Fixed assets* are resources which have a relatively long economic life and are acquired not for resale in the normal course of business, but rather for use in producing other goods and services. They can be subdivided into intangible and tangible assets, the latter including land and buildings, plant and machinery, and vehicles.

(b) *Goodwill* is the excess of the purchase price paid by a parent company for its investment in a subsidiary over the net book value of the

Table 9.3 Consolidated balance sheet for CW Plc at 31 March 19. .

		£m	£m
(a)	*Fixed assets*		
	Intangible assets		
(b)	Goodwill		100
	Tangible assets		
	Land and buildings		250
	Plant and machinery		250
(c)	Investments		50
			650
(d)	*Current assets*		
	Stock and work-in progress	400	
(e)	Debtors	250	
	Cash	75	
		725	
(f)	*less* Creditors due for payment within one year		
	Bank overdraft	75	
	Trade creditors	300	
	Current taxation	40	
	Proposed final dividend	25	
		440	
(g)	Net current assets		285
(h)	Total assets *less* current liabilities		935
(i)	*less* Creditors due after one year		225
	Net assets		710
	Capital and reserves		
	50m 8% cumulative preference shares issued fully paid		50
	200m ordinary £1 shares fully paid	200	
(j)	Share premium account	50	
	Other reserves	410	
	Ordinary shareholders' interest		660
	Minorities		—
			710

subsidiary's assets less its liabilities at the time of its acquisition. It is considered as an 'intangible' asset and must be written off over its economic life, not exceeding twenty years.

(c) *Investments* are usually trade investments, which represent holdings of shares (or other securities) in other companies; they are investments made for the purposes of the business and are therefore not readily realizable. Interests in customers, suppliers, or even competitors are included under this heading.

(d) *Current assets* generally include cash in hand and at the bank, together with assets expected to be converted into cash (such as debtors) or consumed in the business (such as stocks of raw materials) within twelve months from the balance-sheet date.

(e) *Long-term debtors* are included in this category, but identified separately in a note to the accounts, and must be deducted before calculating liquidity ratios.

(f) Strictly speaking, that part of the tax liability which is payable more than a year hence should be shown as a separate item. Bank overdrafts are included because in theory they are recallable on demand, but in practice they are frequently 'rolled over' from year to year.

(g) *Net current assets* represent 'working capital' – that part of current assets which must be financed from longer-term funds.

(h) *Total assets less current liabilities* represents those assets financed by the longer-term (permanent) funds of the business.

(i) In the case of CW Plc, these consist of

£50 million 10% mortgage debenture 2005
£100 million secured medium-term bank loan – variable rate 2000
£75 million 12% unsecured loan stock 2010

(j) *Share premium account* is the excess of the actual proceeds of share issues over their nominal ('par') value. It is treated in the accounts as a capital reserve which, in contrast to a revenue reserve, is not available for distribution as dividends. The note to the accounts will indicate which of the 'other reserves' are revenue reserves and which are capital reserves.

(k) If CW Plc had one or more partially owned subsidiaries, the outside shareholdings – the minority interests – would be shown as the final item in the balance sheet.

9.5.3 Sources and application of funds statement

All listed companies are now required to provide a consolidated sources and application of funds statement. These statements show the internal and external sources of funds, and the ways in which they have been invested. The statements are useful, taking several years together, for predicting external fund-raising operations, dictated by the inability of internal funds alone to sustain the company's planned investment programme.

One important internal 'source' of funds is *depreciation*, which is a deduction from profit but which does not represent an actual outflow of cash. Cash is expended only when an asset is bought; depreciation is part of the accrual system of matching revenue and expenditure period by period. Analysts frequently use retained earnings and depreciation allowances as a proxy for *cash flow*, and this figure can then be compared with future capital commitments, whether contracted yet or not. Unfortunately, the notes to the accounts normally give details only of fixed-capital expenditure intentions, so some forecast needs to be made of likely changes in net working capital.

Changes in tax liabilities will also affect the cash flow position.

9.5.4 Inflation accounting
Some companies produce inflation-adjusted accounts. Because of the use of replacement cost for both fixed and current assets, current-cost accounting tends to produce a lower reported profit than historic-cost accounting, but an increased balance-sheet value of the assets. Despite attempts in the 1970s and 1980s to introduce an agreed method for dealing with the effects of inflation, inflation accounting was never widely accepted by either the users or producers of accounts. By the early 1990s the majority of companies had reverted to only historic-cost accounts.

9.5.5 The directors' report
This gives certain factual information relating to the year under review which has to be disclosed by law. The most interesting points are the recommended final dividend, the directors and any change in their shareholdings, the current valuations of properties relative to their book value, details of any interests of over 3 per cent in the company, and any breakdown of the profit figures.

9.5.6 Report of the auditors
One of the first tasks of any user of accounts is to check to see that the auditors have not 'qualified' their approval in any way. Any proposed change of auditors should be noted in the directors' report.

9.6 Ratio analysis

Ratio analysis is an important tool in investment, enabling the analyst to highlight the salient figures in the accounts and to make comparisons with previous years (to establish trends) or with rival companies or some industrial average, although ratios rarely tell the user much when considered in isolation. They are usually grouped into four main categories: *liquidity*, *gearing*, *activity*, and *profitability*.

9.7 Liquidity ratios

Generally the investment analyst's first concern is liquidity: has the company sufficient cash to meet its immediate trading needs? Although, on the 'accruals' system of accounting, income and expenditure may appear stable, actual payments and receipts of cash are frequently more irregular and differ in their actual timing. The bank overdraft is ideally suited to accommodate fluctuations in financial flows, enabling the company to meet its bills as they fall due.

Most companies to some degree make use of short-term sources of finance, principally trade creditors and the banks. Normally, both of these are willing to continue such lending on a 'revolving' basis, providing the company is trading profitably. If there is any suspicion about the company's ability to meet its debts, however, supppliers might refuse to continue to trade with it except on a cash basis, and the bank might refuse to extend further overdraft facilities. It is therefore essential that a company retains the confidence of its trade creditors and bankers. One way of doing this is by demonstrating that it could repay their lending if necessary. The two most commonly used measures of liquidity are the *current ratio* and the *quick assets ratio*.

9.7.1 Current ratio

The *current ratio* or *working capital ratio* is computed by dividing current assets by current liabilities. It indicates the extent to which the claims of short-term creditors are covered by assets that are expected to be converted to cash during the next year. For CW Plc (see Table 9.3),

$$\frac{\text{current assets}}{\text{current liabilities}} = \frac{£725 \text{ million}}{£440 \text{ million}} = 1.65 : 1$$

9.7.2 Quick assets ratio

The disadvantage of the current ratio is that it treats all current assets as being equally liquid. The *quick assets ratio* (sometimes called the *liquid* or *'acid test' ratio*) excludes stock. The reasons for this omission are

(a) stock is at once the least liquid of the current assets and the current asset on which losses are most likely to occur in the event of a disposal;
(b) the company could not continue to trade effectively with stocks below a certain minimum level.

For CW Plc,

$$\text{quick assets ratio} = \frac{\text{current assets} - \text{stock}}{\text{current liabilities}}$$

$$= \frac{£725 \text{ million} - £400 \text{ million}}{£440 \text{ million}} = 0.74 : 1$$

The traditionally acceptable minimum values for current and quick assets ratios are 2 : 1 and 1 : 1 respectively. By present-day standards, however, these appear rather high.

9.8 Gearing ratios

Gearing (or leverage, as the Americans refer to it) shows the relationship between a company's creditors and its shareholders. There are two main types of gearing ratio: *capital* and *income*. Capital ratios show the proportion of funds supplied by the creditors as compared with those from the owners. The higher the proportion of borrowings, the higher the capital gearing. This ratio can be expressed in *book value* (balance-sheet) terms, or by using *market values* if the securities are quoted.

Income gearing shows the distribution of income among the holders of the different classes of capital. If a company has a high proportion of interest payments relative to shareholders' earnings, it again is said to be highly geared. There are no agreed definitions of gearing, however, and within each of the two main categories there are several different ratios. The main difficulty lies in deciding what types of prior-charge capital to include.

9.8.1 Capital gearing

(a) **Capital gearing ratio**   This is designed to give lenders some indication of the protection for their loans. If the company were to go into liquidation, would the assets be sufficient to repay the creditors in full, given that some items, such as plant and machinery, are unlikely to realize their book values? Goodwill is usually deducted, as it is an intangible asset. The ratio is defined as

$$\text{capital gearing ratio} = \frac{\text{borrowed funds}}{\text{total funds} - \text{intangibles}}$$

$$\text{or} \quad \text{capital gearing ratio} = \frac{\text{borrowed funds}}{\text{equity funds} - \text{intangibles}}$$

The difficulty lies in deciding what items to include in the numerator and denominator. One view is that capital gearing should measure simply the capital structure – that is, it should be restricted to the long-term financing of the company represented by long-term debt, preference shares, and net worth (ordinary shareholders' funds). In this way, 'capital structure' is distinguished from 'financial structure', which also includes all forms of short-term debt.

Most analysts include preference shares as part of borrowed funds because they are fixed-return securities, although, unlike loan capital interest, preference share dividends can be 'passed' with relative impunity. Bank borrowings are generally more important than preference shares. Often medium-term bank loans have replaced debentures and loan stocks, and there is no case for omitting them from 'borrowed funds'. Likewise, there is a very strong argument for including bank overdrafts, especially if in practice they are of a semi-permanent nature. Indeed, any contractual obligation, such as leasing, should be capitalized and included. The inclusion of short-term liabilities (such as taxation, trade creditors, and accruals) is more debatable, particularly if they fluctuate a great deal.

Difficulties arise not only from having to decide what items to include in the ratio, but also from how to value them. For example, should shares and loans be included at balance-sheet values or stock market values? Shareholders' funds in the balance sheet can be expressed in terms of either historic or current (inflation-adjusted) costs. There are arguments for and against each approach, but traditionally the ratio has been restricted to permanent sources of funds, shown at historic-cost balance-sheet valuations. For CW Plc,

$$\text{capital gearing ratio} = \frac{\text{£275 million}}{\text{£935 million}-\text{£100 million}} = 0.33$$

(Preference shares are included in the 'borrowed funds' in the numerator, but short-term bank borrowings have been excluded.)

(b) Capital cover and priority percentages   Debt-holders and other lenders may be more interested in the security of their particular loan than in the indebtedness of the company as a whole. It is possible to calculate capital cover for each type of loan, but this should be done on a cumulative basis. In this way it is never possible for a lower-ranking security to have a greater cover than a higher-ranking one. For CW Plc, we can list the prior-charge capital in descending order of priority and calculate capital cover for each:

	Amount	*Capital cover*
10% mortgage debenture	£50m	$\dfrac{\text{£835m}}{\text{£ 50m}} = 16.7 \text{ times}$
Medium-term bank loan	£100m	$\dfrac{\text{£835m}}{\text{£150m}} = 5.57$
12% unsecured loan stock	£75m	$\dfrac{\text{£835m}}{\text{£225m}} = 3.71$
8% cumulative preference shares	£50m	$\dfrac{\text{£835m}}{\text{£275m}} = 3.04$

Note that, for reasons of simplicity, current liabilities and their equivalent assets have been ignored in the calculation.

An alternative way of presenting the same information is in terms of *capital priority percentages*. These tables show what proportion of assets belong to different types of capital, again in descending order of priority. Thus:

	Percentage of assets	*Priority percentage*
10% mortgage debenture	$\dfrac{\text{£ 50m}}{\text{£835m}} \times 100 = 6$	0–6
Medium-term bank loan	$\dfrac{\text{£100m}}{\text{£835m}} \times 100 = 12$	6–18
12% unsecured loan stock	$\dfrac{\text{£ 75m}}{\text{£835m}} \times 100 = 9$	18–27

8% cumulative preference shares	$\dfrac{£\ 50m}{£835m} \times 100 = 6$	27–33
ordinary shares	$\dfrac{£560m}{£835m} \times 100 = 67$	33–100

9.8.2 Income gearing

While capital ratios are very much akin to 'shutting the stable door after the horse has bolted', in that they are concerned with the ability to repay loans in the event of a liquidation, income ratios have the merit of measuring directly the ability of a company to service the interest on borrowed funds. The two most popular types of income ratios are *interest cover* and *income priority percentages*.

(a) Interest cover   This is defined as

$$\text{interest cover} = \frac{\text{profit before interest and tax}}{\text{gross interest payments}}$$

This measures the extent to which profits can decline without resulting in financial embarrassment to the company because of an inability to meet annual interest costs. For CW Plc,

$$\text{interest cover} = \frac{£140\text{ million}}{£40\text{ million}} = 3.5\text{ times}$$

The £140 million is derived from operating profit of £118 million, associated companies' profit of £17 million, and investment income received of £5 million.

With high rates of interest, it is usually the interest cover constraint that limits further borrowing, rather than asset cover.

(b) Income cover and priority percentages   Income priority percentage tables are similar to the capital cover versions, except that they show the particular slice of the total profits that is used to remunerate a specific stock, rather than the percentage of assets relating to that stock. For CW Plc, we can list the income priority percentages and income cover as shown in Table 9.4.

Profits and interest on borrowings are taken net of tax at 35 per cent. The net-of-tax cost of servicing the interest, £26 million (i.e. £40 million$\times(1-0.35)$), is added to the net-of-tax profit figure, £65 million, to determine the available profits of £91 million.

Taking the reciprocal of the priority percentages gives a much sounder indication of cover than that obtained by comparing the profits available for a particular item of capital with its individual income requirement. If we take CW Plc's ordinary shares, for example, a 'naïve' comparison of 'available

Table 9.4 Income priority percentages and income cover for CW Plc

	Available profits (£m)	Net income required for charge (£m)	Cumulative total (£m)	Percentage of profit taken (rounded)	Priority percentage (rounded)	Income cover
£50m 10% mortgage debenture	91.00	3.25	3.25	4.00	0–4	25 times
£100m medium-term bank loan (15% gross)	87.75	9.75	13.00	10.00	4–14	7 times
£75m bank overdraft (14⅜% gross)	78.00	7.15	20.15	8.00	14–22	4½ times
£75m 12% unsecured loan stock	70.85	5.85	26.00	6.00	22–29	3½ times
£50m 8% cumulative preference shares	65.00	4.00	30.00	4.00	29–33	3 times
200m ordinary £1 shares, ordinary dividend	61.00	31.00	61.00	34.00	33–67	1½ times
Retentions	30.00	30.00	91.00	33.00	67–100	

profits' (£61 million) with 'income required' (£31 million) suggests a cover of
2. Indeed this figure would be the figure quoted in the press. But dividend
cover calculated on a cumulative basis (total available profits of £91 million
divided by total charges of £61 million) is only 1.5. This tells the investor
more about the security of the dividend – that total profits are currently only
1½ times more than is required to cover the present distribution and prior
claims.

9.9 Activity ratios

Activity ratios measure how effectively the company employs the resources at
its command. These ratios all involve dividing the sales figure by the level of
investment in various categories of asset. A ratio that is low compared to the
average from the past, or to that of rival companies, suggests that there is an
underemployment of assets and usually reflects poor management. A high
ratio may indicate that the company's asset base is too narrow, that recent
investment has been inadequate, and that further capital may be required to
finance sales. Overhasty conclusions should not be drawn, however, as
changes may simply reflect shifts in company policy in accounting practice,
factoring of debtors, leasing of assets, or revaluations.

9.9.1 Total assets turnover

The ratio is defined as

$$\text{total assets turnover} = \frac{\text{sales}}{\text{net tangible assets}}$$

For CW Plc,

$$\text{total assets turnover} = \frac{£1625 \text{ million}}{£835 \text{ million}} = 1.95 \text{ times}$$

9.9.2 Stock turnover

This ratio is defined as

$$\text{stock turnover} = \frac{\text{sales}}{\text{stocks}}$$

For CW Plc,

$$\text{stock turnover} = \frac{£1625 \text{ million}}{£400 \text{ million}} = 4.06 \text{ times}$$

9.9.3 Credit granted to debtors

The relationship between trade debtors and sales can be expressed in terms of *either* the number of times debtors are turned over in a year *or* the average number of days a debt is outstanding. For CW Plc the ratios are

$$\text{Trade debtor turnover} = \frac{\text{sales}}{\text{trade debtors}}$$

$$= \frac{£1625 \text{ million}}{£250 \text{ million}} = 6.5 \text{ times}$$

$$\text{Average collection period} = \frac{\text{trade debtors}}{\text{sales}} \times 365$$

$$= \frac{£250 \text{ million}}{£1625 \text{ million}} \times 365 = 56 \text{ days}$$

(Long-term debtors have been excluded.)

A reduction in debtor turnover (increase in the average collection period) may be indicative of inefficiency in credit control, and may lead an analyst to suspect an increase in the proportion of bad debts.

9.10 Profitability ratios

9.10.1 Return on capital employed
This is the prime measure of profitability, and one of the key ratios overall. It is defined as

$$\text{return on capital employed (ROCE)} = \frac{\text{profit before interest and tax}}{\text{capital employed}-\text{intangibles}} \times 100\%$$

For CW Plc,

$$\text{ROCE} = \frac{\text{£140 million}}{\text{£835 million}} \times 100\% = 16.8\%$$

To be more precise, bank overdraft interest (£11 million) should be deducted from the profit figure, as the bank overdraft is not included in the figure for capital employed.

9.10.2 Profit margin
The profit margin is the profit expressed as a percentage of sales. Using the same profit figure as before, for CW Plc,

$$\text{percentage profit margin} = \frac{\text{profit}}{\text{sales}} \times 100\%$$

$$= \frac{\text{£140 million}}{\text{£1625 million}} \times 100\% = 8.6\%$$

Some analysts would argue that 'profit' should be operating profit, before deducting such items as depreciation, auditors' remuneration, and directors' emoluments, and adding investment income. Sales of associated companies are not normally consolidated, so there is a strong case for omitting 'share of results of associated companies'. But the case for adopting the simple approach is that it illustrates the fundamental relationship determining return on capital employed (ROCE), that is:

$$\text{ROCE} = \frac{\text{profit}}{\text{assets}} = \frac{\text{profit}}{\text{sales}} \times \frac{\text{sales}}{\text{assets}}$$

Provided that these three ratios are defined consistently, it should be possible to diagnose the causes of changes in the return on capital employed.

The relationship between the profit margin and the asset turnover demonstrates that no one ratio should be considered in isolation. In retailing, for example, discount warehouses tend to have a much higher asset turnover than traditional department stores, but their 'stack 'em high, sell 'em cheap' philosophy means a lower profit margin. It is the overall impact in terms of return on capital that matters.

9.10.3 Return on ordinary shareholders' funds

This will differ from ROCE because of the effect of gearing, and also because it is usually expressed net of the total corporation tax charge. For CW Plc it is calculated as follows:

$$\frac{\text{return on ordinary}}{\text{shareholders' funds}} = \frac{\text{equity earnings}}{\text{ordinary shareholders' funds} - \text{intangibles}} \times 100\%$$

$$= \frac{\text{£61 million}}{\text{£660 million} - \text{£100 million}} \times 100\% = 10.9\%$$

9.10.4 Net asset value per share

The *net asset value per share* is the value of shareholders' assets (minus intangibles) divided by the number of shares outstanding. For CW Plc the values are

$$\text{net asset value per share} = \frac{\text{£660 million} - \text{£100 million}}{200 \text{ million}} = £2.80$$

That part of the proposed final dividends relating to the ordinary shares could also be added to the numerator.

A share would normally be expected to sell at a premium to its net asset value, as investors would be willing to pay something for 'goodwill' – the company's management, expertise, and reputation. But sometimes, because of low returns on capital, some companies have share values significantly below their net asset values per share, especially in current-cost terms. Under such circumstances the asset backing may give an underpinning to the share price, as the share is valued more on the basis of its assets than on its earnings.

Attention to the net asset value per share presumes either that sooner or later the company will earn an acceptable return on capital, or that it will be taken over, or that the assets will be liquidated. The *equity valuation ratio* (the market value of the share divided by its net asset value) can be a good indicator of a take-over 'victim'; if so, the bid price will be influenced by the net asset value per share, and will usually exceed the historical cost value. For CW Plc, if the current market value of the shares is £2.50,

$$\text{equity valuation ratio} = \frac{£2.50}{£2.80} = 0.89$$

Many companies manage to remain independent despite a persistent low valuation ratio, however. The extent of directors' shareholdings may give some indication of their ability to frustrate any take-over approach. They are unlikely to liquidate the company voluntarily, for reasons of self-interest or concern for their workers, or because of heavy redundancy and other closure costs. Moreover, both historical-cost and current-cost valuations are based on the 'going concern' assumption. One would need to examine the constituents of the shareholders' assets to make an estimate of possible liquidation values.

9.11 Sources of information

It is not necessary to send for copies of the accounts in order to obtain the required information: it is published in the card services of Extel Financial Services Ltd. These *Extel cards* and fact sheets are produced for every company listed on the Stock Exchange, and also for a large number of unquoted companies and overseas companies – see fig. 9.3. Most broker/ dealers subscribe to one of these services and they will make cards available to their clients. Many of the large bank branches also subscribe, and a customer requiring a card of a particular company can always ask his or her branch to obtain it from their broker/dealer if they do not hold it themselves.

The information shown on annual cards includes:

(a) the main business of the company;
(b) the names of the directors;

ANNUAL CARD | EXTEL FINANCIAL U.K. LISTED COMPANIES SERVICE | CARD ISSUED MAY 1989

CE-CH 15   **CHURCH & CO. PLC**   **CHU**

COMPANY HISTORY
Registered January 1926 as a Private Company; Registered No 211135; Made Public December 1951; Re-registered February 1982 as a Public Limited Company under the Companies Act 1980
The Company was formed to acquire the business of Church & Co.
In December 1951 Ordinary shares of 5/- were introduced to The Stock Exchange.
REGISTERED OFFICE
St James, Northampton NN5 5JB Tel: 0604 51251 Telex: 312110
REGISTRARS
National Westminster Bank PLC, PO Box 82, Caxton House, Redcliffe Way, Bristol BS99 7NH   Tel: 0272 306600   Telex: 445845
Fax: 0272 306509.
ACTIVITIES
The Group is principally engaged in manufacture, wholesale and retail distribution of footwear.
COMMERCIAL DATA
OUTLETS

CLOSE COMPANY
Income and Corporation Taxes Act 1988: No
DIVIDEND PAYMENT DETAILS – ORDINARY Year end December 31

		% Payable		Per Share		Tax	Shares Ranking				
		Gross	Net	Gross	Net	Rate	For Dividend(000's)	Announced	Paid	Holders	Ex Date
1984	Int	17.143	12	4.286p	3p	30%	5,217	31-8-84	19-10-84	27-9-84	17-9-84
	Fin	68.571	48	17.143p	12p	30%	5,217	21-3-85	13-5-85	9-4-85	25-3-85
	Cap	100		-	-	-		21-3-85	-	17-4-85	13-5-85
1985	Int	14.286	10	3.571p	2.5p	30%	10,437	30-8-85	21-10-85	26-9-85	16-9-85
	Fin	33.803	24	8.451p	6p	29%	10,437	20-3-86	12-5-86	11-4-86	1-4-86
1986	Int	14.085	10	3.521p	2.5p	29%	10,450	1-9-86	20-10-86	25-9-86	15-9-86
	Fin	38.356	28	9.589p	7p	27%	10,450	19-3-87	11-5-87	10-4-87	23-3-87
1987	Int	16.438	12	4.11p	3p	27%	10,450	26-8-87	22-10-87	24-9-87	14-9-87
	Fin	45.333	34	11.333p	8.5p	25%	10,708	17-3-88	9-5-88	8-4-88	21-3-88
1988	Int	16	12	4p	3p	25%	10,765	1-9-88	21-10-88	23-9-88	5-9-88
	Fin	48	36	12p	9p	25%	10,765	17-3-89	8-5-89	13-4-89	3-4-89

DIVIDENDS OF EARLIER YEARS – ORDINARY
Net: 1979, 7.5p; 1980, 8p; 1981, 8.5p; 1982, 9.5p; 1983, 11p
PER SHARE RECORD OF 25p ORDINARY - Adjusted for Capital Changes

	Dec 31 1984	Dec 31 1985	Dec 31 1986	Dec 31 1987	Dec 31 1988
EARNINGS based on Reported Profits					
Basic	31.1p	25.6p	29.1p	35.3p	33.4p
EARNINGS based on Adjusted Profits					
Net Actual	29.755p	24.856p	27.727p	32.051p	27.673p
Net Maximum	24.224p	23.266p	26.502p	30.529p	26.744p

Source: Extel Financial UK listed companies service

Fig. 9.3   An extract from an Extel card

(c) the company's registered office, and registrars;
(d) the company's broker;
(e) the company's capital history;
(f) major shareholdings;

and a five-year record of

(g) profit and loss accounts;
(h) balance sheets;
(i) earnings per share;
(j) dividend payments;
(k) dividend cover;
(l) net asset value per share;
(m) share price highs and lows;
(n) sources and uses of funds;

plus

(o) income priority percentages for the current year;
(p) a summary of the chairman's last statement.

The *news card* provides updating information, and for most companies there is an *analyst's service* which provides a ten-year record. This provides certain other information in a readily accessible form – for example, key accounting ratios and dividend and earnings yields, including 'relative to the *FT*–Actuaries indices', over the last ten years.

Those investors who deal directly with a stockbroker/dealer should receive regular circulars and company studies, which are restricted to broker/dealers' clients (see fig. 9.4). In addition, the *Financial Times* and the financial pages of other quality newspapers are important sources of information, together with weekly publications such as the *Investor's Chronicle*, and the more general *The Economist*, and monthly magazines such as *Money Management*. A press-cuttings service is provided by *McCarthy Information Services*, which keeps a constant watch for news and comment on listed companies in the leading newspapers and magazines. Now a subsidiary of the *Financial Times*, McCarthy Information Services is available from an on-line database. This service is taken by some major libraries.

For the investor who is determined to be closely involved, the *Stock Exchange Fact Service* deals with securities generally, and the *Stock Exchange Official Year Book* gives details of individual quoted companies. Copies of the latter are available in the reference section of most public libraries. It is extremely useful because it summarizes the mass of information recorded in a company's file at Companies House, with the exception of the list of members and the annual report and accounts. Whereas Extel provides a detailed statistical summary of a company, *Datastream* – a subsidiary of Dun and Bradstreet Corporation – provides a detailed graphical presentation and manipulation of financial data. The information is available on-line in statistical and graphical form. It can immediately produce the

				Year End	Pretax Profit £mn	EPS (P)	PE ratio	Net div. (P)	Gross dividend yield (%)
TESCO	**BUY**	**Price** 193p	**1989 H/L** 219p/131p	**Feb 1989**	265.3	11.7	16.5	3.5	2.4
			Next Results Apr(F) **Mkt Cap** £3,040m	**1990E**	330.0	14.0	14.2	4.2	2.8

Food retailer. Tesco's investment in new space and distribution continues to bear fruit. The interim results saw pre-tax profits rise 30%, generated by strong sales up 14% and further strengthening of margins. Tesco is continuing in the restructuring of its store portfolio in favour of "conforming" stores, which contribute well above average margins, and in the focus of supply management and distribution systems. With two of its leading competitors currently preoccupied, Asda with ex-Gateway stores and Argyll with integrating Safeway, Tesco has seen it as an appropriate time to accelerate its store development programme and with much of 1989/90's 23 store openings geared to the year end, significant sales benefits will arise next financial year. Continue to buy for long-term growth in a defensive sector ☐ AK

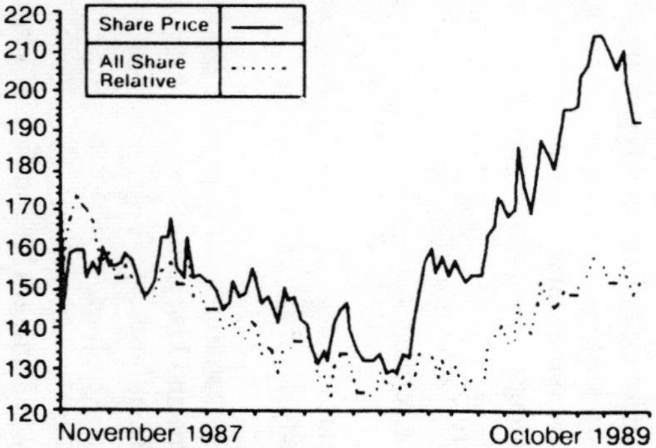
Share Price
All Share Relative
220
210
200
190
180
170
160
150
140
130
120
November 1987
October 1989

Source: NatWest Stockbrokers. Contributor: Alastair Kendall

Fig. 9.4 A broker's recommendation

answers to questions such as 'Which shares have earnings per share growth of more than 10 per cent per annum over the last five years, and currently sell on P/E ratios of less than 10?' Many of the tables and graphs in the financial press are supplied by Datastream. However, its cost is likely to be prohibitive for most personal investors. The *Hambro Company Guide* is an annual guide which provides useful statistical summaries and diagrams of share price performance for all companies' ordinary shares dealt in on the Stock Exchange.

At Companies House, in Cardiff and in London, a separate file is kept for every registered company (the London ones are on microfilm). A file may be inspected by any member of the public for the payment of a small fee. The file contains the memorandum and articles of association, the prospectus, mortgages and charges, the annual return, and the annual report and accounts. An analyst who feels that the consolidated accounts are inadequate can extract the names of the subsidiaries from the annual report and investigate the subsidiary accounts at Companies House if they are companies registered in the United Kingdom (in Edinburgh for Scottish registered companies). The accounts of limited liability subsidiaries must comply with company law in the same way as those of the parent company.

A company must also maintain at its registered office certain registers which again may be inspected by the general public, for a small fee for each register inspected. All of them are included in the annual return at Companies House, but those at the registered office will be more up to date – especially the register of shareholdings.

9.12 Arriving at a conclusion

For anyone other than the specialist analyst concentrating on only a handful of companies, there is a danger of being overwhelmed by accounting information. Ratio analysis makes it possible to extract the key points in the report and accounts. But ratios are not an end in themselves – they simply provide a means of judging the present and future risks and return prospects of a company generally, and of its equity capital in particular.

The hardest task in fundamental analysis is not analysing the accounts, but rather deciding how far your assessment of them, and other sources of information, is already reflected in the current share price. Supporters of the *efficient market hypothesis* (discussed in chapter 10) believe that share prices fully 'discount' most, if not all, published information almost as soon as it becomes available.

Most amateur investors will rely on the verdict of specialist commentators, such as the 'Lex' column in the *Financial Times*.

9.13 Technical analysis

> A trend is a trend is a trend
> But the question is, will it bend?
> Will it alter its course
> Through some unforeseen force
> And come to a premature end?

Technical analysis is the study of stock exchange information principally in the form of price and volume data. The word 'technical' implies a study of the market itself, and not of those external economic factors that are reflected in the market. Many technical analysts would claim that a knowledge of the company and industry is a positive disadvantage. Some would prefer not to know the nature of the underlying asset, claiming it is immaterial whether they are predicting the price of ICI shares, gold, or postage stamps!

Technical analysis is essentially based on trends and patterns. Mechanical trading rules in the main are concerned with deciphering major turning-points, but they are based on the belief that there is a certain momentum in share prices both upward and downward.

9.13.1 Relative strength
This approach is based on the belief that a share or sector which is outperforming the market will probably continue to do so; it embodies the 'momentum idea' or 'bandwagon effect'. It may also reflect the gradual dissemination of good or bad news to a progressively wider investing public. In one study, relative strengths were determined by dividing the current market price by the average of the previous 26 weeks; these ratios were computed weekly, and the highest 10 per cent were bought and the lowest 10 per cent sold. Success was claimed for such a policy.

9.13.2 Filter rules
Filters are designed to isolate the primary trends from minor price changes arising from random factors. Figure 9.5 illustrates their use: if the price of a share moves up at least x per cent from a low point, it should be bought and held until its price moves down at least x per cent from a subsequent high, at which time it should be sold. The share is not repurchased until it moves up again at least x per cent from the subsequent low point.

The problem with using this technique is deciding on the size of the filter. If x is small (3 to 5 per cent say), the investor is constantly buying and selling and thus spending heavily on broker/dealer's commission and stamp duty. If x is large (perhaps 20 to 25 per cent), much of the price movement has taken place before the investor acts. The so-called 'Hatch' system is basically a 10 per cent filter.

9.13.3 Chartism
Most analysts use charts at times as a method of keeping track on the price movements of particular shares, or of the market as a whole. In the case of

Fig. 9.5   The filter method

individual shares, charts can alert the analyst to any sharp upward or downward movement or any persistent trend relative to the market and he or she may then decide to investigate the fundamentals of the company.

Chartists are a special breed, however, in that they rely on charts alone, and have their own ways of plotting share prices. The essence of chartism is the belief that share prices trace out patterns over time. These are a reflection of investor behaviour and, if it can be assumed that history tends to repeat itself in the stock market, a certain pattern of activity that in the past produced certain results is likely to give rise to the same outcome should it reappear in the future.

There are three principal forms of chart that plot the movement of the prices of individual shares and of market indices.

(a) The simplest form of chart is a *line* chart (see fig. 9.6). This consists of a line connecting the closing prices of the share, or average prices over a period of perhaps a week, to show the price movements over a period of months or, more probably, years. Those analysts who use line charts usually plot other lines on the same chart. These may show the movement of the share price relative to an index for the appropriate market sector or for the market as a whole. They may also show the price movement relative to earnings or, with investment trusts, the price as a percentage of asset value.

(b) Another form of chart is the *bar* chart (see fig. 9.7). This shows the highest and lowest prices a share reaches each week, joined by a vertical line or bar. Bar charts usually attempt to indicate the volume of business each week in the share.

(c) The third form of chart in common use is the *point-and-figure* chart (see fig. 9.8). In this type there is no time scale and only price movements are plotted. As a share price rises, a vertical column of crosses is plotted.

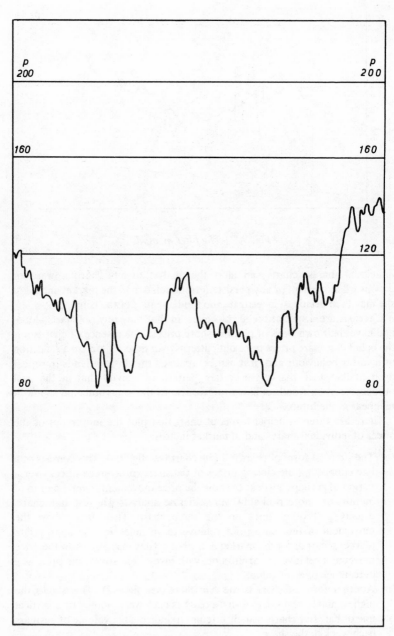

Source: Investment Research, Cambridge

Fig. 9.6   A line chart showing a double bottom

Fig. 9.7   A bar chart showing a 'head and shoulders' top

When it falls, a circle is plotted in the next column, and this is continued downward while the price continues to fall. When it rises again a new vertical line of crosses is plotted in the next column, and so on. A point-and-figure chart that changes column on every price reversal is cumbersome, and many show a reversal only for price changes of three units or more (a unit of plot may be a price change of, say, one penny).

In all charts, different patterns are produced by use of arithmetic or logarithmic scales. An arithmetic scale is calibrated in equal sections for equal absolute changes, whereas the calibration in a logarithmic scale gives equal sections for equal percentage changes.

Virtually all chartists employ colourful, and sometimes almost mystical,

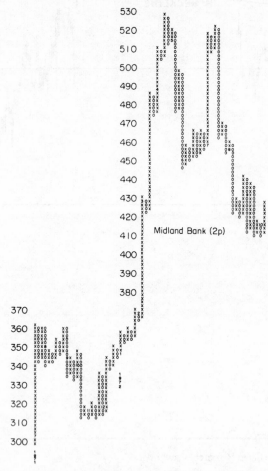

Fig. 9.8   A point-and-figure chart showing a double top

terminology. For example, if the share price persistently fails to rise above a certain level this is known as a *resistance level* (fig. 9.9). This is perhaps because at this price people who bought previously, but then saw the share price fall, took the opportunity to sell at the price they previously paid. Likewise, a *support level* is a price at which buyers constantly seem to come forward to prevent the share price dropping any lower.

A *line* (fig. 9.10) is a period of consolidation, when the share price moves sideways within a range of about 5 per cent of the share price. Eventually a *break-out* will occur, and it is often suggested that, the longer the period of consolidation, the greater will be the extent of the ultimate rise or fall.

A *trend line* is a line joining at least two points (often three or more). Advances or declines sometimes appear to be composed of a series of ripples around a straight line. Chartists reckon that in a rising market the trend line is likely to be the one connecting the minor bottoms (fig. 9.11), and in a declining market the one connecting the tops of the minor rallies. If another line is drawn in parallel, a *channel* is created which can supposedly be used for predicting the extent of the minor rallies and falls.

Probably the best-known pattern is the *head and shoulders* pattern shown in fig. 9.7. Here the share price rises on buying pressure from investors who

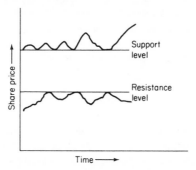

Fig. 9.9   Chart patterns: support level and resistance level

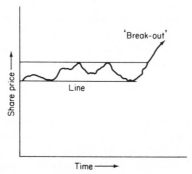

Fig. 9.10   Chart patterns: line and break-out

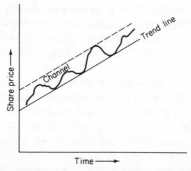

Fig. 9.11   Chart patterns: trend line and channel

have specialist knowledge of the company, and this is later reinforced by other investors 'jumping on the bandwagon'. A major top is formed at A. Then a reaction sets in as some investors decide to take their profits. Another upsurge then takes place, as the share is still very much in the limelight and no doubt the subject of press comment. A new high top is formed at C. Again buying support is exhausted, as some investors believe the upward trend has been overdone. A reaction takes place back to D; although there is a further rise to E, it is based on very little volume of deals and fails to reach C. The crucial point is reached when the third reaction takes place from E – if this penetrates the *neckline*, it signals (according to the chartists) a significant change in sentiment for the share and the beginning of a major decline in price.

Another pattern, the *double bottom*, is illustrated in fig. 9.6. This is very much like the 'head and shoulders' in reverse!

Pure chartists have frequently been the object of ridicule by fundamentalists, who have compared them to astrologers, palmists, and readers of tea-leaves. The scepticism of the mainstream analysts is due to the absence of any economic foundation to the chartist methodology. Chartism seems to imply that there is no learning process, that there are always 'leaders' and 'followers', and that information about a company is only slowly disseminated through the market. Attempts to measure chartist performances have been inconclusive, as the chartists consistently maintain that their role is not simply a mechanistic one but rather that it is interpretative. Unfortunately, different chartists frequently receive different messages from the same chart!

9.14 Timing

Even fundamentalists may use price data so as to judge the right time to buy or sell a share. The secret of short-term success in equity investment is *when* you buy and sell rather than *what* you buy and sell, as nearly all shares tend to move upwards in price during a 'bull' market and downwards in a 'bear' market. All investors would like to buy at the bottom of a bear market and sell, or 'go liquid', at the top of a bull market. In this respect the personal investor and the small unit trust have much greater flexibility than most other investors, particularly large insurance companies and pension funds, who would find it both very difficult and imprudent to reduce their share holdings suddenly and drastically.

For the personal investor, the difficulty lies in knowing when the top or bottom has been reached. Is he watching a primary change in the trend, or merely a temporary aberration? One can say only with hindsight. Although bull and bear markets seemingly regularly follow each other, their duration and amplitude are not consistent enough for a regular pattern to be discerned.

9.15 Questions

1. (a) The theoretical basis of the intrinsic value of a share is the discounted value of:

   A all future dividends.
   B all future earnings.
   C the previous dividend and all future dividends.
   D the last reported earnings and all future earnings.

   (b) Which of the following is true of the capital asset pricing model:

   $$E(r) = R_f + \beta(R_m - R_f)$$

   (where $E(r)$ = the expected return, R_f = the risk-free return, and R_m = the market return)?

   A $E(r)$ will be higher the lower the level of β.
   B R_f is influenced by the value of β.
   C The investor is rewarded for assuming market (i.e. systematic) risk and not for specific risk.
   D Specific risk cannot be diversified away.

   (c) In which of the following sectors is 'net asset value' a particularly important concept?

   A Stores.
   B Property.
   C Banks.
   D Electronics.

   (d) Three of the following conditions are necessary for an item in the profit and loss account to be deemed an extraordinary item. Which *one* is *not* necessary?

   A It is material.
   B It involves losses.
   C It is non-recurring or infrequent.
   D It is outside the ordinary activities of the business.

(e) Return on capital employed is calculated by dividing (net profit before interest ×100) by:

  A loan capital+preference shares+ordinary shares+reserves.
  B preference shares+ordinary shares+reserves.
  C ordinary shares+reserves.
  D loan capital+preference shares+ordinary shares.

(f)

		£000
Ordinary share capital (25p)		1000
Preference share capital (£1)		100
Share premium		250
Profit and loss account		850
		2200
11% unsecured loan stock 1993/97		500
		2700
Fixed assets		1790
Current assets		
Stock	1580	
Debtors	840	2420
Current liabilities		
Creditors	640	
Bank overdraft	870	1510
Net current assets		910
		2700

Notes: (1) Fixed assets are stated net of depreciation £900 000, of which £400 000 relates to current year.
  (2) Profits attributable to the ordinary shareholders were £715 000, of which £350 000 was paid as dividends.

Calculate:

  (i)   working capital,
  (ii) the acid test ratio,
  (iii) the gearing ratio,
  (iv) the net asset value per (ordinary) share,
  (v)   the cash flow.

(g) The graph in fig. 9.12 shows that, over the period in question, British Gas Plc shares:

  A showed good defensive qualities during the crash of October 1987.
  B were priced a little lower in June 1988 than they were a year earlier.

Fig. 9.12   British Gas share price relative to the FT–Actuaries All-Share
Index

    C were volatile, while the market generally was relatively steady for
    most of the period.

    D saw a small decrease in earnings per share over the 12 month
    period.

2. The issued capital of AZ Plc consists of 10 million ordinary shares of 50p
   each, 3 million 4.2% (net) preference shares of £1, and £1.5 million 6½%
   debenture stock 1994. Its capital and revenue reserves amount to £200 000
   and £3.63 million respectively. For the year ended 30 September 1990,
   profits, before interest and corporation tax, amounted to £6 million, and
   the directors propose to pay a dividend of 8.4p (net) per share for the
   year.

  (a) (i) Calculate the capital gearing ratio, using book values, by **one** of
   the recognized methods.

      (ii) How would this calculation differ if it were based on market
   values as follows?

          Ordinary shares   257p
          Preference shares   56p
          Debenture stock   £82

     (iii) Comment on the usefulness for investors of the figures produced
   in (i) and (ii) above.

  (b) Calculate the income priority percentage and the overall (i.e. cumulative) cover for each claim.

                            (CIB 10/88)

3. In assessing the ordinary shares of a quoted public company, what
   importance would you attach to the following factors: (a) earnings, (b) net
   asset value, (c) management?

                            (CIB 4/83)

4. (a) An investor, who uses the filter system known as 'Hatch', has been following a particular share for some months. After a period when the price did not move much, either up or down, the share price rose 10 per cent above its 'low' and he purchased 5000 shares at 230p. The share price (weekly averages are used) then moved as follows:

Week	0	1	2	3	4	5
Share price	230p	252p	248p	295p	264p	282p

    (i) Set out these prices in the same form as above, and underneath each of weeks 1–5 indicate, with reasons, whether Hatch signals that the investor should 'Hold', 'Sell', or 'Buy' (more shares).

    (ii) What is the 'theory' behind the Hatch System and what, if any, do you consider to be its disadvantages?

  (b) Interpret the information contained in the Earnings and Dividends chart of Ladbroke Group Plc shown in fig. 9.13.

(CIB 5/90)

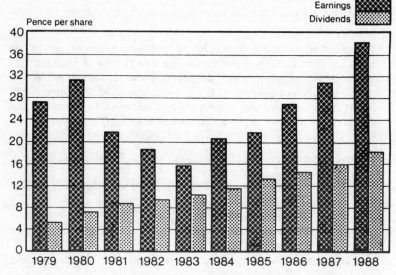

Fig. 9.13   Ladbroke Group Plc, earnings and dividends

10 Indices and the efficient market hypothesis

Stock market indices show the movement over time in aggregate share prices, or the prices of other securities. In the United Kingdom the best-known and the most widely used are those published by the *Financial Times*. There are four main share price indices: the *FT Ordinary* (or *30 Share*) *Index*, the *FT–Actuaries Share Indices*, the *FT–SE 100 Index*, and the *FT–Actuaries World Indices*. Their functions and methods of calculation are outlined below.

10.1 The *FT* Ordinary (30 Share) Index

This is the 'original' *Financial Times* index, begun in 1935, and the one which used to receive most publicity. It is a price index of the equities of 30 leading industrial, commercial, and financial companies in Britain. The 30 are chosen to give a wide range of industry and commerce, each being a leader in its field, and together they have always represented a relatively large part of the equity market as a whole. Table 10.1 shows the constituents of the Index in November 1989.

The scope of the Index has been extended in recent times with the inclusion of oil (British Petroleum), financial companies (National Westminster Bank and Royal Insurance), and privatization issues (British Airways, British Gas, and British Telecom).

From its inception, the purpose of the Index has always been to show the 'mood' of the equity market – whether it is 'bullish' or 'bearish', or 'flat' – and the strength of these moods. Thirty was considered the optimal number because index readings on a few shares had little stability but as the number was increased beyond 30 the readings flattened out because of the inactivity in dealing in many second-line shares (the New York Dow-Jones Index uses the same number). This factor, together with the tendency of these shares to 'follow' the leaders, meant that with their inclusion the desired sensitivity of the Index to changes in sentiment would have been lost.

The *FT* 30 Share Index is an *unweighted geometric mean* of the price-

Table 10.1 Constituents of the FT Ordinary Share Index

Allied-Lyons	Grand Metropolitan
ASDA Group	GKN*
BICC	Guinness
Blue Circle Industries*	Hanson
BOC Group	Hawker Siddeley*
Boots	ICI*
British Airways	Lucas Industries
British Gas	Marks & Spencer
British Petroleum	National Westminster Bank
British Telecom	P & O
BTR	Royal Insurance
Cadbury Schweppes	Smith Kline Beecham
Courtaulds*	Tate and Lyle*
General Electric*	Thorn-EMI
Glaxo Holdings	Trusthouse Forte

Companies marked * have been in the Index since its compilation began.
Source: *Financial Times*.

relatives of the individual constituents. The *price-relative* of a share is the current share price divided by the price at a base date. The geometric mean is obtained by multiplying these 30 values together and taking the thirtieth root of the result; in practice, it is necessary only to multiply the 30 current prices together and then divide by a constant, before taking the thirtieth root. Because of its construction, the *FT* 30 Share Index places equal weight on each fractional price change, irrespective of the original market capitalization of the company. The value of the Index on the base date, 1 July 1935, is taken as 100.

Except where all the numbers have equal values, a geometric mean always understates an arithmetic one. The difference between the two averages is larger the wider the distribution of numbers. The *FT* 30 Share Index is less affected than an arithmetic index would be by exceptionally large price increases for a small number of shares, but more so should they show abnormal falls in price. In the extreme case, one share price falling to zero would reduce the Index to zero, but in practice such a share would be replaced well before that point was reached. Some shares have been replaced because of take-over, either by another company or through nationalization. A new share is then introduced at a base price that leaves the Index unchanged.

Another advantage of having only 30 shares in the Index is that it can be calculated frequently, from 8.30 opening and then every hour on the hour from 9 a.m. to 4 p.m. inclusive, and at the 'close', 4.30 p.m.

The Index reflects movements in the stock market as a whole reasonably well. As illustrated in fig. 10.1, it reached low points in June 1940 (an all-time low of 49.4) and in January 1975 with a fall to 146. By September 1989 it had breached the 2000 mark.

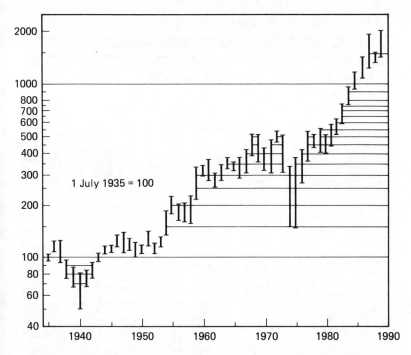

Fig. 10.1   The FT *Ordinary Index, 1935–89: annual highs and lows*

10.2 The *FT*–Actuaries Share Indices and World Indices

The *FT*–Actuaries Share Indices are designed specifically to measure portfolio performance and are so named because they are jointly compiled by the *Financial Times*, the Institute of Actuaries, and the Faculty of Actuaries. A large number of these indices are published in the *Financial Times* every day except Mondays (see Table 10.2). Each index shows in parentheses the number of companies included in it. The indices are designed to cover a sufficiently large number of shares to facilitate their subdivision into groups and subsections with adequate representations in each. Dividend yields, earnings yields, and P/E ratios are provided for most subsections and major groupings. The exceptions are some of the financial groups – merchant banks, life assurance companies, and investment trusts – which do not provide earnings yields and P/E ratios. Consequently, the 500 Share Index is the broadest index to provide these figures.

The *FT*–Actuaries Share Indices' principal function is to serve as a reliable measure of portfolio performance. They are *weighted arithmetic means*. These are found by calculating a price-relative for each share in an index which is then *weighted* by multiplying it by the equity market capitalization (the total market value of the ordinary shares) of the company at the base

Table 10.2 *FT*–Actuaries share indices

© The Financial Times Ltd 1990. Compiled by the Financial Times Ltd in conjunction with the Institute of Actuaries and the Faculty of Actuaries

EQUITY GROUPS & SUB-SECTIONS Figures in parentheses show number of stocks per section	Thursday July 5 1990						Wed Jul 4	Tue Jul 3	Mon Jul 2	Year ago (approx)
	Index No.	Day's Change %	Est. Earnings Yield% (Max.)	Gross Div. Yield% (Act at 25%)	Est. P/E Ratio (Net)	xd adj. 1990 to date	Index No.	Index No.	Index No.	Index No.
1 CAPITAL GOODS (196)	875.02	−1.1	13.22	5.31	9.23	19.75	884.90	897.43	899.78	959.67
2 Building Materials (26)	1107.22	−1.5	13.83	5.44	8.93	27.29	1124.50	1141.48	1154.15	1180.20
3 Contracting, Construction (36)	1427.03	−0.8	16.66	5.76	7.81	34.92	1438.73	1457.54	1477.32	1622.61
4 Electricals (10)	2473.11	−1.1	11.62	5.38	10.59	61.43	2499.89	2515.45	2531.44	2818.65
5 Electronics (26)	1806.62	−1.0	10.45	4.46	12.46	26.12	1825.33	1852.66	1817.05	2196.28
6 Engineering-Aerospace (8)	468.39	−0.3	13.84	5.02	8.61	9.54	469.63	474.52	475.69	0.00
7 Engineering-General (46)	490.04	−0.8	11.99	5.21	10.09	10.10	493.80	496.90	498.48	0.00
8 Metals and Metal Forming (6)	477.53	−2.7	24.39	7.04	4.98	16.45	490.56	495.64	500.85	513.59
9 Motors (14)	364.54	−1.5	15.25	6.31	7.64	9.81	369.92	375.69	376.90	326.92
10 Other Industrial Materials (24)	1565.24	−0.9	11.21	5.14	10.30	36.58	1580.13	1611.53	1619.67	1644.39
21 CONSUMER GROUP (178)	1295.54	−1.3	9.40	3.90	13.13	20.52	1312.46	1319.07	1320.45	1240.70
22 Brewers and Distillers (22)	1604.49	−0.7	9.49	3.63	12.65	23.38	1616.21	1623.32	1620.67	1357.70
25 Food Manufacturing (20)	1104.28	−0.9	10.38	4.34	11.93	19.91	1114.08	1119.26	1120.80	1127.76
26 Food Retailing (16)	2500.06	−1.8	9.27	3.29	13.81	33.61	2545.42	2551.37	2542.48	2377.14
27 Health and Household (15)	2532.00	−1.4	6.79	2.74	17.51	25.10	2566.86	2597.01	2600.94	2223.40
29 Leisure (32)	1486.41	−1.2	9.82	4.15	12.39	24.42	1504.56	1515.34	1518.68	1654.70
31 Packaging & Paper (12)	605.45	−0.2	10.96	5.67	11.25	12.94	606.76	607.79	607.23	567.81
32 Publishing & Printing (16)	3542.18	−1.2	10.17	5.21	12.29	81.93	3583.78	3593.35	3559.50	3539.81
34 Stores (34)	788.24	−2.1	11.27	4.75	11.42	15.80	805.00	803.60	813.78	817.37
35 Textiles (11)	496.17	−2.5	12.41	7.25	10.17	18.26	508.90	511.55	504.64	541.61
40 OTHER GROUPS (106)	1188.22	−0.9	10.95	4.99	11.00	17.19	1198.87	1207.23	1205.66	1114.32
41 Agencies (17)	1715.69	−0.7	5.80	2.22	20.88	15.27	1727.33	1735.87	1715.64	1352.53
42 Chemicals (23)	1267.90	−0.7	11.12	5.23	10.52	31.39	1277.12	1287.12	1291.06	1260.73
43 Conglomerates (15)	1623.26	−1.9	10.58	6.14	11.33	31.95	1654.37	1669.67	1690.22	1661.26
44 Transport (13)	2278.57	−0.4	10.78	4.52	11.77	47.77	2287.80	2312.52	2311.05	2458.54
46 Telephone Networks(2)	1246.03	−0.7	10.77	4.52	12.08	3.78	1254.99	1267.06	1241.96	1060.83
47 Water(10)	1955.03	−0.9	16.41	6.93	6.82	0.00	1972.82	1956.75	1958.83	0.00
48 Miscellaneous (24)	1806.96	−0.5	12.08	4.96	9.44	37.62	1816.16	1823.17	1841.31	1669.91
49 INDUSTRIAL GROUP (480)	1169.17	−1.1	10.81	4.58	11.30	19.89	1182.43	1191.68	1192.50	1152.33
51 Oil & Gas (20)	2283.85	−0.6	12.33	5.40	10.71	46.50	2298.27	2297.91	2296.01	2095.70
59 500 SHARE INDEX (500)	1262.91	−1.1	11.01	4.69	11.21	22.08	1276.36	1284.96	1285.58	1232.25
61 FINANCIAL GROUP (108)	797.20	−0.5	–	5.74	–	21.09	800.97	803.35	805.62	730.41
62 Banks (9)	837.00	+0.8	19.57	6.45	6.69	25.62	830.01	830.95	833.18	710.92
65 Insurance (Life) (7)	1446.46	−2.0	–	5.08	–	36.94	1476.46	1483.59	1504.49	1082.96
66 Insurance (Composite) (6)	691.96	−1.3	–	5.98	–	19.43	701.18	707.45	709.78	573.99
67 Insurance (Brokers) (8)	987.99	−2.0	8.78	6.51	15.01	31.64	1008.38	1016.66	1016.15	954.97
68 Merchant Banks (7)	437.98	−0.3	–	4.63	–	10.76	439.43	438.87	437.86	332.70
69 Property (47)	1104.19	−0.9	7.98	4.27	16.05	19.54	1114.71	1113.20	1107.72	1312.57
70 Other Financial (24)	289.12	−0.7	10.68	6.76	12.16	7.47	291.26	293.02	294.99	362.19
71 Investment Trusts (67)	1206.86	−0.7	–	3.23	–	15.35	1215.91	1222.50	1225.16	1158.90
91 Overseas Traders (5)	1459.88	−0.5	9.65	6.26	12.38	44.49	1467.74	1479.49	1456.62	1336.27
99 ALL-SHARE INDEX (680)	1151.07	−1.0	–	4.81	–	21.57	1162.19	1169.35	1170.25	1110.00

	Index No.	Day's Change	Day's High (a)	Day's Low (b)	Jul 4	Jul 3	Jul 2	Jun 29	Jun 28	Year ago
FT-SE 100 SHARE INDEX	2331.4	−24.1	2352.2	2327.8	2355.5	2371.7	2372.0	2374.6	2355.7	2161.2

date. These figures are then added together for all the shares in the relevant index, and the sum is divided by their total equity market capitalization at the base date. The resulting quotient is then expressed in terms of the base date values of 100.

From time to time the weights are modified to take account of capital or constituent changes. For this purpose a 'chain-index' procedure is used, the first 'link' in the chain being the movement in the index from the base date – usually 10 April 1962 – to the date of the first capital change. The index is restarted at 100 with new weights, reflecting the new market capitalizations after the change, but this 'new' index is adjusted by a constant factor reflecting the value of the 'old' index at the change-over date, thus preserving continuity.

The indices reproduce the performance of 'model' portfolios in which the holdings of each constituent is always proportional to the total market value of its ordinary shares. The model portfolio will 'take up' any 'rights', increasing its holding of that particular constituent and reducing those of all the others, so that the resulting holding of each constituent is still proportional to the new equity market valuations (the implication is that no dividend income is reinvested).

The *All-Share Index* (fig. 10.2) is usually regarded as the yardstick by which to measure the performance of an equity fund. It represents around three-quarters of the total market value of UK equities listed on the Stock Exchange. Certainly it provides a much better measure than the *FT* 30 Share Index, comparisons with which are grossly misleading because of the latter's geometric constitution. Any fund simply investing in the same proportions as those in the All-Share Index should always 'beat' the *FT* 30 Share Index over the long run.

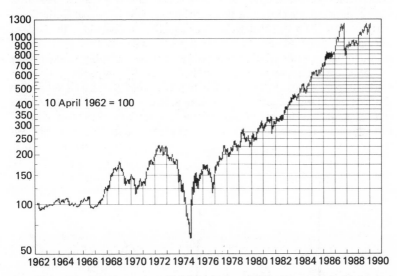

10 April 1962 = 100

Fig. 10.2   The FT–*Actuaries All-Share Index, 1962–89: monthly highs and lows*

For worldwide fund performance measurement, the best yardsticks are the *FT–Actuaries World Indices*. These are weighted arithmetic means based on the prices of around 2400 equities of major companies drawn from 24 countries, accounting for around 70 per cent of the capitalization of the world's main equity markets. A table published daily in the *Financial Times* provides indices for each country, for regional areas (such as the Pacific

Basin), and for the overall *World Index*. The indices are produced in terms of dollar, sterling, yen, or Deutschmarks, and also in the local currency, so it is possible to see to what extent performance is due to movement in the local share price and to currency changes. The base date was 31 December 1986, with a base figure of 100.

The World Indices provide the best yardsticks for measuring the performance of international funds, such as specialist unit trusts. The indices deliberately exclude shares that are not available to overseas investors, and the indices also exclude companies where 75 per cent or more of the shares of a company are controlled by dominant shareholders.

10.3 The *FT*–SE 100 Index

The *Financial Times–Stock Exchange 100 Index* was established in 1984 primarily to meet the needs of the Stock Exchange and the London International Financial Futures Exchange (now the London Derivatives Exchange) for an index which would provide a sound basis for options and futures contracts based upon the United Kingdom equity market. An index was required which moved in line with the value of a typical institutional portfolio, yet could still be calculated frequently. Consequently, the basis of calculation of the *FT*–SE 100 Index is very similar to that used for the All-Share Index – that is, it is a weighted arithmetic mean, but based on only 100 companies, initially almost precisely the top 100 companies in terms of market capitalization. A key figure is that the Index is recalculated almost continuously at one minute intervals from 8.30 a.m. to 5 p.m. The base level was set at 1000 at the end of business on 30 December 1983. The 'Footsie' index provides a good proxy for the All-Share Index, and has now replaced the *FT* 30 Share Index in popular usage. Its performance is shown in fig. 10.3.

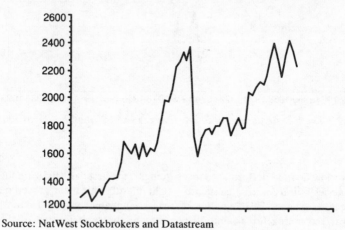

Source: NatWest Stockbrokers and Datastream

Fig. 10.3   The FT–SE *Index, April 1985 to March 1990*

10.4 Other *FT*–Actuaries Indices

In addition to the share indices, there are five British Government Fixed-interest Price Indices, three Index-linked Price Indices, ten British Government Fixed-interest Yield Indices, four Index-linked Yield Indices, and similar sets of indices for debenture and preference shares.

The British Government Indices were introduced in May 1977 to provide a comparison measure for the gilts market, equivalent to that provided by the *FT*–Actuaries Share Indices in the equity market. The gilts market is not homogeneous, but has separate sectors requiring separate analysis. The price indices subdivide the market by maturity period (0 to 5, 5 to 15, 15-plus years, undated, all stocks) and by whether the coupon and par value are fixed or index-linked. The yield indices have a three-way division, being separated by maturity period (0 to 5, 5 to 15, 15 to 25 years, and undated), coupon (low, medium, or high) and whether fixed-rate or index-linked. The various sectors are of interest to different investors, depending on their status.

Since the number of gilt-edged stocks on the market is comparatively small, the price indices represent the complete market value of all stocks in each sector expressed in the form of an index the base for which was 100 on 31 December 1975.

10.5 Other indices

The *Financial Times* also publishes a *Government Securities Index* and *Fixed-interest* and *Gold Mines* indices.

The Government Securities Index is an unweighted geometric mean of approximately eleven gilts, from one-year to undated stocks. The index was started at 100 in 1926. The Fixed-interest Index, on the other hand, is an unweighted arithmetic mean, comprising the six undated gilts plus local authority and public board fixed-interest stocks and corporate loanstock and preference shares. It was started at 100 in 1928. See Table 10.3.

Specialist indices are also produced for Smaller Companies, the USM, and the Third Market, by Hoare Govett, Datastream, and Buckmaster and Moore respectively.

Overseas share indices need to be treated with caution, because they are not all of the same type. The best-known – the *Dow-Jones Industrial Average* – is an unweighted arithmetic mean of 30 leading shares on the New York Stock Exchange. It includes oil and commodity companies and even a public utility – American Telegraph and Telephone. Because of its method of construction, the performance of the Index corresponds to that of a portfolio in which the relative value of each holding is proportional to share price rather than market capitalization. There are Dow-Jones averages for transportation and utilities as well as industrials. (Chartists pay particular attention to the relationship between the transportation and industrial indices.) More useful measures for portfolio comparison purposes are the *Standard and Poors* indices, which are weighted arithmetic indices similar to

Table 10.3 *Financial Times* indices (excluding *FT*–Actuaries indices), 5 July 1990

FINANCIAL TIMES STOCK INDICES

	July 4	July 3	July 2	June 29	June 28	Year Ago	1990 High	1990 Low	Since Compilation High	Since Compilation Low
Government Secs	79.34	79.39	79.80	79.97	79.89	85.72	84.20 (2/1)	74.13 (30/4)	127.4 (9/1/35)	49.18 (3/1/75)
Fixed Interest	88.06	88.05	88.19	88.22	88.19	96.52	92.91 (8/1)	83.80 (30/4)	105.4 (28/11/47)	50.53 (3/1/75)
Ordinary Share	1881.1	1894.7	1896.6	1899.9	1887.8	1798.0	1968.3 (3/1)	1653.6 (30/4)	2008.6 (5/9/89)	49.4 (26/6/40)
Gold Mines	183.4	181.3	182.6	176.8	176.1	199.1	378.5 (6/2)	167.9 (15/6)	734.7 (15/2/83)	43.5 (26/10/71)
FT-SE 100 Share	2355.5	2371.7	2372.0	2374.6	2355.7	2162.9	2463.7 (3/1)	2103.4 (30/4)	2463.7 (3/1/90)	986.9 (23/7/84)

Ord. Div. Yield	4.93	4.88	4.88	4.87	4.91	4.47	Basis 100 Govt. Secs 15/10/26, Fixed int. 1928,
Earning Yld %(full)	10.87	10.78	10.76	10.75	10.83	10.52	Ordinary 1/7/35, Gold mines 12/9/55. Basis 1000
P/E Ratio(Net)(☆)	11.15	11.24	11.26	11.27	11.19	11.47	FT-SE 100 31/12/83. ☆ Nil 11.03

SEAQ Bargns 4.45pm	21,517	23,823	22,505	23,661	22,288	19,615
Equity Turnover(£m)†	-	786.74	563.07	783.76	761.42	956.05
Equity Bargains†	-	23,810	22,342	22,587	21,924	22,880
Shares Traded (ml)†	-	417.4	263.9	343.3	373.2	346.9

GILT EDGED ACTIVITY

Indices*	July 3	July 2
Gilt Edged Bargains	101.0	92.2
5 – Day average	99.6	100.8

Ordinary Share Index, Hourly changes   Day's High 1890.8   Day's Low 1879.0

Open 1890.8	9 am 1888.8	10 am 1884.5	11 am 1880.0	12 pm 1882.1	1 pm 1881.0	2 pm 1879.1	3 pm 1880.3	4 pm 1880.7

*SE Activity 1974.
†Excluding intra-market business
& Overseas turnover.

FT-SE, Hourly changes   Day's High 2366.8   Day's Low 2352.7

Open 2366.8	9 am 2364.3	10 am 2357.4	11 am 2353.4	12 pm 2355.8	1 pm 2355.0	2 pm 2353.8	3 pm 2354.9	4 pm 2355.3

London report and latest
Share index: Tel. 0898 123001.

the *FT*–Actuaries Indices. There are indices for 400 industrials, 20 transportation, 40 public utility, and 40 financial shares, which together make up the *Composite 500 Stock Index*.

10.6 Influences on share indices

Determinants of individual share prices were discussed in chapter 9. Share price indices reflect changes in share prices in aggregate. It should be remembered that the stock market is a 'barometer' of corporate performance, rather than a 'thermometer'. This means that investors look to the future, and attempt to anticipate changes in corporate fundamentals, not simply reacting to them when they occur. This applies both to the performance of individual shares and to the stock market in general.

The investment community anticipates changes in the level of unemployment, inflation, money supply, balance of payments, Government spending, and overseas interest rates because all of these will have important implications for aggregate profits, dividends, and domestic interest rates. Other important influences on the stock market in general are changes of Government; imposition or removal of direct controls on wages, prices, or dividends; nationalization or privatization; changes in dealing costs; changes in the attraction of alternative investments, such as building societies or property; the size of new flotations or rights issues; and changes in investor sentiment. The last was dramatically illustrated when the fall on Wall Street on 'Black Monday' – 19 October 1987 – was almost immediately followed by falls on all the other major stock markets, including the UK's.

10.7 The efficient market hypothesis

The *efficient market hypothesis* (EMH) is a theory that capital markets operate to a high degree of perfection. Its roots lie in the *random walk hypothesis* (RWH), which postulates that share price changes are of a random, rather than correlated, nature.

Technical analysis – whether using chartism or mechanical trading rules – is essentially based on the premise that past share prices can, in some way, be used to predict future share prices. This is denied by the 'random walkers', who have subjected the evidence to very extensive statistical tests both in the United Kingdom and, primarily, in the USA. Serial correlation (the connection between price changes in successive periods, or after a time-lag) was generally found to be insignificant, and the numbers of successive positive and negative price changes were close to those that could be expected from chance. After all, if you toss a fair coin, you may experience a run of 'heads' or 'tails' purely by chance. If 'red' comes up six times in a row at roulette, the outcome of the next spin of the wheel is no more likely to be red than black, provided the wheel is unbiased. Similarly with share prices: stock market cycles, showing both 'bull' and 'bear' markets, can be simulated purely by using a random-number machine.

The RWH has been summarized by one American writer as: 'Prices have no memory, and yesterday has nothing to do with tomorrow. Every day starts

'He's an economic forecaster and I don't like the way he's eating, drinking, and being merry.'

out fifty–fifty. Yesterday's price discounted everything yesterday.' In other words, the best 'guesstimate' of the share price tomorrow, or next week, is the share price today. In the longer run, there will be random movements about an upward trend.

Advocates of technical analysis have argued that the type of tests conducted were unfair because they were too rigid: they simply extrapolated price trends, and did not allow for the subtlety of chartism. But whenever trading rules, such as relative strength and filters (see chapter 9), were tested, they almost invariably failed to generate sufficient profit to cover expenses. The EMH was developed to explain these statistical results. In its 'weak form' it says that any information conveyed by the series of past prices of a share is recognized by investors and is discounted in the current share price.

The 'semi-strong form' of the EMH is a much more serious challenge to conventional beliefs in investment analysis. It asserts that current prices fully reflect not only past prices but all publicly available information about companies, and that efforts to acquire and analyse this knowledge cannot be expected to produce superior investment results. It suggests that the analysis of the annual report and accounts, for example, is largely a waste of time – not because analysts are no good but because they are too good. All leading companies are under the constant examination of a large number of highly skilled analysts who peruse and constantly reassess all the available information, and this is reflected in their investment recommendations. The share price is a consensus of their advice to investors, particularly fund managers. Greater weight is given to analysts with the best track records in each sector. Consequently, at any time, the actual share price approximates to its 'intrinsic' (or true) value.

One of the bases of fundamental analysis is the search for shares that are significantly under- or overvalued. But, according to the EMH, competition between expert analysts and rational profit-seeking investors ensures that such discrepancies are insignificant. The marginal analyst is, in effect, redundant. The degree of efficiency is greater in the USA than in the United Kingdom because of the larger number of analysts and the fuller disclosure of information, both by companies and by the stock exchanges. Academic ideas tend to be better received by the financial community in the USA than in the United Kingdom. Even in the USA, however, although some were willing to assent to the weaker assertion and seriously question technical analysis, very few indeed could accept the implications of the stronger form, and thereby abandon fundamental analysis. The irony is that if they did so to any substantial degree the market would cease to be efficient.

The 'semi-strong' approach supposes that the share reflects and encapsulates all that is publicly ascertainable about a company, and that its price instantaneously adjusts to any new economic information that becomes available. Technical analysis, on the other hand, generally assumes that information is only gradually disclosed, filtering from one group of investors to another.

The 'strong form' of the EMH is the hypothesis that share prices fully reflect not only what is generally known through public information but also private information. It seems almost to suggest that 'insider knowledge' is of no use, which could be the case if that information could have been anticipated from other sources. Appropriate tests have consisted of analyses of the performances of portfolios managed by groups that might have special information, and logging the share predictions of investment analysts.

The conclusion, from numerous studies of unit trusts in the United Kingdom and mutual funds in the USA, is that, allowing for differences in risk, no fund does consistently better than average. If any fund could do so, it would indicate an element of inefficiency in the price-making process. This conclusion has been confirmed, less rigorously but more vividly, by commentators picking shares from the *Financial Times* or the *Wall Street Journal* with the aid of a pin or a dart: on average the portfolios thus selected performed no better and no worse than professionally managed funds.

The EMH was subject to much ridicule at the time of 'Black Monday'. How could shares be worth one-quarter less at the end of a week when no dramatic news had been announced? Moreover, in recent years, a number of anomalies in relation to the EMH have been identified. These can be grouped together under the following headings: the 'weekend' effect, the 'January effect', the 'small-company' effect, and the 'low P/E ratio' effect.

Studies in numerous countries, and over different time-periods, have shown that share returns on a Monday consistently appear to be below average, while those in January are consistently higher on average than in any other month. These results are inconsistent with the 'weak' form of market efficiency, but are unlikely to be of sufficient magnitude to outweigh dealing expenses.

The 'small-company' effect and the 'low P/E ratio' effect are likely to be of greater importance. The small-company effect refers to evidence that small companies' shares appear to outperform large companies' shares, even after allowing for differences in risk. The Hoare Govett Smaller Companies Index, which consists of the smallest 10 per cent of fully listed companies on the UK Stock Exchange, has outperformed the *FT*–Actuaries All-Share Index by an average of nearly 6 per cent per year between 1955 and 1989. Smaller companies find it easier to expand at a fast rate as compared with well-established companies, who may already dominate their market sector. Moreover, many small firms are too small for institutional shareholders to show great interest, and therefore they are not so fully researched. One other reason why small firms offer higher returns is their poorer marketability, reflected in wider dealing spreads. Because of their greater risk of liquidation, and highly volatile share prices, small companies require greater diversification.

A number of unit trusts specialize in small companies. However, investors should be reminded that the very fact that such results have received considerable publicity, and attracted institutional interest, means that they are less likely to be achieved in the future. Many small companies sell on relatively high P/E ratios. As Lex in the *Financial Times* commented, 'It could be that the very fact of it becoming known will put an end to it, and that its promoters will end up like travel writers who publicize a select little fishing village only to see it turn into Torremolinos.'

Similarly, it has been found that shares on low P/E ratios have on average consistently outperformed those on high P/E ratios, even after allowing for differences in risk. This may be because investors are over-optimistic with regard to shares selling on high P/E ratios, while being overpessimistic with shares on low P/E ratios.

Both the 'small-company' and the 'low P/E ratio' effect are apparently in contradiction with the semi-strong form of market efficiency.

However, despite these apparent anomalies, the investor should realize that the general concept of an efficient market remains valid. What then are the implications for investment policy?

First, the EMH emphasizes the incompleteness of fundamental analysis that fails to consider whether the share price already reflects the substance of the analysis. A very optimistic forecast of a company's future earnings is no justification in itself for buying a share; it is necessary that the analyst's forecasts be significantly more optimistic than other forecasts. In which case, is it credible?

The investor is best advised to split his or her equity portfolio into two – one part 'active', the other 'passive'. The exact proportions will depend on the investor's attitude to risk, but the 'passive' one should normally be the larger. The 'passive' part is a recognition of the futility of scrutinizing leading shares: it accepts that they are fairly valued. These funds will be essentially invested 'in the Index'. The largest hundred companies in terms of market capitalization account for around 70 per cent of the *FT*–Actuaries All-Share Index. If these are reasonably efficiently valued, it is almost impossible to 'beat the Index' by partial selection from them. It is far better to gain the full benefits of diversification by investing 'across the board' in a broad-based unit trust, investment trust, or insurance fund. This is already widely accepted in the UK with the growth of '*index*' or '*tracker*' funds which are specifically designed to replicate the performance of a chosen index (see fig. 10.4).

The 'active' element of the portfolio can be devoted to second-line shares. Small companies in particular are likely to be of less interest to institutions and subject to less close analysis, and offer a chance of discovering valuation discrepancies. 'Recovery stocks' are another type of share that may be partly overlooked because of their high risk and low capitalization. Some unlisted shares may offer opportunities for discovering inefficiencies in the pricing mechanism if they are quoted on the Unlisted Securities Market.

Those investors or fund managers who are sceptical of the EMH believe it is possible to make above-average returns by operating an 'active' investment policy. One version of this approach is to buy or sell 'sectors'. The basis of this approach is to buy sectors that are expected to perform well against an index such as the *FT*–Actuaries All-Share Index and to sell those that are expected to do badly. A variety of techniques can be used. Technical analysis

95%
did not.

Morgan Grenfell's UK Equity Index Tracker Trust maintains a fully invested position to track the FT-A All Share Index. 🦋 As at 1st November 1989, 95% of all UK invested unit trusts had failed to outperform this fund since its launch on 8th November 1988.* 🦋

Callfree 0800 282465.

UK Equity Index Tracker

*Source: Micropal, offer to bid, income reinvested. The value of this investment may fluctuate and is not guaranteed. Past performance is no guarantee of future returns. Issued by Morgan Grenfell Unit Trust Managers Limited. Member of Lautro, IMRO and the UTA.

Source: Morgan Grenfell

Fig. 10.4   An advertisement for a UK Equity Index Tracker fund

can be employed to determine which sectors have shown relative strength and weakness over some past period, such as the last six months. Some investors would argue that such trends can be expected to continue; others would advocate a policy of 'contrary thinking', on the basis that the worst-performing sectors are likely to show the most recovery in the longer term. Fundamental analysis involves choosing sectors according to the state of the economy, particularly the course of the business cycle.

Some words of warning are apposite at this juncture, however. Firstly, not all sectors are homogeneous, particularly as companies increasingly diversify. Most of the variation in an individual share price is either specific to that company or general to the stock market, rather than being attributable to the industry or sector. Secondly, it is easy to be beguiled by stockbroker/dealers' short-term enthusiasm for a sector but fail to realize any subsequent profits at the appropriate time. This is particularly a danger for the insurance companies and pension funds, where the shares become 'locked' in the funds.

For the investor with a shorter-term perspective, the fundamental approach suggests that the leading sectors at the start of a potential bull market are those benefiting most from the fall in interest rates and easing of credit that usually precede the upturn in the economic cycle. Lower interest rates give a boost to discount houses and hire-purchase companies, both of which usually lend longer-term than they borrow. Hire-purchase firms, too, benefit from the new business generated by consumer durable sales (television sets, washing machines, hi-fi, cars), which are heavily influenced by the availability of credit. This improvement in business also provides a direct benefit to the stores sector. Other beneficiaries will be contracting and construction (in the form of house-building, which is sensitive to the cost and availability of mortgage finance – see fig. 10.5); building materials; and

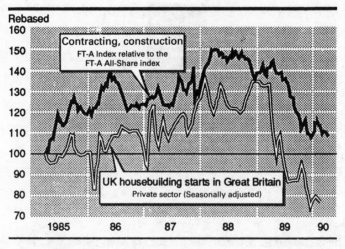

Source: *Financial Times*

Fig. 10.5 Relative performance of the contracting and construction sector

property, which, like contracting and construction, tends to have high levels of borrowing, although less short-term than in the early 1970s.

Banks traditionally suffered when interest rates fell, because of the so-called 'endowment element' in their borrowed funds. This is interest-free money obtained from current accounts. A fall in interest rates lowers the margin between the rate the banks can charge for such money and its zero cost. In recent years this effect has become less noticeable, however, because of the greater proportion of funds obtained from the wholesale money markets, the interest paid on current accounts to be offset against bank charges, and the diversification into areas such as hire purchase.

Increased economic activity at the retail level may initially be met largely by a rundown in stocks, but the impetus will soon be felt by manufacturing industry – especially industries with high operating gearing, such as chemicals. Eventually the capital goods sector, with items such as machine tools, will have increased business with the need to expand and re-equip industry. Investment expenditure is much more unstable than consumer expenditure, and capital goods industries tend to oscillate from relative prosperity to depression.

Short-term speculation 'in and out' of different sectors of the market is a very hazardous business, involving frequent and unpredictable changes in sentiment that do not necessarily coincide with changes in fundamentals. The average investor who adopts an active dealing policy is more than likely to fare worse than by following a 'buy-and-hold' policy, taking into account dealing expenses, including the market-makers' turn.

10.8 Questions

1. (a) The *Financial Times* Ordinary Share Index:

   A provides a general overview of the strength of the market.
   B is based on an unweighted arithmetic mean.
   C is the basis for options in the traded options market.
   D was launched in 1962, more than 20 years before the *FT*–SE 100 Share Index.

   (b) The mathematical basis of the *Financial Times* Ordinary Share Index is the unweighted geometric mean. The geometric mean (average) of the following four share prices – 47p, 67p, 78p, and 96p – (to the nearest penny) is:

   A 70p.
   B 72p.
   C 74p.
   D 76p.

   (c) The *Financial Times*–Actuaries indices include two principal equity price indices, the All-Share Index and a sub-index containing the Industrial Group and the Oil and Gas shares.

	The All-Share Index has approximately:	The sub-index is called:
A	1000 constituents.	the 750 Share Index.
B	900 constituents.	the 750 Share Index.
C	800 constituents.	the 500 Share Index.
D	700 constituents.	the 500 Share Index.

(d) The semi-strong form of the efficient market theory:

A states that the current share price reflects all the market's current knowledge about the share in question.

B confirms that technical analysts can predict turning points in share price behaviour.

C implies that fundamental analysis is invalid.

D suggests that it is impossible to out-perform the market even with insider information.

(e) An index fund is an investment fund:

A consisting mainly of gilts with a small weighting of options.

B linked specifically to index-linked gilts.

C based on the constituents of a specific equity index.

D whose principal aim is to provide a real return – in equities or gilts.

2. (a) List the strengths and weaknesses of the Food Retailing sector, a sub-section of the Consumer Group of the *Financial Times*–Actuaries All-Share Index.

(b) The questions set out below are based on the following extracts from the *Financial Times*–Actuaries Indices on 30 March 1988:

	Index No. on 30.3.88	Earnings Yield (%)	Gross Dividend Yield (%)	P/E ratio	Index No. on 30.3.87
CONSUMER GROUP (185)	1031.75	8.78	3.67	14.52	1144.34
Food Manufacturing (23)	816.64	9.83	4.19	13.01	866.12
Food Retailing (16)	2053.92	7.82	3.12	17.21	2122.54
Health and Household Products (10)	1784.73	6.81	2.73	17.39	2203.35
Textiles (18)	561.46	12.32	4.46	9.32	696.98
ALL-SHARE INDEX (714)	904.13	—	4.35	—	988.79

(i) Which of the four Consumer Group sectors above performed worst (i.e. fell by the greatest percentage) over the period 30 March 1987 to 30 March 1988? Show your calculations.

(ii) State with reasons which of the sectors you consider to be the most growth-oriented on the basis of the information provided.

(iii) Why is no earnings yield or P/E ratio provided for the All-Share Index?

(iv) What is the mathematical basis for these indices? Why is it important that this basis is used?

(CIB 10/88)

3. A new client says he knows virtually nothing about investment, and asks you to explain what precisely is meant by the term 'equities', and the influences on them both individually and in aggregate. Summarize your answer.

(SIE 12/88)

4. Joe Campbell, the personnel director of a small quoted company in the Midlands, comes to London to discuss the transfer of the management of the company's pension fund, currently valued at more than £30 million, to one of the large financial conglomerates.

Joe is himself a very active investor, frequently buying and selling shares, and over lunch he talks to Jane Fraser, the fund manager concerned, about his personal investment problems. He mentions *inter alia* that, while he has usually felt quite pleased with his results, he recently compared his performance with a well-known index and was surprised to find that his own portfolio had underperformed the index in each of the last three years. In the course of their conversation, Jane comments on the sheer difficulty of 'picking winners', even for professionals like herself, and adds that the majority of fund managers fail to 'beat the market'.

Required:

(a) With which index is Joe most likely to have compared his performance? State, with reasons, why Joe would have used this index?

(b) Suggest probable reasons (apart from the selection of poor investments) why Joe's investment record has not been very successful.

(c) Write brief notes on the investment theory which Jane is hinting at.

(d) Briefly describe the investment vehicle which relies upon 'passive', in contrast to 'active', investment. Could this meet Joe's or the company's needs?

(CIB 5/89)

11 Options, warrants, and convertibles

An *option* is a right to buy or sell a security at a fixed price at some time in the future. Some can be traded, but most – known as *traditional*, *conventional*, or *negotiated* options – cannot.

11.1 Traditional options

Traditional options are contracts by which a 'giver' pays a sum of money, called *option money*, to a 'taker' for the right to buy (*call option*) or the right to sell (*put option*) a stated amount of a particular security at a stated price, known as the *striking price* or *exercise price*. As well as 'call' and 'put' options, there are *double options* which confer the right to buy *or* sell. This right lasts at the most for two and a half to three months (to be more precise, for a period encompassing no more than seven ensuing account days). Furthermore, during this period the exercising of the right under the option is restricted to certain specified days, known as *declaration days* (normally the second Thursday of each fortnightly account period). The 'account' is discussed in section 15.2.

With a call option, the exercise price is the offer price of the security in the market at the time of dealing, plus about $2\frac{1}{2}$ per cent for *contango*, which is the cost of financing the option over the period until its expiry date. For example, if the price of ICI ordinary shares is shown at £10.83, this represents the middle-market price – the midpoint of the prices at which market-makers were willing to buy and sell. The actual bid–offer prices might have been £10.75–£10.91. The exercise price could therefore be approximately £10.91+27p = £11.18.

The exercise price of a put option is usually simply the bid price of the security, although it is sometimes increased by part of the contango interest being passed on to the potential seller.

The exercise price of an option is *cum all*, but any rights which accrue to the security become effective only if the option is exercised, in which case they follow the security from the seller to the buyer. The exercise price of a double option is fixed somewhere between the ruling bid and offer prices of the security.

In general the amount of option money (or *rate*) that is paid for an option depends on demand and supply; in bull markets call options are more expensive than put options, whereas in bear markets the reverse is true. Three-month call rates and details of option deals are published daily in the *Financial Times*. The rate for a three months' option on a blue-chip company is probably around 5 to 10 per cent of the share price; for instance, on 2 February 1990 a three-month call option in ICI cost 90p, while the middle-market price of the share was £10.83.

The attractions of options to the investor are:

(a) They are high-risk, high-return investments. The gearing effect can be enormous. In our ICI example, assuming that the exercise price was £11.18, a 20 per cent increase in the share price to £13.00 would mean the option was worth £1.82 (i.e. £13.00−£11.18) if exercised immediately – a capital profit of 102 per cent, ignoring expenses. Equally, if the share price fell, or if it failed to reach £11.18 during the three months, the option would be worthless. These features are nevertheless attractive to short-term speculators and investors seeking capital gain rather than income.

(b) They provide a means of 'hedging one's bets'. For example, suppose that an investor had made a reasonable gain on shares in ICI and believed that the time was ripe to take the profits, but felt that the shares might go still higher. In order to protect the gain while still retaining an interest in any further capital appreciation, he or she could take out an option as an 'insurance policy' – either retaining the shares and taking out a put option, or selling them and buying a call option. Put options are sometimes used in this way to provide protection against a fall in the market when securities in a deceased's estate cannot be sold immediately because of a delay in the granting of probate. Selling shares and simultaneously taking out a call option also provides a means of raising short-term funds, as an alternative to using the shares as collateral for borrowing.

Options are more the province of the professional market operator, close to market information and able to keep a careful eye on trends, than of the amateur. The share price must move by about 12 to 15 per cent before any profit can be made. This is partly because of the cost of the option itself, but also because the broker/dealer's commission (for conventional options of more than one account) is assessed on the exercise price rather than the option price. Commission on sixteen-day options is usually lower than on the three-month option. Similarly, because of the shorter period, the option itself is cheaper – usually around 3 per cent for a put or call in a leading share. Sixteen-day options run from the second Tuesday of one account to the second Thursday of the next.

Many options are bought which are never taken up.

11.2 Traded options

Dealings in traded options – options that can be bought and sold before their expiry dates – began in London in April 1978, five years after the successful introduction of such a system in Chicago. The market deals in both call and put options for individual ordinary shares. Traded options in individual shares are allocated to one of three possible expiry cycles: January, April, July, October; or February, May, August, November; or March, June, September, December.

For each of the three expiry dates there is at least one exercise price below the price of the underlying security and at least one above it. In the case of call options, these are referred to respectively as *in the money* and *out of the money*; with puts, the reverse applies. 'In the money' means that the option has *intrinsic value* – that is, value if exercised immediately. In Table 11.1 the right to buy at 360p when the share price is 384p has intrinsic value of 24p. The call option premium for the March 360 call was 35p. The difference between the option premium, 35p, and the intrinsic value, 24p, is 11p – this is known as *'time value'* and it will gradually depreciate over the life of the option – see fig. 11.1.

Table 11.1 Traded options – Midland Bank Plc

Share price	Exercise price	Call premiums			Put premiums		
		March 1990	June 1990	September 1990	March 1990	June 1990	September 1990
384p	360p	35p	43p	53p	14p	17p	27p
384p	390p	13p	29p	38p	31p	37p	43p

Source: *Financial Times*, 3 February 1990.

Note that the time value is greater the later the expiry date of the option. The 390 calls are 'out of the money' – they have no intrinsic value; the whole of the premiums are time value. 'Out-of-the-money' options have the greater risk because they will be worthless at expiry if the share price does not move from its present level, but they also offer the greatest potential reward, because the option premium is small in relation to the underlying share price.

The six permutations of expiry date and exercise price are officially designated as six *series* of the same *class* of option. As the price of the underlying security moves, a new series is introduced whenever the share closes outside the range of exercise prices for at least two days. Series are also replaced as they expire with the passage of time.

The initial seller of a call option is said to be the *writer* of the option. 'Writers' are investors who accept premiums for taking the risk that they will have to deliver stock in the event of an option being exercised. Note that writing an option is much riskier than buying an option: the writer is obligated to fulfil the contract if it is exercised. Particularly risky is writing call options on shares which the writer does not possess. If the option is

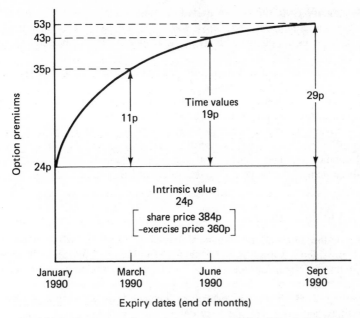

Fig. 11.1   Intrinsic value and time value, Midland Bank 360 Calls

exercised, the 'naked' writer will have to pay the prevailing price in the market to acquire the shares and deliver them to the buyer of the call option.

The difference between the traditional and traded option markets lies not only in the extension of the option period but also in that both buyers and sellers of traded options can close their bargains whenever they like during the life of the options, simply by completing a counterpart transaction. The writer buys an equivalent option; the buyer sells one. This is not possible with traditional options, where both parties are 'locked in' until the option is exercised or expires. This secondary market for traded options can exist only because of the common exercise prices and expiry dates of series within a particular class.

Option contracts on individual shares relate to 1000 shares; deals for amounts larger than this figure require multiple contracts. Unlike traditional options, traded ones can be exercised at any time except on the last day of an account. Unlike trading in company and Government securities, the London Derivatives Exchange (incorporating the former London Traded Options Market (LTOM)) is conducted by means of an auction system of bids and offers made in open competition on the trading floor. There is a facility for members of the public whereby any frustrated orders can be placed on the Public Limit Order Board (PLOB) and they then take precedence over all other business at their price. They must, however, be designated either *good for the day* (GD) or *good till cancelled* (GTC).

By January 1990, there were traded options in nearly seventy major UK and overseas companies, the *FT*–SE 100 Index, and two currency contracts; and their prices are published daily in the *Financial Times*. Their details are illustrated in Table 11.2.

All bargains except for currency options were registered and settled at the London Options Clearing House (LOCH), which was a wholly owned subsidiary of the Stock Exchange. When a holder exercised a contract, LOCH selected a writer, by a random selection process, to deliver or receive the securities in accordance with the terms of the contract. Writers were required to deposit a margin on written options with LOCH as security for performance of their obligations. Arrangements may change with the establishment of the London Derivatives Exchange.

11.3 Financial futures

The London International Financial Exchange (LIFFE), which began in 1982, provided a market in both financial futures and options. A financial future differs from an option in that with a financial future both the buyer and the writer of the contract are obligated to fulfil the contract; the contract cannot lapse. However, the features of financial futures – such as standard quantities, agreed prices, delivery dates, and a clearing house – are very similar to traded options. Consequently, in order to avoid overlap, the LTOM and LIFFE amalgamated at the end of 1990, to form the *London Derivatives Exchange*, housed in a building over Cannon Street railway station in the City.

LIFFE provided a variety of financial futures contracts in UK and overseas short- and long-term interest-bearing securities, the *FT*–SE 100 Index, and exchange-rate contracts. It has also provided a market in traded options on interest-rate futures – that is, an option on a futures contract relating to the movement in the prices of short- and long-term domestic or overseas interest-bearing investments, such as three-month sterling and Eurodollar, long-dated gilts, and German and US Government bonds. In addition, LIFFE offered US $/£ sterling, and US $/Deutschmark contracts which were directly competitive with those of the LTOM.

11.4 Share options and profit-sharing for directors and workers

If share options are granted to directors or other employees of a company, an income tax liability is normally incurred on the difference between the market value at the time of exercising the option and the cost of the shares. However, there are two specially approved schemes which provide for remission against the income tax liability.

11.4.1 SAYE-linked share option scheme
Gains made at the time an option is exercised are exempt from income tax

Table 11.2 Summary of traded options contracts

Type of traded option	Based on	Normal contract size	Expiry cycles	Maximum life	Expiry day	Hours of trading
UK equity	Ordinary shares of UK publicly listed companies	1000 shares (N.B. Vaal Reefs: 100 shares)	Jan., April, July, Oct.; or Feb., May, Aug., Nov.; or Mar., June, Sept., and Dec.	9 months	Normally two days before last day of dealings for last complete Stock Exchange account of expiry month	9.05 to 4.05 on business days
Index	FT–SE 100	£10×index value	Nearest four months	4 months	Last business day of month	9.05 to 4.05 on business days
Currencies	US$/£ US$/DM	US$/£–£12 500 US$/DM–DM62 500	Mar., June, Sept., Dec., plus two nearest months	12 months	Refer to your broker	9.00 to 4.05 on business days
International equity	Ordinary shares of certain listed large foreign public companies	100 shares	Jan., April, July, Oct.; or Feb., May, Aug., Nov.; or Mar., June, Sept., and Dec.	9 months	Refer to your broker	Please consult your broker

Source: The International Stock Exchange, London (1989)

provided that the scheme satisfies a number of conditions, in particular:

(a) The scheme must be available to all directors and employees with five or more years full-time service.
(b) The maximum monthly contribution into an approved Save-As-You-Earn scheme with a bank, building society, or National Savings is limited to £150 per month.
(c) The option must normally be exercised at the end of five or seven years.
(d) The exercise price must not normally be less than 80 per cent of the market value of the shares at the time the option is granted.

If the shares are subsequently sold, a liability for capital gains tax is incurred on the difference between the market value at the time of sale and the price paid by the investor at the time of exercising the option. Nevertheless, this remains an attractive scheme because the interest on the SAYE contract is tax-free, and, if the share price performs poorly during the period of the option, the investor can simply let the option lapse and take the tax-free interest to invest elsewhere. The rate of interest is 8.86 per cent compounded rate over five years, and 9.15 per cent if held for seven years.

11.4.2 Senior executives' share option scheme
Another scheme is available which provides for greater benefits. As with the previous scheme, no tax is levied when the option is exercised, but when the shares are sold capital gains tax is levied on the difference between the exercise price and the price at which the shares are sold. The scheme does not have to be available to all employees. The main requirements are:

(a) The value of the shares (at the time the option is granted) on which a person holds options must not exceed the greater of £100 000 or four times salary.
(b) The exercise price must be fixed and not significantly below the market value of the shares at the time the option is granted.
(c) The scheme must be restricted to full-time directors and employees.
(d) The options must normally be exercised only between three and ten years after they have been granted, and not more frequently than once in three years.

11.4.3 Approved profit-sharing schemes
Under this type of scheme, shares can be given free of tax to employees by trustees. The shares which are allocated are limited to the lower of 10 per cent of the employee's salary or £6000. In order to receive Inland Revenue approval, the scheme must be available on similar terms to all employees with five or more years full-time service. No income tax liability is incurred if the shares are transferred by the trustee to the employee after five years. Any subsequent sale by the employee will result in a liability for capital gains tax based on the difference between the sale price and the value of the shares at the time they were transferred by the trustees.

11.4.4 Employee share ownership plans (ESOPs)

These ESOPs are encouraged under the provisions of the Finance Act 1989. They can be run in conjunction with approved profit-sharing schemes. However, the general rules applying to ESOPS give trustees more flexibility than is permitted under the approved schemes. Distributions out of the trust must be on similar terms to all beneficiaries, but allow for different distributions according to length of service and level of remuneration. The trustees must distribute the shares to employees within seven years of acquisition. There are no special tax reliefs either for the trust or for the employees receiving shares out of it, unless it operates in conjunction with an approved profit-sharing scheme trust.

11.5 Warrants

A *warrant* is a quoted option certificate issued by a company, entitling the holder to subscribe for a given number (or fraction) of ordinary shares in the company at a predetermined price (the *exercise price*) on any one of a selection of specified future dates. A share warrant is in effect a long-dated call option 'written' by the company instead of an investor. Most companies that have issued warrants have done so as part of a 'package deal', with the warrants having been originally attached to loan stock. Subsequently the warrants have been detached, quoted, and dealt in separately from the loan stock, but usually such warrants can be exercised either by subscribing for shares in cash or by exchanging the loan stock.

Warrants produce no income; they are not part of a company's share capital, although they threaten to dilute the equity. In the balance sheet they are normally shown as part of capital reserves. They usually have a limited life, although a very few are perpetual. The company is required by the Stock Exchange to protect warrant-holders from suffering loss due to rights issues or bonus issues reducing the price of the ordinary shares.

At or near any of the stipulated exercise dates, the floor to the market price of the warrant will be its intrinsic value – the difference between the share price and the exercise price (multiplied by the number of shares to which the warrant entitles the holder). But warrants frequently sell for considerably more than their intrinsic value. For example, Ladbroke Group had warrants outstanding that give the holders the right to buy one ordinary share at a cash price of 171.2p for every warrant held. At one point, the warrant was selling for 30p when the ordinary shares were quoted at 95p, giving a *conversion premium* (warrant price plus exercise price minus share price) of 106.2p. It may seem incredible that the warrant was worth anything when the exercise price was nearly double the share price itself! The answer lies in the fact that at that time the warrant had a remaining life of over thirteen years, while the company's growth prospects were above average. In this example there was no intrinsic value in the price of the warrant at 30p – the whole price represented 'time value'. It was in effect an 'out-of-the-money' option. As long as there is any probability of the share price exceeding the exercise price during this period, the warrant will have some value. But a warrant can never sell for more than the value of the shares into which it can be converted.

The size of the conversion premium depends on the remaining life of the warrant, the volatility of the share, and the exercise price relative to the share price. The greater these three factors, the larger the conversion premium, as all three features are attractive to warrant-holders. Obviously, as the end of the warrant's life approaches, the premium will disappear as the warrant must either be exercised or become worthless. As the share price and the dividend income increase, the *gearing attraction* (the extent to which the price of the warrant changes more than proportionately to that of the underlying share) is reduced and it becomes increasingly expensive to forgo income by not exercising the option. Sometimes the exercise price increases periodically, and this may encourage early exercise of the warrant.

In fig. 11.2 we plot on the vertical axis the price of an equivalent warrant, by which is meant the price of that fraction of, or multiple of, a basic warrant which will enable one share to be purchased.

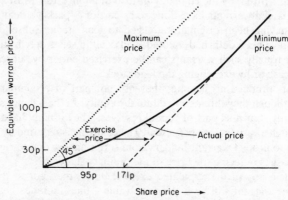

Fig. 11.2   The price range of a warrant (figures for the Ladbroke Group are applied to the model)

If it can be exercised in the very near future, the warrant should never sell for less than its intrinsic value – the difference between the share price and the exercise price – and never for more than the share price.

The attractions of warrants are as follows:

To the company

(a) No initial servicing costs are involved, as no interest or dividends are paid on the warrant itself. As warrants are not normally converted early in life (as long as the premium exists), this situation may extend many years into the future.

(b) They are an attractive supplement for unsecured loan stock where adequate security is lacking.
(c) They provide a means of selling deferred equity to 'outsiders', particularly when the company believes its share price to be overvalued. It the market is grossly over-optimistic, the proceeds of the issue may be obtained without conversion taking place – that is, the warrants become worthless. The Stock Exchange regulations, however, provide that quoted companies must obtain the consent of their ordinary shareholders in general meeting to an issue of warrants other than to existing shareholders.

To the investor

(a) As warrants provide no income, all return is in the form of capital gain.
(b) Warrants offer high risk/return opportunities to the investor, particularly where the exercise price is close to the share price. For example, if the share price is £1 and the exercise price 90p, then the intrinsic value – the minimum value for the warrant – is 10p. A 10 per cent rise in the share price would lead to a 100 per cent increase in the value of the warrant (that is, minimum value of warrant = £1.10−90p = 20p). The ratio of the market price of the ordinary share to the adjusted market price (per share) of the warrant is one which some technical analysts calculate and refer to as a measure of gearing.

11.6 Convertible stocks

Convertible debentures or loan stocks are fixed-interest securities with rights for conversion into ordinary shares at the holder's option and under specified terms and conditions.

There are many different convertible loan stocks, with various conversion rights, and it is impossible to generalize about them. Some have a short conversion period, such as a month, in each of a number of consecutive years. Some have a precise date on which conversion can be carried out. Some may be converted a few years after the stock is first issued, others not for many years ahead. All convertible loan stocks have redemption dates, but these are often of only academic interest as the company usually retains a right to redeem any stock outstanding once a certain percentage of the stock has been converted.

The *conversion ratio* is the number of shares the holder of a convertible receives when his or her security is surrendered on conversion. This number can be fixed, or may vary depending on when conversion takes place. The *conversion price* is the effective price paid for a way into the ordinary shares; that is:

$$\text{conversion price} = \frac{\text{market value of convertible}}{\text{conversion ratio}}$$

This can then be compared with the actual market price of the ordinary shares to determine the *conversion premium*:

$$\frac{\text{conversion}}{\text{premium}} = \frac{\text{conversion}}{\text{price}} - \frac{\text{market price}}{\text{of ordinary share}}$$

The larger the conversion premium, the more expensive the convertible is as a way of buying ordinary shares.

The *option cost* or *rights premium* is how much more expensive a convertible is as compared with a 'straight' debenture or loan stock (that is, one without conversion rights):

option cost per share =

$$\frac{\text{market value of convertible} - \text{value as straight loan stock}}{\text{conversion ratio}}$$

Conversion rights are worth having, but the likelihood of exercising them will depend on the remaining life of the convertible and the size of the conversion premium. If the convertible has a long conversion period remaining and the conversion premium is small, the conversion rights are valuable, and the convertible will sell at a substantial premium over a comparable straight issue.

As an illustration, at one time Wilkinson Match had £11.1 million 10 per cent convertible outstanding, redeemable between five and nineteen years in the future. The stock, selling at a market price of £80, could be converted into 40 ordinary shares for a further four years. The ordinary shares were selling for £1.70. The conversion price was £2.00 per share and the conversion premium was therefore 30p a share, or 18 per cent. The convertible had a high redemption yield, suggesting that at the time investors did not consider the conversion rights particularly attractive and were not willing to buy the stock on a much lower yield than comparable straight debentures.

Because convertibles can be valued either as a straight loan stock or as a means into the equity, the minimum price tends to be set by the higher of these two figures. In an efficient market the convertible should never sell for less than an otherwise identical straight loan stock, and as the share price rises it tends to pull the convertible's price up with it. In our example, if Wilkinson Match's share price rose to £3.00, the convertible would be worth a minimum of £120 (40×£3.00).

The valuation of a convertible is illustrated in fig. 11.3. The conversion premium exists because of the *downside protection* – the 'floor', provided by the convertible as compared with direct ownership of the equity – and because of the income differential, as the interest yield on the convertible usually exceeds the dividend yield from the equivalent shares. As the share price increases and the remaining conversion period shortens, so the conversion premium narrows.

When a possible conversion day is imminent, the convertible should never

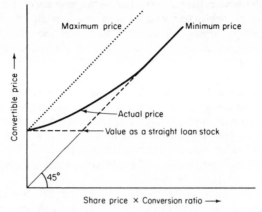

Fig. 11.3   The price range of a convertible stock

sell for less than the value of the shares into which it is convertible, or the straight loan stock, and never for more than the shares plus the loan stock.

The attractions of convertibles are as follows:

To the company

(a) Convertibles are issued as unsecured loan stock by companies without sufficient assets for a full mortgage debenture. The extra risk is compensated for by the opportunity to participate in the success of the business, through conversion, without the full risks of equity-holders.

(b) The cash-flow implications are good, in that convertibles can be sold on lower yields than straight loan stocks if the conversion rights are attractive. Allied to tax relief, this means that the debt servicing can be relatively light in the early years, and so may be useful in the finance of projects with long gestation periods.

(c) It is sometimes suggested that convertibles are a way of selling deferred equity at a premium when the stock market is depressed. This can be misleading, however, since, although the conversion price is at a premium over the share price at the time of issue, it may well be at a significant discount when compared with the price of the equity at the time of conversion. Moreover, the company cannot set the conversion price totally independently of the prevailing share price, since the initial conversion premium will determine how much investors are willing to pay for the option element and the convertible as a whole. In fact, since the company is in reality selling a loan stock and a call option, it should logically issue convertibles at a time when it believes its share price is *overvalued*. After all, a 'writer' of a call option – which the company is in this circumstance – may take the opposite view to a buyer of a call option as to the future performance of the shares.

(d) Convertibles have in the past been part of the currency of take-over bids. In this respect they have provided an indirect method of selling highly priced equity to 'outside' investors. The convertible gives the vendor shareholders a continuing, but secure, stake in the business taken over.

To the investor

(a) There is no limit to the 'upside' potential of a convertible, but the downside is generally limited to the value of a straight loan stock. This can be a more effective protection against risk than a 'stop-loss' order placed with a broker/dealer. Convertibles are most suitable for investment in enterprises where the outcome is uncertain.

(b) They are attractive to trustees of funds where there are restrictions on the equity content of the portfolio. They are regarded as 'narrower-range' investments in the Trustee Investments Act 1961 (see chapter 22). When converted they must be transferred into the wider-range section of the portfolio, but in the meantime they provide a 'back-door' way of boosting the equity content of the fund.

11.7 Conclusion

Options and warrants are sometimes referred to as 'geared' investments, because they are more volatile than the underlying ordinary shares into which they can be converted. Options will tend to be more risky than warrants because of their shorter lifespan. The most risky options are 'out-of-the-money' ones, since their premium consists entirely of 'time value', which will waste away over the life of the option. The reduction in the highest rate of income tax has diminished the relative attraction of options and warrants on the basis of tax efficiency.

Convertibles are more volatile than a simple, straightforward debt security, but less risky than holding the equivalent shares directly. Thus the investor is offered a choice of investments more volatile than the equivalent equity – options and warrants – or less – convertibles. The choice will partly depend upon the risk/return preferences of the investor.

11.8 Questions

1. (a) In the traded options market a contract represents:

   A 100 shares.
   B 500 shares.
   C 1000 shares.
   D 5000 shares.

   (b) 'In-the-money' options:

   A have only 'time value'.

B include put options where the share price is less than the exercise price.

C are more risky than 'out-of-the-money' options.

D are always 'negotiated' options.

(c) A company has issued warrants which are exercisable on the basis of one warrant for one ordinary share. The subscription price for the ordinary shares is 200p and the first exercise date is in 1993. The current price of the ordinary shares is 197p and that of the warrants is 15p. What is the warrant premium?

A 3p.

B 9p.

C 12p.

D 18p.

(d) State *two* differences between traded options and warrants.

2. The prices of the following securities (and other relevant details) have been taken from two editions of the *Financial Times*, for Wednesday 7 December 1988 and Monday 6 February 1989 respectively. They relate to three separate issues of The Peninsular and Oriental Steamship Company (P & O). One of Britain's oldest companies, P & O was incorporated by Royal Charter in 1840. The deferred stock (£1 units) is, in reality, ordinary shares and should be considered as such in your answers.

Wednesday 7 December 1988

Deferred (£1)	α	536p
6.3% Conv. Red. Pref. (£1)	γ	148p
Warrants 1988/92	β	46p

Monday 6 February 1989

Deferred (£1)	α	654p
6.3% Conv. Red. Pref. (£1)	γ	185p
Warrants 1988/92	β	78p

The convertible redeemable preference shares (CRPS) are convertible into deferred stock on 1 July from 1985 to 1990 inclusive, the terms being £340 of the CRPS for £100 of deferred stock.

The warrants entitle holders to subscribe for units of deferred stock at 750p per unit within one month of the distribution of the annual report in the years 1988 to 1992.

Required:

(a) Calculate and comment upon the changes in price of all three issues over the two-month period.

(b) Calculate and explain, using the prices at 6 February, the following:

   (i) the conversion premium/discount on the CRPS; and

   (ii) the warrant premium.

(CIB 10/89)

3. In 1991 a customer has received notification of impending conversion dates in respect of two convertible unsecured loan stocks:

  (i) ABC plc 12% convertible unsecured loan stock, 2003, is convertible into 25p ordinary shares on 25 May each year from 1991 to 2001 inclusive at the rate of 30 shares for every £100 stock. The market price of the ordinary shares is 280p. The market price of the convertible is £105. Net dividends per ordinary share in respect of the year ended 31 March 1991 totalled 9.8p a share.

  (ii) XYZ plc 5% convertible unsecured loan stock, 1998, is convertible into 25p ordinary shares on 28 May each year from 1982 to 1991 inclusive at the rate of 38 shares for every £100 stock. The market price of the ordinary shares is 370p. The market price of the convertible stock is £142. Net dividends per ordinary share in respect of the year ended 31 March 1991 totalled 7.77p.

  (a) Calculate the conversion premium (or discount) in each case.

  (b) What action would you advise your customer to take? Give reasons for your advice and show any relevant calculations.

  (c) What are the advantages of convertible unsecured loan stocks from the point of view of the issuing company?

(CIB 4/83)

4. At a time when the equity markets are volatile, a long-established client asks you how convertibles and options might be used to hedge risk. Draft a response, explaining their main features and how they can be used to hedge the downside risk of an equity portfolio.

(SIE 7/88)

12 New issues

In this chapter we shall discuss mainly two types of new issue:

(a) the bringing to the market of companies that require a full Stock Exchange listing;
(b) the raising of additional capital by companies that already have a quotation.

12.1 Going public

Most large companies have had modest beginnings. Except for companies which have been floated off larger concerns and certain investment companies, most of today's household names started as small businesses, sometimes a very long time ago. Many companies whose names will be equally familiar to the next generation are now small businesses and obscure private companies.

The small business is often turned into a company because of tax considerations. All profits made by a sole trader or a partnership are taxed as the income of the proprietor or partners. With certain restrictions to avoid abuse, the profits of a company are taxed as company profits at the rate of corporation tax, and profits may be carried forward. In addition, the company structure enables friends and relatives of the founder to put their money into the business to facilitate expansion by means other than private loans. They can take up ordinary capital which gives them in return for their investment at least the nominal right to have a say in the way the company is run.

There comes a time with a successful and expanding company when both the resources of the founder's friends and relatives and the willingness of the company's bankers to extend credit facilities come to an end, and it is necessary to look elsewhere for funds for further expansion. At this point a merchant bank may be persuaded to take a financial interest in the company, or perhaps stock or shares will be taken up by a company in the 3i group, such as the Industrial and Commercial Finance Corporation, or in the Estate Duties Investment Trust Ltd, which is managed by 3i.

Once outside finance from sources like these has been brought in, the next step must be the eventual flotation of the company. At some time in the future, the general public will be offered shares to enable the merchant bank or other institution to realize part, at least, of its investment, and for further outside finance to be raised. As mentioned in chapter 7, 'Company securities', there is a distinction between private, public, and publicly quoted companies. A public company must have a minimum issued share capital of £50 000. But most public companies are not quoted on the Stock Exchange.

'He passed away unlisted and unquoted.'

The advantages of quotation may be summarized as follows:

(a) shares become more readily realizable;
(b) share valuation depends on market forces, rather than negotiation or the subjective views of people like accountants, surveyors, or stockbroker/dealers;
(c) the existence of a ready market facilitates the disposal of shares on death for inheritance tax purposes;
(d) the company itself will find it easier and less expensive to raise capital;
(e) it will facilitate take-over activity.
(f) it improves the status of the company.

The procedure for companies seeking a Stock Exchange listing is laid down in the Financial Services Act, which incorporates the European Community's legal requirements for the listing of securities.

12.2 Types of quotation

12.2.1 First tier (the 'Official List')

This market is for companies which require a full listing. It is in effect the 'first division'. Companies are required to offer a minimum of 25 per cent of the ordinary shares to the general public, and the company must have a minimum trading record of three years. A minimum market capitalization of £700 000 is also required, but the *de facto* minimum size requirement is much larger – at least £10 million. The Stock Exchange's listing rules set out both the requirements which must be met to obtain a full UK listing and the 'Continuing Obligations' which must be adhered to after entry. These rules and requirements are to be found in the Stock Exchange's *Admission of Securities to Listing* – commonly referred to as the 'Yellow Book'.

12.2.2 Second tier

This is known as the *Unlisted Securities Market* (USM) and was established in 1980 to meet the needs of the smaller but fast-growing entrepreneurial type of company. Its requirements differ in three principal respects from those of the first tier:

(a) Companies are required to offer only 10 per cent of their equity to the general public.
(b) Only a two-year minimum trading record is required.
(c) There is no minimum market capitalization.

Apart from these three points, second-tier companies are treated almost exactly as first-tier, fully listed companies. They must sign a 'General Undertaking', which is a commitment to follow a set of rules of future behaviour, disclosure, dealings, and financial probity, very similar to those in the Continuing Obligations. The initial requirements and General Undertaking are contained in a Stock Exchange publication *The Unlisted Securities Market*, colloquially known as the 'Green Book'. In fact the very name 'Unlisted Securities Market' is a misnomer, as the *Stock Exchange Daily Official List* carries records of bargains made, although various fiscal and legal provisions distinguish between 'listed' and 'unlisted' securities and could limit institutional investment in this market. The Stock Exchange has therefore deliberately maintained the distinction between the USM and listed securities, both to provide an incentive for companies to 'move up' and to maintain the status of listed companies. For the personal investor, from the dealing point of view, there is virtually no difference between dealing in the first- and the second-tier markets.

12.2.3 The Third Market

The Third Market was established in 1987 to provide an even freer regime than the USM for small, entrepreneurial-type companies to come to the market. It laid down no minimum percentage of equity to be released and no minimum size requirements, and, although there was normally a requirement of at least one year's audited trading record, new fully researched ventures were permitted. One particular advantage was that Business Expansion Scheme (BES) companies – discussed in section 12.14 – were permitted on the Third Market, but not in the Official List or the USM.

In the case of the Third Market, the Stock Exchange relied on a sponsor – usually a member firm of the Stock Exchange – to vet the issue, instead of its own Quotations Department. Companies had to sign a *Third Market General Undertaking*, covering a range of issues, such as releases of information, holding of meetings, share transfers, and restrictions on share dealings by directors.

An amalgamation of the USM and the Third Market took place at the end of 1990, partly to comply with European Community regulations and partly because the Third Market had not grown at the rate expected. By the end of 1989 there were over 400 companies remaining on the USM, from over 750 who had come to that market at some time since its inception. The Third Market consisted of little more than 60 companies.

12.2.4 Other methods of quotation

Rule 535(2) of the Stock Exchange provides a means of investing in unquoted companies. It enables relatively infrequent transactions to take place in shares of small public companies, often with sporting connections, such as Aston Villa Football Club Plc or Wimbledon Lawn Tennis Club. Each company is briefly scrutinized by the Stock Exchange and each deal requires specific approval. This is not a Stock Exchange guarantee; it is simply an attempt to ensure a fair 'arm's length' price for each transaction. Companies whose shares are traded under this rule are themselves unregulated by the Stock Exchange.

There is also a smaller 'over-the-counter' (OTC) market operated by investment bankers, such as Granville & Co. Ltd. They provide a market in a small number of securities, and their prices are quoted in a daily advertisement in the *Financial Times*.

12.3 'Offers for subscription'

Formerly known as 'prospectus' issues, this method of issue was predominant in the early twentieth century but has now largely been superseded by the offer for sale. In the case of an offer for subscription, the company itself invites applications from the public. One disadvantage of this method is that, unless underwriting is arranged, the issuing body cannot be certain that the total number of shares will be applied for. If underwriting is to be arranged, it is far simpler to have a specialized issuing house arrange the whole issue. Another drawback is that an offer for subscription does not provide for the offer of *vendor* shares – shares already owned by existing shareholders – but is restricted to the offer of new capital.

Offers for subscription are now almost entirely restricted to the issue of Government and public authority stocks, except for BES issues and occasionally for the launch of a new investment trust company.

12.4 Fixed-price offers for sale

The most common method of bringing new companies to the Official List is the offer for sale. A City institution, such as a merchant bank that is a member of the British Merchant Bankers Association, buys a block of shares from the existing shareholders and offers them to the general public at a fixed price. The listing particulars of the issue are published together with an application form which the investor can fill in and send off with a cheque to the bank or other institution handling the issue. Copies of the form can also be obtained from other leading banks and financial institutions.

Usually about three to five days elapse between the date of the advertisements and the closing date for applications. All applications submitted by 10 a.m. on that day are accepted if they are in order, but if the offer is oversubscribed at that time the subscription lists close officially after about one minute. If the offer is not fully subscribed, the lists remain open in the hope of further applications arriving, although only applications delayed in the post are likely to be received. Oversubscription means that the offer is a success, and the extent of the oversubscription is some guide to the price at which dealings will open on the Stock Exchange.

If the offer is oversubscribed, the issuing house scales down the applications and quite often the smaller applications are subject to a ballot. Many small investors thus receive no shares and their money will be returned to them. Applications for very large numbers of shares, usually those from institutions, will receive only a small percentage of the shares applied for.

If the offer is undersubscribed, all applications are allotted in full and the issuing house could find itself left with a large block of shares. To avoid this, the issue may be underwritten by certain institutions.

12.5 Underwriting new issues

Underwriting commission is payable to those who undertake to subscribe for a certain number of shares or debentures if shareholders and members of the public do not take up the whole of the issue for which subscriptions are invited. It is usual for issues to be underwritten: in the first case to ensure that the issuing house is not left with a large number of shares it cannot easily sell and, in the second, so that the company concerned is sure of obtaining the cash it requires. Even when an issue appears certain to succeed, an unforeseen event, such as the death of one of the promoters or a sudden slump in share prices generally, may endanger the issue's success. Hence the practice of underwriting an issue.

The issuing house arranges the underwriting contracts, and the underwriting commission of perhaps 2 per cent on the total amount to be subscribed is paid direct to it. The issuing house does not usually take on all the responsibility of the issue, but shares it out among other issuing houses, insurance companies, investment trusts, and stockbroker/dealers: it pays these sub-underwriters a commission on the amount each of them is willing to underwrite, say 1½ per cent. The sub-underwriters are primarily responsible for accepting, *pro rata* (in proportion), shares not taken up by the public; if they fail to do this, the issuing house accepts responsibility. The issuing house receives an *overriding commission* for this contingent liability, in our example ½ per cent.

When the underwriter or a sub-underwriter considers an issue to be a good investment, it may underwrite so much of the issue *firm*; this means that, if the whole issue is subscribed for by the public so that the underwriters are not called upon to take up any of it, the underwriter may be allotted the shares which it has applied for 'firm'.

12.6 Stags and stagging

A *stag* is generally defined as a speculator on the Stock Exchange who subscribes to a new issue with no intention of holding the shares allotted to him or her permanently but hoping to sell the allotment at a profit as soon as dealings begin. The public 'offer for sale' is said to be the most democratic method of issue, because the general public is given the opportunity of subscribing. It is, however, always difficult to fix the 'right' price and, while orthodox opinion holds that the perfect issue is one that goes to a small premium, others maintain that a heavy oversubscription is good publicity – the share gains popularity and the issuing house is regarded as successful.

The abuse of stagging is brought about by multiple applications – perhaps dozens of applications by a single applicant – and, worst of all, applications accompanied by cheques either only partly covered or not covered at all by cash at the banks. In order to curb these abuses, the following remedies have been suggested or attempted:

(a) a requirement that all cheques sent with applications should be cleared before allotment is made:
(b) the exclusion of multiple applications;
(c) a requirement that applicants should send bankers' drafts or certified cheques with their applications;
(d) tender issues.

12.7 Offers for sale by tender

A tender is an offer for sale except that the price of the shares is not fixed in advance. Tender issues are not common but they have been used from time to time, and are sometimes used by the Government to launch a new issue. Their principal advantage to the issuing body is that they avoid difficulties over fixing the issue price. Such difficulties can occur in volatile markets on an offer for sale, as the issue price has to be decided far enough in advance for all the printing and advertising to be arranged. With a tender issue, the applicant has to state the price at which he or she is prepared to purchase the number of shares applied for. To take a very simple example, assume that 1 000 000 shares are offered at a minimum tender price of £1 and applications are received as follows:

> 200 000 shares tendered for at £1.25
> 300 000 shares tendered for at £1.20
> 500 000 shares tendered for at £1.15
> 800 000 shares tendered for at £1.05
> 700 000 shares tendered for at £1.00

The issue is oversubscribed, and the one million shares offered will be allotted at £1.15 per share to those who tendered at or above this price. Those who tendered more than this will receive a refund with their allotment.

Usually the number of shares applied for at the striking price exceeds the number available and a ballot of those tendering at that price may have to be held, although those tendering more will receive allotments in full. Occasionally, when allotment by this method would produce a narrow range of allottees, the Stock Exchange may require the larger allotments to be scaled down and the striking price reduced accordingly to increase the number of successful applicants.

12.8 Placings (or 'selective marketings')

A placing is sometimes used to bring new companies to the market and is most often used for the issue of fixed-interest stocks. A City institution may buy the stock or shares and arrange for the placing of the issue with various funds or companies known to be interested in taking up such issues. Alternatively, the company itself may ask its stockbroker/dealers to place the issue with their own clients. There is also a Stock Exchange requirement to place one quarter of a share issue with the clients of another broker/dealer in the case of larger placings.

Placings are allowed only where there is not likely to be a significant demand for the securities and where the market value of the securities being placed does not exceed £15 million for a full listing or £5 million on the USM. This is the most popular method for companies coming to the USM or the Third Market. Although a prospectus or 'listing particulars' are required (see section 12.10), advertising and other costs are much lower than for an offer for sale. Shares that are placed frequently go to an even more substantial premium than shares offered for sale, however, suggesting that one of the 'costs' – too low an initial price – is not always fully taken into account.

12.9 Introductions

An introduction to the market is used when a company already has a fairly large number of individual shareholdings. It involves only the granting of a quotation by the Stock Exchange for the company's shares. Overseas securities which are well-established public companies in their own countries frequently come to the market by way of an introduction – see fig. 12.1.

Because no capital is being offered for sale, no published prospectus is required under the Companies Act 1985, although the Stock Exchange does insist on a similar document being made available so that the intending shareholder has a measure of protection. It may be that a number of shares will be made available to the market at the time dealings begin, but in any

---

This advertisement is issued in compliance with the regulations of the Council of The International Stock Exchange of the United Kingdom and the Republic of Ireland Limited. It does not constitute an offer or invitation to any person to subscribe for or to purchase any securities of Millicom Incorporated ("Millicom").

MILLICOM INCORPORATED
(Incorporated in the State of Delaware, USA)

INTRODUCTION TO THE
INTERNATIONAL STOCK EXCHANGE IN LONDON

Sponsored by
JAMES CAPEL & CO. LIMITED
and
BEAR, STEARNS INTERNATIONAL LIMITED

Share Capital	Authorised	Issued*
Shares of Preferred Stock of $1.00 each	$2,000,000	–
Shares of Common Stock of $0.01 each	$200,000	$152,133.30
*net of $18,680.06 nominal of Common Stock in Treasury	$2,200,000	$152,133.30

Millicom is the holding company of a diversified international group that concentrates on establishing and enhancing asset values in telecommunications and related businesses. Millicom is developing cellular telephone and personal messaging systems as well as satellite television services in a number of countries worldwide.

Application has been made to the Council of The International Stock Exchange for the issued shares of Common Stock of $0.01 par value in the Company to be admitted to the Official List and it is expected that dealings in such shares will commence on Monday, 4th December, 1989. Details are available in the statistical services of Extel Financial Limited. Copies of listing particulars relating to Millicom and the introduction may be obtained during normal business hours on any weekday up to and including 1st December, 1989 from The International Stock Exchange, 46-50 Finsbury Square, London EC2 and during normal business hours on any weekday up to and including 12th December, 1989 from:

James Capel & Co. Limited	Millicom Cellular (U.K.) Limited	Bear, Stearns International Limited
6 Bevis Marks	South Bank Business Centre	9 Devonshire Square
London EC3A 7JQ	Ponton Road	London EC2M 4YL
	London SW8 5BI	

29th November, 1989

Source: Millicom Incorporated

Fig. 12.1   A formal notice of an introduction

event this method does permit the sale of large numbers of shares by a few shareholders to the general investing public over a period of time.

12.10 'Listing particulars' and prospectuses

Admission to the Official List requires the preparation of *'listing particulars'*, which give investors information about a company and the securities for which it is seeking a listing. The contents are laid down in the 'Yellow Book' and the Financial Services Act 1986. A similar document, simply called a *'prospectus'*, is normally required for the USM and Third Market. 'Listing particulars' and prospectuses provide a detailed history of a company, including audited accounts for the requisite number of years.

12.11 Advertising

'Listing particulars' and prospectuses have to be made available to investors. The mass of information may not materially assist the average investor to assess the merits of the issue, but the fact that it has been published does provide protection since it will have been carefully prepared and checked and will have passed through the hands of many expert professional people. The prospects for the shares at the time and price of issue will be discussed by financial journalists in the daily papers, and to the average investor their comments may be more readable and more interesting than the 'Listing particulars' or prospectus.

The advertising requirements vary according to the size and method of the issue, and the tier of the market to which it applies. An offer for sale on the Official List in excess of £15 million will require the 'listing particulars' to be published in full in two daily newspapers. At the other extreme, a small placing or introduction will require only one formal notice (for example, a 'box' advertisement) in the daily press, with full details of the issue being available from Extel.

12.12 The cost of flotation

The cost of an offer for sale or an offer for subscription greatly exceeds the cost of either a placing or an introduction, and the costs of entry to the USM or Third Market tend to be lower than for the Official List. Expenses include sponsor's fees, broker's fees, underwriting or placing commission, account-ants' fees, tax advisers' and solicitors' fees, advertising and printing costs, Stock Exchange charges, registrars' and bankers' fees, and stamp duty. On average, costs absorb at least 5 per cent of the sums raised.

12.13 Privatization issues

In selling off State enterprises, the UK Government in recent years has been concerned more with ensuring a successful take-up than with extracting the maximum financial return. This is illustrated in Table 12.1, which shows the 'stagging' profits that short-term investors could have made on privatization issues.

Table 12.1 Privatization – the first weeks of trading (premium to partly paid offer price)

Date	Issue	Premium (%)	
		After 1 day	After 1 month
1982	Britoil	−19	−35
1984	Enterprise Oil	0	−4
1984	British Telecommunications	+86	+113
1986	British Gas	+23	+32
1987	British Airways	+68	+82
1987	Rolls Royce	+68	+41
1987	BAA	+37	+32
1987	BP	−29	−42
1988	British Steel	+4	+2
1989	Water (average of all stocks)	+45	+58

Source: Price Waterhouse.

Most privatization issues have been offers for sale, in partly paid form, aimed at the smaller investor. Some have included a tender element for the larger investors. The promise of vouchers or bonus shares were included in some issues in an attempt to discourage personal investors from taking quick profits.

12.14 The Business Expansion Scheme (BES)

This is a scheme which enables investors to obtain significant tax advantages when subscribing to new issues. It is possible to claim relief against income tax for investment in such schemes, and exemption from capital gains tax when the shares are first sold.

The BES was designed to encourage investment in small, unquoted businesses. To be eligible for tax relief,

(a) the investor must not be connected with the company – he or she cannot be an employee, director, or close relative of a paid director, nor hold more than 30 per cent of the shares;
(b) the investor must be a UK resident;
(c) the shares must be new issues;
(d) the shares must not be quoted on the main market or the USM for at least three years;
(e) the business must not be involved in

  (i) property development where the company has more than 50 per cent of its assets in land or property, unless it is a company letting property on 'assured tenancies';

    (ii) commodities, securities, or futures;
    (iii) banking, insurance, or other financial activities;
    (iv) legal or accounting services;
    (v) farming or forestry.

The minimum investment is £500 for a single company issue and £2000 for a 'fund' issue, where the investment is diversified across a number of schemes. The maximum investment is £40 000 per year. The cost to a 40 per cent taxpayer of contributing the maximum £40 000 could be a net £24 000, since, if income were sufficiently high, £16 000 could be saved in tax by offsetting the contributions against income before computing the income tax liability. Moreover, provided that the shares were held for at least five years, any capital gain realized would be free of capital gains tax.

Set against the tax advantages are a number of disadvantages. These are:

(a) lack of a track record in most cases;
(b) failure and liquidation in many cases;
(c) management charges are often high, and 'cream off' much of the tax advantage;
(d) difficulties in finding buyers for the shares, particularly if the investor needs to realize the investments within the initial five-year period;
(e) poor diversification, even within the 'fund' issues.

The reduction in the rates of income tax and the remissions against capital gains tax have reduced the attraction of BES investments, particularly for basic-rate taxpayers. If inclined to such investments, investors would be well advised to restrict themselves mainly to the assured-tenancy leasehold property schemes, where the risk is less, unless they have thoroughly researched a scheme.

12.15 Unquoted shares

Shares in unquoted companies, where there are no regular purchases and sales of the shares, is generally unattractive to personal investors. Although there are special tax rules which allow investors to claim income tax relief on interest charges incurred on borrowings to finance such investments, and realized losses can be offset against taxable income, the disadvantages of such investments are usually more critical. Small, unquoted companies are generally high-risk investments. The articles of association may restrict the transfer of shares, and may require the shares to be offered to the directors of the company. There is no straightforward method of valuing the shares; sometimes the value is arbitrarily determined by the auditors. The dividend payments may be restricted by the directors for tax reasons. Furthermore, unquoted shares are usually unacceptable to banks and other lenders as collateral. Finally, if the investor is an employee of the company there is the risk of simultaneously losing both employment and capital if the company should go into liquidation.

On the other hand, there have been cases – particularly in respect of management buyouts – where worker shareholders have made far greater capital profits on a subsequent quotation than could ever have been achieved through normal stock market investment in equities.

12.16 Rights issues

Rights issues are the issue of new shares to existing shareholders for cash. Companies often find it necessary to raise additional funds for general expansion, for particular projects, or for the repayment of short-term borrowing which has been incurred for these purposes. Banks and insurance companies in particular have to maintain adequate capital bases and thus quite frequently raise new capital in this manner. This can be done in several ways, and one of them is the issue of additional equity capital.

Additional equity capital must be issued at less than the market price, or else no one would buy the new shares. An issue below the market price to the public at large would adversely affect existing equity-holders, so the issue is made to existing holders in proportion to their holdings. They may either take up the new shares offered to them or dispose of the rights to them to another person. A person acquiring rights pays the market price of the right (the *premium*) to the allottee and the issue price (the *call*) to the company.

12.16.1 The theoretical value of rights
When rights issues are announced, the value of the rights to existing holders and the anticipated premium on the market can be calculated. Assume that a company whose shares are quoted at 180p each is about to make a rights issue of one new ordinary share for every five held, at 120p per share. A holder of ordinary shares would then have this position:

5 old shares at £1.80 each would cost	£ 9.00
1 new share will cost	£ 1.20
6 shares therefore would cost	£10.20
Each share is therefore worth ('ex-rights' price)	£ 1.70

The rights are said to be worth 10p per share, as this is the amount by which the value of each old share will fall when the issue is made. The rights would be expected to command a premium of 50p on the market, as this is the amount by which the value of a share (£1.70) exceeds the sum payable to the company (£1.20). This 50p is known as the *'nil-paid'* price. In fact, of course, prices fluctuate as a result of supply and demand and these calculations are only theoretical.

12.6.2 Market factors
A rights issue generally has the effect of depressing the market price of the underlying shares, for several reasons. One is that, initially, many shareholders will sell their rights, thus depressing the theoretical price of those

rights. The mere fact that the supply of shares has been increased relative to demand is a depressing factor. More fundamental, however, is the investor's reaction to the purpose of the issue. Quite frequently the issue is made to replace short-term borrowings and represents a reduction in the company's gearing. This is good for the company but it may reflect adversely on its future distributions by way of ordinary dividends. (Of course, if the announcement of the rights issue is accompanied by news of future highly profitable projects, the price of the underlying shares could well increase.)

Any fall, however, is likely to be only a short-term phenomenon and the rights issue can therefore provide a good buying opportunity for the investor.

12.6.3 Dealing with rights

A rights issue is made by means of a *provisional letter of allotment* which acts as a receipt for moneys paid to the company as well as a negotiable document on the stock market. Provided that a premium is quoted for the rights, an investor should take up his or her entitlement, or sell it, or sell part of it and take up the balance. If he or she fails to act on the allotment letter, the value of the rights may be lost. Sometimes an issue is made in adverse market conditions and the rights prove to have no value. In this case the shares should not be taken up and the rights will prove unsaleable.

The net 'cost' to a shareholder of taking up the rights or of selling them is exactly the same if the costs of sale are ignored. Sometimes lack of finance prevents a shareholder from taking up all the shares, but shareholders should nevertheless generally base their decision not on the cost of the issue but on the investment merits of the shares themselves. Consider the case of a shareholder holding 1700 shares (quoted at £1.80) and £940 cash:

	Shares		Cash		
	Pre-rights value	Post-rights value	Pre-rights value	Post-rights value	Total value
	£	£	£	£	£
(a) All rights sold	3060	2890	940	1110	4000
(b) All rights taken up	3060	3468	940	532	4000
(c) 100 rights taken up, 240 rights sold	3060	3060	940	940	4000

In case (a), the 340 rights are sold at the premium of 50p, realizing £170, and the price of the share falls to £1.70. In case (b), 340 new shares are purchased at £1.20. The 2040 shares now held are worth £1.70 each. In case (c), the shareholder chooses to take up just as many rights as he or she can afford using the proceeds of the sale of some of the rights. Whereas the shareholder formerly had 1700 shares worth £1.80 each, he or she now has 1800 shares valued at £1.70. The cost of taking up the shares (100×£1.20) is found by selling 240 of the rights (240×50p). Where the shareholder wishes to take up some of the rights without depleting his or her cash, or, to put it another way, to maintain the same proportionate interest in his or her portfolio, the number of rights that should be taken up is found by the formula

$$\text{number of rights taken up} = \frac{\text{nil-paid price}}{\text{'ex-rights' price}} \times \text{number of rights allotted}$$

Only when the shareholder takes up his or her full entitlement does he or she maintain the same proportionate stake in the company.

Occasionally a rights issue fails because for some reason the share price falls dramatically just before or after the issue is announced. If the price drops below that of the new shares, the rights will command no premium and the shareholder will allow them to lapse. As rights issues are usually underwritten, however, the company will receive the money from the underwriters.

Sometimes a company will undertake a '*deep discounted*' rights issue, whereby shares are offered at a larger discount to the previous market price than is the usual practice. By offering the shares at more than say a 25 per cent discount, the company can save on underwriting expenses because it is virtually certain that someone will be willing to take up the rights if there is no likelihood of the market price falling below the offer price.

12.17 Allotment letters

In offers for sale, successful applicants receive *letters of acceptance* or *allocation*, but for subscription offers and rights issues the document received is an *allotment letter*. There is no practical difference between the two documents, and we shall term them both 'allotment letters'.

Allotment letters all follow a fairly standard form (see figs 12.2, 12.3, and 12.4). Apart from the name of the company, the name of the allottee, and details of the issue, there are several important sections. First, there is the calculation of the allotment, based on either the underlying holding or the amount applied for. Secondly, there is the timetable: the date and time by which payments (if any) must be made; the place where payment must be made; the last dates for splitting, renunciation, and registration (see below); and the date when the certificates will be issued. There is, thirdly, a form of renunciation and, fourthly, a registration application form.

12.17.1 Renunciation and splitting

If the original allottee signs the form of renunciation, he or she converts the allotment letter into a valuable, negotiable document. During the period up to the last date for registration, the document may pass *by delivery* (that is, no transfer form is required) in the same way as a bearer security but subject to stamp duty if it is an equity allotment letter. After that date the shares represented by the allotment letter can be transferred only by a transfer form in the usual way.

Splitting is a means of facilitating negotiation of the allotment. A re-

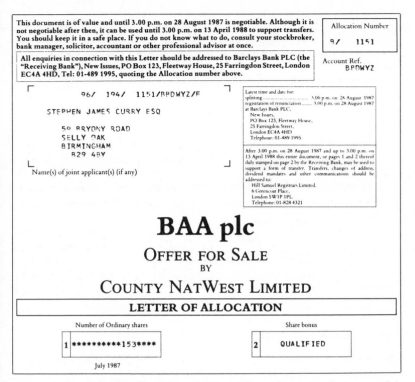

Fig. 12.2   A letter of allocation sent to notify an investor of a successful application for shares

nounced allotment letter can be lodged with the company or its registrar with a request for a number of separate letters in smaller demoninations. This is necessary to complete market deliveries or when the allottee wishes to take up part of the allotment and dispose of the rest.

12.17.2 Calls

Payment is normally made in full on application. Sometimes, however, further payments known as *calls* also have to be made. Where calls have to be paid in respect of an allotment, the most important part of the allotment letter is that dealing with the date and place of payment. Strictly speaking, any earlier payments can be forfeited if a later payment is overdue, but even issuing houses have hearts and by concession often accept later payment. Failure to make a first payment on time, however, will result in a lost allotment.

12.17.3 Registration

If the shares are being taken up and retained by the original allottee, it is not

THIS DOCUMENT IS OF VALUE AND IS NEGOTIABLE. IF YOU DO NOT UNDERSTAND IT YOU SHOULD CONSULT YOUR STOCKBROKER/DEALER, BANK MANAGER, SOLICITOR, ACCOUNTANT OR OTHER PROFESSIONAL ADVISER IMMEDIATELY WHETHER OR NOT YOU WISH TO TAKE UP ANY NEW SHARES. THE OFFER EXPIRES AT 3 p.m. ON 15 SEPTEMBER, 19...

To: *No.* ....

X Y Z COMPANY PLC

Issue of 1 000 000 ordinary shares of 25p each at 80p per share
Payable in full on acceptance not later than 3 p.m. on 15 September 19..

PROVISIONAL LETTER OF ALLOTMENT

Number of Shares held 1 Aug. 19.	Number of new Shares provisionally allotted	Amount payable at 80p per share	At ABC Bank Plc, New Issue Dept., London EC99 .	
			Last date for:	**at 3 p.m. on:**
			SPLITTING (nil paid)	13 September
			ACCEPTANCE	15 September
			SPLITTING (fully paid).	10 October
			REGISTRATION OF RENUNCIATION	12 October

To the Holders of Ordinary Shares.

20 August 19..

DEAR SIR (*or* MADAM).
    As explained in the Company's Circular Letter dated 20 August, and enclosed herewith, your Directors have decided to issue 1 000 000 Shares of 25p each at 80p per Share. You have been provisionally allotted the number of Shares shown above being in the proportion of one new Share for every twenty held by you on 1 August 19.. fractions of a new Share being disregarded.
    The new Shares, when fully paid, will rank *pari passu* with the existing ordinary shares of the Company.
    If you wish to accept this provisional allotment this Allotment Letter, together with a remittance for the sum shown above, must be lodged with ABC Bank Plc, New Issue Dept., London EC99 not later than 3 p.m. on 15 September 19.. This Allotment Letter will be appropriately marked and returned to the person lodging it. Cheques must be payable to 'ABC Bank Plc'.
    Share Certificates will be available in exchange for this allotment letter on and after 15 November 19.. After 31 December 19.. any remaining certificates will be despatched to the registered holders and Allotment Letters will cease to have any value.

By Order of the Board,
T.O. MANN,
Secretary.

Payment received for ABC BANK Plc	XYZ COMPANY PLC
....	Payment due £ ....

Fig. 12.3   A specimen allotment letter for a rights issue

FORM OF RENUNCIATION

FORM X

To the Directors of
  XYZ COMPANY PLC
  I/We hereby renounce my/our right to the Shares comprised in this Allotment Letter in favour of the person(s) named in the Registration Application Form relating to or including such Shares.

  Dated .... day of .... 19 ......

SIGNATURE(S) ....
OF   ....
ALLOTTEE(S) ....

  (In the case of joint holdings ALL must sign. A corporation must affix its seal.)

FORM Y

REGISTRATION APPLICATION FORM

  If Form X is completed this Allotment Letter must be lodged for Registration with Form Y completed.

To the Directors of

  XYZ COMPANY PLC

  I/We request registration in the following name(s) of the shares specified in this Allotment Letter.
  This form must be lodged by an Authorized Depositary unless the following Declaration can be made.
  I/We declare that the person(s) in whose name(s) the Shares are to be registered is/are not resident outside the Scheduled Territories and is/are not acquiring the Shares as the nominee(s) of any person(s) so resident.

      Signature of Declarant ....

      Dated this .... *day of* .... *19* ....

Full name(s) and address(es) of the persons in whose name(s) the shares are to be registered.	
Lodged by:	

Fig. 12.4 Specimen forms of renunciation and registration to be found on the reverse of the allotment letter in fig. 12.3

usually necessary for application for registration to be made. But if the allotment letter is disposed of on the market or by gift, the eventual owner must complete the registration application form and lodge the document where indicated to ensure that a certificate in his or her name is issued in due course. This is usually seen to by the investor's stockbroker/dealer on his or her behalf. Once the registration application form has been completed, the document cannot pass by delivery.

12.18 Capitalization issues

Capitalization issues may be referred to as *scrip* issues or *bonus* issues. They represent only an adjustment to the share capital of a company.

In the course of its normal activities the reserves of a company may increase – perhaps as a result of retaining part of its earnings or of an upward revaluation of fixed assets such as land and buildings. As a consequence, the value of the assets permanently employed in the business may come substantially to exceed the nominal value of the issued capital, the balance forming part of the various reserves. At this stage the company may decide to *capitalize* part of the reserves – that is, to convert reserves into issued share capital. As the reserves belong to the owners of the equity, this normally means that new ordinary shares are issued to existing ordinary shareholders in proportion to their holdings. No payment is due from the shareholder.

The effect of a capitalization issue on the market price of ordinary shares is, other things being equal, to reduce the price in exact proportion to the issue. Thus, if a company with 2 000 000 ordinary shares of £1 in issue decided to reduce its reserve accounts by £1 000 000 and to create £1 000 000 of new ordinary capital, it would issue to shareholders one new ordinary share of £1 for every two such shares already held, and the price of the ordinary shares on the market would fall by one-third. In fact other things are rarely equal, and usually the price after a bonus issue is slightly more than the equivalent price beforehand. This is mainly because a bonus issue is usually accompanied by either a profit statement, an increased dividend rate, an encouraging forecast of future profits, or an upward revaluation of fixed assets – any of which would have the effect of increasing the price of the shares – or by more than one of these. Another reason is that the reduction in the price of a share has the effect of increasing its marketability. There is a freer market for lower-priced shares, for no good reason except that many private investors seem to be put off by 'heavy' (high-priced) shares.

No investment decisions need to be made with capitalization issues. The shares are received in the form of a renounceable share certificate, and no specific action has to be taken unless the holder wishes to sell or otherwise dispose of the bonus shares. In this case all the holder should do is to sign the certificate in the place indicated on the reverse side and hand it to his or her broker or to the transferee.

A bonus issue has only marginal benefits for a holder. If a dividend rate is being maintained on capital increased by a capitalization issue, this is only equivalent to a corresponding increase in rate without an issue. The making of a capitalization issue should not of itself be understood as good news for shareholders, although good news frequently accompanies such an issue.

A capitalization issue, in which new fully paid shares in the same denomination are issued, must be distinguished from a *share split* or subdivision. The share split involves the creation of a larger number of shares with a lower nominal value – for instance, 100 000 £1 shares might become 400 000 25p shares.

12.19 Fractional allotments

Bonus and rights issues often involve fractions of shares. The terms of issue do not usually produce whole numbers of shares to be allotted, except of course with bonus issues on a one- or two-for-one or similar basis. Where a bonus issue gives rise to fractions, these are not allotted to holders but the shares representing fractional allotments are sold by the company and the proceeds are distributed to the holders entitled.

Fractions arising on rights issues are not usually allotted or sold. Sometimes a form is sent to shareholders with their allotment letter enabling them to apply for *excess* shares – shares in excess of their *pro rata* entitlement – at the same price as the rights issue. To those applying, allotments are made out of unallotted fractions and from shares not dealt with by original allottees. Allotments of excess shares are always small but they do represent a genuinely cheap purchase where a reasonable premium applies on the market.

More often, a company sells rights that are not taken up and distributes their value to the shareholders entitled. In these cases no excess share application forms are issued and fractions are ignored altogether. The allotment letters will indicate what is being done, but an allottee should always take action personally if able to do so.

12.20 Offers of different classes of capital

Sometimes holders of equity capital are sent forms or allotment letters in respect of issues of other classes of capital. Where the recipient is the holder of ordinary shares and the document represents a bonus issue of preference shares, there is no problem as only a capitalization of reserves into non-voting capital is taking place. From time to time, however, application forms are received giving the right – sometimes a preferential right over the general public – to apply for an unsecured loan stock or similar issue. Sometimes allotment letters or application forms are received in respect of issues of shares in other companies.

All these documents require careful consideration. A document that has value must say so at the top of the first page. Other application forms may or may not present opportunities for investment on favourable terms and may or may not be negotiable. Any document of this nature requires careful evaluation before any action is taken or before a decision to do nothing is made.

12.21 The timing of new issues

With companies coming newly to the market, the question of timing is fairly simple. Unless it is essential for the issue to be dealt with as soon as possible, most companies try to avoid the troughs of the market fluctuations and wait until a firm bull trend is established before considering a flotation. Not only does this give a better chance of success, but a higher price can be obtained as investors inevitably compare companies new to the market with others already quoted for a guide to a valuation of their shares.

When a company wishes to raise additional capital, there is the question not only of general timing but also of the class of capital to be selected. When equity prices are depressed, a rights issue is to be avoided because of the high cost of paying a dividend on increased capital at the same rate as previously. If a period of moderate interest rates accompanies a depressed equity market, it is probably cheaper to issue a prior charge, as the interest payable costs the company only the equivalent of the initial yield, net of corporation tax.

When equity prices are high, a leading company can make a rights issue which gives only a low initial yield, and this can be cheaper, in the short term, than a prior charge issue. In the long run, however, the company has to take into account the overall cost. Ordinary dividends are normally expected to increase as time goes by, and for tax reasons are much more expensive to the company than interest payments.

In assessing the investment merit of new issues, it is desirable to look at the reasons for the issue being made. All companies making issues take advice from leading City broker/dealers and institutions. If a company chooses to make a rights issue at a time when it appears that fixed-interest issues are more appropriate, extra care is called for in deciding whether to invest. This situation may mean that the company is already overgeared. On the other hand, a fixed-interest issue could indicate that it is unable to support an equity issue with an attractive profit forecast. In any event, a warning signal is sounded for the prospective investor.

12.22 Questions

1. (a) A company may be admitted to the Official List or to the Unlisted Securities Market in various ways.

   (i) Which method involves no marketing of shares?
   (ii) What fundamental condition must be fulfilled before the Stock Exchange will allow this concessionary method of obtaining a quotation?

(b) In an offer for sale by tender:

   A a minimum tender price is set.
   B a maximum tender price is set.
   C both minimum and maximum tender prices are set.
   D tenders will be allowed at any price.

(c) 1 000 000 shares are subject to an offer for sale by tender. The minimum tender price is 125p. Shares are subscribed for as follows:

     150 000   125p   250 000   145p
     200 000   130p   100 000   150p
     350 000   135p   50 000   155p
     250 000   140p

Assuming that the basis of the offer is that the shares will all be issued at the same price, what would be the striking price?

(d) A company's 50p ordinary shares are priced in the market at 100p. The company makes a one-for-two rights issue of new ordinary shares at 70p, ranking *pari passu* with the existing shares. Following the rights issues, the theoretical market value of the old shares will be:

   A 70p.
   B 90p.
   C 60p.
   D 80p.

(e) Stock Exchange Rule 535(2):

   A is to be abolished.
   B applies only to USM securities.
   C permits limited dealings in unquoted shares.
   D concerns suspended shares.

2. Discuss the various methods by which companies may obtain a quotation on the International Stock Exchange (ISE).

                                                (CIB 10/89)

3. (a) Rights issues involve the raising of new equity funds from a company's existing shareholders. Give *two* distinctly different reasons why a company may wish to make a rights issue.

  (b) AKZ plc decided to make a rights issue and, at the date it was announced, the 25p shares were standing at 397p. The announcement caused the price to fall some 10 per cent and, prior to the old shares being marked 'xr' (ex-rights), the price of the old shares ranged from 352p to 370p.

     What explanations can you give for this price behaviour?

  (c) The terms of the rights issue were one new share at 320p for every four shares then held. At the 'xr' date the old shares were quoted

365p–370p. Calculate:

  (i) The theoretical 'ex-rights' price of the old shares on the day they were quoted 'xr' for the first time. (Base your calculation on the 'bid' price quoted above.)
  (ii) The value of the rights per old share and the value of the 'nil-paid' new shares.

(d) The company decided against making a 'deep discounted' rights issue. Why is this type of issue so called and what advantage could it have for the company?

(e) A shareholder who does not want to keep up his allotted shares in full or sell them has two other choices. Briefly describe these two choices.

(f) The new shares are usually traded in 'nil-paid' form for a matter of a few weeks. As such they have the potential to rise or fall in value much faster than the old shares. They are said to have 'gearing' or 'leverage'. Name *three* other *types* of investment which have similar qualities.

(CIB 5/88)

4. A customer of yours who has recently become interested in investment seems rather excited because a company in which he holds shares is making a 'bonus' issue.

(a) What is the correct term for a 'bonus' issue? Explain fully its implications for the financial structure of the company.

(b) The news that the company would shortly make a 'bonus' issue – two new shares for every five existing shares – was immediately followed by an increase in the share price. Suggest possible reasons why the increase in the share price could have been caused by this announcement.

(c) Immediately prior to the old shares being quoted 'xa' they were 812–840p. What does the abbreviation 'xa' mean and what will be the theoretical bid price of the shares now? Indicate clearly any additional assumptions you make and show all calculations.

(CIB 9/87)

13 Take-overs and mergers

13.1 Reasons for take-overs and mergers

A shareholder may at any time encounter a take-over bid, either for a company whose shares he or she owns or by such a company for the shares of another. The small shareholder is unlikely to be able to exercise very much influence in the latter case, but, where an offer is made for the shares which are owned, he or she and fellow shareholders will have a significant influence on the result of the bid.

The terms 'take-over' and 'merger' are often used interchangeably, but there is a technical difference in accounting terms: a merger is a coming together of equals, forming a new company, whereas a take-over involves one company absorbing another. However, a take-over is sometimes referred to as a merger in the financial press, in order to soothe the bruised egos of the victim company's directors and management. Mergers are usually agreed at the outset, but this is by no means always the case with the take-over. The bidder is known as the 'offeror'; the victim company is the 'offeree'.

Often take-over bids arise when a company's earnings are too low to maintain a market price at or near the net asset value. This situation prompts a second company to bid for the first company's voting capital at a price more in line with net asset value, so that it may use the assets to expand its own business. This is often a far cheaper and quicker way of expanding than issuing new capital for cash and then setting up new factories to extend operations. When it takes over another company, an offeror company acquires not only assets but an existing market and an experienced workforce. By merging the interests and operations of the two companies, it should be possible to effect economies and to produce greater efficiency than could be achieved by the two companies operating separately.

Take-overs and mergers usually fall into one of three categories: *horizontal*, *vertical*, or *conglomerate*. Horizontal take-overs involve an amalgamation of companies which are competitors in the same industry. Vertical ones are combinations of companies from different stages of the production process – an example would be an oil company owning businesses involved in oil extraction, refining, and retailing through service stations to the motoring public. Proposed horizontal and vertical take-overs and mergers are strictly monitored by the Office of Fair Trading and the Monopolies and Mergers Commission (MMC), and in most cases a bid is referred to the MMC and permission is refused if the resulting company is likely to control 25 per cent or more of the market.

Conglomerate take-overs and mergers involve companies from often unrelated business areas. The rationale for such combinations is much less obvious, except for the transfer of general managerial expertise from a successful to a less successful company. Such bids generally encounter less opposition from the MMC, but, with one or two notable exceptions – such as Hanson and BTR – the results have often been disappointing. In fact, by the late 1980s the trend towards conglomeration had been to some extent reversed, to be replaced by 'unbundling', sometimes by means of a *management buyout*.

13.2 Hostile bids

A hostile bid for a company is one not welcomed by and opposed by the directors of the target company. The classic defence of a company that is the subject of a hostile take-over bid is to announce profit forecasts for current and future years, in an attempt to prove that the depressed market price is based on a mistaken view of its prospects. Usually increased dividends are forecast, often a bonus issue is announced, and the company sets out to re-establish a higher market rating in order to persuade its shareholders not to accept the bid. Not all bids are defended in this way, and many take-overs go through quietly, but a sufficient number become take-over 'battles' to feed the headlines of the popular press. Often more than one company is bidding at the same time for the shares of the same company. Sometimes a 'victim' company will actively seek another bid from a company to which it is more favourably disposed – often referred to as a 'white knight' – in order to frustrate a hostile predator.

Uneasiness has been expressed about the amount of information available to directors which is not passed on to shareholders, because a considerable number of take-overs fail or the bids have to be raised before they are successful. If a company can defeat a bid by announcing profit forecasts that raise the share price substantially, it is reasonable to ask why these forecasts were not given to shareholders before the bid was made. It may be argued that it is not in the interests of shareholders to disclose detailed forecasts and information except when they are being asked to accept a bid which is too low, but the ordinary shareholders of a company are its proprietors and have a right to be informed of a company's situation – especially if ignorance might cause them to sell their shares on the market too cheaply. Directors have as much duty to shareholders who wish to sell their shares as to those who are buying them. Sometimes a take-over defence reflects more the directors' fears for their jobs than the interests of the shareholders, who might benefit from exchanging their shares for those of a more dynamic company.

Directors sometimes grant themselves long-term service contracts which have to be bought out in the event of a bid. These are colloquially referred to as 'golden parachutes'.

13.3 The City Code on Take-overs and Mergers

Take-over activity is both necessary and healthy in an advanced economy. Sometimes a proposed take-over may seem sensible when viewed from the economic aspects of efficiency and resource allocation but may be questioned because of its adverse effect on jobs. The activities of the 'asset-strippers', who obtain control of companies only to wind them up and make quick profits for themselves, come into this category.

Because the take-over, by its very nature, involves the making of an offer above the current market price for the shares, it is clearly a prime area for activities and manipulations by the unscrupulous. Adverse publicity resulting from this kind of activity does the Stock Exchange and City institutions no good, and in the late 1960s the larger institutions, encouraged by the Bank of England, formed the *Panel on Take-overs and Mergers* to regulate take-over activity. In March 1968 the first City Code was published by the Panel. This has been revised and strengthened several times.

The Code does not prescribe the precise manner in which take-over bids should be made: it states certain general principles and elaborates these in some specific rules. Four of its main principles are

(a) that all shareholders of the same class should be treated equally;
(b) that shareholders should be given adequate information to form a proper judgement;
(c) that directors of the offeree company (the company whose shares are being bid for) should act in the best interests of their shareholders and obtain independent advice, and there must be no unilateral frustration of the bid by the offeree board;
(d) that there should be no false markets in securities during the period of the offer.

It is a cardinal rule that the spirit of the Code, and not merely its letter, be observed. The underlying principle is that there should be equal treatment of all shareholders. For instance, before the Code was introduced, a company might make a generous offer for the directors' and their families' shares, thus acquiring control, and then at a later date make a lower offer to the other shareholders. Such practices are not permitted by the Code.

There are three rules relating to levels of shareholdings. If any company (including its associates and other parties 'acting in concert') acquires through the stock market *10* per cent or more of any class of shares in the twelve months before it makes a take-over bid and during the offer period, then it must offer a cash alternative to all shareholders of that class at the highest price paid during that period. Moreover, if any company acquires *30* per cent or more of the shares in another company (this proportion being regarded as sufficient to give it effective control), then it is required to make a general offer to all shareholders with a cash alternative of at least the highest price paid for these shares in the past twelve months. This is known as a 'mandatory' bid.

All persons owning or controlling *1* per cent or more of the shares involved in a take-over must disclose any dealings made during the offer period. They cannot hide behind nominee names.

If an offer is made which, if successful, would result in the offeror company gaining control, then it must be a term of the offer that it will not become 'unconditional' until the offeror has acquired control. The percentage of the voting shares which a bidder requires before declaring the bid 'unconditional' will be stipulated in the offer document. In the case of a 'mandatory' bid this is 50 per cent, but in other bids this can vary between 50 per cent and 90 per cent. Once the offer has been declared unconditional, the offer must remain open for at least fourteen days more.

Since the authority of the Panel is not statutory, its own powers are limited. It can admonish an offender in private; reprimand the offender publicly; refer the matter to the offender's own professional body or SRO for disciplinary action; or, in the most serious cases, refer the matter to the Serious Fraud Office for further investigation. Recently the Panel has extended its powers by imposing severe financial penalties on companies involved in illegal share-price-support operations, although such fines are subject to judicial review. More generally, appeals against disciplinary rulings can be made to an Appeals Committee.

The behaviour of directors is one of the main concerns of the Code, since it is essential that, as they are in a position of trust, they should always put the interest of shareholders before those of themselves and their associates. The dangers of the unscrupulous use of price-sensitive information – what is widely known as *insider dealing* – have been highlighted in a number of well-publicized take-over scandals, notably in the Guinness take-over of Distillers.

The Take-over Panel can investigate cases of 'insider dealing', but this offence is dealt with outside of the Take-over Code.

Insider dealing involves the purchase or sale of securities, including options on those securities, on the basis of *privileged price-sensitive information* by persons *connected* with a company – including directors, employees, and their close relatives – either at the time of the deal or within the previous six months. It is a criminal offence under the *Companies Securities (Insider Dealing) Act 1985*. The penalties available are an unlimited fine and/or a period of imprisonment of up to seven years.

The Stock Exchange and the Take-over Panel monitor movements in share prices which may indicate insider dealing, particularly as a prelude to the announcement of a bid. Where there is such evidence, the share price quotations of both companies may be temporarily suspended pending a formal announcement.

13.4 Obtaining control

Legally, a company has control of another when it has an absolute majority (over 50 per cent) of the voting shares, but a company needs 75 per cent of the votes to pass special and extraordinary resolutions. In practice, however, it does not need anything like such a large proportion of the shares to obtain *effective* control – the Take-over Code deems 30 per cent to be sufficient. Nevertheless, many companies like to obtain total ownership, for various reasons, and there are provisions in the Companies Act 1985 (section 429 as amended by the Financial Services Act) which prevent a small minority of shareholders from defeating this aim.

For the bidding company to obtain absolute (100 per cent) ownership, it must have received acceptances of 90 per cent of the shares other than any that it held at the date of the bid. If, for example, it already held 5 per cent of the shares, it must receive further acceptances of at least 85.5 per cent of shares (90 per cent of 95 per cent) to invoke section 429.

Whatever the situation, the bidding company must receive the required acceptances within four months of the bid. It must then within two months give notice to the remaining shareholders to acquire their shares, any dissenting shareholders having six weeks to apply to the court to retain their holdings. There is generally little point in a shareholder refusing the offer, as minority shareholders are in a very weak position.

Conversely, a minority shareholder has the right to demand to be bought out by the offeror. If the offeror has acquired 90 per cent or more of the outstanding shares, it must inform any minority shareholders of this fact within one month, and then the minority shareholders have a minimum of three months after the close of the final offer period to exercise their right to be bought out at the same price.

13.5 Take-overs: the shareholders' response

Take-over bids are almost always of short-term benefit to the shareholders of the company bid for. Whether the bid succeeds or not, the price of their shares will rise and, if they do not wish to accept the bid, they have the opportunity to dispose of their holdings on the market at an enhanced price. In any event, the affairs of the company bid for are ventilated, and this can rarely do harm to the shareholders.

If the proposal is for a merger, it is likely to be beneficial to the former shareholders of both companies, in the long run. In the short run, one company's shareholders may gain at the expense of the other's as market prices reflect the merger terms. If the merger really seems to make economic sense, however, the merger will be a 'bull point' and the shares of both companies could rise, reflecting the market's view of improved business and profits prospects. A merger will result in an exchange of shares in the old company for shares in the new one, and there are no capital gains tax considerations.

With a take-over bid the position is rather different. Because the bidding company is offering more than the current market price for the shares of the other company, its shares usually fall in price in the short run. If the directors have got their sums right, however, this should not depress the bidding company's shares unduly, since in due course an expansion of profits should justify the bid. In many contested bids, however, the price ultimately paid is determined more by corporate rivalry than by economic logic.

The main difference between the two offers is in the terms. In a merger, only shares are offered in exchange for shares. In a take-over, the bid may be entirely for cash, or for cash and shares, or it may include a fixed-interest element – perhaps a convertible loan stock.

If the offer is for cash, the shareholder can easily calculate the immediate profit in prospect, taking into account the fact that a cash sale represents a disposal for capital gains tax purposes. Of course the offer, while being immediately attractive, may still fall below the price originally paid.

If the offer is in shares only, the calculations are fairly straightforward. Suppose, for example, that company A, whose shares stand at 200p, offers one of its shares for every two of company B, whose shares are quoted at 80p; the bid is worth 100p a share and there are no capital gains tax considerations. The shares of company A will not remain at 200p, however, nor will company B's automatically rise to 100p. There are two main possibilities. If the bid seems likely to fail, the market may not mark up the shares much beyond the initial 80p. On the other hand, the share could rise well beyond 100p in the belief that either an increased offer or other bidders will appear on the scene, and at this point the shareholders must decide whether to sell in

Table 13.1 Take-overs and mergers

Company bid for	Value of bid per share**	Market price**	Price before bid	Value of bid £ms**	Bidder
Prices in pence unless otherwise indicated					
AMI Healthcare	370*	371	378	245.65	Co.Gen.des Eaux
Br Kidney Pnts IT	✠	305	290	✠	N'thumberl'd Tst
Camford Eng.	305*	315	244	57.92	Markheath
Chemoxy Intl.	450*	443	268	13.30	Suter
City Gate Estates	140*	135	92	19.46	Accura B.V.
Contl.& Ind. Tst.	960	900	843	164.00	Transatlantic
Dunloe House‡	Ir45*§	52	49	7.82	Clayform Props.
Hatfield Estates	230*	239	225	17.32	Lilley
Intl. City Hldgs‡	31	31	34	21.07	York Trust Grp.
Jitra Rubber	52¼	50	50	5.80	Rowe Evans Invs.
Just Rubber	140*	135	72	10.5	Scapa Group
Laing Properties	650*§	682	564	390.80	Pall Mall Props.
Paragon Comms.	153¾	149	128	8.35	Shandwick
Really Useful Grp	233*§	234	218	77.4	Jorraban (No.26)
Regentcrest	15*	14¼	12½	6.8	Wolverhampton
Runciman (Walter)	520*§	548	472	46.8	AB Avena
SAC Intl.‡	105	107	117	21.45	Ricardo Grp.
Sketchley	262	273	249	94.73	Compass
Western Motor	789*	785	675	95.59	Tozer Kemsley

*All cash offer.††Cash alternative. ‡Partial bid. §For capital not already held.‡Unconditional.**Based on 2.30pm prices 23/3/90.†At suspension. §§Shares and cash. ✠ Offer is 105pc of fav of BKPAIT.

Source: *Financial Times*, March 1990

the market or wait in the hope that a better offer will materialize.

If the bid is accepted, the shareholder must make another important decision, namely whether to keep the new holding or to sell in the market. This decision will depend very much on his or her view about the bidding company.

Where the offer is in cash and shares, the cash element is subject to capital gains tax. Suppose that company A's terms were two shares and £1 cash for every five shares of company B – the same offer based on the 200p valuation of company A's shares – and consider the holder of 2000 company B shares purchased at 60p:

Original cost (or March 1982 value, if later)	Acquisition value of company A shares	Capital gain (before inflation adjustment)
2000 shares of company B at 60p £1200		

Acceptance of offer:

800 shares of company A at £2 £1600	£ 960 $\left(£1200\times\dfrac{1600}{2000}\right)$	Deferred until sale of company A shares
Cash £ 400	£ 240 $\left(£1200\times\dfrac{400}{2000}\right)$	£160
£2000 £1200		

Where the offer also concerns, say, a fixed-interest stock, the position is still more complicated. A new loan stock is something of an unknown quantity, and valuing it is not always easy, especially if conversion rights are attached. Many shareholders will not want it, anyway.

Other factors the offeree's shareholders must consider are:

(a) What is the premium over the previous market price of the shares before the bid was rumoured or announced? In the case of quoted companies, this can be found in the *Financial Times* – see Table 13.1. What is the 'exit' P/E ratio, and how does it compare with those of similar companies?

(b) How does the bid price compare with the net asset value of the shares?

(c) Is a higher bid likely? If the market price of the shares stands at a higher level than the offer price, it is indicative that the market is already discounting a higher bid.

(d) If the bid involves a share-for-share exchange, what is likely to happen to the offeror's share price in the immediate future?

(e) Is a referral to the Monopolies and Mergers Commission likely? If so, the market price is likely to be below the offer price.

(f) Is the bid agreed and recommended by the offeree company's directors, or is it to be contested? In most cases, agreed bids will go through with little fuss, but in the case of a hostile bid the shareholder is likely to be bombarded with literature from both the offeror and the offeree.

(g) Has the bid gone unconditional?

Shareholders will normally have 21 days to consider an initial offer document, and a further fourteen days for any revised offer. At the first closing date, the offeror must reveal the level of acceptances, and if it has not gained control it must decide whether simply to keep the offer open in the hope of further acceptances, or to raise the bid, or to let it lapse. On Day 42 from the date of the issue of the original offer documents, shareholders who have accepted the original offer may withdraw acceptances if by this date it has not gone unconditional. Normally by Day 60 the bid must have either been declared unconditional or lapse. However, the timetable can be extended in the event of a rival bid. If it lapses, any remaining acceptances become void.

13.6 Vendor placings and vendor rights issues

A vendor placing is an arrangement to satisfy the offeror who wishes to issue shares and the offeree's shareholders who may wish to receive cash. The offeror company's brokers place the securities acquired on behalf of the offeree's shareholders with institutional and other investors at a predetermined price. The cash realized from the placing passes to the offeree company's shareholders. Sometimes a variant called a *'bought deal'* is used. Bids for the shares are invited from banks and brokers, and the whole issue is sold to the highest bidder.

Shareholders in the offeror company may be concerned at the price at which the shares are placed, or sold as a bought deal. A vendor rights issue is similar to the above except that the offeror's shareholders have the right to claw back shares if they wish to take them up themselves, *pro rata* to their existing holdings.

13.7 Questions

1. (a) State *two* of the general principles of the City Code on Take-overs and Mergers.

   (b) Under the City Code on Take-overs and Mergers, an offer is mandatory when a company holds a specified percentage of the target company's shares. This percentage is:

   A 10 per cent.
   B 15 per cent.
   C 25 per cent.
   D 30 per cent.

(c) A vendor placing is:

    A the popular term for a 'selective marketing'.
    B a technique used in some take-over situations.
    C a form of rights issue.
    D an alternative term for an introduction.

(d) Explain what is meant by 'insider dealing' and state the legislation dealing with this offence.

2. Take-over bids are an almost daily feature in the activities of the Stock Exchange in London. Spectacular battles, involving vast sums of money, often result.
    Required:

(a) What measures are available for the protection of the UK investor who has shares in a company involved in a take-over bid? What penalties can be imposed on companies involved in take-over situations?

(b) Outline the main items which should be contained in the offer document.

(CIB 4/86)

3. Discuss the factors you would take into account when advising a client who is an ordinary shareholder in a company which is subject to a take-over bid.

(SIE 12/87)

4. Jeremy Shilton is a wealthy self-made man whose share portfolio alone is worth in excess of £1 000 000. Recently, following the death of a relative, he received under the will 24 000 ordinary shares of £1 each in EFG Plc. The company, his broker informs him, is not listed on the Stock Exchange, nor are its shares quoted on the Exchange's 'junior markets'. He was intrigued, nevertheless, to learn that trading in the shares does take place from time to time with the approval of the Stock Exchange. The most recent deal was executed at 120p which assumes a P/E ratio (net) of 4.
    Mr Shilton describes the company as 'sleepy but with amazing prospects'. He has seen the accounts for the last five years and the most recent show net asset value per share to be 210p. The main problem, he believes, is the management. The two directors are known to have resisted two take-over approaches within the last three years. Mr Shilton would like to increase his stake in the company to 35 per cent and obtain a seat on the board.
    The other shareholders and their respective holdings are as follows:

James Carlton	Managing Director	60 000
Brian Gough	Director	20 000
Mary Farmer		72 000

Abel Davis	48 000
Elizabeth White	24 000
3 holdings of 3 per cent	36 000
6 holdings of 2 per cent	48 000
59 other shareholders	68 000
(holdings of 1 per cent or less)	

(a) (i) What did Mr Shilton's broker mean by 'junior markets'. State *one* major way in which these markets differ from each other.

(ii) Explain the circumstances (and any conditions) under which dealings in the shares of EFG Plc would appear to have taken place.

(b) Two of Mr Shilton's rights as a shareholder are to attend meetings and vote on resolutions.

(i) List *four* of Mr Shilton's other rights as a shareholder, and any legal obligations he incurred when he inherited the shares.

(ii) At what kind of meeting would a special resolution be put? If all but the 59 very small shareholders attended such a meeting, what would be the minimum number of votes required to pass such a resolution?

(iii) If Mr Shilton wanted voting to take place otherwise than by a show of hands, he could ask four other shareholders to join him in demanding a poll. What alternative measure of support could he attempt to obtain?

(c) (i) Mr Shilton considers the most promising way of increasing his holding to 35 per cent will be to offer 155p a share to the two largest non-director shareholders. Because EFG is a public company, it is subject to the City Code on Take-overs and Mergers, despite its being unlisted. State in what ways Mr Shilton might be breaching the City Code if he follows this course of action.

(ii) On the basis of the limited information provided, comment briefly on the price Mr Shilton is prepared to pay. State clearly any assumptions you make.

(CIB 5/89)

14 The Stock Exchange dealing system

14.1 The International Stock Exchange of the United Kingdom and the Republic of Ireland Ltd (ISE)

Many people still think of the Stock Exchange as the tower block on a piece of land in the City of London surrounded by Threadneedle Street, Old Broad Street, Throgmorton Street, and Bartholomew Lane. Although this building is the administrative centre, its trading floor is redundant, as is the visitors' gallery. Nowadays, dealing in securities is done by means of computer-based visual display units (VDUs) and the telephone, rather than through face-to-face contact. This change came about with the so-called 'Big Bang', in October 1986. Thus the location of Stock Exchange member firms is becoming increasingly irrelevant, apart from contact with their clients.

Up to now, in this book we have often referred to the 'Stock Exchange' but its formal title, since October 1986, when it became recognized, under the Financial Services Act, as a 'recognized investment exchange', has been the 'International Stock Exchange of the United Kingdom and the Republic of Ireland Ltd', abbreviated to 'ISE'.

Before 1965 there were separate trading floors throughout the United Kingdom and the Republic of Ireland. Each was a self-governing institution. Then, in that year, the Federation of Stock Exchanges was formed and, although each exchange maintained a large degree of autonomy, there was more co-operation between them with a movement towards a single national exchange, which came about in March 1973.

Further change was brought about by a combination of two factors. Firstly, in 1978 the Office of Fair Trading began action against the Stock Exchange because of the restrictive practices identified in its rule book. Secondly, foreign-exchange controls were abolished in 1979, and, as a result of the New York Stock Exchange having 'deregulated' in 1975, it became possible for large-scale UK investors to deal in major UK companies either through London or New York. Consequently, the UK Stock Exchange had to be competitive in order to retain business.

In 1983 a deal was struck between the Government and the Stock Exchange, whereby the Government agreed to the withdrawal of its reference to the Restrictive Practices Court provided that the Stock Exchange undertook voluntary reform.

In March 1986, 100 per cent outside ownership of existing and new Stock Exchange member firms was permitted, and member firms no longer had to be in the control of individual members. This was known as the 'Little Bang'.

On 27 October 1986 came the 'Big Bang'. Overnight the dealing system changed, and fixed-scale commissions were abolished, to be replaced by commissions at the discretion of the broker.

The prefix 'International' was added because the Stock Exchange merged with the International Securities Regulatory Organization, an association of major dealers in international securities. The UK had become a major centre for dealing in overseas securities, and this trend has continued since 'Big Bang'. Partly it is due to the geographical position of the UK within the increasingly global market. The UK time-zone conveniently overlaps with the Tokyo and New York markets. This has been helped as English has increasingly become the world language for business. A further factor has been the sophistication of the UK Stock Exchange, and freedom from bureaucratic controls, particularly as compared with the stock exchanges in Continental Europe.

14.2 Changes to the dealing system

The 'Big Bang' also brought about another change in terminology. Before October 1986, stock*brokers* acted on behalf of investors and bought and sold securities on their behalf as their agents. Stock*jobbers* were not permitted to deal directly with the public; they could only transact business with other jobbers and with brokers – that is, they acted as *principals*. Brokers made their living primarily from commissions earned by acting on behalf of clients. Jobbers made a market in particular investments by buying lines of shares and other securities which were for sale, and selling lines for which there were buyers. But the resources of the jobbers were inadequate to finance the amount of capital necessary to satisfy the dealing requirements of the institutional investors. This had led over the years to mergers of many jobbing firms seeking to spread their risks and pool their resources.

The complete separation of the broking and jobbing functions, known as the *single-capacity* system, had taken place in 1908, and from then until October 1986 members had carried on business as either brokers or jobbers but not both. The essence of the system was that jobbers should provide a competitive market for the more popular shares, with competition between them for brokers' business forcing down the jobbers' 'turn' – the difference between the bid and offer price – while also providing a continuous market for securities in which deals occurred less frequently. In addition, because jobbers dealt on their own account, it was often claimed that they performed an essential function by counterbalancing speculative price movements and thus stabilizing the market.

However, this model became increasingly unrealistic as the competitive nature of the market was undermined by the contraction in the number of jobbing and broking firms (see Table 14.1).

Table 14.1 Numbers of brokers and jobbers on the Stock Exchange

Year	Jobbing firms	Broking firms
1920	411	475
1950	187	364
1960	100	305
1970	31	192
1975*	21	284
1982*	17	221
1985*	17	199

* After amalgamation.
Source: *Stock Exchange Quarterly*, March 1985.

The traditional single-capacity system was replaced at 'Big Bang' by a *dual-capacity* system (see fig. 14.1) modelled along the lines of the National Association of Securities' Dealers Automated Quotations System (NAS-DAQ) operating in the United States. All firms are deemed to be dual-capacity *broker/dealers*, combining the functions of both agent and principal. Broker/dealers are able to apply to act as *market-makers* in specific securities, similar to the traditional jobbing function. Those that do not have a market-making side are known as '*agency*' brokers. Market-makers are committed to maintaining continuous two-way prices in shares in which they have agreed to trade. They are required to maintain a market of 'at least a prescribed minimum size in all securities' in which they have chosen to trade.

The new dealing system provided more scope for conflicts of interest to arise within member firms, particularly in the case of integrated firms, such as Barclays de Zoete Wedd (BZW), which brought together banks, brokers, and market-makers. A conflict of interest could arise, for example, in the case of a take-over bid where the bank, in its advisory capacity, was privy to confidential price-sensitive information which could not be disclosed to the broking or market-making sides of the business. '*Chinese walls*' were introduced to prevent such seepage of information: they are an established arrangement whereby information known to persons in one part of a business is not available to persons in another part of the business. Decisions are taken in each part of the business without reference to the interests in the other parts of the business. Thus Chinese walls are designed to prevent many of the benefits that might be expected to follow from integration! They usually mean geographical separation of the different parts of the business, but there may also be separate incorporation of the different activities and independent boards of management.

Unfortunately, Chinese walls have been breached in a number of take-over bids where insider dealing has been detected. Chinese walls can only be precautionary and cannot prevent people talking on the telephone or

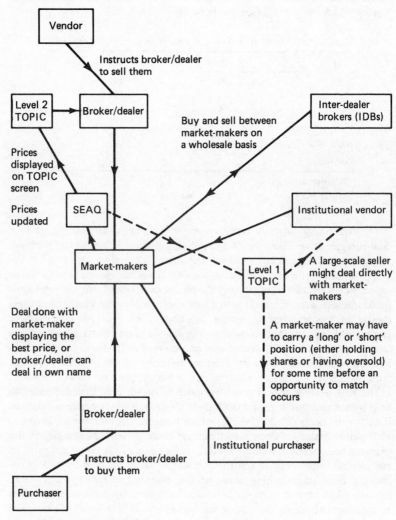

Fig. 14.1   *The International Stock Exchange at work – the equity market*

meeting in a quiet pub, even though insider dealing is a criminal offence.

Another possible conflict of interest arises from the nature of 'dual capacity'. The investor requires protection because, under the post-Big-Bang dealing system, the agent can also act as a principal – even as a market-maker. To counter the possibility that the investor might be offered prices inferior to those available elsewhere in the market, the *'best execution'* rule was introduced. This is a requirement imposed upon firms acting as agents to effect transactions on the most advantageous terms for their customers.

For The Securities Association (TSA) – the self-regulating organization overseeing the International Stock Exchange – 'best execution' means dealing at the best price displayed on the TOPIC screen where 'firm' bids and offers are available, from at least two market-makers, at the appropriate time and in the appropriate size. Thus a market-maker which receives an order from its broking side must at least match the best price currently displayed in the size if it is to keep the deal 'in-house'. Agency brokers have a stiffer requirement: they are required to better the best price on TOPIC (discussed later) if they wish to act as a principal. An *agency cross* is where an agency broker matches a buy and sell order directly. All contract notes record the time of the deal, so any suspected irregularity can be checked against the computer tapes of the prices displayed.

In the case of large orders, for greater amounts than the sizes displayed on the TOPIC screen; or when prices quoted are only indicative; or when prices are changing faster than the market-makers can revise their screen prices – a 'fast market' – a looser requirement, called *'best advantage'*, applies. This simply requires, under the general principles of agency law, that the broker/dealer obtains the best price it reasonably thinks that it can obtain for its client.

The price transparency available through the TOPIC screens enables large-scale investors with this facility, such as institutional investors, to contact the market-maker directly if prices in the required size are displayed. To counter this action, broker/dealers have reduced commissions to small margins on large-scale deals.

Equity *inter-dealer brokers* (IDBs) buy from and sell to the market-makers exclusively. They provide a facility whereby market-makers can deal indirectly with each other, for a very fine margin, and at the same time preserve their anonymity with the other market-makers and thereby not have to disclose important information about their 'long' or 'short' positions.

The market-makers input the data into *SEAQ* – the Stock Exchange Automated Quotations system – and this information is then relayed into *TOPIC* – the Teletext Output of Price Information by Computer system. An investor or member firm merely has to call up the correct teletext page to see the comparative prices for each security. The new system is said to be *'quote-driven'*, rather than *'order-driven'*, because the prices are determined by competing market-makers rather than by bids and offers from investors.

A similar system to that operating in the equity market has been introduced for the gilt market (see fig. 14.2). The basis of the new system is that the Bank of England deals with a large number of gilt-edged market-makers (GEMMs), who in turn supply broker/dealers acting as agents for the general public. Gilt turnover increased from around £1.4 billion per day before 'Big Bang' to around £4.5 billion per day after 'Big Bang'. Initially, the new dealing system in gilts began with 27 GEMMs, but in early 1990 the number had fallen to nineteen, following losses of over £200 million. Only

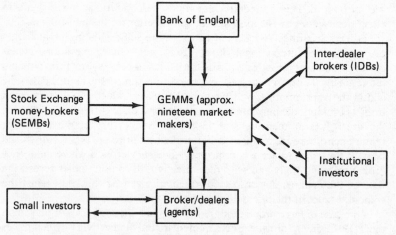

Fig. 14.2   The dealing system for gilt-edged securities

'indicative' mid-prices are quoted on the TOPIC screens. Institutional investors are also able to deal directly with the GEMMs.

Inter-dealer brokers exist in the gilt-edged as well as in the equity market. About half of gilt turnover involves IDBs. Their commission is as low as $\frac{1}{128}$th of 1 per cent. *Stock Exchange money brokers* (SEMBs), which exist in the gilt-edged but not the equity market, provide liquidity by lending and borrowing stock from GEMMs.

14.3 The market at work

The market for stocks and shares is one of the best examples of a pure market existing today. The price of shares, like that of everything else, depends upon supply and demand. If the demand for manufactured goods or farm produce falls far enough, supply will be cut off completely. Competition among manufacturers ensures that artificial shortages cannot be created. With the market in stocks and shares, prices rise and fall entirely as a result of supply and demand (actual or anticipated) and no other factors apply.

When a broker/dealer has an order to buy, say, 1000 ordinary £1 shares in a particular company, it will be able to see the current bid–offer spread quoted by the market-makers displayed on the TOPIC screens, for standard quantities of shares. For example, it may be quoted as follows:

Market-maker A   298–301
Market-maker B   299–303
Market-maker C   296–300

Each of these pairs of figures means that the market-maker is prepared to buy that particular share at the lower of the two prices and to sell it at the higher. As, in this example, the broker/dealer wishes to buy 1000 shares, it will deal with market-maker C, which is required to sell it that number at the price quoted (300p). As the price is quoted in pence, the cost to the broker/dealer's client is £3000. Had the broker/dealer had an order to sell instead of to buy, it would have dealt with market-maker B, which is bidding the highest price of 299p.

Once a market-maker has displayed a 'firm' price for a share, it must deal at those prices – although only in the indicated size. For example, it may quote a share as '75–77p for 10 000 only'. This means that it will buy up to 10 000 shares at 75p each or sell up to 10 000 shares at 77p each. If the broker/dealer wishes to deal in a larger number, it must telephone the market-maker and say so, and the quote may be altered – probably widened, perhaps to 74–78p – which will discourage business in a large number of shares. If it wishes, the broker/dealer may still accept the original quote and deal in the smaller number of shares.

If a broker/dealer's price is higher than that of other market-makers in the same share, all the shares being sold will come to it. If its offer price is lower than that of its competitors, it will be selling shares continually but not buying any. As the aim of a market-maker must be to *balance its book* – that is, to match buying orders with selling orders as far as possible – it cannot afford to have all its dealing in one share going in the same direction. If it buys shares continually without selling any, it must lower its bid price and its offer price to discourage sellers and encourage buyers. Equally, if broker/dealers are buying shares from it continually and no shares are being sold to it, it must raise both bid and offer price to correct the balance. Thus prices move according to supply and demand.

A market-maker naturally moves its prices in anticipation of a change in the balance of buyers and sellers. Thus a press recommendation that a share is cheap causes market-makers to raise prices in anticipation of buyers appearing. An announcement of lower profits than expected may cause market-makers to drop prices in anticipation of sellers. The expected does not always happen, however, and often prices have to be returned to previous levels very quickly to offset a rush of trading in the opposite direction.

14.4 The market-maker's turn

The difference between the lower and upper prices in a market-maker's quote – that is, between the bid and offer prices – is called the *market-maker's turn*, and, if prices remained stable and the market-maker's book remained even, this is the profit it would make on each share dealt in. With an active share its price may be moved quite often and the actual profit on shares purchased and then sold may be very different from the 'turn' quoted at any time. For instance, a market-maker may quote 95–100p for a particular share and sell 100 000 of them in two or three deals when it has only 5000 shares in that company on its book. As the deals are all in one direction and it has oversold its book, it may have to raise the price to discourage buyers and bring out sellers. If its quote is raised to, say, 98–105p it may be able to buy 20 000 shares but it may be necessary to raise the price again, to 99½–107p say, before it can buy enough shares to balance its book. It will then have had to pay an average of over 99p per share for them. Its 'turn' therefore on those shares is less than 1p per share, although the quoted 'turn' has been 5p to 7½p during the operation.

Making a living at market-making is clearly only for skilled market operators, able to assess the probable trends in the demand for particular shares and to react quickly and accurately to market influences. Changes in the prices of shares are made by market-makers but are caused principally by the operations of the large financial institutions in the market. Their decisions to buy or sell large numbers of shares on the market determine the level of prices in the long run.

14.5 SEAQ and the TOPIC information service

The SEAQ service has replaced the trading floor and provides the basis for a totally integrated market within the UK and Ireland, and increasingly with markets outside. SEAQ has both a domestic and an international service.

From the time of 'Big Bang' in October 1986, to January 1991, the International Stock Exchange grouped company securities into four categories – alpha, beta, gamma, and delta – according to their degree of marketability. Alpha shares were the most marketable, delta the least. Alpha shares were shares of companies which normally had an aggregate equity market capitalisation of at least £625 million, a share turnover of at least £100 million per three months, and ten or more market-makers. All shares in 'Footsie' were classified as alpha shares. Beta shares were slightly less marketable, and normally required a minimum of four market-makers. Gamma were less actively traded with at least two market-makers.

However, in January 1991 these designations were formally dropped by the ISE, and replaced by a new classification system, replacing the old categories with a 12 level system. The new system is based on a company's *normal market size* (NMS). This is the number of shares traded in a normal-sized market transaction, and can range from 500 to 200,000.

To take two examples: British Gas initially had a NMS of 100,000 while British Bloodstock Agency had a NMS of only 500 shares. These represent the maximum-size deals which could normally be done without affecting their market prices.

Normally details of bargains must be reported within 5 minutes, and publicised through SEAQ. However, in order to protect the market-makers, details of a deal involving more than three times a company's NMS can be withheld from the market for up to 90 minutes.

A further change to the rules is that the practice of broker/dealers matching buying and selling orders from clients ('agency cross'), rather than putting the business through the market-makers, is replaced by a rule that all such business should be shown to the market-makers in order to give them the opportunity to compete for the deal.

Shares listed in the *Financial Times* do not specify the NMSs. However, the *Financial Times* retains the alpha and beta categorisations for its own purposes. The alpha symbol is now used to indicate a NMS of between 2,000 and 200,000, and beta means a NMS of either 500 or 1,000 shares.

Subscribers to the TOPIC service can see the prices on offer – see fig. 14.3. *Level Two* service shows all the competeting bid–offer prices for all the registered market-makers in each share. In addition, the best current bid and offer prices are displayed at the top of the screen on the '*Yellow Strip*'. *Level One* service, which is designed more for the investment community outside of member firms, shows only the best quote for the most frequently traded securities.

Using the old terminology, alpha shares, although only about 150 in number, accounted for approximately 67 per cent of turnover in domestic equities. Alpha shares also had the narrowest '*touch*' – the spread between the best buying and selling prices. The touch percentage for alpha shares increased from less than 1 per cent to around 2 per cent at the time of 'Black Monday' in October 1987. But at such 'bearish' times gamma shares became even more illiquid, and their average touch widened from 3 per cent to over 6 per cent. There has been a general widening of spreads since deregulation and this has been most severe in the case of the less marketable shares. In many cases they are more than 10 per cent.

14.6 SAEF – SEAQ Automatic Execution Facility

For most security transactions, a broker/dealer has to contact a market-maker by telephone in order to execute a deal. However, *SAEF* allows broker/dealers to complete orders quickly and efficiently at the best price available on SEAQ, for leading securities. SAEF automatically matches an order against a market-maker making the best price at the time. Both parties are immediately notified by SAEF that they have traded, and a trade report is generated automatically. The whole process is completed within seconds.

At present, bargains involving more than 1000 shares still need to be arranged over the telephone and confirmed manually. However, SAEF was devised to accommodate larger orders, and the size limit is likely to increase in the near future. SAEF is open for trading throughout the ISE's mandatory quote period, 8.30 a.m. to 4.30 p.m.

Although reproduced here in black and white, these pictures are in reality in colour.

Referring to the white strip (actually yellow) towards the top of the first screen, when more than three market-makers quote the same price, priority on the strip is given to those quoting in the largest size; if several are identical, priority goes to the earliest quotes.

It can be seen that, for British Airways, bid quotes highlighted were from:

HOAE = Hoare Govett
BZWE = Barclays de Zoete Wedd Equities
P&DT = Phillips & Drew Trading

All quoted 167p.

The offer prices highlighted were from

SBRO = Salaman Brothers
GSCO = Goldman Sachs
SVTL = Scrimgeour Vickers

All offered to sell at 169p.

Each firm quote stock has a minimum size displayed on the screen, but market-makers have the facility to display sizes larger than the minimum.

The following codes appear:

Size	Code	Size	Code
100	.1	1 000	1
250	Q	99 000	99
500	H	100 000	IL
750	T	900 000	9L
900	.9	>9000 000	XL

LxL indicates that a market-maker is prepared to deal in 100 000 shares on both their bid and offer prices.

The British Airways page also shows that, up to 2.35 p.m., 8.1 million shares had been traded – the last trades being at 168p, 169p, 168, 169, 168p – and that the previous day's closing price spread had been 169–172.

Alpha shares – one to a page

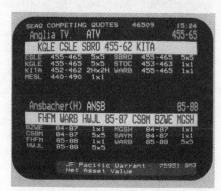

Beta shares – two to a page

Gamma shares – four to a page

Source: International Stock Exchange, London (1989)

Fig. 14.3   SEAQ Domestic

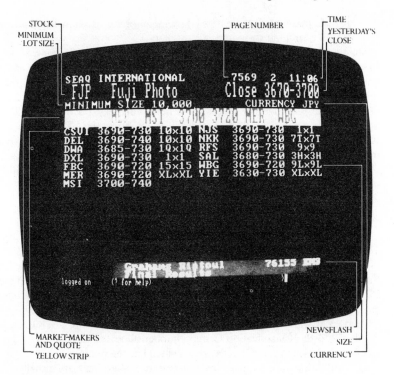

Source: International Stock Exchange, London (1989)

Fig. 14.4   SEAQ International – key features

14.7 SEAQ International

SEAQ International is a screen-based trading system in non-UK equities. It began in June 1985, when UK equities were still being traded on the trading floor, and since its inception the International Equity Market (IEM) has grown to be the world's largest market for non-domestic equities. Some 700 leading international 'blue-chip' shares are displayed, with over 300 quoted on a 'firm' dealing basis. The liquidity of this market is often greater than that of the home market, enabling investors to trade in large sizes. In 1988 turnover was one-third of that in UK shares, but in January 1990 the £33 billion of business done through SEAQ International was one-third more than in UK shares. Approximately 70 per cent of the business done was in Continental European shares. For example, as much as one-half of the business done in some blue-chip French shares is done in the UK.

Non-UK securities are eligible to appear on SEAQ International if the market upon which they are principally listed has met certain minimum standards. In many cases these non-UK companies are also fully listed on the ISE, as well as in their own domestic markets.

Shares can be quoted on either a firm or an indicative basis. For a SEAQ International eligible share to be quoted on a firm basis, three or more market-makers must register to make a market in it. An indicative quote requires only one market-maker. Market-makers are all members of the ISE. Quotes are displayed in US dollars or the home currency, but market-makers are usually prepared to deal in other leading currencies. The prices are displayed and continuously updated on screens throughout the world, so that investors and market-makers can trade no matter where they are located – see fig. 14.4. The trading hours cover the late afternoon in Japan, the whole of the European day, and the morning in North America.

14.8 The *Stock Exchange Daily Official List*

The *Stock Exchange Daily Official List* (SEDOL) is published by the Council of the Stock Exchange on each working day. It provides a much fuller list than is available in the *Financial Times* of all stocks and shares quoted on the ISE and gives particulars of the last dividend paid, the date last quoted 'ex-dividend', the dates of dividend payments, the quotation at 2.15 p.m., and prices at which business was transacted. It also shows the SEDOL code number and the Classification Group Number allocated to each issue. For USM securities, the same details are provided bar the quotation.

The quotations are supplied by the market-makers and are usually far wider than a normal business quote. That is to say, the difference between buying and selling prices (the market-maker's turn) is greater than any market-maker would normally quote to a broker/dealer seeking to do business. The quotations listed are the 'official' quotations at the close of business, however, and are the basis of valuations for inheritance tax and capital gains tax.

14.9 Investors and broker/dealers

Stockbroker/dealers are permitted to advertise, but the majority of investors may not know whom to approach when they want to carry out their first transactions. Many small investors may have acquired shares for the first time through privatization issues, or employee schemes, and have had no direct contact with a broker/dealer. Many investors deal through their banks and, if the sums involved are relatively small, this is a reasonably satisfactory way of going about matters. Some of the clearing banks now have their own broker/dealer subsidiaries.

An investor wishing direct contact with a broker/dealer should preferably be introduced to one by either a friend or a relative, or through his or her bank. Alternatively he or she can write to Investor Research and Education, the International Stock Exchange, London EC2N 1HP, which will, on request, send out lists of broker/dealers willing to accept business introduced in this way. A prospective investor should write to one of these firms, mentioning that its name has been supplied by the Stock Exchange. He or she should check the commission-rate tariff and determine whether an 'advisory', 'management', or 'execution only' (no advice) service is required. Each will have its own rates of commission (see chapter 15).

When placing an order with a broker/dealer, an investor must ensure that the order is clear and that there can be no misunderstanding as to his or her requirements. If the order is for ordinary shares, it is usually necessary only to give the name of the company to identify the shares, and this can often be abbreviated to an acceptable Exchange nickname. For example, if he or she wished to buy 1000 ordinary shares in BAT Industries plc, there would be no misunderstanding if the order to the broker was 'Buy 1000 BATs'. If the order related to Imperial Chemical Industries 5 per cent cumulative preference shares, it would be necessary to say 'Buy 1000 ICI 5 per cent pref' to avoid confusion with other stocks and shares issued by that company. In the case of fixed-interest stocks, the investor should clearly specify whether the sum concerned is nominal value or market value. The investor would also have to make clear to the broker/dealer whether any shares were to be bought at the best available market price at the time of dealing ('at best'), or if he or she wished to place a limit on the price to be paid ('300 or better'). These same details would be required in the case of sales.

As a general rule, broker/dealers tape-record all conversations with clients so that the tape can provide decisive evidence in the event of any subsequent dispute concerning an order.

14.10 Questions

1. (a) Which of the following statements about alpha stocks is *not* true?

   A All shares in the *FT*–SE 100 Share Index are alphas.
   B Alpha stocks are required to have a minimum number of market-makers.
   C Alphas are characterized by a close spread and narrow touch prices.
   D Alphas do not have to meet any market capitalization or volume requirements.

   (b) Which of the following statements is true?

   A All Stock Exchange firms are broker/dealers.
   B Most firms are also market-makers.
   C A small minority of firms are agency brokers only.
   D A broker/dealer must opt to act in one capacity only.

   (c) What is the minimum permitted number of market-makers for a gamma stock?
   (d) Which single-volume publication contains (as well as other information) concise details of all listed securities?
   (e) What are 'Chinese walls' and what purpose do they serve?

2. Outline the market-making and dealing systems for securities quoted on the International Stock Exchange following deregulation ('The Big Bang').

(CIB 4/87)

3. Briefly explain the meaning of *two* of the following terms which have come into use following 'Big Bang':

   (a) agency broker;
   (b) touch prices;
   (c) equity market-maker;
   (d) inter-dealer broker.

(CIB 10/88)

4. Give the main differences between alpha, beta, gamma, and delta securities.

(SIE 7/88)

15 The transfer and settlement procedure

15.1 Cash and account transactions

The date on which a bargain should be settled is shown on the contract note. There are two main types of settlement: *for cash* and *for the account*. The following securities are almost always dealt in for cash – that is to say, settlement is theoretically due on the following business day:

(a) British Government stocks;
(b) Commonwealth Government and provincial securities;
(c) United Kingdom corporation and county stocks;
(d) new issues in allotment letter or renounceable certificate form.

Most securities other than these are dealt in for the account, unless special arrangements for settlement are made.

15.2 The account

The *account* system is used for securities that are not dealt in for cash. The account is normally a fortnight – from Monday to Friday week – although there are three-week accounts at holiday times such as Christmas and Easter. All transactions taking place within an account are due for settlement on *settlement day* (also known as *account day*), which is the second Monday after the end of the account.

Account day is the earliest day on which a broker/dealer can receive stock for delivery to its client, and the client should ensure that the broker/dealer receives payment on or before account day. If shares are bought and sold within the account, brokerage and stamp duty reserve tax are payable and the client receives the net difference between purchase and sale price, minus charges, on or shortly after account day. If the difference is negative, this sum must be forwarded to the broker/dealer by account day. As an example, one typical autumn account worked as follows:

	September					October				
Sunday		2	9	16	23	30		7	14	21	28
Monday		3	10	17	24		1	8	15	22	29
Tuesday		4	11	18	25		2	9	16	23	30
Wednesday		5	12	19	26		3	10	17	24	31
Thursday		6	13	20	27		4	11	18	25	
Friday		7	14	21	28		5	12	19	26	
Saturday	1	8	15	22	29		6	13	20	27	

The account days were 3 and 17 September and 1, 15, and 29 October. Taking that 1 October account day as an example, the first dealing day was Monday 10 September and the last was Friday 21 September. All transactions for the account between 10 and 21 September inclusive were due for settlement on 1 October. By that date, of course, the market was into the second week of dealings for settlement on 15 October. Dealing for *new time* (next account) is not allowed except during the last two dealing days of the account, when special bargains may be done for the following account. Thus bargains for the 1 October settlement could have been made from 8.30 a.m. on Thursday 6 September as new-time dealings. New-time dealings may cost fractionally more than the normal offer price, for the privilege of the extended settlement time.

The two most famous words of Stock Exchange jargon, and the best-known animals in the market, are the *bull* and the *bear*. Both are speculators looking for quick profits from short-term market fluctuations. A bull buys shares during an account in the hope of being able to sell them at a profit before the end of the account. The credit given by the account system enables him or her, if successful, to profit with no cash outlay at all. A bear sells shares in the hope of being able to buy back at a lower price before the end of the account. Thus the account system allows him or her to sell what he or she does not own as delivery is not required at the time of sale – a *naked bear*. A bear who owns the shares in question is referred to as a *covered bear*. Thus a bull is looking for a quick increase in price and a bear for a quick fall in price. From this has derived the application of the words to market movements in general: a *bull market* is a rising market and a *bear market* is a falling one.

A bull may take up the shares purchased if the hoped-for quick profit does not materialize and he or she has the money available to do so. If a bull is very wrong and no price rise comes, he or she may be termed a *stale bull*. If the bull does not have the cash available at the end of the account and wishes to 'carry over' (or 'continue') the bargain to the next account, this may be possible by arranging a 'cash-and-new'. This expression is something of a misnomer, because no cash settlement is involved. The term is used when shares bought during the account are sold again at the end of the account and are immediately repurchased 'new time' for the new account. Normally a premium is payable when shares are bought for 'new time', but, at the market-maker's discretion, this is reduced for dealing 'cash-and-new'. The operation is much the same as an old technique called contango, as it postpones full payment for the shares from the next account day to the following one.

15.3 The contract note

The contract note (see fig. 15.1) gives the investor the details of the transaction carried out on his or her behalf. The following information is shown:

(a) the name and address of the broking/dealing firm;
(b) the names of the partners in the firm;
(c) whether the transaction was a purchase or a sale;
(d) the number of shares or amount of stock;
(e) the name of the company or authority and the type of share or stock dealt in;
(f) the price at which the bargain was done;
(g) the consideration – that is, the number of shares or amount of stock multiplied by the price;

A. BROKER/DEALER & CO.

Partners

In accordance with   A. PARTNER   789 COPTHALL COURT   Telephone 071-001-0010
your instructions we   B. PARTNER   LONDON E.C.2.
have today   A. N. OTHER   and Stock Exchange.
                       C. PARTNER

BOUGHT   This contract note should be carefully preserved
                       for tax purposes.

I. INVESTOR ESQ.
10 HIGH STREET
ANYTOWN

Reference	Date	Settlement
AS2914	13 MAR 19..	12 APRIL 19..

2 000 A COMPANY and SONS PLC Ordinary Shares of 25p each @ 150p	3 000.00
Commision @ 1.65% 49.50 Transfer Stamp 15.00	64.50
Total Cost £	3064.50

Yours faithfully

A. Broker/dealer & Co.

MEMBERS OF THE INTERNATIONAL STOCK EXCHANGE LONDON
MEMBERS OF THE SECURITIES ASSOCIATION

Subject to the Rules and Regulations of the International Stock Exchange including any temporary regulations made by, or under the authority of the Council of the Stock Exchange.

Fig. 15.1   A specimen contract note

(h) the commission charged by the broker/dealer;
(i) the transfer stamp duty or stamp duty reserve tax, if any;
(j) PTM levy, if applicable – payable on equity bargains with a considera-
    tion in excess of £5000;
(k) the total cost of the purchase or the net proceeds of sale, whichever is
    applicable;
(l) the settlement date (no date is given where settlement is for cash);
(m) the contract date;
(n) the client's name;
(o) the time of the deal – all deals done after 4.30 p.m. are marked 'early
    bargain' (EB) as technically they are business of the following day.

The investor should retain the contract note as evidence of the existence of
the contract for the sale or purchase between him or her and the broker/
dealer. It will also usually be required in connection with liability for capital
gains tax.

15.4 Commission

15.4.1 Equities
Strict minimum scales of commission were laid down by the Rules of the
Stock Exchange and enforced until 27 October 1986 (the day of the 'Big
Bang'). For small investors the most relevant rate charged was 1.65 per cent
on equity deals up to £7000 consideration.

Immediately following 'Big Bang', a number of broker/dealers introduced
cut-rate no-frills 'execution only' dealing services for those investors who
simply wanted a dealing service, with no advice provided. However, with one
or two notable exceptions, many of these services have been curtailed, and
the tendency has been for the costs of small deals to rise as compared with
before 'Big Bang', while the commission rates on large deals, particularly
involving institutional investors, have been drastically reduced.

The cost of small deals is usually more dependent on the minimum
commission charged by a broker/dealer rather than on the initial commission
rate. Most provincial broker/dealers charge a minimum commission of £25 to
£35, but some London ones charge in excess of £50. On the other hand, for
deals of more than £50 000 the average rate is 0.2 per cent.

Charges levied by a cross section of broker/dealers in early 1990 are shown
in Table 15.1.

The rates indicated in Table 15.1 are subject to revision from time to time.
The rates quoted are for the relevant 'tranche' of consideration – that is, a
bargain of £10 000 might be assessed at one rate on the first £7000 and at a
lower rate on the balance of £3000.

When enquiring about commission rates, investors should realize that
direct comparison is not always easy, as each broker/dealer may offer a
slightly different range of services for the rates quoted. For example, in the
case of 'closing bargains', where an investor buys and sells the same shares

Table 15.1 Commission rates on equities, early 1990

	£ consideration	%	Minimum £
Barclayshare	0–5 000	1.40	18.50
(For dealing-only service there is	5 000–15 000	0.85	
an additional charge of	15 000+	0.50	(maximum £250)
£12.50+VAT per 6 months; for			
advisory service it is £18.75+VAT			
per 3 months)			
Midland Bank	0–7 000	1.50	20
	7 000–15 000	0.55	
	15 000–130 000	0.50	
NatWest Bank	0–5 000	1.65	25
	5 000–12 500	1.50	
	12 500+	0.50	
Lloyds Bank		1.65	20
			(maximum £165)
			+£5 administration
			fee
Sharelink (dealing-only service)	0–2 500	1.50	17.50
	2 500–5 000	0.75	
	5 000+	0.10	
Albert E. Sharpe	0–5 000	1.25	
	5 000–10 000	1.00	
	10 000+	0.25	+£30 bargain fee
Allied Provincial	0–7 000	1.85	28.50
	7 000–15 000	0.50	
	15 000–50 000	0.35	
	50 000+	0.25	+£1.40 bargain fee
National Investment Group	0–10 000	1.95	30
	10 000–15 000	1.25	
	15 000–25 000	0.80	
	25 000+	0.60	
Henry Cooke Lumsden			
Advisory Service	0–7 000	1.90	28
	7 000+	0.60	
Dealing only	0–5 000	1.75	23
	5 000–10 000	1.00	
	10 000+	0.50	

within a single account period, some broker/dealers charge two lots of brokerage, while others charge a reduced rate or nothing at all on the second bargain.

Banks' rates appear competitive for small deals, but dealing through agents such as solicitors and accountants normally costs more than dealing directly with a broker/dealer.

15.4.2 Gilts
The rates of commission on gilt-edged securities are considerably lower than for equities. On small deals, broker/dealers are in competition with the National Savings Stock Register, which charges approximately 0.4 per cent. Broker/dealers usually start at around 1 per cent, but the rate rapidly reduces on larger deals. The typical rate on a large deal – £1 million, for example – is around 0.2 per cent, and in some cases the deal is done on a 'net' basis – that is, free of commission – the integrated firm making its profit through its market-maker's 'turn', rather than through brokerage.

15.4.3 Other securities
Separate rates of commission may apply to other securities, such as preference shares, debentures, options, and unit trusts. Most prices quoted on SEAQ International are on a 'net' basis – that is, free of commission.

15.5 Transfer stamp duty

Stamp duty must currently be paid when most UK-registered marketable securities are purchased. However, an exemption applies to British Government and other fixed-interest securities and any allotment letters on them. But convertible securities are specifically not exempted from transfer stamp duty. Bearer securities – including American Depository Receipts (ADRs) – are unregistered, and therefore exempt on transfer. The Finance Act 1986 introduced stamp duty reserve tax of 0.5 per cent on purchases subsequently sold within the same account and on purchases of equity renounceable allotment letters, both of which had previously been exempted. Charities and pension funds are exempted, as are gifts passing between individuals for no consideration. The rate of stamp duty is 0.5 per cent – 50p per £100 or part thereof – payable by the transferee (the purchaser). It is charged on the consideration.

In the 1990 Budget, the Chancellor announced the total abolition of stamp duty and stamp duty reserve tax on security transactions as soon as the ISE's paperless settlement procedure, known as TAURUS, is introduced. This will be in late 1991 at the earliest.

15.6 PTM levy

This levy is used to finance the Panel for Take-overs and Mergers. The current rate is 10p on bargains for purchase or sale of equity holdings with a consideration in excess of £5000. Gilt bargains are exempt from the charge.

15.7 Transfer of registered securities

Almost all the securities issued in the United Kingdom are *registered* securities, meaning that a register of holders is maintained by or on behalf of the issuing body. The register shows the name and address of the holder, the amount of stock or the number of shares held, and any instructions which the holder may have given in connection with the payment of interest or dividends. When stocks or shares pass from one holder to another, the register must be amended, and this is usually effected by the completion either of a *stock transfer form* (see fig. 15.2) or a *Talisman sold transfer form* (see fig. 15.3). When the change of ownership arises as a result of a transaction on the Stock Exchange, the procedure differs from that used in respect of a gift, a private sale, or the distribution of an estate.

If a holder of shares in a company agrees to sell them to another person without the deal going through a broker/dealer, all the vendor needs to do is to fill in and sign a stock transfer form and hand it, with his or her stock certificate, to the purchaser against payment of the agreed proceeds. The purchaser then completes his or her own name and address on the form and pays the transfer stamp duty, if any, at an Inland Revenue Stamp Office. The duty paid is shown by means of impressed stamps on the form. He or she then lodges the certificate and stock transfer form with the registrar of the company and in due course receives a new certificate in his or her own name.

This type of transaction usually takes place in shares that are not quoted on the International Stock Exchange. Where the transfer arises from a gift, no stamp duty is payable and the stock transfer form – available from any law stationers – is simply completed and sent to the company's registrar.

As a stock transfer form does not have to be signed by a purchaser, any fully paid stocks and shares can be transferred into anyone's name without his or her knowledge, as the transferrer can lodge the form with the registrar. This was not possible before the passing of the Stock Transfer Act 1963, as it was then necessary to complete a *transfer deed* where the signatures of both transferrer and transferee were required and had to be witnessed. A transfer deed is still required with the stocks and shares of overseas companies and bodies to whom the 1963 Act does not apply, and in the case of partly paid securities.

The procedure necessary for transactions dealt with on the Exchange is described in section 15.8.

15.8 Talisman

Talisman (Transfer Accounting Lodgement of Investors, Stock MANagement for principals) covers the settlement of most securities with a United Kingdom, Irish, Australian, or South African register that are listed on the Stock Exchange and normally dealt in for account settlement. It excludes new issues and gilts, both of which are normally dealt in for cash, and bearer securities, but it is being extended to include certain other foreign-registered securities – namely those of the USA and Canada.

The basis for Talisman was the establishment of a Stock Exchange nominee company – SEPON Ltd (Stock Exchange POol Nominees) – into which all sold stock is registered during the course of settlement. SEPON has a single undesignated shareholding account in the register of every company

STOCK TRANSFER FORM			
	(Above this line for Registrars only)		
	Consideration Money £	Certificate lodged with the Registrar **(For completion by the Registrar/Stock Exchange)**	
	Full name of Undertaking.		
	Full description of Security.		
	Number or amount of Shares, Stock or other security and, in figures column only, number and denomination of units, if any.	Words	Figures (units of)
	Name(s) of registered holder(s) should be given in full; the address should be given where there is only one holder. **If the transfer is not made by the registered holder(s) insert also the name(s) and capacity (e.g., Executor(s)) of the person(s) making the transfer.**	In the name(s) of	

Source: International Stock Exchange, London (1989)

Fig. 15.2   A stock transfer form (Continued opposite)

participating in the scheme. All sold stock is transferred from the seller into the 'pool' account, and purchasers receive their stock by transfer out of SEPON. The Talisman Centre maintains separate accounts for each market-maker dealing in the stock, and these record the movement of stock during the settlement process.

When the selling broker/dealer receives the share certificate and the signed Talisman 'sold transfer' (see fig. 15.3) from its client, it applies its office

I/we hereby transfer the above security out of the name(s) aforesaid to the person(s) named below *or to the several persons named in Parts 2 of Brokers Transfer Forms relating to the above security.* **Delete words in italics except for stock exchange transactions.**	**Stamp of Selling Broker(s) or, for transactions which are not stock exchange transactions, of Agent(s), if any, acting for the Transferor(s).**
Signature(s) of transferor(s) 1 .... 2 .... 3 .... 4 .... **Bodies corporate should execute under their common seal.**	Date ....

Full name(s) and full postal address(es) (including County or, if applicable, Postal District number) of the person(s) to whom the security is transferred. **Please state title, if any, or whether Mr., Mrs. or Miss.** **Please complete in typewriting or in Block Capitals.**	

I/We request that such entries be made in the register as are necessary to give effect to this transfer.

Stamp of Buying Broker(s) (if any)	**Stamp or name and address of person lodging this form (if other than the Buying Broker(s))**

stamp, as before, to warrant the genuineness of execution and the general validity of the documents. It then passes them to the Centre, where they are checked for 'good delivery' (that they are in proper order) and then forwarded to the registrar for registration into SEPON. Although the legal title passes to SEPON only on registration, the ISE is a trustee of the stock from the moment it comes into its hands and holds the stock to the order of the seller (that is, effective voting control remains with the seller) until account day and to the order of the buyer afterwards. On account day the

TALISMAN SOLD TRANSFER

This transfer is exempt from transfer stamp duty by virtue of section 127 (1) of the Finance Act 1976

Above this line for Registrar's use only

Bargain Reference No:

Certificate lodged with Registrar

Name of undertaking

Description of Security

(for completion by the Registrars/Stock Exchange)

Amount of Stock or number of Stock units or shares or other security in words

Figures

In the name(s) of

Account Designation (if any)

Name(s) of registered holder(s) should be given in full; the address should be given where there is only one holder.

If the transfer is not made by the registered holder(s) insert also the name(s) and capacity (e.g., Executor(s) of the person(s) making the transfer.

I/We hereby transfer the above security out of the name(s) aforesaid into the name of SEPON LTD and request the necessary entries to be made in the register.

Bodies corporate should affix their common seal and each signatory should state his/her representative capacity (e.g. 'Company Secretary' 'Director') against his/her signature.

PLEASE SIGN HERE

1 ______

2 ______

3 ______

4 ______

Balance Certificate Required for (amount or number in figures)

Stamp and Firm Code of Selling Broker

Date

SEPON LTD is lodging this Transfer at the direction and on behalf of the Member Firm whose stamp appears herein ('the Original Lodging Agent') and does not in any manner or to any extent warrant or represent the validity or genuineness of the transfer instructions contained herein or the genuineness of the Transferor's signature. The original Lodging Agent by delivering this Transfer to SEPON Ltd authorises SEPON Ltd to lodge this Transfer for registration and agrees to be deemed for all purposes to be the person(s) actually lodging this Transfer for registration.

Stock Exchange Operating Account Number (if applicable)

TAL 112/1

Source: International Stock Exchange, London

Fig. 15.3 A Talisman sold transfer form

stock is transferred to the market-maker's trading account and the selling broker/dealer receives payment from the Centre on the market-maker's behalf. The stock in the market-maker's trading account is then allocated to its sold bargains in the correct sizes by a process known as *apportionment*.

The registration details of the buying clients must be submitted to the Centre by the broker/dealer by the last business day before account day.

Once apportionment has taken place, the stock is held to the order of the various buyers, and 'bought transfers' authorizing the removal of the stock from the SEPON account into the name of the buyers are prepared by the Centre and lodged for registration. When the *Talisman bought transfer* is registered, legal title passes from SEPON to the buyer and a new share certificate is issued by the registrar through the Centre.

The Stock Exchange (Completion of Bargains) Act 1976 allowed for the introduction of new transfer forms for Talisman settlement. A further provision of the Act was introduced for the benefit of trustees and ensures protection from action for breach of trust by reason only of their having deposited stock at the Centre in advance of receiving payment or having paid for purchased stock in advance of obtaining transfer of the securities.

One of the main objectives of Talisman was to smooth the peaks of work for member firms, institutions, and registrars, and a key factor in achieving this is the facility for sold stock to be deposited at the Centre before account day. The Talisman 'sold transfer' includes the name of SEPON Ltd pre-printed as the transferee, and registrars reject any Talisman 'sold transfer' which is not received directly from the Centre or on which any alteration has been made to these words.

Plain stock transfer forms are still used for non-Talisman transactions on the ISE – principally those in gilt-edged securities. The selling broker/dealer has a stock transfer form signed by its client for the total amount of stock sold. (This will have been sent to the client with the contract note.) If the stock sold has to be delivered to more than one buying broker/dealer, the selling broker/dealer cancels the transferee part of the stock transfer form. It then completes separate *broker/dealers' transfer forms* and takes the certificate, the stock transfer form, and the broker/dealers' transfer forms to the Certification Office of the ISE, where the broker/dealers' transfer forms are certified to the effect that a certificate has been deposited to cover them. The broker/dealers' transfer forms once certified are good delivery and they are presented to the buying broker/dealers for payment. The stock transfer form and certificate are sent by the ISE to the Bank of England to await the presentation by the buying broker/dealers of the broker/dealers' transfer forms completed with the details of the purchasers. In due course the Bank of England sends each buying broker/dealer a new certificate showing the purchaser as the registered holder.

Sometimes a certificate provided by a seller is for more stock than has been sold. When this happens, the stock transfer form or Talisman transfer is certified and the certificate sent to the registrar by the ISE. In due course, a balance certificate is sent to the selling broker/dealer (for Talisman deals, via the Talisman Centre) for returning to its client.

15.9 Certificates

An investor in registered stocks or shares (unless he or she sells his or her holding very soon after acquiring it) receives a certificate showing the details entered in the register of holders. The certificate shows the name of the company or undertaking, the type of stock or share, the holder's name, the amount of stock or number of shares which the certificate represents, and the address of the company's registrar. It may or may not show the holder's address.

A certificate is merely a record of an entry in the register of holders. Transfers are not normally registered without production of the certificate, as a protection against fraud. As the signature of a transferee is not required on a stock transfer form nor on a Talisman sold transfer form, however, the registrar has no record of the signature of a holder. Thus anyone coming into possession of a stock certificate could fraudulently complete a transfer form out of the holder's name in order to negotiate the holding. The risk is small, as it would be comparatively easy to trace anyone acting fraudulently. Any cheque issued by a broker/dealer for proceeds would have to be negotiated. Nevertheless, a prudent investor keeps his or her certificates in a safe place.

If a certificate is lost, or destroyed by accident, a registrar issues a duplicate or registers a transfer of the holding on receipt of an indemnity signed by the holder and guaranteed by a bank, an insurance company, or sometimes a stockbroker/dealer. Many holders, when asked to get their bank to join in an indemnity, feel that this is unnecessary, but, as the registrar has no means of knowing whether the person completing the indemnity is the real holder or an impostor, the request is intended as much for the protection of the holder as of the registrar. A guarantee of an indemnity is a continuing liability and, as a claim based on the original certificate could theoretically be made at any time, banks or insurance companies often make a charge for joining in. Where a certificate is lost in the post to the holder and has never come into his or her possession and his or her bank wishes to make a charge for joining in an indemnity which only he or she, as the registered holder, can complete, an understandable difference of opinion can arise between the bank and its customer. It is difficult, however, to arrive at a compromise solution to a problem of this kind which protects all parties from the consequences of a possible misappropriation of a certificate.

The ISE proposes to make share certificates a thing of the past in the near future. TAURUS (Transfer and Automated Registration of Uncertified Stock) will enable participants to hold and transfer most UK securities in uncertified form. Records of shareholdings will be held in TAURUS electronically and will be amended by book-entry transfer. The transfer of ownership will take place without share certificates, just like movements in a bank or building society account.

As a company is transferred on to TAURUS – *'dematerialized'* – each of its shareholders will receive a statement showing how many shares they hold. At the same time, their certificates will cease to be a document of title. At least every six months, shareholders will receive a statement showing their total holdings.

A further effect of dematerialization will be that Talisman forms will be abolished – broker/dealers will effectively transfer shares on their client's behalf, without having to send out and wait for sold forms to be completed and returned. It is argued that the absence of a signed form should not increase the risk of fraud because, as mentioned above, registrars currently do not have the means to check signatures under the existing scheme.

A further aspect of TAURUS will be the abolition of account settlement, and its replacement by 'rolling' settlement, initially five working days after the bargain, and later reduced to three days.

TAURUS is an attempt by the ISE to answer the oft-repeated criticism that, while the UK has one of the most efficient dealing systems in the world, it also has some of the worst settlement mechanisms.

15.10 Questions

1. (a) Ownership of shares bought and sold is effective from:

   A the date on which the buyer pays the purchasing broker.
   B the date on which the shares are registered in the name of the buyer.
   C the date of the share certificate.
   D the date of the contract note.

   (b) The transfer stamp duty on a 'bought' bargain with consideration of £21 024 would be:

   A £105.12.
   B £105.25.
   C £105.50.
   D £106.00.

   (c) In which of the following situations is stamp duty reserve tax *not* payable?

   A Transfer of 'nil-paid' new shares (in allotment letter form) arising from a rights issue.
   B A purchase of shares closed out by a sale within a Stock Exchange account.
   C The purchase of a convertible loan stock.
   D The conversion or transfer of shares into ADR form.

   (d) A Talisman transfer form:

   A should be executed before account day.
   B has to be executed before giving an order to sell shares.
   C is always printed on the back of the share certificate.
   D has to be executed before giving an order to purchase shares.

2. (a) What changes have taken place since 'Big Bang' in the International Stock Exchange's rules and regulations affecting buying and selling costs? Explain how these changes affect both the personal investor and the institutional investor.

(CIB 4/87)

   (b) Leslie Adams purchased £8000 Treasury 14% Stock 1996 at $119\frac{17}{32}$ on Monday 9 October 1989. Show how the total cost of this transaction would be made up if he used a Stock Exchange broker. Assume commission to be 0.8 per cent on the first £2500 consideration and 0.4 per cent thereafter.
   (N.B. Interest payable 22 July, 22 January.)

(CIB 10/89)

3. James Kenyon reads in his newspaper that Bloggs Chemicals Plc is due to announce its final results in about a week's time. According to the report, 'investors are due for a pleasant surprise.'

   Although he has purchased and sold shares from time to time, he has always taken a medium- to long-term view. He decides, for the first time in his life, to purchase some shares in the company on the International Stock Exchange (London) for the next account with a view to selling them before the end of the account. The account begins on 5 February 19–.

   Required:

   (a) (i) On which date (and day of the week) will the account end?
       (ii) On which date (and day of the week) will settlement take place?
       (iii) Which is the earliest date (and day of the week) before the start of the account that he could purchase the shares for settlement on the same day as (ii) above? What is this process called?
       (iv) On which date (and day of the week) during the account is declaration day. What is its purpose?

   (b) What advantages (to investors) are associated with 'account dealing'?
   (c) Analyse the total cost of the purchase of 4000 shares at 257p. (James's brokers charge commission at 1.65 per cent on the first £7000 and 0.6 per cent on the balance. Their minimum commission is £25.)
   (d) Shortly before the end of the account he is able to sell the shares for 277p. What will be the breakdown of his net sale proceeds?
   (e) On learning towards the end of the account that Bloggs Chemicals' results will not be announced until early in the next account, Mr Kenyon feels he has been 'somewhat premature' in purchasing the shares when he did. Comment on his assumption that the purchase ought to have been delayed.

(CIB 5/88)

4. (a) Distinguish registered securities from bearer securities.
   (b) Outline the procedure for the transfer of UK registered shares from the standpoint of an individual investor selling shares through a Stock Exchange broker/dealer.

(CIB 5/90)

16 Unit trusts, investment trust companies and PEPs

Indirect investment in stocks and shares or in property means the purchase of an interest in a managed fund. Instead of making direct purchases of stocks and shares on the market or through new issues, or buying land and buildings, the indirect investor entrusts his or her money to professional investment managers who themselves place the total amount entrusted to them in direct investments. The indirect investor has no rights of ownership over the individual investments made by the investment managers, whereas a managed private portfolio belongs to its owner at all times.

There are two traditional modes of indirect investment: *investment trusts*, which first came to the fore in the 1860s, and *unit trusts*, which had their fullest flowering a century or so later.

16.1 What is a unit trust?

The unit trust is one of the best-known forms of managed fund investment. The law controlling its operation is not company law, but the law of trusts. The purchaser of units in a unit trust – the *unit-holder* – becomes a beneficiary of a trust fund and his or her interests are safeguarded by the *trustee* of the fund. Unit-holders can at any time require that their share of the fund be paid to them in cash.

A unit trust is constituted by a trust deed made between the managers and the trustee, who must be independent of each other. The *managers* of a unit trust are its promoters. They try to persuade the investing public to entrust its money to them for investment, they are responsible for the day-to-day management of the fund, they make a market in the units, and they are entitled to charge the fund for their services. And, of course, they aim to make a profit out of promoting the trust. The *trustee* – invariably a bank or insurance company – has custody of the trust assets, controls the issue of units, maintains a register of holders, and generally watches over the management of the trust. The trustee does not interfere with the day-to-day management of the trust unless the actions of the managers conflict with the interests of the unit-holders.

The money entrusted by the public to the managers of the trust is invested in stocks and shares. The investments are chosen so as to achieve the expressed objects of the trust. Some units aim at maximum capital appreciation and others at maintaining a reasonably high level of income return with some prospects of appreciation of capital value; still others concentrate on achieving the highest possible income return. Some specialize in certain sectors of the market. Most of the money invested in unit trusts is placed in the equity share market, although many trusts at times hold cash and Government and other fixed-interest stocks, and a few specialize in fixed-interest issues.

At any time, the price of units reflects the value of the investments and cash held. A demand for units in a particular trust does not result in a rise in price as with direct investments: it merely means that more cash is available for investment in the shares selected by the investment managers, and it is the fluctuations in prices of those underlying investments which cause the price of the units to move.

A unit trust has no capital and therefore it cannot have a capital structure such as investors in companies are accustomed to. The whole of the fund and the income received from it belong to the holders of units in proportion to their holdings. At any time, the value of a unit is the value of the investments and cash held, together with the income in hand and receivable, divided by the number of units issued.

Any attempt at gearing by means of borrowing or over-investment is not permitted. If foreign currency is borrowed for investment overseas, a deposit in sterling of equivalent amount has to be made in the United Kingdom.

The Department of Trade and Industry regulates the borrowing powers and permitted investments of a UK authorized unit trust. The constitution of UK authorized unit trusts is regulated by the DTI and SIB, but the management of trusts is regulated by the Investment Management Regulatory Organisation (IMRO), and the marketing and selling by LAUTRO and FIMBRA.

16.2 The issue of rights

A unit trust is an *open-ended* fund. The number of units in issue changes as units are created by the managers to meet purchases by the public, or are liquidated as a result of sales of units by the public back to the managers. Most unit trusts are not quoted on the Stock Exchange, and the market in the units is made by the managers.

16.2.1 Purchases
When an investor decides to invest in a unit trust, he or she contacts the managers either directly or through his or her bank, broker/dealer, or other agent. The managers issue a contract note showing the number of units the investor has purchased, the price, and the total amount payable. No commission or transfer stamp duty is payable, as this has been allowed for in

the bid–offer spread. A name ticket is included and this must be completed and returned; a certificate will be issued in due course showing the details on the name ticket.

An investor who has been persuaded to purchase unit trusts as the result of a 'cold call' normally has the right to cancel the contract within fourteen days of receiving the cancellation notice. If he or she does so, the investor recoups either the original sum invested or the prevailing offer price at the time of cancellation, whichever is less.

16.2.2 Sales

When an investor is selling units, it is the managers who buy them. A contract note is issued showing the price and total proceeds. The investor must sign an endorsement on the back of the certificate giving up his or her rights of ownership of the units and send this to the managers, who then send the investor a cheque for the proceeds. Settlement should normally be within five working days.

16.2.3 Creations and liquidations

Creations and liquidations of units represent transactions between the managers and the trustee. To *create* units, the managers prepare a calculation showing the cost of the units to be created and lodge this with the trustee. They must then pay the trustee the total cost, usually by the next Stock Exchange settlement day. This transaction increases the number of units in issue. To *liquidate* units a similar calculation is prepared and lodged with the trustee. The trustee reduces the number of units in issue accordingly when it has received endorsed certificates to the total number of units to be liquidated, and pays the managers the proceeds out of the fund to enable them to settle with the unit-holders.

The progress of the unit trust movement over the ten years to 1989 is shown in Table 16.1.

Table 16.1 Unit trusts: a ten-year picture

Year	Value of funds (year-end) (£m)	Sales (£m)	Repurchases (£m)	Net investment (£m)	Number of unit holdings (million)
1980	4 968	532	424	108	1.72
1981	5 902	955	428	528	1.79
1982	7 768	1 155	564	591	1.80
1983	11 689	2 460	960	1 500	2.04
1984	15 099	2 920	1 476	1 444	2.20
1985	20 307	4 485	1 947	2 538	2.55
1986	32 131	8 718	3 483	5 235	3.41
1987	36 330	14 544	8 215	6 330	5.05
1988	41 574	7 676	5 880	1 796	4.89
1989	58 159	10 609	6 744	3 864	4.85

Source: Unit Trust Association/*Financial Statistics*.

16.2.4 Certificates

It is an important part of the trustee's duty to ensure that at no time are there certificates in issue for more units than those for which it holds assets in the fund. So, when units are created, it issues no certificates until it has received the moneys for the creation from the managers. When units are liquidated, it does not pay the managers until endorsed certificates are lodged with it. When units are bought and resold by the managers, it does not issue certificates to the new holders until it has endorsed certificates from other holders to an equivalent number of units. This protects the investor against the possibility of fraud by the managers when dealing in their units with the public.

16.3 The pricing of units

All creations of units by the managers with the trustee must be on an *offered*-price basis. All liquidations must be on a *bid*-price basis. The Department of Trade and Industry requires these two methods of calculating the price of units to be in accordance with prescribed formulae laid down in the trust deed.

The offered price is the maximum price at which units are sold by the managers to the public, and the bid price is the minimum price at which the managers will repurchase units from the public – the 'cancellation price'. They are the notional figures for establishing or realizing the entire fund. The offered price is based upon each investment in the fund at the lowest offered price in the market. To this is added a percentage for expenses, including a percentage for broker/dealers' commission on the purchase of the investments, the amount of the managers' initial charge, and the income in hand and receivable. The cancellation price is based on each investment in the fund at the highest bid price in the market, less a percentage for broker/dealers' commission on the sale of the investments.

Until December 1979, initial and annual management charges were governed by Department of Trade and Industry regulations. Since that date, unit trusts have been free to set their own charges. As a general rule the percentages charged have tended to increase, and many unit trusts now levy a 6 per cent initial charge and 1½ per cent annual charge.

Few unit trusts are quoted in line with the official cancellation-price and offer-price calculations, which can give values as much as 8 to 11 per cent apart. Quoted prices usually give a spread of between 5.5 and 7.5 per cent. If the trust is a net seller of units, the offer price often tends to be fixed at or near the maximum permitted level – 'offer basis' – the bid price being somewhat higher than the minimum cancellation price. If, on the other hand, the managers face heavy demands for repurchases, the price structure will reflect their need to sell units, the minimum price being paid on repurchases – 'bid basis' – with units being offered at below the maximum formula price.

Following the Financial Services Act, unit trust managers publish both their bid–offer prices at the last valuation and the initial charge included in that spread. Unit trusts can be priced on either a *historic* or a *forward* pricing basis. Trust managers are required to state a precise time during the day when valuations will be carried out. For example, the financial press may carry the code *12.00H* against a particular management company. This indicates that the funds are revalued every day at 12.00 noon, and dealt with on an historic basis – that is, any deal done after 12.00 is at the price fixed at 12.00. On the other hand, if the code had been *12.00F* this would have indicated a forward pricing basis. In this case, the investor would not know the precise price at which he or she had dealt until the *next* 12.00 hours revaluation.

If a trust is priced on an historic basis, it must temporarily move to a forward pricing basis, or a new price must be calculated, if the managers believe that prices have moved by more than 2 per cent since the last valuation. If an order is dealt with by post, or the investor requests it, it must also be dealt with on a forward pricing basis.

Fund managers must publish the *cancellation price*, even when the units are quoted on an offer basis. In such a case the cancellation price – the bid price on a bid basis – will be less than the actual bid price on an offer basis. If the fund is already on a bid basis, the bid and cancellation prices will be the same.

16.4 Regulation of authorized unit trusts

The Department of Trade and Industry, SIB, and IMRO are the regulatory authorities which share responsibilities for authorizing the operations of any UK unit trust which seeks to attract money from the general public. Any trust which the managers wish to make available to investors at large must be an *authorized* unit trust, as defined by the Financial Services Act.

16.4.1 Investment powers of managers
The investment powers of UK authorized unit trusts are currently being extended as a result of the Financial Services Act. Traditionally, authorized unit trusts have been restricted to stocks and shares, almost all of which had to be quoted on an approved market. The approved markets are the Official Lists of the European Community countries, plus the principal markets of the remainder of Europe, North America, and the Far East, and include the USM. Up to 10 per cent of a fund can be invested in transferable securities that are not approved. The rules are being relaxed to allow for new types of authorized unit trust investing in money securities, property, options and futures, and commodities. Previously these had only been available offshore in unauthorized form. Now they can be marketed directly to the general public, with appropriate wealth warnings.

In the case of UK authorized unit trusts investing in ordinary shares, there are restrictions on the amount which can be invested in individual holdings. Generally, no more than 5 per cent of the fund can be invested in any one investment, although there are certain exceptions to this. If, because of changes in the value of the investments, one holding becomes larger than the limits laid down in the deed, the holding need not be reduced until the fund is reduced by reason of liquidation of units. Then a sale of part of the overlarge investment should be made.

A deed must also limit the amount of capital of one company that can be purchased in the unit trust. Usually this limit is 10 per cent of the issued equity capital.

16.4.2 Requirements of the Act
The Financial Services Act lays down certain requirements for the deeds of authorized unit trusts, including provisions for price and yield calculations, control of advertising, audit and circulation of accounts, and the powers of trustees, but the regulatory authorities exercise a far larger measure of control on the content of the trust deed of every authorized unit trust.

16.4.3 Approval of managers
Perhaps the most important part played by the regulatory authorities in the authorization of unit trusts is their examination of the two companies which propose to act as manager and trustee. Both must be limited companies, and they must be controlled independently of each other. In practice, trustees are invariably banks and insurance companies. Anyone with sufficient capital to set up a unit trust can do so and can, in fact, employ specialist companies to carry out all functions of the managers. The regulatory authorities will wish to be satisfied as to the probity of the persons controlling the operation before granting the authorization which enables the managers to solicit funds from the general public.

The regulatory authorities exercise a general supervision over the operations of authorized unit trusts, including examination of accounts and a watch on advertising standards. Their protection of the interests of the public investing in authorized unit trusts is invaluable.

16.4.4 Designated-territory status
A 'designated territory' is one which the UK authorities consider has investor protection legislation equivalent to that available in the UK. The main offshore centres – Jersey, Guernsey, the Isle of Man, and Bermuda – have all been granted this status. Any fund based in a 'designated territory' can apply for permission under the Financial Services Act to market its offshore funds in the UK. Such funds are known as 'authorized offshore funds'.

16.4.5 UCITS
An 'Undertaking for Collective Investments in Transferable Securities' (UCITS) is a unit trust that has received recognition within one of the member countries of the European Community. Having received approval, it can be marketed throughout the EC, including the UK. The most popular country for registration is Luxemburg.

16.5 The duties of the trustee

The primary duty of the trustee of an authorized unit trust scheme is to ensure that the terms of the trust deed are complied with. This includes the duties relating to the issue of certificates, the creation and liquidation of units, and the general supervision of the administration on behalf of the unit-holders already discussed. The trustee may agree with the managers to enter into supplemental trust deeds to amend the provisions of the trust deed if it is satisfied that the interests of unit-holders are not prejudiced by the amendment. If it is not so satisfied, it must require the managers to call a meeting of unit-holders to which the proposed amendments will be put.

16.5.1 Advertising

In the early days of unit trusts, advertising – sometimes less than 'full and fair' – was responsible for substantial sales of units, but today the volume of advertising is much reduced. LAUTRO's rules provide that its members must state the aims and objectives of funds, initial and annual management charges, and distribution dates. Furthermore, statements to the effect that the investment must be considered long-term, and that the price of units may go down as well as up, must also appear. Where past performance records are quoted, they must be for a reasonable period – at least five years in the case of established trusts – and a representative market index must be used. Graphs, if employed, should not be misleading.

The trust deed will require all advertising matter to be submitted to the trustee before publication if it contains an invitation to buy units or any reference to the price at which units may be purchased or the yield from the units. In practice, trustees see advertisements, circulars, and reports before issue, and they naturally require amendments to be made from time to time. A trustee's concern must be that all statements are true and that there is nothing misleading in the content of such material.

16.5.2 Pricing

By the terms of most trust deeds, the trustee is not required to check the price calculations produced by the managers unless specifically requested by a unit-holder to do so. From time to time, however, a wise trustee will check carefully the calculation of the unit price, as errors can arise in the portfolio of investments, or in the broker/dealers' valuation of the securities, or in the balance of cash held. Similarly, the trustee is not required to check yield calculations, but it will check that distributions bear a close relation to published yields.

16.5.3 Custody

The most time-consuming and labour-intensive part of the trustee's duties is the custody of the assets of the trust. The investment managers of a unit trust deal through their broker/dealer in the name of the trustee. The trustee is nominally the principal in all purchases and sales on behalf of the trust. Many trusts are actively managed funds, with as many as a hundred stock or share transactions in a year for every £1 000 000 of value.

Some holdings will be held for only a short period and, in an active fund, many holdings may be purchased and sold within a six-monthly accounting period. All these transactions have to be recorded and settled with the broker/dealers by the trustee. Active dealing also gives rise to problems in the collection and payment of dividends. Purchases normally outnumber sales, especially where a trust is expanding. The cost of dealing may discourage investment activity, although in practice the managers of unit trusts are substantially more active than are the pension fund managers.

16.5.4 Control of investments

One of the functions in the operation of a unit trust that is definitely not the trustee's province is the investment management. The trustee has no jurisdiction over the selection of shares for investment, and in consequence the investment performance of the fund is entirely the responsibility of the managers. This having been said, however, the trustee should watch the investments made by the managers to satisfy itself on five points.

(a) The trustee should ensure that all investments made are in accordance with advertised policy. It should not, for example, permit a purchase of a stores share in a trust which advertises that it invests exclusively in shares in the financial sector.
(b) It should ensure that purchases do not bring holdings above the permitted limits on investments and, if they do, that the trust does not lose on their sale.
(c) It should check that purchases are of freely marketable investments and not, for instance, in other types of managed funds where sales back to the managers can be suspended.
(d) It should ensure that no 'bear' transactions are entered into and, if shares which the trust does not hold are inadvertently sold, that the trust does not suffer on their subsequent purchase.
(e) No transactions should be carried out by the managers with themselves or any associated company, not even through the Stock Exchange.

16.5.5 Registration

The maintenance of a register of unit-holders is the responsibility of the trustee, although in these days of computerized registers this function is often delegated to the managers themselves or to a specialized register. The trustee remains responsible for the correctness of the register and usually arranges for checks to be carried out to ensure its accuracy.

16.5.6 Liaison

The managers of a unit trust normally maintain close contacts with the trustee, consulting with it on any unusual matter and discussing problems as they arise. The agreement of a reputable trustee to a course of action is a valuable support to a management company. The co-operation of regulatory authorities, the trustees, and the managers in the interests of unit-holders has proved a real protection to the investor.

16.6 Investment in authorized unit trusts

Several arguments are put forward in favour of investment in unit trusts as opposed to direct investment in stocks and shares on the market. Firstly, there is the argument that, for the small investor, investment in a managed fund gives a spread of interest over industries and companies that cannot be achieved with direct investment of a modest amount of cash. Secondly, it is argued that investment in a unit trust gives the small investor professional investment management that is not otherwise available. Neither of these two arguments is entirely valid.

16.6.1 Spread of interest
The first is a sound argument in many cases, but an investor buying units for this reason should choose his or her trust with special care. Many unit trusts specialize in certain sectors of the market, and an investor seeking spread of interest should be sure to choose a general trust with a relatively large number of holdings. The valuation of portfolios of unit trusts is based on the theory that all the shares held could be sold at the prevailing prices. This would not be so in practice. Where many different holdings are included in the portfolio, quite a high proportion of repurchases can be accumulated without upsetting the prices of the underlying holdings by the sale of smaller holdings and small parts of large holdings. But where there is undue concentration in relatively few holdings, there is a danger of severe price falls unless the holdings are in large companies with a free market in their shares.

16.6.2 Management
There is no real evidence that an investor obtains better value for money by investing in unit trusts than by using some other form of professional management, such as investment trusts or property bonds. Many unit trusts are used as 'shop-windows' by institutions providing investment management services, to show the public at large what they can achieve. Merchant banks generally do not accept private portfolios of less than £100 000, but run unit trusts for their smaller clients. Many unit trust management companies offer fund management in other types of investment, such as investment trusts and insurance schemes. There is no evidence from the performance records of unit trusts to suggest that the quality of the investment management offered by merchant banks is in general any better or worse than that offered by investment companies or other institutions offering private portfolio management. The performance of unit trusts managed by the clearing banks and by insurance companies is steady and unspectacular, these trusts appearing only infrequently among the top and bottom performers.

16.6.3 Charges

The initial charge imposed on unit trust investments can prove expensive where quite large sums are involved. An investor who is proposing to place a sum exceeding, say, £25 000 in one authorized unit trust would be well advised to try to negotiate a reduced initial charge with the managers. Some trusts in fact reduce the initial charge automatically on large investments; others, by the imposition of a high minimum investment, have low initial charges. In return, the investor may have to agree to accept limits on the numbers of units that can be resold to the managers on any one day.

16.6.4 Timing

The most important point about investment in unit trusts – as for all equity investment – is that of timing. Unit trusts make regular investment easy, in a way which is not available to the direct investor, through the operation of savings schemes.

16.7 Timing of unit trust purchases

Unfortunately, the public at large tends not to invest in unit trusts when prices are depressed, and has usually waited until a rising trend has been clearly established before entrusting funds to the unit trust industry. As a result, very many people have become disenchanted with unit trusts. They have seen the value of their investments fall to below their cost during the first bear market after purchase, and have had to wait a long while to see a profit in their units.

Management companies have frequently been criticized for advertising for funds when markets are high and refraining when they are low. They cannot entirely be blamed for this: too many of them have lost money by advertising extensively in depressed markets to encourage a reversal of the trend. Unless the initial charges paid on units sold through an advertisement are sufficient to cover the cost of its insertion, there is no encouragement to advertise frequently. Unfortunately, many people do not realize that units are almost always available for purchase at the daily quoted price. The regulatory authorities require that managers must buy back on any dealing day.

16.8 Savings schemes and pound cost averaging

One argument in favour of the unit trust as a form of investment is wholly valid, and that is the facility it offers for the regular investment of small sums. Some trusts have a relatively high minimum investment requirement, and few permit the investment of less than £500 initially, but most provide savings schemes which accept monthly sums from about £20 upwards. This is an ideal way to invest in the share market for investors who can provide only a few pounds each month from their income. Direct investment out of savings is possible only by the purchase of one holding every now and again. At present Stock Exchange commission levels, a minimum of £100 a month would have to be set aside to make one new equity purchase a year at an economic cost. This is unsatisfactory in many ways. The regular purchase of units in an authorized unit trust scheme not only gives a spread of interest with the smallest sum but also levels out the fluctuations in the market, disposing of the problem of timing. In addition, the monthly investment of a fixed sum, as opposed to the purchase of the same number of units, brings in the benefits of what is known as *pound cost averaging*. This merely means that more units are bought when prices are low. Its advantages are illustrated in Table 16.2.

The figures in Table 16.2 are hypothetical, but, whatever figures are taken, the average cost per unit is always less than the average of the prices over the period, and in the long term substantially less. Obviously the average cost per unit is higher than if the total investment were made at the time that prices were at their lowest, but no investor can be certain of recognizing that moment. In practice, units bought through savings schemes are either calculated to three places of decimals, to absorb fully the monthly subscription, or else they are allocated as whole units with any cash balance remaining carried forward to the next month.

Table 16.2 Pound cost averaging: investment of £10 in a unit trust per month for ten months

Month	Unit price (pence)	Number purchased
1	50.0	20.000
2	49.2	20.325
3	47.8	20.920
4	45.0	22.222
5	42.0	23.810
6	39.5	25.316
7	40.0	25.000
8	44.0	22.727
9	47.5	21.053
10	50.0	20.000

Total units purchased	221.373	
Total cost of units	£100	
Average cost per unit	45.17	
Average unit price	45.50	

16.9 Withdrawal plans

Many unit trusts offer withdrawal plans, under which the investor receives not only his or her share of the income of the trust but also a regular realization of his or her capital. With such a scheme in operation, the investor is paid a regular sum which is made up of the income to which he or she is entitled together with the proceeds of sale of part of the fund.

Most commonly, either a half-yearly payment is fixed by the management company in offering the plan, or else the payment is selected by the

unit-holder from a range offered by the managers. The payments are usually
between 3 per cent and 8 per cent per annum of the amount invested, paid in
half-yearly instalments of one-half the agreed rate. The sums received consist
of income after tax plus the proceeds of sufficient of the holding units to
make up the agreed half-yearly percentage. A tax certificate is issued to the
unit-holder in respect of the income proportion of the payment and can be
used to support a repayment claim where this is relevant. The big disadvantage of this type of withdrawal plan is that the unit-holder loses the facility of
timing the sales of units. During bull markets the plan works satisfactorily,
but during bear markets the sales of units take place at depressed prices and
therefore eat severely into the value of the investment.

The problem is partly overcome by using the withdrawal unit method, in
which the payment consists of a fixed percentage of the value of the units
held, rather than of the amount invested. Each half-year the predetermined
percentage of the fund is paid to unit-holders, and this consists of both
income and capital, as in the other method. Because the payment is related
to the value of the fund, the distribution is less when prices are depressed
than it is when prices are high, and so the holder cannot be certain of a
particular return. On the other hand, approximately the same proportion of
the fund is realized each time, varying only by the amount of income
available, so overcoming in part the disadvantage of using the other method
of operation in bear markets.

Although withdrawal plans seem to appeal to some people, the disadvantages of forced sales at times of low prices make them unattractive in general.

16.10 Share exchange schemes

The drift of the private investor from the stock market has been encouraged
by share exchange schemes. Many unit trust companies are prepared to
accept quite small quantities of shares – perhaps as little as £1000 worth – in
exchange for units. Usually these schemes are attractive because the terms
offered are better than a straight sale of the shares and a purchase of the unit
trust. For the unit trust managers, some of the shares acquired in this way are
of little interest, and for these the terms offered may not be so good. If, on
the other hand, the shares can be taken into their existing portfolio they
could pay as much as the market 'offer' price. For capital gains tax purposes a
share exchange represents a disposal, and the tax implications must therefore
be taken into account.

16.11 The choice available

Once a decision has been made to invest in a unit trust, the choice available is
bewilderingly wide. With over 1300 authorized mainland funds from over 160
management companies to choose from, there is likely to be a trust to suit
any requirement. The Unit Trust Association has tried to simplify matters by
categorizing unit trusts in the following way:

(a) UK funds   At least 80 per cent invested in the UK:

- *General* – at least 80 per cent of their assets in equities; have a yield of between 80 and 110 per cent of the yield of the *FT*–Actuaries All-Share Index; and which aim to produce a combination of both income and growth.
- *Equity income* – at least 80 per cent of their assets in equities; and which have a yield in excess of 110 per cent of the yield of the *FT*–Actuaries All-Share Index.
- *Growth* – at least 80 per cent of their assets in equities; and have a primary objective of achieving capital growth.
- *Gilt and fixed-interest* – at least 80 per cent of their assets in gilt and fixed-interest securities.
- *Balanced* – less than 80 per cent of the portfolio invested in either equities or gilt and fixed-interest securities.

(b) International funds   Less than 80 per cent invested in one geographical area:

- *Equity income* – at least 80 per cent of their assets in equities; and have a yield in excess of 110 per cent of the relevant yield for the *FT*–Actuaries World Index.
- *Growth* – at least 80 per cent of their assets in equities; and have a primary objective of achieving capital growth.
- *Fixed-interest* – at least 80 per cent of their assets in fixed-interest stocks.
- *Balanced* – less than 80 per cent of the portfolio invested in either equities or fixed-interest securities.

(c) Japan   At least 80 per cent of their assets in Japan.

(d) Far East

- *Including Japan* – at least 80 per cent of their assets in Far East securities, with a Japanese content of less than 80 per cent.
- *Excluding Japan* – at least 80 per cent of their assets in Far East securities but with no Japanese content.

(e) Australasia   At least 80 per cent of their assets in Australia or New Zealand securities.

(f) North America   At least 80 per cent of their assets in North American securities.

(g) Europe   At least 80 per cent of their assets in European securities but not less than 50 per cent in Continental European securities.

(h) Specialist

- *Commodity and energy* ⎤
- *Financial and property* ⎬ At least 80 per cent of their assets in relevant securities or instruments.
- *Money markets* ⎦
- *Investment trusts* – investing only in investment trust shares.
- *Fund of funds* – investing only in other authorized unit trust schemes.

(i) Exempt – unit trusts This sector is for those trusts set up as vehicles for pension funds and charities to invest in. They are exempt from corporation tax as well as capital gains tax.

(j) Exempt – free-standing additional voluntary contributions (FSAVCs) These trusts are available to personal investors in a unit trust personal pension or FSAVC scheme.

Some of the sectors include several types of fund. For example, a major subsector of 'UK growth' is 'smaller-companies' trusts, and the sector also covers 'special situations' (such as take-overs, new issues, etc.) and 'recovery funds' (which invest in shares which have fallen substantially in price). Growth funds will have a low income yield, as will most of the overseas funds – particularly in the Far East.

A unit-holder in a growth fund often requires income to be reinvested. This can usually be arranged by one of two methods: either through a *reinvestment scheme*, under which distributions are retained by the management company and used to buy additional units, or else through *accumulation units*. The latter do not qualify for distributions, but the income is reinvested in the trust, increasing the value of each unit. Some trusts provide only accumulation units. In both cases, reinvested income is subject to tax, and the higher-rate taxpayer using such a scheme must find the additional tax due out of other income.

Equity income funds, although providing a higher income return than general funds, normally do not yield more than around 6 per cent. For higher yields the investor must seek a fund consisting partly or entirely of gilts and other fixed-interest and preference shares.

For an investor without an existing well-balanced portfolio, the most sensible course of action would be to invest in a UK general or an international balanced fund. Both types of trust will provide diversification – the international-type trusts providing spread of risk across countries as well as securities. 'Fund of funds' trusts provide additional diversification, usually within the family of trusts offered by a management company. On the other hand, for those investors looking for high risk/return possibilities, there are specialist sector trusts in areas such as gold shares, or single-country funds investing in small, volatile markets, such as those of the emerging economies of the Far East.

Full details of all authorized unit trusts can be found in the *FT Unit Trust Yearbook*. It provides a basic introduction to each trust and a review of its track record. The Unit Trust Association publishes performance statistics, and statistical reviews are available in the daily press and personal finance magazines, among which *Money Management* has one of the most comprehensive coverages, giving details of performance over one and six months and one, two, three, five, and ten years.

There is no agreed approach to selecting unit trusts for performance – just as there is no single method of selecting individual shares – but the following are some of the methods suggested:

(a) *New trusts*   There is a certain amount of evidence to suggest that newly established funds do better than average. This may be because they have greater freedom of action in buying, or that managers are under greater pressure to demonstrate performance when the fund still needs to attract funds. Also, the sector or type of fund chosen may reflect the prevailing mood at the time of inception.

(b) *Small trusts*   The arguments for using a trust from a small management company are similar to those for (a). Such funds have greater flexibility than large funds, and can buy or sell large proportions of the portfolio without moving share prices.

(c) *Contrary performance*   Proponents of this approach believe that the performance of specialist unit trusts very much depends upon what particular sector they are in. Sectors move in and out of fashion, and it may well be that the worst-performing sector one year will improve, while the best-performing sectors are less likely to repeat their performance.

(d) *The fund manager*   The financial press usually features its own 'beauty contest' once a year, when a straw poll is taken to determine the most highly rated analysts and fund managers. However, like footballers, such personalities are footloose, and can move to the highest bidder, thus undermining continuity of performance for a particular management group.

(e) *Management group*   It may be better to concentrate on a particular management group, on the basis that it may have particular research methods, staff training, and investment philosophies which are applied across the range of funds. Some management groups have earned a reputation for performance in certain sectors, but generally they should be judged by their performance across a range of categories. It is possible for a management group to 'fluke' a winning performance in a small sector which fortuitously outperforms the market as a whole. However, it is much harder for a management company to do consistently better than average across a range of types of fund.

(f) *Expenses and management charges*   Another factor that the investor should not ignore is the level of management charges. Some managers have decried the fact that there is little point in maintaining lower charges than their rivals, since investors seem indifferent to them. 'Index' funds (discussed in section 10.7) are promoted partly on the basis that they offer reduced charges because of the lower level of research and dealing charges incurred.

(g) *Ethical funds* For those investors with a particular concern for the environment and for ensuring that business does not override deeper social issues, there are 'ethical' and 'green' unit trusts. They usually have an advisory panel appointed to vet the constituents of the trust to ensure that they conform with certain guidelines. Usually outlawed are companies involved in nuclear power, armaments, tobacco, alcohol, animal experimentation, gambling, pornography, and involvement in certain countries with undemocratic governments. Positive criteria adopted imply investment in companies involved in pollution control, waste recycling, acid-rain control, health care, housing for the elderly, good labour relations, and contribution to the community. Details of ethical funds can be obtained from the Ethical Investment Research Information Service (EIRIS). The performance of ethical trusts to date has not been inferior to that of comparable conventional trusts.

16.12 Distributions and reports

Most unit trusts distribute income received at half-yearly intervals, and for a few weeks before the date of distribution the units are dealt in *ex-distribution* in the same way as stocks and shares are quoted ex-dividend. Some trusts distribute quarterly, some only annually, and, of course, accumulation units have no distributions. In all cases unit-holders are supplied with a tax-credit certificate at the end of the accounting period. Distributions are rounded off to a convenient figure and any balance of income is carried forward.

One feature of unit trust distributions is *equalization*. The distribution is in respect of dividends and other income received and is not like a dividend declared by a company. The price of a unit at any time is calculated by including income received and receivable at that time. A purchaser of units is entitled to his or her share of income received after the date of purchase. Part of the price paid for his or her units is in respect of income received before his or her money was introduced to the trust. On the first distribution date, he or she receives the same income as all other holders. Part of this is taxed income and represents his or her share of income received after the date of purchase. Part is not taxed and is in effect a return of part of the purchase price – that part which represented income receivable up to the date of purchase. This sum is termed 'equalization'. It is similar to 'accrued interest' when purchasing gilts.

At least once a year, and in most cases every half-year, a report is sent out to unit-holders. This shows the calculation of the distribution, the composition of the trust portfolio, the managers' report for the period covered, the auditors' report, and the names of the managers, trustees, auditors, and solicitors to the trust. Copies of the last report of any trust may be obtained from the managers, who are also required to publish annually accounts for the trust showing the amount of their charges and expenditure on the trust.

16.13 The taxation of unit trusts

Income received by trustees on behalf of unit-holders of an authorized unit trust consists mostly of dividends paid by companies. It is therefore net of tax when received. Some income may be received without tax having been deducted – for example, interest on moneys on deposit. Other income may be interest received on holdings of Government or other gilt-edged stock, or company debentures and loan stocks. This interest is normally taxed before receipt, but will not have borne corporation tax in the hands of the payer.

The income of unit trusts is liable for corporation tax, as the trust is treated as a corporation for tax purposes. But from January 1991 authorized mainland unit trusts pay a special rate of corporation tax of 25 per cent on unfranked income. This is reclaimable by non-taxpayers, who receive a tax credit for the tax paid. This brings mainland funds into line with the taxation of income in UCITs. Dividends are not taxed again, as they represent franked income to the trust. The Finance Act 1980 freed unit trusts themselves from tax on capital gains, thus transferring the onus for this tax entirely to the unit-holder. This change was advantageous for the many small

'What do you mean, Them? We are Them.'

investors who are unlikely to pay capital gains tax because of the annual exemption. However, the capital gains tax indexation allowance does not apply to an investor's holdings in unit trusts which are at least 90 per cent invested in assets which themselves do not qualify for indexation – for example gilts and bank deposits.

Offshore funds are taxed somewhat differently from UK mainland funds. All offshore funds are classified as either '*roll-up*' or '*distributor*' funds. Roll-up funds are those which normally distribute less than 85 per cent of their income. Tax is deferred until the investment is encashed, when the whole of the gain is subject to income tax at the investor's marginal rate in the year of encashment. Distributor funds, on the other hand, distribute at least 85 per cent of their income each year. This is subject to income tax in the normal way, and any capital gain is subject to capital gains tax in the year of encashment.

16.14 Unauthorized unit trusts

The main remaining type of unauthorized unit trust is a 'house' fund. Many stockbroker/dealers, merchant banks, and other institutions run funds on unit trust lines which are designed for their own clients. Some of these are in fact authorized unit trusts, although not advertised or promoted, and their prices do not appear in the newspapers. Many of them, however, are not authorized and the unit principle is used for these funds only because it is a convenient and efficient way of running an open-ended fund, maintaining fairness between incoming, outgoing, and continuing investors. Investors whose advisers encourage them to place moneys in an unauthorized trust should realize that they have none of the protection afforded by authorization. The trustee need not be independent of the managers, and the investment powers may be unrestricted.

There are also a number of unauthorized offshore funds. Their details are shown in the *Financial Times*, but they cannot be advertised to the general public.

16.15 What are investment trusts?

Unlike unit trusts, investment trusts are not trusts but companies, subject to the provisions of the Companies Acts like all other companies. The Companies Act 1980 created an entirely new class of public company – the *investment company*. Investment companies provide another way in which the small investor can obtain a spread of interest and professional investment management. They use their capital and reserves for direct investment, and a holder of ordinary shares in such companies has an indirect interest in the underlying portfolio.

Investment trust companies are a long-established form of indirect investment – some were formed over a century ago. But they have suffered many problems in recent years and have not grown anything like as quickly as their

Table 16.3 Assets held by investment trusts 1987–89

Investment trusts

			United Kingdom					
			Listed company securities					
	Total invest-ments	Total	British Govt. securities	Total	Loan capital	Prefer-ence	Ordinary	Unlisted company securities
Holdings at end of year: market values £m								
1987	19 066	10 782	595	8 910	218	175	8 517	728
1988	19 298	10 431	360	8 764	249	383	8 132	931
1989	23 526	12 395	196	11 141	157	512	10 472	849

			Overseas company securities		
	Property	Total	Loan capital	Preference	Ordinary
Holdings at end of year: market values £m					
1987	61	7 958	408	68	7 482
1988	75	8 697	506	75	8 116
1989	60	11 024	346	91	10 587

Source: *Financial Statistics* January 1991.

more popular rivals. While the number of unit trusts has increased, invest-ment trusts have contracted and currently number only around 200, although they are larger on average than a unit trust. Their merits are less well known to the average personal investor, and most of their shares are owned by other institutions, whereas most units in unit trusts are owned by the general public.

There are investment trust companies to suit most investment require-ments, from above-average income return to nil income return, from specialized investment to a wide-ranging general investment policy, and from those concerned principally with UK investment to those that concentrate their attention overseas. Overall, investment trusts are more diversified than unit trusts, and display less variation in performance. Around 90 trusts provide regular savings schemes from about £25 per month.

16.16 Split-level trusts

The split-capital company – often called a *split-level trust* or a *dual trust* – was first introduced in 1965. In this type of investment trust company there are two classes of equity capital: *income shares* and *capital shares*. During the life of the company, which is usually a fixed period (often twenty years), the income shares are entitled to most or all the income received from the underlying portfolio and the capital shares are entitled to most or all of the assets. At the end of the company's life the income shares are paid out at a pre-arranged figure – usually their par value – and the value remaining is paid out to the capital shareholders.

Split-level trust shares are an interesting investment. During the life of the company the income shareholders should receive a growing return to help offset the reduction in purchasing power caused by inflation. Some capital growth can be achieved by the sale of income shares fairly early in their life, as the increasing yield on the value ultimately to be repaid makes the price of the shares on the market rise above the nominal value, although the price must fall again towards the end of the company's life. The income shares give a gearing element to the capital shares which, at the end of the period, are entitled to the value of the investments, less the repayment value of the income shares.

Capital shares may be useful to the higher-rate taxpayer who finds income an unwelcome embarrassment. Their volatility, because of the gearing, makes them an investment to be in and out of rather than one to stick to through the usual succession of bull and bear markets. Sometimes additional gearing is introduced by the issue of fixed-interest capital, which makes a *triple trust*. Triple trusts can be very highly geared indeed, and their capital shares are the most volatile of all.

16.17 Comparison with unit trusts

There are several differences for the investor between an investment in an investment trust company and an investment in a unit trust, as follows:

16.17.1 Closed funds

An investment trust company is a *closed-end* fund, whereas a unit trust is *open-ended*. Issues of new capital can be made as in any other company but, unless there are prior charges which increase the gearing, only to existing ordinary shareholders by way of rights issues. Unit trusts, however, being open-ended, may grow in size as new unit-holders buy themselves into the trust at asset value.

16.17.2 Gearing

Investment trust companies usually have an element of *gearing* – that is, part of their capital consists of fixed-interest issues such as debenture stocks. This gives shareholders an advantage during periods of rising market prices. Conversely, in bear markets the shareholders suffer from a fall in the value of their shares greater than the fall of prices generally. Unit trusts may not borrow, and the price of units moves in line with the value of the underlying portfolio.

Gearing by investment trust companies is sometimes achieved by the issue of convertible debenture stocks or loan stocks, giving a right to convert into the ordinary capital at some future date. Gearing can also be introduced by means of foreign-currency loans. Investment trust companies can use their equity portfolios as security for the borrowing of foreign currency, thus increasing the total amount available for equity investment. Investment trust gearing has declined in recent years, because of high interest rates.

16.17.3 Prices and costs of dealing

The price of shares in investment trust companies is governed by the market forces of supply and demand. Unit trust prices are governed by the value of the underlying portfolio. Many investment trust company shares are dealt in on the Stock Exchange and therefore may be priced at above or below their asset value.

Investment trust company charges vary considerably from company to company, but generally the annual management charge, at around 0.5 per cent, is less than the equivalent for unit trusts. As shares are purchased on the market, there is no initial charge as such, but the normal expenses of the purchase of shares apply. Generally, investment trust company investment is cheaper than other forms of indirect investment.

16.17.4 The discount on net asset value

When share prices are rising, investment company shares are a particularly strong market and it is at such times that new issues abound. For many years, it has been more usual for investment company shares to sell at a substantial discount, and this can be viewed as a cheap way of buying shares – see fig. 16.1. However, certain specialist trusts in small overseas markets sometimes sell at a premium to net asset value.

16.17.5 Income

Except in the case of accumulation trusts, unit trusts generally distribute all their income. Investment trust companies, like other companies, declare dividends which may or may not exhaust the available income.

16.17.6 Investment powers

The investment powers of unit trusts are limited by the terms of the trust deed: only a certain proportion of the fund may be invested in a single stock, and only a percentage of the share capital of a company may be acquired. The investment powers of investment companies may instead be limited by their articles of association and the Stock Exchange Continuing Obligations.

16.17.7 Marketability

Marketability is no problem with a unit trust: only rarely are sales to the public suspended, and the managers are required to repurchase any units offered to them. The shares of many investment trust companies are tightly held by institutions and just not available for purchase. This creates a very narrow market in some smaller companies, and it is often difficult to deal. This problem does not arise in the larger companies.

16.17.8 Information

Unit trust management companies supply information on all their trusts to enquirers. Because only a few trusts are quoted on the Stock Exchange, stockbroker/dealers' advice on unit trusts is usually restricted to a small number of trusts where they have special connections. Information on investment trust companies in general is available from the Association of Investment Trusts, and details of all trusts can be found in the *FT Investment Trust Yearbook*. Certain broker/dealers specialize in investment trust companies, and can provide up-to-date advice.

16.17.9 Taxation and approval

In order to qualify for exemption from tax on capital gains, the company must be approved by the Inland Revenue as conforming with the definition of an investment trust company contained in the Income and Corporation Taxes Act 1988. The vast majority of investment trust companies do so conform.

The chief requirements of the Act are that:

(a) the company's income is derived wholly or mainly from securities (this is interpreted as about 70 per cent or more);
(b) no holding must represent more than 15 per cent of the investment trust company's investments;
(c) its own shares are quoted on the International Stock Exchange;
(d) the company is debarred by its own memorandum or articles of association from distributing as dividends profits arising from the sale of investments.

New applicants for a Stock Exchange listing are required to state an investment policy under which no more than 10 per cent of the fund is invested in the securities of any one company and no more than 25 per cent is invested in securities not listed on a recognized stock exchange or NASDAQ.

Investment trusts are at a disadvantage to unit trusts in terms of taxation of unfranked income. They pay the full rate of corporation tax (35 per cent 1990/91), whereas unit trusts become subject to basic-rate tax, reclaimable by non-taxpayers from 1991.

16.18 The decline in the status of investment trusts

Investment trust shares were a strong market in the early 1970s, and this gave rise to a number of new issues. Several of the better-managed companies' shares were selling at a premium, and the average discount narrowed to around 3 per cent. Yields were low, in line with their growth-oriented portfolios.

After the spate of new issues and the general market euphoria of the earlier period, a reaction set in. The oversupply of investment trust company shares coincided with investors' disillusionment both with the 'cult of the equity' and with the mistakes of many investment trusts in overseas markets. The drift of the private investor from the stock market and the counter-

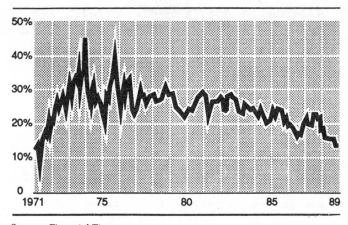

Source: *Financial Times*

Fig. 16.1   Investment trusts – average discount (share price/net asset value)

attractions of unit trusts also occasioned heavy selling of investment trust shares. By 1976 the discount to net asset value had widened to over 40 per cent (see fig. 16.1). With the growth of other institutional investment – particularly the pension funds – managers have tended to make direct investments rather than rely on the expertise of the investment trust managers.

In recent years there have been signs that the situation is improving. Several pension funds have invested in the purchase of the whole of the issued capital of some investment trusts, and the excess supply problem has been assisted by a number of liquidations. At the same time, several investment trust companies have been 'unitized' – that is, converted into unit trusts. In recent times the discount has narrowed to less than 20 per cent on average.

16.19 Judging performance

Performance naturally varies, and the investor will examine the market price of different companies over a period when selecting established trusts. The *FT*–Actuaries Investment Trust Index forms a useful yardstick. With newer trusts it is now often possible to examine the record of other trusts under the same management, as investment trust companies have largely become concentrated in the hands of several specialist investment management concerns.

Table 16.4 and fig. 16.2 compare the performance of unit and investment trusts and building society investment over the ten-year period from 1980 to 1990 and intervening periods. It is quite apparent from the two separate studies that the average investment trust signficantly outperformed the average unit trust over the whole period, by as much as 25 per cent. While

Table 16.4 Comparative performance – theoretical £1000 invested over given periods to 1 March 1990: offer to bid, income reinvested

	Value (£) after				
	1 year	2 years	3 years	5 years	10 years
Average unit trust:					
MM unit-holder average	1038	1206	1125	1833	4980
Bank:					
Lloyds deposit account	1076	1138	1179	1363	2051
Building society:					
Halifax Index	1095	1178	1270	1527	2607
Stock market:					
FT All-Share Index	1073	1273	1192	2032	5611
Investment trusts:					
FT–A Investment Trust Index	1069	1345	1221	1929	6248
Inflation:					
RPI, 31 December 1989	1077	1157	1195	1310	1921

Source: *Money Management*.

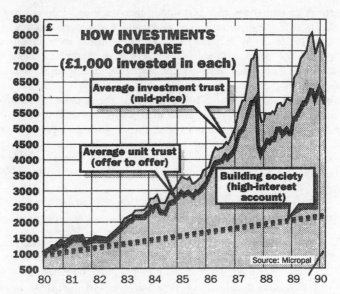

Fig. 16.2　Comparative performance of unit trusts, investment trusts, and building society accounts, 1980–90

both outperformed inflation and a bank or building society investment, only the investment trusts bettered the performance of the *FT*–Actuaries All-Share Index. The investment trusts' superior performance was largely accounted for by their gearing in a rising market, greater exposure to overseas stock markets, and lower level of management charges.

16.20 Personal Equity Plans (PEPs)

Personal Equity Plans were introduced in the Finance Act 1986 in an attempt (along with privatization) to encourage direct ownership of equities. Instead of simply buying a diversified portfolio indirectly through a unit trust or investment trust, investors were to be encouraged to identify personally with individual companies, although the shares would be bought through a pooled arrangement.

The main attraction of PEPs is that dividend income and capital gains earned in a plan are tax-free. But, unlike pension contributions or the Business Expansion Scheme, there is no tax relief on the sums invested. Since its introduction, a number of the original restrictions have been relaxed. The maximum investment for 1990/91 is £6000 per person; £12 000 for a married couple. Investors must be resident and 'ordinarily resident' in the UK, and at least eighteen years of age.

PEPs are operated by 'approved managers' authorized to deal in securities – broker/dealers, banks, building societies, unit trusts and investment trusts. There are a large number of schemes on offer – nearly 200 in late 1989 – and they differ in a number of respects. 'Self-select' PEPs allow investors to choose their own shares; others offer discretionary management. They can cater for lump sums or regular savings. Some take advantage of the possibility of using a PEP to buy into a unit or investment trust.

The 'self-select' PEPs usually offer only a restricted list of shares, and can be expensive in terms of management charges. The managers are required to restrict the shares to UK-registered shares which are fully listed or quoted on the USM. Privatization issues can be transferred into a PEP within 30 days of the announcement of the allocation. They must be included in the annual investment limit. PEP investors have the same rights as ordinary shareholders – to receive the annual report and accounts, to attend meetings and vote, etc. – but some managers charge exorbitant fees for supplying the relevant material.

Some companies have used a 'corporate PEP', which holds only a single company's ordinary shares, as a means of encouraging the small investor.

For most investors the most attractive option is to use the PEP as means of obtaining a unit or investment trust. Up to £3000 per person per year can be invested through a PEP into a 'qualifying' unit or investment trust, which must have at least 50 per cent of its underlying holdings in UK-quoted shares. The limit for 'non-qualifying' trusts is £900 (1990/91).

The unit trust or investment trust version of a PEP really defeats the original objective of the PEP, which was direct share ownership. But it has the virtues of tax advantages, lower management charges, and much greater diversification than other PEPs.

16.21 Performance measurement

How do you measure performance of a unit trust or investment trust? The answer is that it depends on the purpose for which the exercise is being undertaken. If it is to see what is the overall return on capital invested over a specified period, we use the *money-weighted* rate of return. On the other hand, for comparing the performance of one fund manager with another, the *time-weighted* rate of return is more satisfactory. In both cases we calculate the total return on the fund in terms of increase in capital value plus income received. The total return is negative at times when the capital value decreases by an amount greater than the income received.

16.21.1 Money-weighted rate of return

The simplest method of measuring the return on a portfolio is to value the investments on the two days between which the performance is to be compared, and adjust for items such as sales and purchases, including rights issues, capital gains tax, and income received. To take a simple exercise, suppose that an equity fund was worth £10 000 at the beginning of the year. Dividend income of £600 was received at the end of the year and was immediately reinvested in the fund, which was then worth £12 000. The portfolio thus achieved a return of £2000, and the 'total' rate of return was 20 per cent – 6 per cent dividend yield plus 14 per cent capital growth.

The example would have been more complicated if additional capital had been invested or withdrawn during the course of that year. Imagine the following timetable:

	Invested	Withdrawn
End of February	£1000	
End of June		£2000
End of September	£1500	

During the year there has been a 'net' investment of £500. If this is deducted from the closing valuation, the rate of return is reduced to 15 per cent – that is, total return = £12 000−£10 000−£500 = £1 500.

If greater accuracy is required, the calculation could be modified to allow for differences in timing of capital injections and withdrawals, weighting each by the number of months of the year remaining at the time they are effected:

$$\text{Total rate of return} = \frac{£12\,000-£10\,000-£500}{£10\,000+(\tfrac{5}{6}\times£1000)-(\tfrac{1}{2}\times£2000)+(\tfrac{1}{4}\times£1500)}$$

$$= \frac{£1500}{£10\,208} = 14.7 \text{ per cent}$$

Where a personal investor withdraws his or her capital for spending purposes, any capital gains tax should be counted as a charge on the portfolio but is effectively paid out of the sum withdrawn. But when the liability results from a 'switching' operation, only the 'net' sum – that is, net of any capital gains tax – counts as a withdrawal. The argument in favour of a switch must be that, notwithstanding the tax that will be payable, the shares purchased will show better prospects than the shares sold. The tax payable is a penalty for the ability to manage the portfolio, as any *FT*–Actuaries index is equivalent to an unmanaged portfolio. The All-Share Index suffers the 'penalty' of having to remain in unsuccessful sectors and companies. If a sale gives rise to an allowable loss against capital gains tax, this is ignored until it is used to reduce tax payable, when only the net amount of any tax will need to be allowed for in the calculations. If income is received throughout the year and immediately reinvested, it can be ignored in simply calculating the total return on the portfolio, but it should be treated in the same way as any other capital injection if comparison is to be made with the *FT*–Actuaries indices (which, of course, do not reinvest income).

The rate of return produced by this method is the actual return on the fund and can be thought of as the rate of interest which the initial portfolio, plus net new money, would have had to earn in a deposit account in order to accumulate to the actual value of the portfolio at the end of the year. This is useful for the individual but is inadequate, and sometimes misleading, for institutional investors.

16.21.2 *Time-weighted rate of return*

Pension funds and insurance companies need to pay attention to the performance of their assets relative to any change in their liabilities. Thus they generally emphasize growth in investment income more than possible short-term changes in capital values. To long-term investors, with growing funds, capital values can appear largely irrelevant if assets are never likely to be sold on any substantial scale. It is none the less sometimes necessary to measure the performance of fund managers – particularly those of unit trusts and investment trusts.

In making such an assessment, the effect of new money must be eliminated; otherwise it cannot be clear whether the overall return was the sole responsibility of the investment manager or whether it was affected by the timing of the new money over which he or she had no control. A unit trust fund manager, for instance, may be faced with the problem of the greatest inflow of cash when the market is near its peak, and may be under great pressure to invest when he or she may not wish to do so; the equity fund manager in an insurance company may find that the amount of 'new money' to be invested has been determined by an investment committee. The advantage of the time-weighted rate of return is that it eliminates this effect.

Suppose the *FT*–Actuaries index has the following values:

1 January	100
30 June	80
31 December	130

The return over the year is obviously 30 per cent, ignoring dividend income. If an institutional investor had invested £10 million at the beginning of the year and then invested a further £10 million on 30 June, the value at the end of the year would have been £29.25 million (that is, £10 million $\times \frac{130}{100} +$ £10 million $\times \frac{130}{80}$). Then:

$$\text{money-weighted return} = \frac{£29.25m - £10m - £10m}{£10m + (\frac{1}{2} \times £10m)}$$

$$= \frac{£9.25m}{£15m} = 61\frac{2}{3} \text{ per cent}$$

The reason why the portfolio so dramatically outperformed the index – $61\frac{2}{3}$ per cent as compared with 30 per cent – is that the 'new money' invested on 30 June achieved a much higher return than the initial fund. Thus the apparent good performance relative to the index had nothing to do with the shares selected, but was solely due to the 'accident' of the timing of the new money.

The problem is partly resolved by breaking down the return for a particular period into subperiods, with a separate subperiod for every injection or withdrawal of capital. In our example, the new money was received half-way through the year, so the year can be simply divided into two six-month subperiods. The return for the first half-year was −20 per cent, as the value of the investment, ignoring dividend income, fell to 80 from 100 – a price-relative of $\frac{80}{100}$ – but in the second part of the year the investment rose from 80 to 130 – a price-relative of $\frac{130}{80}$. The time-weighted rate of return is derived from the product of the price-relatives: $(\frac{80}{100} \times \frac{130}{80}) - 1 = 0.3 = 30$ per cent. Obviously, this is the same annual return as that on the 'index', despite the timing of the cash inflows. If the investor had not modelled his or her portfolio on the constituents of the index, but had bought different shares, or given different weightings to the shares, success or failure relative to the 'index' could be identified using this method, without timing distortions.

There are two drawbacks to this method. Firstly, by eliminating the effect of the new money, fund managers are no longer penalized by factors beyond their control. But where they have discretion over timing, this approach deprives them of any credit for successfully predicting 'bull' and 'bear' markets; equally they are not 'punished' for getting the market wrong. Secondly, a precise calculation of the time-weighted rate of return requires a valuation of the fund, to measure capital change, every time new money is introduced. One approximation is to calculate the money-weighted rates of return quarterly rather than annually and then combine these returns together to give a fairly good approximation of the time-weighted rate of return for the year.

Alternatively, we may use the *unitization* approach. A unitized fund is revalued every time there is a flow of money into or out of the fund, in order to calculate the unit price. The change in the unit price over a particular period automatically gives the precise time-weighted rate of return.

For funds not unit-linked, the easiest solution to the problem of timing is to calculate the money-weighted rates of return for both the fund and the chosen index – that is, to assume funds were invested in the index in exactly the same amounts and at exactly the same time. A notional fund can be established with the same opening value as the actual fund. Every time cash is added to or withdrawn from the actual fund, the notional fund can be revalued in line with the index, and the appropriate addition or deduction can be made. A 'chain index' can be used to provide continuity when alterations are made. For example, if the fund starts with £10 million when the index is 200, and at the end of the first month the index is 210, the value of the notional fund will be £10 million$\times\frac{210}{200}$ = £10.5 million. If £500 000 is now invested, the notional fund is worth £11 million. At the end of the second month the index stands at 220, and the fund is now worth £11 million$\times\frac{220}{210}$ = £11.52 million. If £500 000 is again invested the fund is worth £12.02 million. With each injection or withdrawal of funds, the closing index level becomes the base for the next period. Every time the actual fund is revalued, it can be compared with the notional fund.

16.21.3 Base portfolios

The notional fund outlined above is an example of a 'base portfolio'. The term refers to an unmanaged fund against which the performance of the managed fund can be compared. It can be used for equities, gilts, property, or any other type of asset, or any combination of them.

The base portfolio might be the existing fund, taken in order to see the outcome of an inactive, non-switching policy. It could be an 'index fund' or it could be constructed independently where no existing index is felt to reflect the requirements of the fund as dictated by the nature of its business, the investment committee, or the trustees.

16.21.4 Risk

So far we have discussed portfolio performance measurement without mentioning risk. This is not unacceptable in the case of long-term investors, such as life assurance and pension funds, for whom all that really matters is the overall rate of return – year-to-year fluctuations in returns can be ignored. This is not true of most other managed funds – particularly unit and investment trusts: where the investor may hold the portfolio for no more than a few years, the *volatility* of the annual returns needs to be considered. The greater the volatility, the less the reliance that can be placed on the mean expected return, particularly over the short-to-medium term. 'League-tables' of unit trusts and other unit-linked investments used to offer a crude ranking of fund performance by rate of return alone. More sophisticated techniques incorporating risk and return are increasingly being used.

For instance, a leading authority on investment, W. F. Sharpe, calculates the average return and the variability of returns on a wide range of funds over a given number of years. Risk can be plotted against return for all funds on a single graph (as in fig. 16.3). Clearly, a good fund offers a lot of extra return for a given amount of risk, whereas a poor fund offers much less extra return for the same amount of risk, or offers the same extra return for a much greater degree of risk.

The 'best' fund is fund A. This is because it offers a steeper line from i, the risk-free rate (such as a one-year Government bond), than any other fund

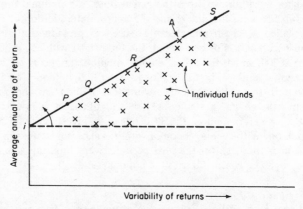

Fig. 16.3   The Sharpe model

plotted on the graph. The risk/return combinations shown by points P, Q, and R could have been obtained by holding a combination of risk-free asset and fund A and varying the weights. Point S could have been achieved if it had been possible to *borrow*, rather than invest, at the risk-free rate, i, and invest one's own proceeds plus the borrowed funds in fund A. Therefore any other fund can be shown to be inferior, no matter what its risk level.

Sharpe's method can be adopted to establish relative rankings for unit trusts and similar funds, or to see whether a particular fund has 'beaten the market', by plotting the *FT*–Actuaries All-Share Index, or a similar index, as a notional fund.

It would be rash to presume that past performance can be used to identify the best-performing funds for the future. The efficient market hypothesis – in particular the 'strong form' – casts doubt on continuity of performance. Often the worst-performing trust in one period is the best performer in the next, and vice versa, especially when the fund is concentrated heavily in one sector of the market.

16.22 Protection for the investor

The controls on advertising, 'cold-calling', and cancellation rights for investors in unit and investment trusts and PEPs are similar to those for investors in life assurance. These are discussed in section 17.10, in the following chapter on life assurance.

16.23 Questions

1. (a) What is the usual maximum percentage of an authorized unit trust fund which may be invested in any one company?

   A 2½ per cent.
   B 5 per cent.
   C 10 per cent.
   D 15 per cent.

   (b) Which of the following is *not* true of personal equity plans (PEPs)?

   A A PEP must be held for over 12 months for the tax benefits to be enjoyed.
   B Holders of PEPs can attend meetings of the relevant companies.
   C Husband and wife can each take out one plan each year.
   D Direct investment is restricted to UK companies.

   (c) All unauthorized unit trusts are:

   A very risky.
   B based offshore.
   C outside SIB/DTI regulation.
   D insurance-based.

   (d) Explain the meaning and relevance of: (i) 'designated territory' status, (ii) UCITS. (SIE)
   (e) Outline *four* differences between authorized unit trusts and approved investment trusts. (SIE)
   (f) Outline the income and capital gains tax treatment of offshore 'roll-up' and 'distributor' funds. (SIE)

2. (a) Recently published figures show that investment in investment trusts has been more successful than investment in unit trusts over a period of ten years. What are the reasons for this?
   (CIB 5/89)
   (b) An investor has capital of £120 000 to which he adds £60 000 after three months. Exactly six months later he withdraws £30 000. At the end of one year his total fund together with income reinvested is worth £180 000. Calculate his return on a money-weighted basis. How satisfactory is this method of measuring portfolio performance?
   (CIB 5/88)

3. Your customer, Mr B, has inherited £10 000 and wishes to invest this amount in a unit trust offering a reasonable yield and prospects of medium-term growth of capital and income. He is bewildered by the large number of unit trusts available. Explain how you could help him:

   (a) to identify unit trusts which meet his requirements; and
   (b) to make a final selection. (CIB 4/81)

4. (a) What are the attractions to investors of personal equity plans (PEPs)?
   (b) What arguments could be put forward to support the case for investment in unit trusts rather than PEPs?

(CIB 5/88)

17 Life assurance

17.1 Life assurance

The term 'assurance' is reserved for this kind of insurance only. Every *life assurance* policy consists of a contract between an insurance company and its customer. The contract covers an agreed sum of money – the *sum assured* – and a period of time – *the term*. The policy-holder agrees to pay certain sums – the *premiums* – usually at regular intervals over the term. The company agrees to pay the sum assured in the event of the customer's death before expiry of the term or, in certain cases, on survival at the end of the term.

There are three basic types of life assurance:

(a) *Term* Premiums are paid throughout a limited period and the sum assured is payable only on death before the term ends. The best-known example is the mortgage protection policy.
(b) *Whole-life* Premiums are paid throughout life or to a specified age and the sum assured is payable only on death.
(c) *Endowment* Premiums are paid for a specified number of years only. The sum assured is payable on completion of the term or on earlier death.

Whole-life and term policies are similar in that the sum assured is normally payable only on death, whereas endowment assurance premiums have to take into account the probability of survival to the end of the specified term. Term assurance is generally inexpensive, whereas endowment assurance is by far the most costly of the three kinds.

UK life assurance companies are not subject to investment limits in the same way as authorized unit trusts or approved investment trusts, but their overall portfolio mix is controlled by the Insurance Companies Regulations 1981 and the Insurance Companies Act 1982. The retail side of life assurance business is controlled by the relevant SRO – LAUTRO or FIMBRA, for tied or independent business respectively.

17.2 Endowment assurance

Assurance policies that provide only for payment of the sum assured at death can hardly be regarded as investments, although they should be an important feature of any investor's overall financial strategy. Endowment policies, however, contain a very substantial savings and investment element.

On taking out a policy, the customer knows for certain the minimum sum that would be payable should he or she die before the end of the term. The endowment policy may be *with profits* or *without profits*, the former type giving the customer the right to share in the life assurance profits of the insurance company. The life companies commonly set sums assured conservatively, and a 'with-profits' policy is usually much the better investment of the two. The premium is of course higher, though not in proportion to the anticipated return.

The profits on traditional endowment policies are of two kinds:

(a) *Reversionary bonuses* are based on the sum assured and are usually declared annually during the life of the policy. Over the years they have steadily increased, and life companies are extremely reluctant to cut the bonus rates. Reversionary bonuses are added at each declaration to the sum assured and cannot be revoked.
(b) *Terminal bonuses* reflect the capital value of the investments to the maturity date. Terminal bonuses apply only if the policyholder dies, or the policy matures, in a given year. Terminal bonuses are not cumulative.

'If you care to back your message with money . . .'

The life companies generally invest premium income in a balanced portfolio which usually includes substantial elements of gilt-edged securities and equities. The holder of a straightforward endowment policy does not know how his or her premiums are being used, but a wide variety of life assurance schemes are now linked to some specific type of fund such as equities, property, or gilts or some combination of these investments. Whole-life policies can also be taken out on the same basis.

Policies do not have to be maintained throughout the whole term. The holder of a whole-life or an endowment policy nearly always has the options of *surrender* or *conversion to a paid-up policy*. Companies are now required to publish their terms for surrender or conversion – these vary considerably, although this is often reflected in the level of premiums. Nevertheless, these options are usually on terms that bear harshly on the policyholder. Traditional life assurance contracts should therefore only be entered into for the long term after careful consideration. They should be surrendered or paid up only in circumstances of extreme necessity. An alternative is to sell the paid-up policy to someone else. Foster and Cranfield are specialist auctioneers who sell endowment policies. Others such as Policy Network, Policy Portfolio, and Beale Dobie either link up buyers and sellers or act as principals themselves.

17.3 Unit-linked policies

The development of unit-linked policies owes much more to the unit trust movement than to the life assurance companies. Left to themselves, the latter would doubtless have preferred the greater flexibility which is permitted them in providing traditional policies. The performance of unit-linked policies tends to be more volatile than that of traditional policies. The investor is exposed to the full rigours of gains and losses. Unlike with traditional policies, gains made in earlier years can be lost if unit values fall.

Life assurance as such is one of those essential services that normally require to be actively sold. In general, people do not seek out life assurance and so traditionally it has been sold by the doorstep salesperson calling on homes and offices. The marketing of unit trusts at first depended largely on newspaper advertising, and more recently on sales through agents such as stockbroker/dealers and insurance brokers, but until the introduction of the Financial Services Act unit trusts could not be sold door-to-door. Before the Act, however, either by arrangement with existing life assurance companies or by forming their own companies, unit trust managers could very effectively promote the sales of their products in this way.

Today unit-linked life assurance includes equities, gilts, property, cash, and managed funds, on either a lump-sum or a regular-premium basis. The single-premium policies are generally known as *'investment bonds'*.

The selection of a single 'best' linked scheme is virtually impossible, in view of the vast number of specialist funds within each of these categories and the problems of assessing future performance.

An advantage sometimes claimed for unit-linked policies is the ability to switch between the constituent funds at nil or negligible cost, whereas in the case of unit trusts the full bid–offer spread normally has to be paid, and the investor incurs a potential liability for capital gains tax.

In the case of unit-linked policies, charges consist of firstly the initial bid–offer spread of around 5 per cent on the price of units and secondly the annual management charge of typically 0.75 per cent, both of which are slightly less than usual for unit trusts. But there is also a policy fee each year. In addition some unit-linked funds invest in unit trusts of the same management group and so suffer a double management charge. Life policies make a deduction on maturity of a policy for the contingent capital gains tax liability – that is, for that point in the future when gains are realized and capital gains tax has to be paid. The deduction is usually between 10 and 25 per cent of the accrued gain. The 1990 Budget statement said that life offices' holdings in unit trusts would be assessed for capital gains tax on *accrued* gains each year. But the largest deduction can be in the *allocation rate* – the proportion of the investor's money which actually goes into the funds. In the early years the allocation rate may be very low, although this may not be apparent if the money is simply allocated to 'capital units'. These have a much higher management charge than the standard units.

17.3.1 Property bonds

The attractions of property as an investment have long been recognized, and property bonds have been no exception. As with all investments, the timing of the purchase is of crucial importance and the bonds should be regarded as long-term, or at least medium-term, investments. Property bonds' prices reflect the ups and downs in industrial, commercial, and agricultural property.

The two main problems with the property fund are liquidity and valuation. Property is less readily marketable than are stocks and shares, and the managers must therefore maintain a degree of liquidity to enable them to meet withdrawals as they occur. Very large withdrawal demands could be disastrous for the fund, and the investor should therefore buy only those bonds issued by leading companies that have the backing of, say, a large insurance company.

Property is notoriously difficult to value, and the only real valuation is the ultimate sale price. However, some attempt at valuation must be made for investment and withdrawal purposes. A fund will have all its properties independently valued each year and will subsequently update these valuations on a month-to-month basis by reference to an index such as that reflecting the cost of new construction.

The other dangers to investors in property-linked contracts are similar to those involved in equity-linked contracts: the level of charges and the freedom from supervision of dealings, which are legally permissible between associated companies. A property fund can be used by less scrupulous insurance companies as a 'dump' for their unsuccessful property investments.

As with equity funds, the proof of the pudding is in the eating: it is the medium- to long-term performance that counts. The early performance of new funds should be ignored in making comparisons, as this is almost certainly based on other forms of investment. A substantial sum is needed before the first property can be purchased.

17.3.2 Managed bonds

These are assurance contracts that are linked on the unit principle to a number of underlying funds, the split between them being determined by the promoters. Also known as a *flexible* or *three-way fund*, the typical *managed bond* consists of elements of equities, fixed-interest stocks, and property, but the managers have absolute discretion and some bonds from time to time contain only fixed-interest securities.

In practice these bonds are less flexible than they claim to be. Property, in particular, cannot be acquired or disposed of very quickly. But there is a degree of flexibility in that managers can invest new funds in those areas that currently appear to offer the best prospects for investors. This can be offset if withdrawals for a time exceed new money coming in.

As with most insurance schemes, the operation is organized to deal with an expanding fund. There have been occasions when certain linked funds have experienced a negative cash flow – that is, their new money fell short of surrenders and maturities. This always causes problems, particularly with a mix of equity and property funds, where the equity fund must always be resorted to in the shorter term. The claims of the promoters – to be influenced in their investment policy solely by good prospects in different investment areas – assume a growing fund with a successful record. Sheer force of circumstances could, on occasion, make those claims impossible to maintain.

17.4 Qualifying life assurance policies

Until March 1984, an investor could obtain Life Assurance Premium Relief (LAPR) on gross life assurance premiums on new 'qualifying' policies.

With policies taken out before March 1984, a gross premium of, say, £100 now actually costs the investor £87.50. The insurance company claims back £12.50 from the tax authorities. All life assurance policies are free of capital gains tax in the hands of the investor, because the fund itself pays capital gains tax. This is a reversal of the situation with regard to the authorized mainland unit trusts and approved investment trusts. 'Qualifying' life assurance policies are also exempt from income tax in the hands of the investor, whereas 'non-qualifying' policies may be subject to higher-rate income tax, although exempted from basic-rate tax. Thus for a basic-rate taxpayer there is effectively no difference between a qualifying and a non-qualifying policy.

The main requirements to be a qualifying policy are:

(a) premiums must be payable for at least ten years, except in the case of term assurance;

(b) premiums must be paid annually or more frequently;
(c) the sum assured must be not less than a certain percentage of the premiums payable – 75 per cent for endowment policies. For policyholders over 55 years of age the rule is relaxed somewhat.

All these rules exist to prevent abuse of the tax system. If, for example, a policy is surrendered within ten years or three-quarters of the term (whichever is less), the taxpayer could find that he or she is assessed for income tax at a rate equivalent to higher rate less basic rate.

17.5 Taxation of single-premium policies

On encashment, 'non-qualifying' policies – usually single-premium assurance policies, or 'investment bonds' – are subject to higher-rate tax (if applicable) less basic-rate. The method of taxation is known as *top-slicing*. These bonds are mainly of interest to investors who pay higher-rate tax. The Inland Revenue allows modest withdrawals, up to a cumulative maximum of 5 per cent annually with any higher-rate tax deferred until encashment. These policies can also be of use where an investor's income fluctuates substantially from year to year, involving considerable changes in tax liability.

The following example shows how the principle of top-slicing operates.

Units in a single-premium life policy acquired for			£10 000
Annual withdrawals:			
Years 1 to 3	£1 500 (i.e. £500 p.a.)		
Years 4 and 5	nil		
Year 6	£ 700		
Year 7	£1 300	£ 3 500	
Policy cashed after seven years for	———	£20 000	£23 500
Overall profit on policy			£13 500

Such profit is not tax-free but is exempt only from the basic-rate tax charge. To ascertain the tax payable we must first deal with the overall profit on an annual basis. The overall profit of £13 500 is divided by the number of complete years the band has been held – in this case seven complete years. The 'top slice' is therefore £13 500/7 = £1928. If the investor's other income in the year of final encashment were, say, £15 000 then there would be no tax to pay since the combined income would be £15 000+£1928 = £16 928, which is less than the starting point for higher-rate tax, £20 700 (1990/91).

If the investor's other taxable income happened to be £25 000, the investor would obviously be a higher-rate taxpayer, and the whole of £13 500 would be subject to 15 per cent additional tax. The 15 per cent is the difference between higher-rate tax and basic-rate tax. The additional tax would therefore be £13 500×15% = £2025.

If the investor's taxable income were previously below the higher-rate tax threshold, but would go above it when the 'top slice' was added, the top-slice would be apportioned. Assume the taxable income was £19 000; then

£19 000–£20 700 – exempt
£20 700–£20 928 – subject to higher-rate less basic-rate tax

The additional tax liability would therefore be

£228×15%×7 (years) = £239

If the investor withdraws more than 5 per cent of the original sum – even after allowing for unused withdrawals from previous years – the 'excess' withdrawals are similarly subject to top-slicing. The complete years used as the divisor in the calculation would be the number of years from the purchase of the policy until the date of the 'excess' withdrawal. The 'excess' amounts would not be subsequently included in the final encashment calculation, since this could involve them being taxed twice.

One advantage of these policies that is frequently commented upon is that encashment can be deferred until the investor changes from being a higher-rate taxpayer to a basic-rate or non-taxpayer, due to retirement or moving abroad. However, on retirement the whole of the gain – not just the 'top slice' – is included when calculating entitlement or otherwise to 'age allowance'.

17.6 Guaranteed income and growth bonds

These bonds offer a fixed income net of basic-rate tax (which is not reclaimable) for a set number of years, at the end of which the original investment is returned in full. Several types of income bond are in issue, and each is subject to a different type of tax treatment. One type consists of a combination of a deferred annuity (see section 17.8) and an immediate temporary annuity. The latter provides an 'income', part of which is a return of capital and so is free of tax. The taxable portion is paid net of basic-rate tax, and the holder must of course pay any higher-rate tax. At maturity the investor can receive the deferred annuity or can withdraw his or her investment by taking a cash option instead. The latter course of action is generally preferred, because if an annuity is required it is usually possible to obtain one on better terms from another company. However, the whole of the gain on the deferred annuity is subject to higher-rate tax, but with top-slicing relief.

An example will illustrate how such an income bond works. A 60-year-old man invests £10 000 over a five-year term: £3400 goes to provide the temporary annuity and £6600 is deferred. The temporary annuity is £900 gross, of which only £193 is taxable, giving the 25 per cent taxpayer a net £852 per annum and the 40 per cent taxpayer not much less at £823. The deferred annuity will produce £11 133 – a profit on £6600 of £4533. After basic-rate tax, the amount paid back to the investor will be his original investment of £10 000. Of course, a higher-rate taxpayer must pay the extra tax if he or she is still liable to higher-rate tax in the year the bond matures.

The currently popular type of income bond consists of purchasing either one single-premium endowment policy or a series of them. The single policy has guaranteed bonus additions which are automatically encashed at the end of each year to provide the income. If it is a series of policies, one matures each year to provide the income. The tax treatment, involving top-slicing, is exactly the same as for the investment bonds discussed earlier.

Some guaranteed income bonds have what is described as a 'growth option', which simply involves reinvestment of the income during the investment term. In fact, all the specialist guaranteed growth bonds are variants on the schemes discussed above. A deferred annuity contract with a cash option was once the most popular type of growth bond. The cash option is taken, and the whole gain is subject to basic-rate and higher-rate taxation, but subject to top-slicing relief.

A more common scheme nowadays, however, is one written simply as a single-premium endowment policy with guaranteed bonus additions which are not realized until the end of the endowment period. The liability to higher-rate tax and the top-slicing procedure again apply, but the method of calculation produces net returns higher than the annuity scheme for an investor paying higher-rate tax in the year of encashment. Anyone paying basic-rate tax at the maturity date will obtain the same return under either scheme.

17.7 Friendly societies' bonds

A useful but very limited scheme can be operated by friendly societies, which pay no tax whatsoever and thus can write endowment policies that are entirely tax-exempt. Such policies must not be for less than ten years, with the premiums payable throughout the period, but limited to £150 per year. A person aged eighteen or over can take out one policy.

These bonds must be regarded as a long-term investment, because in case of surrender before the maturity date the societies are not allowed to repay more than the premiums paid. The other disadvantages are the low limit on contributions and the conservative types of asset held, which can result in unexciting performance. The management of the funds is controlled by the Friendly Societies Act 1974.

17.8 Annuities

An *annuity* is really a special form of insurance policy – a sort of 'whole-life' assurance policy in reverse. Instead of paying regular premiums over a period of years in return for a guaranteed sum payable on death or survival to a stated age, the annuitant pays a capital sum to the insurance company and, in exchange, receives regular annual payments for the remainder of his or her life or for a fixed period. As with life assurance, the size of the annuity payable for a given premium depends upon the sex and age of the annuitant.

The annual payments received consist partly of capital and partly of income. The earlier payments are mainly income, but over a period of time the income portion decreases. For convenience the Inland Revenue has agreed fixed proportions based on the life-expectancy tables. There are many variations on the standard contract, known as an *'immediate level annuity'* or *'purchased life annuity'* (PLA).

One disadvantage of level annuities is the possibility of the death of the annuitant soon after entering into the contract. An alternative is the *'joint life, last survivor'* annuity paid, at a lower rate, until the death of a surviving spouse. Another problem is the impact of inflation on a flat-rate annuity – see Table 17.1. It is possible to buy an *'escalator'* annuity, which makes provision for a specified increase of, say, 5 per cent per annum compound, but this may be of little comfort when inflation is running at a much higher rate. Annuities for these contracts quoted by leading companies in early 1990 for a purchase price of £10 000 were as follows:

	Male (age 65) £	Female (age 60) £
Immediate level annuity	1534	1295
Joint life, last survivor annuity	1239	1239
Escalator annuity (5 per cent)	1138	895

Index-linked annuities are available which provide full inflation protection but have a low initial payment. *'With-profits'* and *'unit-linked'* annuities provide variable returns dependent on the performance of their respective funds. Some annuities guarantee payments for a minimum fixed period – a *'capital protected'* annuity – but at the cost of a lower initial return.

Table 17.1 Annuities and inflation

Years later	Number of survivors		Value of £100 at yearly inflation rate of		
	Men of 65 (%)	Women of 60 (%)	5% (£)	10% (£)	15% (£)
0	100	100	100	100	100
5	87	95	78	62	50
10	69	87	61	39	25
15	47	75	48	24	12
20	25	59	38	15	6
25	9	39	29	9	3
30	2	19	23	6	2
35	0	6	18	4	1

Source: *Money Management*.

Home-income plans provide an opportunity to unlock some of the capital tied up in a house while continuing to benefit from its use. These plans usually involve taking a mortgage on the value of the property and using the funds to purchase an annuity. These plans are discussed in chapter 20.

17.9 Investment in life assurance

The removal of the subsidy on all new policies from March 1984 undoubtedly reduced the attraction of regular-premium policies to most investors.

The need for protection against the financial consequences of early death is an important element of financial planning. Term assurance in particular provides a means of ensuring that a family receives a large financial sum for a relatively modest outlay. For a man of 40, a 25-year mortgage protection policy for £30 000 would cost little more than £100 a year. However, how many families take out term cover sufficient to safeguard their standard of living if the breadwinner should die? The cover necessary for someone earning around £20 000 per year, with at least twenty years to retirement, would need to be at least £200 000. Little wonder, it is said, that life assurance is sold rather than bought!

Many investors prefer endowment policies to term ones, on the basis that at least some money is received if the policyholder survives the full term. This is, however, a fallacious argument, since even in the case of endowment policies some of the premium will go towards protection, and only the balance to investment. Ironically enough, while life assurance has a lot to commend it for protection, as an investment it rates quite poorly. When compared with unit and investment trusts, PEPs, and pensions (see chapter 18), the returns on both traditional and unit-linked life assurance policies are consistently worse. This is illustrated in Table 17.2.

The reasons for the inferior performance of life assurance policies are the taxation of capital gains within the fund and their higher expenses ratios due

Table 17.2 Unit trusts versus life assurance: the return on an investment of £20 per month gross by a male aged 29 at the outset. (Figures to 1 February 1985)

	General unit trusts	Unit-linked assurance	With-profits assurance
	£	£	£
After 15 years			
Top return	20 972	16 641	10 616
Average return	14 505	10 709	8 010
Bottom return	9 691	5 333	5 289
After 10 years			
Top return	11 167	7 713	5 440
Average return	7 015	5 003	4 202
Bottom return	4 089	2 959	3 286

Source: *Planned Savings.*

to commissions paid. It is difficult to recommend life assurance *as an investment* when compared to the alternatives listed above.

Table 17.2 shows that, on average, the general-type authorized unit trust outperformed the unit-linked life assurance policy by 35–40 per cent. Even the top-performing unit-linked policies achieved returns which were barely ahead of the median unit trust. The comparison with 'with-profits' endowment policies is even more damning. Even the top performing 'with-profits' policy was barely ahead of the bottom 1 per cent of general-type unit trusts over the fifteen-year period.

17.10 Protection for the investor

The general rules on advertising, projected returns, 'cold-calling', and 'cooling-off' periods were outlined in chapter 2, 'Advice and protection'. The regime for life assurance and unit trusts is characterized by a distinctive set of privileges and responsibilities. The particular privileges are the general freedom to make unsolicited calls, to engage in 'off-the-page' advertising, and to be excused the necessity for written customer agreements. At the same time, projections of future benefits are standardized, 'cooling off' periods are imposed, and advisers are polarized into either company representatives or independent intermediaries.

Authorized persons are free to make unsolicited calls to persuade members of the public to buy life assurance, unit trusts, and 'unit trust only' PEPs. But regulations handed down by SIB require that in all cases the customer be given the product details necessary to make an informed decision. These consist of

(a) at the outset handing over a *'buyer's guide'*, which clarifies the status of the adviser – independent or tied – and indicates to the customer what information should be provided, and at what point in the course of the negotiation;

(b) providing adequate *general information* at the point of sale to enable the customer to make an informed decision, and informing the customer of the basis of the 'cooling-off' period;

(c) supplying *written product particulars*. Where the investor has the right to cancel, product particulars must be sent no later than, and in practice are usually sent with, the notice of the right to cancel. Where the investor has no right to cancel, product particulars must be supplied as soon as is reasonably practical after making the contract. Included among the details will be the effects of commission charges and other expenses. These are shown on a 'soft' disclosure basis. Independent intermediaries only have to reveal their commission as a percentage of the premiums, rather than in absolute cash terms, unless requested. Tied representatives are not required to produce any commission details at all. Both types of intermediary show overall charges as a percentage of investment returns, rather than in cash terms.

Note that these details are not produced at the time the contract is executed, but are only sent to the investor subsequently. These procedures have been criticized by the Office of Fair Trading and are under review at the time of writing. Other details supplied include amounts payable by the investor, a description of the product, consequences of discontinuance of regular premiums, surrender or transfer values in the first five years, taxation aspects, and the bid–offer spread in the case of unit-linked products.

The customer normally has fourteen days to cancel a contract involving unit trusts or life assurance – the fourteen days beginning from the date of receiving the notice of the right to cancel. However, these cancellation rights are extinguished if the customer is an 'execution only' customer (that is, no advice is given) or enters into a written customer agreement in advance. Such an agreement previously entered into may have permitted unsolicited calls. The overriding exception is regular-premium life assurance, for which cancellation rights always remain operative.

Sales of 'unit trust only' PEPs are, unless effected by means of written customer agreement formalities, in general subject to a *delayed entry* mechanism – the buyer is given a seven-day period during which he or she can withdraw his or her application, and the firm cannot accept the application until the seven days have elapsed.

At present there is no 'cooling-off' period in the case of 'off-the-page' sales of unit trusts and single-premium life policies. But again there is an exception for regular-premium life policies sold in this way. 'Off-the-page' (OTP) advertisements are ones to which the investor can respond by making an immediate commitment, usually by sending off a cheque, supplying a credit-card number, or mandating a direct debt. An advertisement is not OTP if a positive response from the investor cannot be converted into an investment agreement without further literature being sent, or a discussion entered into. Clearly in the case of OTP the 'know your customer' and 'best advice' rules do not apply. The OTP provisions thus create a distinction which is analogous to that between prescription-only medicines and those which can be bought over the counter. Adverts must contain 'fluctuation' and 'front-end load' warnings, and a statement that there will be no right to cancel, unless it is regular-premium life assurance.

Projections or illustrations are statements of the possible future value of an investment. Except where the projection relates to a guaranteed fixed rate of return, such estimates are highly conjectural, based upon assumptions about future rates of return, future charges, tax rates, etc. There could easily be a tendency to extrapolate short-term unsustainable performance when the firm is in a highly competitive market. This process of competitive 'bidding-up' was ended by the introduction of standardized projections. LAUTRO prescribes the assumptions on which projections must be based, with the result that all such life assurance companies' projections are identical. Every projection must contain two sets of figures, based respectively on conservative and optimistic assumptions. In this way the hypothetical nature of the projection and the scope for variability are underlined. The same constraints are imposed on unit trusts.

At the time of writing there is a feeling within the investment industry that investment trusts are unfairly treated as compared with unit trusts and life assurance, and that the regulations controlling them should be relaxed to place them on an equal footing with their direct competitors. At present, investment trusts have none of the privileges outlined above relating to unit trusts and life assurance. They cannot be sold on a 'cold-call' basis, and there are tight controls on advertisements. Yet collectively they have provided better returns over most periods than both unit trusts and life assurance.

Other safeguards provided for investors are as follows:

17.10.1 Unit trusts
Every non-professional purchaser of units must be offered *scheme particulars*, as well as automatically being sent *product particulars*. The scheme particulars provide fuller details of the operations of the fund.

If an investor has a complaint about a particular unit trust investment, there are a number of bodies to which the complaint can be addressed:

(a) the unit trust management company itself;
(b) the trustee;
(c) IMRO, which can refer the matter to its own referee if it is to do with the management of the fund;
(d) FIMBRA or LAUTRO, depending upon whether the investment was bought or sold through an independent or a tied intermediary;
(e) SIB, which operates an arbitration service through an independent panel;
(f) the Unit Trust Ombudsman.

(Addresses and telephone numbers are given in appendix 2.)

17.10.2 Life assurance
In the case of complaints against a company or its salespersons, a referral can be made to:

(a) FIMBRA or LAUTRO;
(b) the Insurance Brokers' Registration Council;
(c) the Personal Insurance Arbitration Service (PIAS);
(d) the Insurance Ombudsman.

In addition, there are safeguards for investors if a life assurance company should fail to meet its obligations. Under the *Policyholders' Protection Act 1975*, policyholders receive 90 per cent of the value of their policies in the event of the collapse of a company registered under the Act. Alternatively, arrangements can be made to have business transferred to another company.

17.11 Questions

1. (a) A holder of a single-premium bond, if subject to tax at all, is liable for:

   A CGT only.
   B basic-rate tax (BR).
   C income tax at his or her marginal rate (MR).
   D MR−BR.

   (b) Nearly four years ago £22 000 was invested in a single-premium policy and no withdrawals have yet been made by the policyholder. The maximum amount which can be withdrawn in the fourth year, without immediate tax consequences, is:

   A £1100.
   B £2200.
   C £4400.
   D £8800.

   (c) Friendly-society bonds are:

   A free of all taxes.
   B free of CGT only.
   C subject to corporation tax.
   D taxed as insurance funds.

   (d) What is meant by a 'qualifying' life assurance policy? What tax advantage does it have as compared with a non-qualifying policy?
   (SIE)
   (e) Outline *four* differences between a Guaranteed Income Bond and a National Savings Income Bond.   (SIE)
   (f) Outline the main differences between whole-life and endowment assurance.

2. In assessing the merits of a life assurance policy it is helpful to disentangle three of the main features – life cover, investment, taxation. Discuss the relative importance of these factors for the following major types of policy:

   (a) a managed bond;
   (b) a mortgage protection policy;
   (c) a regular-premium 'with profits' endowment policy;
   (d) a guaranteed income bond.

   (CIB 5/84)

3. The competing attractions of authorized unit trusts and single-premium investment bonds have long been debated by financial writers and planners.

   (a) Describe the similarities between these two types of investment.

(b) Describe the taxation differences. How do these affect the individual investor?

(c) What other differences are there between the two types of investment?

(CIB 9/86)

4. Kenneth Wilson took out a single-premium unit-linked policy – a property bond – in February 1982. He intended to maintain the policy for at least fifteen years. Recently, due to ill health, he decided to retire and cash in the policy.

The policy cost £30 000 and he withdrew £2500 after two years and a further £2500 last year. The total proceeds of the policy at withdrawal in February 1991 amounted to £43 200. His net taxable income (i.e. after all allowances and outgoings) for 1990/91 is £17 700.

(a) What is his tax position in relation to the encashment of the bond?

(b) How would his tax position be changed if, instead of cashing in the entire policy, he withdrew a further £12 500 in January 1991?

(CIB 5/89)

18 Pensions

One of the most important – if not *the* most important – investments for many individuals is their pension. Until recently, many people did not regard their pension entitlement as an 'investment', because they had very little control over it. However, the situation changed dramatically with the Social Security Act [SSA] 1986, which made 'personal' pensions available to everyone for the first time.

Since the SSA 1986, the choices open to an individual are

(a) to rely on the State,
(b) to rely on the employer,
(c) to make his or her own arrangements,
(d) a combination of the above.

18.1 The State schemes

The basic State pension is provided by a contributory scheme which provides a flat-rate pension at statutory retirement age to everyone who has paid sufficient National Insurance contributions. Apart from those on very low incomes, everyone who is working has to contribute to this pension. The amount payable for 1990/91 is £46.90 per week for a single person and £93.80 for a married couple who have both paid full contributions. If one of the partners has not paid sufficient contributions, the couple's pension is reduced to £75.10 per week.

The *State Earnings Related Pension Scheme* (SERPS) was introduced in 1978 to top up the basic State pension. It applies to employees who are not members of a pension scheme which has '*contracted out*' of the State scheme. It is index-linked, but the pension is limited to 25 per cent of a person's *revalued average earnings*, subject to he or she contributing for at least twenty years. 'Revalued average earnings' is the average of the twenty best years over the earnings period for which a person was contributing. 'Actual' earnings are revalued in line with the annual rise in national average earnings. But only earnings between a lower and upper limit for the year in question are used in the calculation. For 1990/91 the lower and upper weekly limits are £46 and £350 respectively. The earnings between these two figures are called '*band earnings*'.

In the early 1980s the Government became concerned about the burden of SERPS in future years, because of the ageing of the population. Unlike company schemes, the State schemes are pay-as-you-go. There is no fund of accumulated investments to pay the pensions; instead, at any particular moment, pensions are directly financed by contributions from the working population. Consequently, the Government determined that from 1999 the maximum pension from SERPS would be gradually reduced until by the year 2009 it would be only 20 per cent of a person's revalued average earnings, which in turn would be based on the average of all years of contributions, not just the best twenty years.

Other features which make SERPS generally unattractive are:

(a) higher-income employees do not receive any pension on their earnings above the upper band limit;
(b) a SERPS pension cannot be taken before the statutory retirement ages of 65 for men and 60 for women;
(c) there is no provision to take part of the pension as a lump sum;
(d) there is no opportunity to build in any life assurance cover.

18.2 Occupational pensions

In recent years, many companies have run their own occupational pension schemes. Some of these act as a top-up to the State schemes, while others are designed to replace the SERPS element. The latter schemes must provide benefits which are at least equal to those of SERPS – that is, provide at least a 'guaranteed minimum pension' (GMP) – in order to opt out of SERPS. These are known as '*contracted-out*' schemes. They can be either '*defined-benefit*' schemes, which provide for a guaranteed pension based on final earnings, or '*contracted-out money purchase schemes*' (COMPS) which offer a pension determined by investment returns. Pensions can be taken at any time between the ages of 50 and 70, or earlier due to ill health.

The Inland Revenue constrains the benefits from and contributions to occupational pension schemes. The limitations on ultimate pension apply to defined-benefit schemes which relate pensions to 'final pensionable remuneration', which is the best year of the last five years, or the average of the best three or more consecutive years in the last ten, allowing for inflation. Defined-benefit schemes are usually constructed as $\frac{1}{80}$th or $\frac{1}{60}$th schemes. With a $\frac{1}{60}$th scheme, a contributor could retire after 40 years' service on two-thirds final pensionable remuneration – that is, $40 \times \frac{1}{60} \times$ final remuneration. In the case of a $\frac{1}{80}$th scheme the pension would be half his or her final remuneration. There is also provision to take a lump sum – usually up to $1\frac{1}{2}$ times final remuneration – but this will result in a reduced pension if the contributor is otherwise entitled to a two-thirds final remuneration pension. For Inland Revenue purposes, the lump sum of $1\frac{1}{2}$ times final remuneration plus a pension of half final remuneration approximates to a pension of two-thirds final remuneration and no lump sum.

Other limitations on benefits are

(a) *Death in service*   Life assurance cover during working life is subject to an upper limit of four times final remuneration. Pensions may also be paid to a surviving spouse and/or dependants, but the pension paid to any one person cannot exceed two-thirds of the maximum pension the employee could have received if he or she had retired on incapacity grounds at the date of death; and the total pensions to a spouse and dependants cannot exceed the total incapacity pension the employee could have received if he or she had retired early owing to incapacity to work.

(b) *Death after retirement*   Separate pensions for a surviving spouse and dependants can be provided, subject to an individual pension not exceeding two-thirds of the maximum pension that could have been approved for the employee and the total pensions not exceeding the whole of that maximum.

The Finance Act 1989 introduced further constraints. For new schemes established after 13 March 1989 and those joining existing schemes after 30 June 1989, a 'cap' was placed on 'final remuneration' for pension purposes. This 'cap' was itself to be indexed, and in 1990/91 the limit was fixed at £64 800. However, this limitation on pension (that is, $\frac{2}{3} \times$ £64 800) does not apply to persons already in a scheme before the deadline. A further restriction introduced at the same time in the Finance Act 1989 was that a maximum two-thirds final salary pension normally requires at least twenty years' service at the rate of $\frac{1}{30}$th for each year's service. For members of a previously existing scheme, the maximum can apply after only ten years' service.

An employee cannot contribute more than 15 per cent of earnings into an occupational pension scheme. These contributions receive tax relief at the investor's marginal rate of tax. Many contributors, with a full contributions record, can achieve the maximum permitted pension by contributing no more than around 6 per cent of income per year. However, certain individuals, who may be late entrants to the scheme, may have a poor pension entitlement and may wish to buy-in extra benefits. This is done by means of *additional voluntary contributions* (AVCs), provided that the total pension contributions, including AVCs, do not exceed 15 per cent of income in a particular year.

AVCs can be either 'in-house' or 'free-standing'. 'In-house' AVCs provide for extra benefits within the company scheme, whereas 'free-standing' AVCs are invested separately outside of the company, with an insurance company, unit trust, bank, or building society. Since October 1987 all occupational scheme members have the right to contribute to an AVC. Members are permitted to vary the amount and timing of AVCs. However, AVCs cannot be taken before retirement and may not be commuted for a lump sum, and benefits must be aggregated with those from the main occupational scheme to determine maximum permitted benefits. Any overprovision due to overfunding is returned to members with interest but subject to a tax charge.

In the case of COMPS there is no limit to the benefits, which depend entirely on the investment returns, but contributions by members of the pension scheme are limited to 15 per cent of earnings (subject to the limit of £64 800) in the same way as for a defined-benefit scheme.

When a person contributing to an occupational pension scheme changes employment, provided that he or she has accrued benefits for at least two years, he or she is entitled to have either a 'preserved' pension, which will become payable on retirement, or a 'transfer payment' to a new scheme, if the scheme will accept it, or to an insurance company or a personal pension plan. Where there is a preserved pension, the potential pension must be increased each year in line with the increase in retail prices, or by 5 per cent if less.

18.3 Personal pension plans (PPPs)

Under the SSA 1986, individuals are free to take out a personal pension plan (PPP) provided that they have the necessary 'relevant' earnings. The right to take out a personal pension was extended to persons in SERPS and/or an occupational pension scheme. A personal pension can normally be taken at any time between 50 and 75 years of age, but at an earlier age for certain professions. The investor receives a pension and can also take a lump sum of up to 25 per cent of the total funds accumulated. PPPs are fully portable regardless of the occupation of the investor, provided he or she has the necessary taxable income.

18.3.1 Contribution limits

The amount that can be paid into a PPP depends upon the age and income of the investor. The current rates are shown in Table 18.1. 'Net relevant earnings' are earnings from non-pensionable employment or business, after deduction of certain business expenses.

Table 18.1 Contribution limits for personal pensions

Age	% of 'net relevant earnings'*	Maximum £ (1990/91)
Up to 35	17.5	11 340
36–45	20	12 960
46–50	25	16 200
51–55	30	19 440
56–60	35	22 680
61+	40	25 920

* Subject to earnings limit of £64 800, 1990/91.

The earnings cap applies to *all* personal pension plans, irrespective of whether or not the contributor was in the plan before limits were introduced in March 1989. Nevertheless the contribution limits are particularly generous for persons in their sixties. Contributions can also be backdated for up to six years, to use previously unused allowances.

18.3.2 Types of plan

Personal pensions use the same types of funds as life assurance and unit trusts – the only difference is that the fund itself is tax-free if it is used to provide pensions – see Table 18.2. Thus the investor has to choose the appropriate type of plan to suit his or her risk/return requirements. There are 'without-profits' policies, 'with-profits' policies, unit-linked policies, and deposit administration schemes.

Most 'without-profits' policies are of the deferred annuity type, which guarantee a specified rate of pension. Some guarantee only a cash sum, so the

Table 18.2 Unit-linked pension plans offered by unit trusts and life assurance companies

Midland Unit Trusts Ltd (1200)F
192 Eyre Street, Sheffield, S1 3RD
0742 529888

	Initial charge	Cancel-lation price	Bid price	Offer price	Change on day	Gross yield
British Tst 6		58.39	58.39	62.45	-0.03	3.41
(Accum Units) 6		60.72	60.72	64.94	-0.03	3.41
Capital 6		107.4	107.4	114.9	+0.5	2.45
(Accum Units) 6		156.5	156.5	167.4	+0.6	2.45
European Growth ...6		161.8	161.8	172.6	+0.5	0.67
(Accum Units) 6		199.5	199.5	212.8	+0.6	0.67
Extra High Inc 6		63.46	64.66xd	69.15	-0.07	7.76
(Accum Units) 6		90.82	92.53	98.96	-0.1	7.76
Gilt & Fxd Int 4		45.60	45.60xd	47.62	+0.05	9.89
(Accum Units) 4		97.13	97.13	101.4	+0.1	9.89
High Yield 6		193.9	197.1	210.8	-0.3	5.92
(Accum Units) 6		382.6	388.9	415.9	-0.5	5.92
Income 6		228.3	231.1	247.2	-0.2	4.83
(Accum Units) 6		420.4	425.6	455.2	-0.4	4.83
Intl High St UT 6		56.38	56.38	60.30	-0.16	1.75
(Accum Units) 6		58.12	58.12	62.16	-0.16	1.75
Japan Growth 6		313.2	313.2xd	335.1	-3.0	0.00
(Accum Units) 6		329.3	329.3	352.2	-3.2	0.00
Mandarin Tst 6		67.97	67.97	72.70	+0.34	1.09
(Accum Units) 6		68.53	68.53	73.29	+0.34	1.09
Mngd P'folio Acc ..6		69.36	70.20	75.08	-0.16	2.68
Money Market UT ...1½		50.22	50.22	50.97	+0.01	13.52
(Accum Units) 1½		57.04	57.04	57.89	+0.01	13.52
North American 6		123.3	125.0	133.7	-0.5	0.68
(Accum Units) 6		152.2	154.3	165.0	-0.6	0.68
Smaller Cos 6		144.0	144.0	154.0	-1.2	2.88
(Accum Units) 6		161.2	161.2	172.4	-1.3	2.88
Meridian Income ...6		102.5	102.5xd	109.6	—	4.13
(Accum Units) 6		108.4	108.4	115.9	—	4.13
Meridian Growth ...6		113.7	113.7	121.6	-0.3	2.24

Midland Personal Pension Unit Trust *

	Initial charge		Bid price	Offer price	Change on day	Gross yield
British 6		60.71	61.43	65.35	+0.17	3.40
European Growth ...6		73.96	74.16	78.89	+0.22	0.67
Gilt & Fixed 6		48.27	48.28	51.36	+0.15	9.88
Income 6		53.58	54.50	57.98	+0.01	4.83
Japan Growth 6		45.97	46.22	49.17	-0.45	0.00
Managed 6		54.92	55.88	59.45	+0.08	2.67
Money Market 6		57.90	57.90	61.38	+0.14	13.50
North American 6		57.71	58.78	62.53	-0.22	0.68

Midland FSAVCS Unit Trust *

	Initial charge		Bid price	Offer price	Change on day	Gross yield
British 6		56.11	56.78	60.40	+0.09	3.41
European Growth ...6		70.54	70.74	75.25	+0.18	0.67
Gilt & Fixed Int ...6		46.73	46.74	49.72	+0.12	9.90
Income 6		52.86	53.81	57.24	-0.04	4.84
Japan Growth 6		46.51	46.77	49.75	-0.47	0.00
Managed 6		52.82	53.75	57.18	-0.12	2.68
Money Market 6		54.60	54.60	57.87	+0.02	13.54
North American 6		56.67	57.74	61.43	-0.26	0.68

Midland Executive Pension Unit Trust *

	Initial charge		Bid price	Offer price	Change on day	Gross yield
British 6		57.48	58.17	61.88	-0.04	3.41
European Growth ...6		69.19	69.38	73.81	+0.21	0.67
Gilt & Fixed Int ...6		45.90	45.90	48.83	+0.04	9.90
Income 6		54.74	55.72	59.28	-0.05	4.84
Japan Growth 6		47.42	47.69	50.73	-0.46	0.00
Managed 6		56.64	57.64	61.32	-0.13	2.68
Money Market 6		54.56	54.56	57.83	+0.01	13.53
North American 6		58.91	60.02	63.85	-0.24	0.68

On a switch, units will be issued at bid price.

Black Horse Life Ass. Co Ltd
Mountbatten Hse, Chatham, Kent.
0634 834000

Life Funds	Bid price	Offer price		
The Managed Invest Fd....	326.94	344.15	......	—
The Income Fund.........	529.27	557.13	......	—
The Extra Income Fund...	467.97	492.60	......	—
The Wrldwd Grwth Fd....	368.64	388.05	......	—
The Balanced Fund......	429.97	452.60	......	—
Smlr Co"s & Rcvy Fd....	494.91	520.96	......	—
The Int Technology Fd..	367.96	387.33	......	—
The Nth Amer & Gen Fd..	268.39	282.52	......	—
The Energy Int Fd......	158.78	167.14	......	—
The Pacific Basin Fund.	297.89	313.57	......	—
The German Growth Fund.	197.78	208.19	......	—
The Japan Growth Fund..	164.74	173.42	......	—
The UK Growth Fund.....	145.50	153.16	......	—
The Contl Eur Gwth Fd..	104.22	109.71	......	—
Nth Amer S.C. & Rcvy..	146.31	154.02	......	—
The Property Fund......	313.71	330.23	......	—
The Fixed Interest Fd..	199.55	210.06	......	—
The Cash Fund..........	217.56	229.02	......	—
The Managed Fund.......	523.20			
Pension Funds				
Managed Pen Fd........	134.88	141.98	......	—
Fixed Int Pen Fd......	100.80	106.11	......	—
Property Pen Fd.......	150.66	158.59	......	—
Cash Pen Fd...........	124.88	131.46	......	—
UK Equity Pen Fd......	122.27	128.71	......	—
Nth Amer Pen Fd.......	124.13	130.67	......	—
European Pen Fd.......	157.09	165.36	......	—
Far East Pen Fd.......	104.57	110.08	......	—

Source: *Financial Times*, April 1990

ultimate pension is dependent on the annuity rate offered by the company at the retirement date. 'With-profits' policies also offer deferred annuities and cash funds, but the minimum guaranteed sums are improved with reversionary and terminal bonuses. Unit-linked policies are riskier because the ultimate cash fund depends on the performance of the units at retirement date. With unit-linked schemes it is normally possible for both the amount already accumulated and future premiums to be switched at low cost between the available underlying investment funds. Consideration should be given to switching into a deposit fund shortly before retirement, to safeguard the returns already achieved. Deposit administration schemes invest in bank, building society, and local authority deposits. They are unlikely to achieve returns as good as with other types of fund over the longer term.

Personal pension plans are available from a range of institutions, including insurance companies, friendly societies, unit trusts, banks, and building societies. Most offer both regular-premium and single-premium versions of the above policies. There is no difference in their tax treatment. Single-premium policies provide greater flexibility to vary the annual premiums; they usually involve lower levels of commission, and the investor can reassess the market each year to determine the best terms available.

All personal pensions plans have to provide an *'open market option'*, which means that the investor can take the accumulated cash sum, or its equivalent, at the maturity of the policy and buy an annuity from whichever insurance company is offering the best rate. Although a variety of institutions can sell personal pension plans, only insurance companies can provide the annuity in retirement.

18.4 Opting-out

Since the SSA 1986 there is no restriction on persons 'opting out' of SERPS or an occupational pension into a personal pension plan.

As mentioned in section 18.1, SERPS is particularly unattractive for many types of individual, and 'opting-out' is an attractive proposition for them. On the other hand, many occupational pension schemes – particularly in the public sector – offer attractive benefits, and it would generally be unwise to switch.

Employees in SERPS can opt out altogether or top-up with a PPP. If the employee decides to opt out of SERPS altogether or out of a 'contracted-out' occupational scheme, he or she must take out a special type of PPP known as an *'appropriate personal pension'* (APP) which provides 'protected rights'. With this type of plan, the National Insurance contributions of the employer and employee which would otherwise be used to fund the SERPS benefits are redirected into the APP. All of the returns from the National Insurance contributions must be taken in the form of a pension for life at State pensionable age. No part can be taken as a lump sum, and the APP must include provision for index-linking and for widow/widowers' pensions. However, additional sums can be contributed to an APP to provide a tax-free lump sum, life assurance, or more generous spouse's benefits. Alternatively, the individual can take out a further PPP, separate from the APP.

An extra incentive for employees in SERPS to opt out and switch into an APP is a 2 per cent incentive payment available until 1993. For such persons the Government, each year until 1993, pays a subsidy of 2 per cent of the relevant 'band earnings' into the APP.

The arguments for opting out of an occupational scheme into a PPP are not so strong, particularly for employees in the public sector who may have fully index-linked pensions. Older employees may prefer the security of a defined-benefit scheme. Employees who are likely to achieve rapid promotion will also generally prefer a defined-benefit scheme linking their pension to final earnings. In addition, some occupational pensions provide for *ex-gratia* benefits, whereby pensioners may share in the success of a company through additional benefits on an *ad hoc* basis. Some schemes may be non-contributory. Also if an employee opts out of the firm's scheme the employer may in future contribute no more than the additional National Insurance contributions. The member may lose widow's or widower's pension and death-in-service benefits, and may not be allowed to opt back into the occupational scheme at a later date. The 'protected benefits' or 'transfer values' may be set at conservative levels. Finally, high earners will be subject to the 'cap' applicable to contributions to a PPP, which would not apply to those who have contributed to occupational schemes since before March 1989.

On the other hand, younger persons – particularly if they are likely to change jobs frequently – may prefer the portability aspect of a PPP. Older persons with a poor contribution record may also benefit from the high contribution limits now available.

18.5 Commutation

On retirement, with both occupational and personal pension schemes, the investor can usually choose whether to have a maximum retirement annuity or a lump sum and a reduced annuity. In the case of occupational defined-benefit schemes, the maximum lump sum will be $1\frac{1}{2}$ times final remuneration; 25 per cent of the value of the fund in the case of a PPP. It is usually advantageous to take the maximum lump sum. This is obviously true if the investor is in poor health. Even if the investor is in good health, the lump sum has advantages. It provides immediate liquidity if the investor wishes to move house, buy a car, or take an extended holiday. It can be used to repay liabilities, particularly if the investor is paying a high rate of interest. In the case of occupational schemes, the lump sum could be used to purchase an annuity from an insurance company. The insurance annuity will receive more favourable treatment for income tax purposes because part of it will be regarded as repayment of capital, and therefore tax-free. The critical question is, 'Can the investor earn a higher net-of-tax return on the lump sum than is likely to be achieved with the pension?' Any increases in the pension –

whether guaranteed, index-linked, or *ex-gratia* – would need to be taken into account in order to make a correct comparison.

18.6 Performance

Unit-linked policies provide a much wider range of performance than 'with-profits' policies. This is true of personal pensions, just as much as it was

Table 18.3 'With-profits' and unit-linked personal pensions – comparative performance to July 1989

Actual results, 5 year term, regular premiums of £1000 p.a.

With-profits		Unit-linked	
Pearl	£10 566	Col Mutual Equity	£19 342
Co-operative	10 264	Prem Life Equity	11 278
Scot Amicable	9 680	Col Mutual Managed	10 800
Friends Provident	9 671	M & G Recovery	10 584
Nat Mut Life	9 508	Target Recovery	10 572
Worst	7 689	Worst	5 823

Actual results, 5 year term, single premium of £5000

With-profits		Unit-linked	
Standard	£14 924	Col Mutual Equity	£40 613
Pearl	13 567	CU Equity	22 726
Legal & General	12 147	Col Mutual Managed	18 514
London Life	11 516	M & G Recovery	18 490
GRE	11 469	Friends Prov S'ship	17 857
Worst	9 094	Worst	4 490

Actual results, 10 year term, regular premiums of £1000 p.a.

With-profits		Unit-linked	
Pearl	£34 430	Confed Equity	£44 666
Standard	33 279	Lon & M'ster IT	35 775
Friends Provident	32 952	Target Managed	33 984
Equitable	32 854	M & G Equity	33 301
Norwich Union	32 173	Albany Equity	33 288
Worst	23 725	Worst	16 082

Actual results, 10 year term, single premium of £5000

With-profits		Unit-linked	
Scottish Life	£29 439	Target Managed	£49 688
Equitable	27 319	Confd Managed	45 851
Equity & Law	27 279	Albany Equity	36 561
Legal & General	26 970	M & G Equity	35 650
GRE	26 635	Save & Prosper Eq	35 022
Worst	16 796	Worst	10 852

Source: *Money Management*.

true of insurance policies in chapter 17. Table 18.3 summarizes the results for
five and ten years, up to July 1989. It is evident that the best-performing
unit-linked policies did much better than the 'with-profits' ones, but conversely the worst-performing unit-linked policies were much inferior to the
worst 'with-profits' policies. Clearly, therefore, choice of a particular unit-
linked policy is a much more critical determinant of performance than is the
case for 'with-profits' policies. Details of performance are published on an
annual basis in the *Financial Times Handbook of Personal Pensions*.

18.7 Protection for the investor

Personal pension plans, except for deposit administration ones, are 'investments' under the Financial Services Act and are subject to the normal rules of
'best advice'. Depending upon the type of scheme, they are regarded as
equivalent to life assurance or unit trusts. Consequently, they can be sold on
a 'cold-call' basis, and can be sold 'off-the-page'. The investor has the same
cancellation rights as for unit trusts and life assurance, as discussed in
section 17.10. Complaints should be addressed to the same bodies mentioned
in section 17.10. In addition, responsibility for occupational pensions rests
with the Superannuation Funds Office (SFO), which is a branch of the Inland
Revenue, and the Occupational Pensions Board (OPB), which was established in 1975.

18.8 Questions

1. (a) Following the implementation of the Social Security Act 1986, the
State Earnings Related Pension Scheme (SERPS):

   A remains attractive for older people who have been contributors
   since its inception.

   B is no longer an attractive option in any circumstances.

   C has been made more attractive and full advantage of the scheme
   should be taken by those who qualify for it.

   D has been made modestly more attractive by incentive payments of
   2 per cent to those entering the scheme before 6 April 1993.

   (b) An employee of a company not operating a pension scheme opts out
   of SERPS and contributes instead to an *appropriate* personal pension
   plan (APPP). What additional pension arrangements can he make to
   supplement the APPP?

   A A further APPP.

   B An *approved* personal pension plan.

   C Additional voluntary contributions (AVCs).

   D Free-standing AVCs.

2. Mark Schofield is a trainee accountant, aged 25, who is finding it difficult

to live in London on his present salary. Because the firm he works for does not yet have a pension scheme, Mark makes regular contributions to the State scheme, which is compulsory for all employees whose employers have not contracted out. The company will shortly be announcing its own pension scheme.

Mark says that he knows he ought to be contributing to a 'proper pension scheme' and that he has already met two pensions salespeople, but he says that he works hard and 'with what little is left over I want to play hard too'.

What are the alternatives open to Mark and what are their advantages and disadvantages.

(CIB 10/89)

3. Your customer, Major-General Blunderbuss, is shortly to retire from the army at the age of 55. He wishes to discuss with you whether he should take his retirement pension (index-linked) in full or whether he should commute part of it for a lump sum.

   Required:

   (a) What further information would you need from General Blunderbuss?
   (b) State, with reasons, the advice you would give him.

(CIB 9/85)

4. Discuss the relative attractions to an investor of personal pensions and PEPs.

(SIE 7/90)

19 Overseas investment and investors

19.1 Investing overseas

For UK investors, the main arguments for investing outside of the UK are as follows:

(a) *Greater diversification* The basic argument in favour of international diversification is that foreign investments offer additional profit potential while reducing the total risk of a portfolio. In other words, it improves the risk/return trade-off in the portfolio. Domestic securities tend to move up and down together, because they are similarly affected by domestic conditions such as interest rates, economic growth, inflation,

Table 19.1 Correlation coefficients of returns between UK equities and overseas equities, 1971–86

West Germany	0.41
Belgium	0.51
Denmark	0.36
France	0.52
Italy	0.35
Norway	0.34
Netherlands	0.61
Sweden	0.36
Switzerland	0.52
Spain	0.26
Australia	0.41
Japan	0.32
Hong Kong	0.29
Singapore	0.40
Canada	0.50
United States	0.47
Gold mines shares	0.08
Gold	0.08
World Index	0.65

Source: Bruno Solnik, *International Investments* (Addison-Wesley, 1988).

and the foreign-exchange rate. This creates a strong positive correlation between most national securities traded in the same market. Foreign capital markets provide good potential for diversification beyond domestic securities and markets.

Table 19.1 shows the correlation coefficients of returns on UK equities with those of other countries between 1971 and 1986. A correlation coefficient of 1 means that returns move perfectly together in the same direction; 0 would imply that there is no relationship; while a figure between 0 and −1 would mean negative correlation – that the returns were inversely related. The lower the correlation coefficient, the greater the scope for diversifying risk.

Although the correlation coefficients vary over time, they are always far from unity. This means that international diversification is a worthwhile activity. It is particularly noticeable that gold and gold-mining shares have a very weak correlation with the UK market, indicating that their inclusion in a UK portfolio should reduce the overall variability of returns.

(b) *Specialist companies and industries*   Certain types of domestic company and industry are not available to UK investors. Obvious examples are gold and diamond mining, rubber plantations, and major railways.

(c) *Exchange rate*   Investing in overseas securities, denominated and quoted in their local currencies, provides a possible hedge against a depreciation in the value of the pound sterling.

(d) *Dynamic economies*   International diversification provides an opportunity to participate in the growth of the more dynamic economies of the world, particularly the 'tiger' and 'dragon' economies of South East Asia – Hong Kong, Singapore, South Korea, Taiwan, Malaysia, Indonesia, the Philippines, and Thailand, as well as Japan. Of the major markets, Japan was the most successful during the 1980s, providing an annual average return of over 32 per cent per year in sterling terms – see fig. 19.1. A major part of the return was due to the depreciation of sterling against the yen.

There are also obvious disadvantages of investing overseas. Among them are the following:

(a) *Risk*   There is a political risk, as evidenced by recent events in China, Hong Kong, and the Philippines, as well as economic risks such as the imposition of exchange controls.

(b) *Delays*   There are likely to be delays and difficulties in obtaining information concerning investments, because of language barriers in many countries and the sheer distance between the UK and these markets. This is known as an 'information gap'.

(c) *Disclosure and controls*   There are less satisfactory accountancy practices in many countries outside of the USA and UK, and also in many cases weak regulatory controls on 'insider dealing'.

(d) *Settlement*   There may be problems of settlement and delivery of

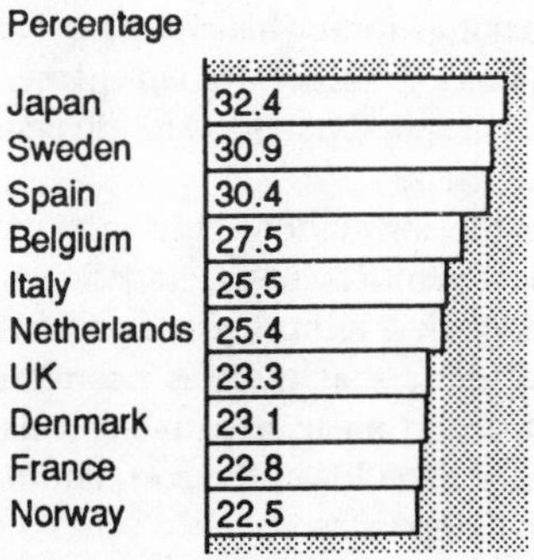

Percentage

Japan	32.4
Sweden	30.9
Spain	30.4
Belgium	27.5
Italy	25.5
Netherlands	25.4
UK	23.3
Denmark	23.1
France	22.8
Norway	22.5

Source: CNWM International Market Returns

Fig. 19.1   Annualized sterling returns in the 1980s from equity markets

certificates for transactions in securities that are not listed on the UK Stock Exchange and covered by Talisman. In some countries there is a very short settlement period (for example, 24 hours in Hong Kong), or a requirement to have the share certificates retained within the country (as in Japan).

(e) *Handling costs*   There may be higher handling costs for safe custody and dividend remittance, including the cost of converting from a foreign currency into sterling.

(f) *Differential prices*   In some countries there is a differential price between shares dealt in standard quantities – called 'board lots' – and amounts which are not a simple multiple of the board lot.

(g) *Limitations on holdings*   Some countries, such as Switzerland and Thailand, have strict controls on the proportion of shares that can be held by foreigners. Consequently foreign-held shares sell at a premium.

(h) *Tax*   There may be tax problems, especially if there is no double-taxation agreement between the UK Government and the country concerned.

19.2 Methods of investing in overseas securities

A UK investor wishing to invest overseas has a choice of direct and indirect means. The problems of investing directly overseas have already been outlined above. As mentioned in section 14.7, around 700 leading international 'blue-chip' companies are quoted on *SEAQ International*. But SEAQ International is mainly for institutional or very wealthy individuals. At the time of writing, the minimum quote for most European shares is around £100 000. In many cases these companies have a listing in the UK as well as in their domestic markets. Those which are not listed in the UK have bargains transacted under Rule 535(4), which is a Stock Exchange rule which permits bargains to be done in any overseas security provided that it is listed on its domestic market. In all cases, settlement is determined by both parties at the time of transaction and is usually carried out in the country in which the share is registered.

To some extent the problems of investing directly in overseas equities can be mitigated by using a UK broker/dealer with overseas connections (such as Nomura Securities), although this may result in two lots of commission on each bargain – one for the UK and one for the overseas broker – or by investing in UK-registered and quoted companies with large overseas interests (for example, Cable and Wireless).

By far the easiest way of investing overseas is indirectly by means of a unit trust, an investment trust, a unit-linked life assurance or pension scheme, or a PEP unit trust or investment trust. These can afford to employ local nationals with expert knowledge; they can provide diversification both within and between the different markets; they can hedge currency risk, if so desired; and dividend and settlement payments will be made in the UK in sterling. Sometimes funds can gain exemption from local withholding taxes.

However, even indirect investment methods are not without their problems. Funds may be large in comparison to their chosen stock market, so creating liquidity difficulties. An advantage of investment trusts – which were the traditional means of overseas investment – is that there can be a reasonably active market in their shares without affecting the underlying investments. However, unlike the UK-orientated investment trusts, which usually trade at a discount to their net asset value, these specialist overseas funds can frequently trade at a premium, which makes them an expensive way into the market. The premium may quickly disappear if the particular market becomes less 'fashionable'. Investors are generally better advised to opt for a more broadly based regional fund rather than a small single-country trust.

19.3 Principal overseas markets

As can be seen from Table 19.2, the two largest equity markets in the world – by a large margin – are the USA and Japan. They each account for about one-third of the total market value of shares traded on the principal stock exchanges throughout the world. The UK comes a poor third, with around 10 per cent. At its peak the Japanese market accounted for 45 per cent of the world's equity capitalization, but Japanese shares suffered dramatic falls early in 1990.

19.3.1 The USA
The New York Stock Exchange is the USA's largest stock exchange, accounting for approximately 80 per cent of all stock exchange volume activity in the USA. Eight major US exchanges – New York ('NYSE'), American ('Amex', also New York), Cincinnati, Midwest (Chicago), Boston, Pacific (Los Angeles/San Francisco), Philadelphia, and NASDAQ – are

Table 19.2 Market capitalizations of the national and regional markets of the *FT*–Actuaries World Indices, 29 June 1990

FT-ACTUARIES WORLD INDICES QUARTERLY VALUATION

The market capitalisation of the national and regional markets of the FT-Actuaries World indices as at JUNE 29, 1990 are expressed below in millions of US dollars and as a percentage of the World Index. Similar figures are provided for the preceding quarter.
The percentage change for each Dollar index value since the end of the calendar year is also provided.

NATIONAL AND REGIONAL MARKETS (Figures in parentheses show number of stocks per grouping)	Market capitalisation as at JUNE 29, 1990 (US$m)	% of World Index	Market capitalisation as at MARCH 30, 1990 (US$m)	% of World Index	% change in $ index since DECEMBER 29, 1989
Australia (80)	93356.2	1.34	88171.0	1.35	− 6.51
Austria (19)	14778.6	0.21	15838.9	0.24	+ 40.67
Belgium (61)	51316.8	0.74	48211.8	0.74	− 2.48
Canada (119)	145580.8	2.09	147337.4	2.26	− 9.63
Denmark (33)	26699.4	0.38	25776.4	0.40	+ 6.39
Finland (26)	3380.6	0.05	3236.5	0.05	+ 1.28
France (124)	230219.9	3.30	217670.8	3.34	+ 2.94
West Germany (92)	306509.4	4.39	318671.0	4.89	+ 7.98
Hong Kong (48)	60501.5	0.87	55091.7	0.85	+ 15.77
Ireland (17)	10716.6	0.15	10179.7	0.16	+ 4.23
Italy (96)	126183.3	1.81	113767.1	1.75	+ 9.88
Japan (454)	2386210.1	34.20	2180441.1	33.48	− 25.40
Malaysia (35)	7773.2	0.11	7817.6	0.12	+ 0.36
Mexico (13)	9796.9	0.14	7614.9	0.12	+ 52.32
Netherland (43)	106792.3	1.53	105186.4	1.62	− 1.43
New Zealand (17)	9533.1	0.14	8657.7	0.13	− 9.90
Norway (23)	8199.7	0.12	7214.4	0.11	+ 17.72
Singapore (25)	16603.0	0.24	15893.8	0.24	+ 13.06
South Africa (60)	50796.4	0.73	54538.9	0.84	− 9.99
Spain (42)	76057.8	1.09	62253.9	0.96	+ 4.82
Sweden (34)	32568.0	0.47	25416.5	0.39	+ 17.07
Switzerland (67)	107611.9	1.54	84233.6	1.29	+ 11.73
United Kingdom (304)	715840.7	10.26	640766.4	9.84	+ 5.71
USA (537)	2381001.4	34.12	2268523.0	34.83	+ 1.14
Europe (981)	1816875.1	26.04	1678423.4	25.77	+ 6.02
Nordic (116)	70847.7	1.02	61643.8	0.95	+ 11.84
Pacific Basin (659)	2573977.2	36.89	2356072.8	36.18	− 23.92
Euro − Pacific (1640)	4390852.2	62.92	4034496.3	61.95	− 13.87
North America (656)	2526582.2	36.21	2415860.4	37.10	+ 0.46
Europe Ex. UK (677)	1101034.4	15.78	1037657.0	15.93	+ 6.28
Pacific Ex. Japan (205)	187767.1	2.69	175631.7	2.70	+ 1.41
World Ex. US (1832)	4597026.4	65.88	4243987.5	65.17	− 13.61
World Ex. UK (2065)	6262181.7	89.74	5871744.1	90.16	− 10.47
World Ex. So. Af. (2309)	6927231.4	99.27	6457971.6	99.16	− 9.04
World Ex. Japan (1915)	4591817.7	65.80	4332069.4	66.52	+ 2.55
The World Index (2369)	6978027.8	100.00	6512510.5	100.00	− 9.04

© The Financial Times LImited, Goldman, Sachs & Co, and County NatWest Securities Limited. 1987

Source: *Financial Times*

linked together by the Intermarket Trading System (ITS), an electronic communications system which enables brokers, specialists, and market-makers to interact with their counterparts on the network whenever the nationwide Composite Quotation System shows a better price.

With the exception of NASDAQ, the US exchanges use the *'specialist'* system, which is an example of an 'order-driven' market. Most member firms are dual-capacity broker/dealers. A minority of firms, however, register as specialists. As such they relinquish their rights to deal with members of the public and take on the responsibility to maintain an orderly market in the securities to which they are allocated – one specialist per security. Each specialist may deal in only one security from a sector. Trading is by 'open outcry' on a trading floor. Broker/dealers wishing to trade in securities allocated to a particular specialist congregate round its 'trading post'. The market is organized as a continuous auction, in which the broker/dealers call out their orders and trade directly with one another. On the NYSE the specialist is often not directly involved in the auction process at all. However, where a broker/dealer enters the crowd and finds no one prepared to make a price in the security, the specialist is under an obligation to do so. The specialist undertakes to buy or sell for its own account and to limit price movements to a 'tick' between successive trades. As the market stabilizer, the specialist may not buy on an 'up tick' or sell on a 'down tick'. The specialist also has custody of the 'limit order' book, with orders left with it by broker/dealers to deal at a price when feasible.

The trading unit in shares is generally set as a 'round lot' of 100 shares or an 'odd lot' of less than 100 shares. Trades of 10 000 shares or more are called 'block' trades.

The National Association of Securities Dealers' Automated Quotation System (NASDAQ) was the forerunner to the SEAQ system used on the ISE in the UK – a system of 'competing market-makers'. Market-makers display their quotes on computer screens; there is no requirement for a trading floor. NASDAQ quotations are available to subscribers in the UK.

Most transactions are subject to five-day settlement in the USA.

19.3.2 Japan

There are eight stock exchanges in Japan, of which Tokyo is by far the largest – accounting for around 80 per cent of total turnover. The membership of each stock exchange is divided into three categories: regular members, Saitori members, and 'special' members. Regular members engage in the buying and selling of securities on the floor of an exchange, both for their customers and for their own account. Saitori members act as intermediaries between the regular members, and they are not allowed to trade on their own account. 'Special' members handle transactions on the Tokyo Stock Exchange for orders that cannot be handled on the regional exchanges.

On the Tokyo exchange, trading in major shares is by auction through a Saitori member who matches bids and offers at trading posts. The selling order with the lowest price and the buying order with the highest price take precedence over other orders. Where there is more than one buy or sell order at the same price, 'time priority' applies, whereby an earlier order takes precedence over later orders at the same price. On the Tokyo Stock Exchange, apart from the 250 or so most actively traded shares, trading in all other domestic shares is conducted through computer screens, with Saitori clerks matching buying and selling orders on the screen for major companies.

Last trade prices are immediately displayed electronically to securities firms and news offices.

Domestic shares are normally traded in board lots of 1000 shares. Almost all transactions are settled on the third business day after the bargain has been made.

19.3.3 Australia

All six stock exchanges in Australia are subsidiaries of the Australian Stock Exchange Ltd, a unified stock exchange formed in 1987. The Sydney and Melbourne Stock Exchanges are the two biggest exchanges, accounting for approximately 90 per cent of total Australian trading volume. The procedures for execution and settlement are identical for all the exchanges. Broker/dealers operate under dual capacity, and under a negotiated-commission structure. There are no specialists or market-makers. Traditionally, broker/dealers dealt with each other at trading posts on the stock exchange trading floor, but Australia introduced a screen-based trading system in 1987, and to date over 200 major shares are traded in this way.

Table 19.3 Equity market size, December 1987

Country	Equity market capitalization as a percentage of gross domestic product
Australia	41
Austria	5
Belgium	26
Canada	47
Denmark	17
Finland	17
France	16
Greece	8
Hong Kong	120
Indonesia	1
Italy	13
Japan	106
Malaysia	67
Netherlands	31
New Zealand	69
Norway	12
The Philippines	10
Portugal	24
Republic of Ireland	22
Singapore	100
South Africa	72
South Korea	28
Spain	23
Sweden	28
Switzerland	66
Taiwan	49
Thailand	14
Turkey	7
UK	79
USA	49
West Germany	16

Source: Peter Gartland, *The Dumenil Guide to International Investment* (Rosters, 1988).

Shares are traded in lot sizes, depending on the market price.

Settlement is normally within ten business days from the issue of the contract note.

19.3.4 The 'tiger' and 'dragon' markets

Apart from Japan, Hong Kong, and Singapore, the South East Asian stock markets are generally small in relation to their economies. This is illustrated in Table 19.3, which shows the equity market capitalization of most markets in relation to their gross domestic products. This illustrates the potential to be found in these smaller, high-growth economies, but at present the number of companies available is quite small, and access for a non-resident other than through a unit or investment trust is difficult.

19.3.5 Continental Europe

Share dealings in stock markets in Continental Europe have been dominated by the International Equity Market, operated by SEAQ International, in the UK. As a consequence, reform of antiquated dealing practices has been taking place in recent years in many of the Continental stock exchanges. Screen-based trading systems have been introduced in France, Spain, Luxemburg, Denmark, and Spain.

Throughout the world, open-outcry systems are being replaced by screen-based trading systems, which are hastening the day when there will be a fully integrated 24-hours-a-day global trading system.

19.4 Major overseas indices

The *Financial Times* publishes daily indices for the main stock markets throughout the world. They are in two forms:

(a) The actual indices used in the countries themselves are listed as shown in Table 19.4. Most of these are weighted indices, taking into account the different market capitalizations of the constituent companies. But, as described in section 10.5, the Dow-Jones indices in the USA are unweighted arithmetic means – less useful for long-term performance measurement than the Standard and Poors indices, which are weighted arithmetic means. The same distinction applies in Japan, where the Nikkei Dow-Jones index, an unweighted arithmetic average of 225 shares on the Tokyo Stock Exchange, is a less useful yardstick of performance than the Tokyo Stock Exchange Index, which is a weighted arithmetic mean of all shares listed on the First Section of the Tokyo Stock Exchange.

(b) Table 19.5 shows the country indices available daily in the *FT*–Actuaries World Indices. These were referred to in section 10.2. Their advantage to the UK investor is that they are all prepared on a consistent basis – they are all weighted arithmetic means with a base of 100 on 31 December 1986 – and they measure the performance of representative shares available to non-residents of the countries concerned.

Table 19.4 Major overseas indices

INDICES

NEW YORK

DOW JONES	July 3	July 2	June 29	June 28	1990 HIGH	1990 LOW	Since compilation HIGH	Since compilation LOW
♦Industrials	2911.63	2899.26	2880.69	2878.71	2935.89 (15/6)	2543.24 (30/1)	2935.89 (15/6/90)	41.22 (2/7/32)
Home Bonds	91.11	91.09	90.77	90.88	93.04 (3/1)	88.48 (2/5)	—	—
Transport	1140.51	1144.16	1144.34	1142.70	1212.77 (6/6)	1031.83 (30/1)	1532.01 (5/9/89)	12.32 (8/7/32)
Utilities	208.94	209.57	210.01	208.63	236.23 (2/1)	203.09 (30/4)	236.23 (2/1/90)	10.50 (8/4/32)

♦Day's High 2925.74 (2908.66) Low 2891.09 (2869.80)

STANDARD AND POOR'S	July 3	July 2	June 29	June 28	1990 HIGH	1990 LOW	Since compilation HIGH	Since compilation LOW
Composite ‡	360.16	359.54	358.02	357.63	367.40 (4/6)	322.98 (30/1)	367.40 (4/6/90)	4.40 (1/6/32)
Industrials	423.73	422.50	420.52	420.25	428.34 (4/6)	371.92 (30/1)	428.34 (4/6/90)	3.62 (21/6/32)
Financial	28.91	29.00	28.93	28.87	31.87 (3/1)	26.59 (27/4)	35.24 (9/10/89)	8.64 (1/10/74)
NYSE Composite	196.61	196.22	195.48	195.18	200.21 (4/6)	178.43 (30/1)	200.21 (4/6/90)	4.46 (25/4/42)
Amex Mkt. Value	360.67	360.14	361.21	358.57	382.45 (5/1)	342.64 (24/4)	397.03 (10/10/89)	29.31 (9/12/72)
NASDAQ Composite	461.76	462.04	462.28	460.38	468.86 (13/6)	410.72 (30/1)	485.73 (9/10/89)	54.87 (31/10/72)

	June 29	June22	June15	year ago (approx.)
Dow Industrial Div. Yield	3.74	3.77	3.67	3.70

	June 27	Jun 20	June13	year ago (approx.)
S & P Industrial div. yield	2.97	2.93	2.90	3.09
S & P Indl. P/E ratio	16.70	16.87	17.07	12.97

NEW YORK ACTIVE STOCKS

Tuesday	Stocks traded	Closing price	Change on day
Philip Morris	2,674,100	48	+ ⅞
Cen Me Pwr (xd)	2,302,700	18¾	+ ⅛
Entergy Corp	1,987,900	20	+ ⅛
Gen Instruments	1,959,000	45⅝	+ ½
SCE Corp	1,470,000	37⅝	+ ⅛
Panhandle	1,451,500	23½	- ⅝
Mattel	1,347,500	22½	+ ⅜
Am T & T	1,240,500	38⅝	- ¼
Am Express	1,187,600	31½	+ ¼
Beverly Ent	1,150,800	6¼	+ ⅛

TRADING ACTIVITY

† Volume (Millions)	July 3	July 2	June 29
New York	130.050	130.200	145.500
Amex	11.552	9.518	13.024
NASDAQ	(u)	114.153	158.811
Issues Traded	1,973	1,981	1,994
Rises	828	780	966
Falls	650	739	572
Unchanged	495	462	456
New Highs	70	52	56
New Lows	41	43	47

CANADA

TORONTO	July 4	July 3	July 2	June 29	1990 HIGH	1990 LOW
Metals & Minerals	3296.80	3262.20	(c)	3208.50	3453.05 (4/1)	2850.80 (23/4)
Composite	3575.30	3560.00	(c)	3544.00	4009.47 (3/1)	3334.20 (1/5)
MONTREAL Portfolio	1852.48	1841.50	(c)	1833.26	2060.90 (3/1)	1720.25 (27/4)

Base values of all indices are 100 except NYSE All Common – 50; Standard and Poor's – 10; and Toronto Composite and Metals – 1000. Toronto indices based 1975 and Montreal Portfolio 4/1/83. † Excluding bonds. ‡ Industrial, plus Utilities, Financial and Transportation. (c) Closed. (u) Unavailable.

	July 4	July 3	July 2	June 29	1990 HIGH	1990 LOW
AUSTRALIA						
All Ordinaries (1/1/80)	1541.1	1512.8	1496.6	1500.7	1713.7 (12/1)	1434.5 (30
All Mining (1/1/80)	734.7	718.6	711.7	715.5	860.8 (5/1)	711.7 (2/
AUSTRIA						
Credit Aktien (30/12/84)	618.99	615.67	605.82	603.80	703.29 (19/3)	526.59(2/
BELGIUM						
Brussels SE (Cash Mkt) (1/1/80)	6274.42	6281.62	6286.20	6263.04	6599.43 (12/1)	5568.16 (2
DENMARK						
Copenhagen SE (3/1/83)	379.82	378.10	376.55	377.14	382.50 (15/6)	352.96 (25
FINLAND						
Unitas General (1975)	537.0	539.0	540.9	546.8	677.3 (23/1)	537.0 (4/
FRANCE						
CAC General (31/12/82)	543.07	543.99	542.08	545.08	564.62 (30/5)	482.94 (26
CAC 40 (31/12/87)	2015.93	2031.98	2029.54	2035.03	2129.32 (20/4)	1800.32 (2
GERMANY						
FAZ Aktien (31/12/58)	814.26	807.32	805.18	795.64	830.92 (3/4)	732.71 (2
Commerzbank (1/12/53)	2355.20	2330.30	2325.6	2297.3	2414.0 (3/4)	2151.5 (2
DAX (30/12/87)	1925.13	1906.23	1915.30	1879.90	1968.55 (30/3)	1756.41 (2
HONG KONG						
Hang Seng Bank (31/7/64)	3363.49	3356.55	3319.47	3278.24	3363.49 (4/7)	2738.24 (
IRELAND						
ISEQ Overall (4/1/88)	1689.21	1687.73	1689.17	1689.11	1893.10 (22/1)	1582.61 (
ITALY						
Banca Com. Ital. (1972)	736.94	741.38	745.11	753.76	763.52 (14/6)	646.73 (26
JAPAN						
Nikkei (16/5/49)	32445.92	32414.60	32160.23	31940.24	38712.88 (4/1)	28002.07 (
Tokyo SE (Topix) (4/1/68)	2363.35	2349.48	2348.70	2343.36	2867.70 (4/1)	2058.82 (5
2nd Section (4/1/68)	4222.84	4203.67	4189.90	4200.81	4284.68 (9/2)	3313.92 (5
MALAYSIA						
KLSE Composite (4/4/86)	586.39	586.36	(c)	584.65	622.20 (20/2)	518.53 (2
NETHERLANDS						
CBS Ttl.Rtn.Gen.(End 1983)	265.3	266.3	266.1	266.5	269.0 (3/1)	240.1 (26
CBS All Shr (End 1983)	197.6	198.3	198.2	198.5	206.3 (3/1)	184.2 (26
NORWAY						
Oslo SE (Ind) (2/1/83)	827.07	824.00	823.94	825.62	859.05 (5/6)	701.67 (2
PHILIPPINES						
Manila Comp (2/1/85)	837.82	852.45	870.17	882.98	1160.70 (21/3)	740.31 (6
SINGAPORE						
SES All-Singapore (2/4/75)	434.03	(c)	432.28	434.20	443.34 (6/2)	401.34 (3
SOUTH AFRICA						
JSE Gold (28/9/78)	1567.0♦	1574.0	1581.0	1522.0	2230.0 (16/1)	1322.0 (2
JSE Industrial (28/9/78)	2984.0♦	2973.0	2966.0	2963.0	3211.0 (6/2)	2794.0 (2
SOUTH KOREA**						
Korea Comp Ex. (4/1/80)	735.30	745.04	713.18	720.00	928.82 (4/1)	688.66 (3
SPAIN						
Madrid SE (30/12/85)	300.10	298.68	297.25	295.80	302.85 (4/1)	248.17 (2
SWEDEN						
Affärsvärlden Gen. (1/2/37)	1328.2	1320.8	1309.0	1309.7	1328.2 (4/7)	1127.20 (
SWITZERLAND						
Swiss Bank Ind. (31/12/58)	844.2	837.3	829.1	830.0	844.2 (4/7)	737.6 (27
TAIWAN**						
Weighted Price (30/6/66)	4677.18	4905.87	(c)	5157.45	12495.34 (10/2)	4677.18 (
THAILAND						
Bangkok SET (30/4/75)	1087.51	1087.53	1082.67	1060.22	1087.53 (3/7)	760.39 (7
WORLD						
M.S. Capital Intl. (1/1/70)	(u)	524.0	523.0	520.4	571.0 (4/1)	468.3 (2/

**Saturday June 30: Taiwan Weighted Price: 5049.58. Korea Comp Ex. 706.79

♦ Subject to official recalculation.

Apr6 Base values of all indices are 100 except: Brussels SE, ISEQ Overall and DAX – 1,000, JSE Gold – 255.7, Industrials – 264.3 and Australia All Ordinary and Mining – 500; (c) Closed. (u) Unavailable.

Source: *Financial Times*

19.5 Bearer securities

Bearer securities are shares or bonds for which ownership is not recorded on a share or stock register. The certificates issued therefore do not include the holder's name. Bearer securities, *prima facie*, belong to the person holding the certificate at any particular time, and ownership passes by delivery alone. Most bearer securities are issued by overseas companies or Governments, but some British companies, such as Shell, have part of their share issues in bearer form. 3½% War Loan and certain other British Government stocks have a small part of their issue in bearer form.

Many investors use a depository – such as a bank, broker/dealer, or solicitor – as a custodian of their bearer securities. Since actual possession of these securities denotes ownership, all that is necessary in order to transfer title in a sale is for the seller to deliver the stock to the buyer. Depositories

Table 19.5 *FT*–Actuaries world indices

Jointly compiled by The Financial Times Limited, Goldman, Sachs & Co., and County NatWest/Wood Mackenzie in conjunction with the Institute of Actuaries and the Faculty of Actuaries

NATIONAL AND REGIONAL MARKETS	WEDNESDAY JULY 4 1990								TUESDAY JULY 3 1990					DOLLAR INDEX		
Figures in parentheses show number of lines of stock	US Dollar Index	Day's Change %	Pound Sterling Index	Yen Index	DM Index	Local Currency Index	Local % chg on day	Gross Div. Yield	US Dollar Index	Pound Sterling Index	Yen Index	DM Index	Local Currency Index	1990 High	1990 Low	Year ago (approx)
Australia (80)	147.02	+2.7	122.11	139.21	125.89	121.69	+1.8	5.73	143.20	119.30	136.82	122.91	119.48	158.31	125.85	133.20
Austria (19)	262.69	+0.8	218.19	248.75	224.94	224.77	+0.4	1.29	260.66	217.09	248.96	223.66		285.63	193.15	124.59
Belgium (61)	152.95	+0.2	127.03	144.82	130.96	127.68	-0.1	4.53	152.67	127.20	145.86	131.04	127.82	160.02	132.11	130.38
Canada (119)	139.13	+0.4	115.56	131.73	119.12	117.07	+0.4	3.46	138.55	115.44	132.37	118.92	116.63	153.61	130.37	141.19
Denmark (33)	262.53	+0.7	218.05	248.60	224.80	223.88	+0.4	1.29	260.71	217.21	249.10	223.78	223.04	262.53	236.69	207.77
Finland (26)	135.57	+0.1	112.60	128.38	116.09	109.70	-0.5	2.50	135.41	112.82	129.38	116.23	110.28	152.29	129.99	141.95
France (124)	161.04	-0.4	133.75	152.48	137.88	139.50	-0.7	2.94	161.65	134.68	154.44	138.74	140.54	168.85	141.69	123.42
West Germany (92)	138.65	+1.3	115.16	131.31	118.72	118.72	+1.0	1.89	136.90	114.06	130.81	117.50	117.50	138.65	122.05	92.83
Hong Kong (48)	139.35	+0.1	115.74	131.95	119.32	139.25	+0.1	4.51	139.16	115.94	132.96	119.45	139.11	139.35	112.24	97.86
Ireland (17)	191.55	+0.6	159.10	181.38	164.02	165.84	+0.3	2.64	190.43	158.66	181.94	163.45	165.43	198.57	172.72	137.99
Italy (96)	106.56	-0.5	88.51	100.90	91.24	96.05	-0.8	2.45	107.10	89.23	102.32	91.93	96.82	109.26	91.85	86.75
Japan (454)	150.82	+1.4	125.27	142.81	129.16	142.81	+0.5	0.59	148.72	123.91	142.10	127.67	142.10	197.26	124.40	179.38
Malaysia (35)	231.81	+0.5	192.53	219.49	198.49	241.36	+0.4	2.25	230.65	192.17	220.37	197.98	240.43	245.32	204.15	182.04
Mexico (13)	497.50	-0.5	413.21	471.09	426.00	1566.22	-0.6	0.33	500.24	416.78	477.95	429.38	1566.16	549.86	324.53	240.13
Netherland (43)	142.61	-0.2	118.45	135.04	122.12	120.64	-0.4	4.67	142.84	119.01	136.47	122.61	121.16	145.66	130.43	121.50
New Zealand (17)	66.34	+1.1	55.10	62.82	56.80	59.53	+1.0	7.45	65.61	54.67	62.69	56.32	58.95	75.36	59.57	66.07
Norway (23)	237.85	+0.7	197.55	225.23	203.67	204.44	+0.3	1.55	236.11	196.71	225.59	202.67	203.74	245.90	202.34	183.80
Singapore (25)	202.46	+1.1	168.16	191.71	173.36	169.83	+0.4	2.05	200.35	166.93	191.43	171.97	169.15	207.93	179.70	157.79
South Africa (60)	181.48	+2.7	150.74	171.84	155.39	159.64	+1.0	3.73	176.79	147.29	168.91	151.74	158.05	251.39	170.00	153.21
Spain (42)	175.62	+0.9	145.87	166.30	150.38	134.38	+0.6	3.98	174.00	145.05	166.34	149.43	133.54	175.82	132.84	151.71
Sweden (34)	232.74	+1.3	193.31	220.39	199.30	206.13	+1.0	1.96	229.83	191.49	219.60	197.28	204.15	232.74	173.89	169.32
Switzerland (67)	108.45	+1.1	90.08	102.70	92.88	93.53	+1.0	2.21	107.27	89.37	102.50	92.09	92.64	108.45	88.75	84.71
United Kingdom (304)	170.19	-0.4	141.36	161.14	145.72	141.36	-0.7	4.82	170.79	142.30	163.17	146.59	142.30	170.79	139.87	144.98
USA (539)	145.52	+0.0	120.87	137.80	124.61	145.52	+0.0	3.34	145.52	121.24	139.04	124.91	145.52	148.55	130.61	130.67
Europe (981)	153.43	+0.1	127.44	145.29	131.38	129.19	-0.1	3.54	153.21	127.65	146.39	131.52	129.38	153.43	135.57	122.23
Nordic (116)	214.73	+0.9	178.35	203.33	183.86	179.11	+0.6	1.69	212.73	177.24	203.25	182.60	178.03	214.73	185.01	166.37
Pacific Basin (659)	150.13	+1.4	124.69	142.16	128.55	141.58	+0.5	0.91	148.03	123.33	141.43	127.06	140.81	192.75	124.63	174.56
Euro-Pacific (1640)	151.87	+0.9	126.14	143.80	130.04	137.16	+0.3	2.00	150.53	125.42	143.81	129.20	136.81	174.18	130.35	153.71
North America (658)	145.04	+0.0	120.46	137.35	124.21	143.64	+0.0	3.34	145.00	120.81	138.56	124.48	143.60	147.87	131.02	131.20
Europe Ex. UK (677)	141.78	+0.5	117.76	134.28	121.42	121.48	+0.2	2.72	141.12	117.57	134.86	121.16	121.26	141.78	124.81	107.74
Pacific Ex. Japan (205)	141.02	+1.5	117.13	133.55	120.76	123.99	+1.0	4.96	138.89	115.72	132.72	119.23	122.70	141.02	122.53	116.89
World Ex. US (1832)	151.93	+0.9	126.19	143.88	130.10	137.08	+0.3	2.06	150.59	125.47	143.89	129.27	136.71	173.77	131.30	153.32
World Ex. UK (2067)	146.41	+0.7	121.61	138.65	125.38	139.61	+0.3	2.23	145.40	121.14	138.93	124.82	139.23	162.00	130.80	144.15
World Ex. So. Af. (2311)	148.32	+0.6	123.19	140.46	127.01	139.59	±0.2	2.48	147.47	122.87	140.92	126.60	139.35	161.84	131.95	144.15
World Ex. Japan (1917)	148.81	+0.2	123.60	140.92	127.44	138.33	+0.0	3.49	148.57	123.78	141.96	127.54	138.32	148.81	134.62	127.57
The World Index (2371)	148.52	+0.6	123.36	140.64	127.18	139.73	+0.2	2.49	147.65	123.02	141.08	126.75	139.48	162.05	132.25	144.21

Source: *Financial Times*

provide some protection against loss, which could mean complete forfeiture of both capital and income rights. Holders receive no direct notice of meetings, circulars, or reports issued by the company. Because of the possibility of forgery of documents, bearer securities must be delivered in a reasonable condition, not badly torn or the wording materially obliterated.

The principal complication arising from the ownership of bearer securities is connected with the payment of interest and dividends. As the registrar does not know who holds the security, it cannot send off a warrant for the amount due as is possible with registered securities. The holder of the bearer security must claim the amount payable from the registrar or paying agent. This is done by detaching a numbered coupon from the bond or certificate and claiming against delivery of that coupon. Normally when a dividend is about to be paid an advertisement appears in the financial press informing holders of which coupon to submit, when to submit it, and to whom; and dates of meetings, new issues of shares, and related matters are similarly advertised. The last coupon is usually larger than the rest and is called a *talon*, and can be exchanged for a new sheet of coupons. Bearer securities must always be 'good delivery' – that is, all remaining coupons and talons should be attached, and the certificate itself must not be defaced.

This procedure makes the holding of bearer securities a troublesome matter, compared with registered securities. On the other hand, they are not subject to transfer stamp duty, which is payable only on the issue of certificates.

19.6 Recognized marking names

Shares in United States and Canadian companies are usually registered securities. The name of a registered holder appears on the face of the certificate, and a register of holders is maintained in the United States or Canada in the usual way. The reverse of the certificate contains a form of transfer which can be completed and the whole certificate sent to the registrar, which will issue a new certificate in the name of the new owner. Dividends are naturally remitted in dollars to the registered holder.

Because of the time and cost factors of transfer and the problems of currency conversion, however, United States and Canadian securities in the UK are usually registered in the name of an institution. If the registered holder signs the form of transfer but the remainder of the form is left blank, it becomes in effect a bearer security, and ownership passes by delivery. Institutions prepared to fulfil this function and which are acceptable to the market are known as *recognized* or *good marking names*. They can be stockbroker/dealers, market-makers, banks, or any other financial institution involved in some way in share dealing. Such status is awarded by the Stock Exchange in return for an undertaking to pay interest and dividends at the approved rate of exchange. Dividends and interest may have to be claimed from the marking name by the beneficial owner.

Anyone purchasing a security registered in a marking name can, if desired, have the holding re-registered in his or her own name and receive the interest or dividends direct. Securities in 'other names' command lower prices than those registered in 'good marking names', however, so this course of action is not to be recommended.

19.7 American Depository Receipts (ADRs)

American Depository Receipts were developed in the 1920s to enable US investors to deal in non-US securities without the risks, settlement delays, and high costs of dealing abroad. ADRs are negotiable receipts in certificate form issued by a US depository bank once the registered shares are lodged with a branch of the depository. The ADRs may be freely traded, but the depository bank remains as the registered holder in the company's share register.

Like marking certificates, ADRs may be cancelled at any time and registration of the ownership be changed to that of the beneficial owner, rather than the depository bank; but this is a rare event. Conversely, registered stock can be converted into ADRs when the facility exists.

An ADR certificate carries on it the duties of a depository bank to the ADR-holder and arrangements for the payment of dividends, proxies, rights offerings, etc. Rights on ADRs are normally sold by the depository through the market, and the proceeds in dollars are then paid to the ADR-holder. A register is normally kept of the holders of the ADRs.

ADRs may be 'unsponsored' or 'sponsored'. An unsponsored ADR issue is undertaken without the prior permission of the company. It is issued to facilitate the trading of an overseas share in the US markets. Because it is unsponsored, full registration of company details with the US Securities and Exchange Commission (SEC) is not required, but investors have to pay the costs of creating unsponsored ADRs as well as charges on the payment of dividends. On the other hand, sponsored ADRs are created with the active knowledge and effort of the company itself. The company meets the costs incurred in creating ADRs and paying dividends. Many companies feel that the cost is justified by the broadening of the shareholder base.

ADRs can be traded freely in both the USA and the UK. Some ADRs are listed on the NYSE, AMEX, and NASDAQ. In the UK, a market in ADRs and other depository receipts was established in 1987. The depositories for UK ADRs are certain leading American banks in London. In the UK, ADRs are treated in an identical manner to the underlying shares. Market-makers display active two-way prices on SEAQ during the mandatory quote period; 'best execution' applies; and, as they relate to alpha securities, bargains are normally reported within five minutes of the trade taking place.

ADR prices are quoted in US dollars, and settlement and dividends will also be in US dollars. Settlement for ADRs is conducted either through a US clearing corporation or, if mutually agreed, via one of the links between Talisman and US clearing corporations. Seven-day settlement – five 'business days' – is required by US clearing corporations. UK ADRs trade free of transfer stamp duty once issued.

19.8 Double-taxation agreements

Income from overseas investment usually has tax deducted at source in the country from which it originates. However, the UK Government has negotiated *double-taxation agreements* with most countries which are likely to be of interest to the UK investor. Under particular double-taxation agreements, certain classes of income are made taxable in only one of the countries which are party to the agreement; certain other income is taxable in both of the countries but the overseas tax – generally known as a 'withholding' tax – is allowed as a credit against any UK tax. If there is no double-taxation agreement then 'unilateral relief' may be available. This means that the UK investor is allowed to set off any overseas tax against his or her UK tax liability in the same way as if there had been an agreement.

Double-taxation relief is also given in respect of overseas tax on capital gains. But, in the case of both income tax and capital gains tax, it is not possible to recover the 'excess' of the overseas tax liability over any UK tax liability. This particularly applies to non-taxpayers in the UK.

19.9 Tax status of non-residents

An individual's liability to UK tax depends upon his or her country of *residence*, '*ordinary residence*', and '*domicile*'. At present these three terms determine an individual's liability to tax in the UK, but the situation is currently under review.

There is a fundamental distinction between domicile, on the one hand, and 'residence' and 'ordinary residence' on the other.

19.9.1 Domicile

Domicile is a concept of the common law, and refers to the country to which an individual 'belongs' – the country which is his or her 'natural home'. It can be determined by the nationality of parents ('domicile of origin'), by marriage ('domicile of dependence') or by self-determination ('domicile of choice'). In order to prove domicile by choice, it is necessary to pay attention to the following matters in regard to the new country: the period of residence, purchase of a home, development of business and social interests, burial arrangements, local education of children, making a will under local laws, and application for citizenship. In addition, regard will be paid to disposal of property in the old country, and severance of all formal ties there.

19.9.2 Residence

'Residence' and 'ordinary residence' are terms derived essentially from Inland Revenue practice. Residence is a question of fact, and usually requires physical presence in a country. It is possible for an individual to be resident in more than one country in a particular year for tax purposes. An investor could be regarded as 'resident' in the UK despite a temporary absence abroad, unless the absence spans a complete tax year, but the rules are generally less restrictive.

A person is considered 'resident' in the UK if

(a) he or she is physically present in the UK for six months or more in a tax year; or
(b) he or she makes substantial and habitual visits to the UK – an average of three months or more each year over four or more consecutive years; or
(c) he or she makes any visit to the UK, no matter how short, at a time when accommodation is available in the UK for his or her use, unless employed full-time abroad; or
(d) he or she is a British or Irish subject who has left the UK for the purpose only of occasional residence abroad.

19.9.3 Ordinary residence

'Ordinarily resident' is broadly equivalent to habitually resident – if a person is resident in the UK year after year, he or she is ordinarily resident in the UK. A person who becomes resident under the three-months rule in section 19.9.2 will also be considered as ordinarily resident, as will anyone with available accommodation who visits the UK in four consecutive tax years, regardless of length of stay, unless employed full-time abroad. If a person leaves the UK and evidence is not available at the start of the absence, it may take three years to establish that he or she is not UK ordinarily resident, although this can be backdated to the time of leaving.

It is possible for an individual to be 'resident' but not 'ordinarily resident', or 'ordinarily resident' but not 'resident' in a particular tax year.

The tax implications of domicile, residence, and ordinary residence for investors are outlined in section 19.9.4.

19.9.4 Tax implications

If an individual remains UK-domiciled but goes abroad, there are certain concessions relating to UK tax on investments. Simply becoming 'non-resident' confers little benefit other than the exemption from UK income tax on income arising outside of the UK, while still remaining liable to any local tax. But being not 'ordinarily resident' in the UK, as well as non-resident, means that exempt gilts, banks, and building societies can pay interest gross of UK tax, although dividend income will be subject to withholding tax. Non-resident British subjects can claim full personal allowances against UK income for which tax has been deducted at source. Furthermore there will be no liability to UK capital gains tax. Note, though, that capital gains tax is charged on individuals who are resident *or* ordinarily resident in the UK.

Inheritance tax liability is determined by domicile, not residence. Any person with a UK domicile is liable to inheritance tax on the value of his or her assets worldwide. Persons who are not UK-domiciled but are resident or ordinarily resident in the UK may be liable to inheritance tax on their UK assets. In fact, domicile has an extended meaning for inheritance tax, and 'deemed domicile' applies to a person who has been a UK resident for at least seventeen of the twenty tax years up to and including the year of transfer, or someone who was domiciled in the UK within three fiscal years of making a transfer liable to inheritance tax.

19.10 Questions

1. (a) Approximately how many companies' shares are represented in the *Financial Times*–Actuaries World Index?

     A 2400   **B** 3000   **C** 3600   **D** 4200

  (b) Name the differences between bearer securities and marking certificates.   (SIE)

  (c) The two largest equity markets in the word are:

    A USA and UK.
    B USA and Germany.
    C USA and Japan.
    D Japan and Germany.

(d) A UK-registered company earns £40 million profits in the UK and £60 million abroad. In both cases, profits are taxed at 35 per cent and double-taxation agreements apply. The company proposes to pay a dividend of £50 million. How well covered will this dividend be? Assume basic rate of tax 25 per cent, ACT $\frac{29}{75}$ths.

    A 1.20   **B** 1.12   **C** 0.88   **D** 0.98.

2. (a) Discuss the advantages of overseas investment for UK investors and also any problems which the investor is likely to encounter in this field. Do the advantages outweigh the problems?

   (b) List the most suitable methods by which small investors in the UK, with little or no knowledge of overseas investment, could add an overseas component to their portfolios.

   (c) List *four* distinctive features of the *Financial Times*–Actuaries World Indices.

(CIB 10/88)

3. Your customer, Mr Dogood, a widower aged 53 years with no children, informs you that he has decided to go to Africa for the next twelve years to help a well-known charitable organization. He has retired early from the company where he has been employed for twenty years. He will receive a deferred pension at the age of 65 and this pension together with his State pension, he feels, will enable him to live comfortably in due course. Meanwhile his house is up for sale and he will receive £180 000 for it after clearance of the mortgage and payment of all costs. He will need a spending income of £12 000 a year for the next twelve years. He will receive no payment from the charitable body for his work.

    He requires your advice. He wishes to keep the real value of his capital as intact as possible, in order to purchase a house in which to live in retirement when he returns to the UK at the end of twelve years. However, he recognizes that it may not be possible for him to purchase a house of the same standard as the one he is selling.

    Required: Discuss the taxation position of Mr Dogood and the implications for investment.

(CIB 4/86)

4. Discuss the main features of SEAQ International.

(SIE)

20 Property and personal possessions

Investments in land, buildings, and the many types of personal possessions are specialized matters requiring specialized advice. It is not possible here to arm prospective investors with sufficient knowledge of the various markets to enable them to operate successfully on their own, and this chapter merely reviews the investment areas available under these headings.

20.1 Investment in property

Direct investment in property can take several forms. An institutional investor can purchase the freehold or leasehold interest in a number of different types of property – commercial (offices, shops, hotels), industrial (factories, warehouses), residential (houses, flats), or agricultural. Owner-occupation has been one of the major, and most successful, investments for most personal investors.

20.2 Freehold property

Ownership of the freehold of a property is the nearest it is possible, in English law, to get to absolute ownership of the property. All land is theoretically leased from the Crown, and this enables Parliament to take away certain rights of ownership from freeholders. Thus, although ownership of land is deemed to include all the air space above the land and everything below the surface down to the centre of the earth, deposits of coal and petroleum are vested in the Crown irrespective of the ownership of the land above them, while aircraft have the right to fly through air space notwithstanding any objections of freeholders below.

Owners of freehold land own everything attached to the land, although it is customary to refer to 'land and buildings' where the land has been built on. Thus a freeholder may occupy the land (and buildings if any) for his or her own use or may let it. If it is let for its full value to a tenant, the rent received

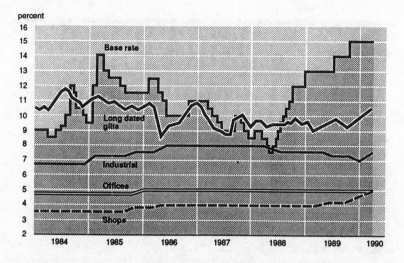

percent

Source: Central Statistical Office and Healey and Baker Research Services

Fig. 20.1   Initial yields on different types of prime property

is called a *rack rent*. Tenancies or leases at rack rents are usually for periods of up to fifty years; where the term of a lease is more than a few years, it usually contains provisions for increases in rent at fixed intervals during the term.

Freehold property is a growth investment. Property values and rents increase with the fall in the value of money. Consequently properties, like equities, have low initial yields, as fig. 20.1 shows.

The advantages of freehold property to large-scale investors, such as the institutions, are as follows:

(a) Property is an excellent hedge against inflation, even of the wage-led variety, which tends to affect equities adversely. Rent is a prior charge on a company's income – even if there is no profit out of which to pay a dividend, the landlord still has to be paid. Rents do not increase annually as equity dividends can, but there are periodic rent reviews – usually every three or five years on a modern lease – and the rent is paid gross and quarterly in advance. Most leases contain 'upward only' rent-review clauses.

(b) Property is a particularly secure investment. It cannot disappear or become valueless (except in the event of fire, earthquakes, or other natural disasters – all of which the investor can insure against). If a company goes into liquidation, the equity-holders may be left with worthless pieces of paper. If a tenant becomes bankrupt, however, the property-owner is left with a building which can be relet.

(c) The average size of deal is very large, and this suits bigger pension funds and insurance companies, which can invest perhaps £50 million in a single property but might find it very difficult to invest the same sum in a single company's shares.

(d) There are no wider responsibilities attached to property investment as there are with equities. Institutional equity investors have reluctantly but inevitably been drawn into involvement with company management, which is not only time-consuming but may also lead to adverse publicity over matters such as redundancies. Only in residential property is the landlord's responsibility likely to attract attention. Most of the insurance companies that used to own sizeable residential portfolios have reduced them substantially over the past fifteen years, investing the proceeds in commercial property.

Property investment also has its disadvantages, however:

(a) Whereas ordinary shares or gilts can be bought simply and quickly, property, although normally marketable, takes time to buy or sell. Lack of liquidity is not a deterrent to institutions, because of the other assets they hold and their positive investment cash flows. There have been occasions when it has been very difficult to sell at all, but the same then also applied to equities. Equities are only liquid if there is a two-way market. All institutions cannot be simultaneous sellers if there are no personal buyers.

(b) The valuation of property is more subjective than that of shares or gilts, because no two properties are the same, simply by differences in location. It is impossible to value a large number of properties every day or every week, and there is no authoritative index against which to measure performance.

(c) The law of property is complicated, and the services of solicitors are frequently required. Apart from the law of landlord and tenant, property-owners may be concerned with compulsory acquisition, planning permissions, the rights of owners of adjacent property, third-party liabilities, and so on. The taxation of income from property is also complicated, while looking after a portfolio of property investments requires professional advice from estate agents and surveyors. A fund investing in property normally has a separate property investment team, therefore. The investor then has some control over the investments, and can help to ensure that they are successful.

(d) Buildings do not last for ever, and extensive repairs, modernization, or rebuilding may be necessary. But it is now normal to grant what is called a full repairing lease, so that the tenant is responsible for repairs and decoration. As the property reverts to the landlord at the end of a lease, the lease normally stipulates that dilapidations must be made good so that the property is returned to the landlord in the condition in which it was handed out.

(e) There is a risk of loss of rent through lack of a tenant. This arises where a tenant vacates the property on the expiry of the lease and no new tenant

'This land has been owned by generations of pension fund managers.'

can be found. Also the bankruptcy or liquidation of a tenant can make it impossible to enforce his or her obligations under the lease. Institutional investors used to set great store by the standing or *covenant* of the tenant. A 'good covenant' means that the tenant's agreement to pay the rent is backed by guarantees from the individuals owning the business or from associated or parent companies, and this gives reasonable security that the rent will always be received. Nowadays, with prime property it is less important.

Prime property is property in a first-class location, suitable for a wide variety of tenants, and having an existing tenant of first-class financial status. Offices are usually considered the safest or best form of property investment, because they can be let to many different tenants without needing any structural work, or indeed without alterations of any kind. Factories have traditionally had a poor rating as investments because they tend to be single-purpose buildings, as are specialist commercial properties such as garages, petrol stations, multi-storey car-parks, cinemas, and hotels. Properties like these should be avoided unless their yield is commensurate with their risk, or unless it would be profitable to pull them down and redevelop the site.

(f) One type of risk that is largely unavoidable is that of changes in supply and demand for the particular item of property. A hotel may have no alternative use, and if demand for hotel accommodation in the area falls off – either through a change in the area itself or by the overprovision of hotels there – the freeholder may find itself with an empty building unsuitable for any other purpose. But even if the property is multi-purpose, such as a town-centre shop, a lost tenant may be difficult to replace if demand has declined because of a shift of population, the 'rundown' of the area, or the building of a competing shopping centre or a new out-of-town hypermarket.

A fall-off in demand may reflect premature obsolescence. The introduction of mechanical handling and pallets rendered many warehouses considerably less valuable. It is not impossible to imagine that office blocks may become obsolete altogether with the computerization of so much 'white-collar' work. The future may well see a return to 'cottage industry', with people working from home, linked to a centre via a television, telephone, and computer network.

20.3 Leasehold property

Leasehold property is land or buildings held on lease from the freeholder. The term is also used for *underleasehold* properties, where the holder of a lease from the freeholder grants a further lease, or underlease. Further leases can be granted to sub-underlessees and so on. Thus a leaseholder may hold the lease in order to use the property for his or her own purposes or to grant further leases at a profit. Underleases must be for periods shorter than those of the leases immediately above them, even if only one day shorter.

Various statutory provisions protect the interests of tenants on the expiry of leases, and possession of the property by the freeholder at that time cannot be relied on.

Where land is suitable for building on, the granting of a building lease of the land, or the granting of a lease of the land and completed buildings, is common. These leases are often for terms of 99 years or even longer, and the rent paid is a *ground rent*. This rent usually represents the rental value of the land only. The cost of the buildings is met by the leaseholder, and the freeholder has no right to those buildings until the lease expires, when the occupation of the land reverts to the freeholder, including all buildings erected on the land. Occupiers of leasehold business premises normally have a right to the renewal of their lease at a current market rent on expiry, under the Landlord and Tenant Act 1954. Occupiers of leasehold residential property in England and Wales are protected by the Leasehold Reform Act 1967, which gave rights to buy the freehold; the Rent Act 1977; the Housing Acts 1980, 1985, and 1988; and the Landlord and Tenant Acts 1985 and 1987.

Leasehold non-residential property is a 'wasting' asset. When the lease comes to an end, the rights of the tenant cease. Even if he or she is entitled to remain in possession, by virtue of statutory protection, there is no investment value in the new lease which may be granted.

20.4 Owner-occupation

Direct investment in property is not usually a suitable investment for the individual of moderate means. Large office blocks, blocks of flats, and shopping precincts are clearly available for investment only to the pension funds, insurance companies, and property companies. The individual is restricted to the smaller type of property and, unless having substantial means, he or she will have a large proportion of his or her capital invested in a single property or a small block of properties. Diversification is difficult to achieve in this type of investment, and the ownership of a small terrace of houses, or a row of little shops, provides all the problems of property ownership with few of the advantages. Small shop property is more likely to be subject to frequent changes of tenant, and consequently more 'empties', than property let to the large multiple stores.

Residential property is subject to the largest number of statutory restrictions. The Rent Acts allow a tenant or landlord to apply to the rent officer – an official of the local authority – to fix a 'fair' rent for the property. It is then illegal to charge more than the 'fair' rent for that property. However, a 'fair' rent is usually well below what might be considered a 'free-market' rent. The Rent Acts give protection to tenants of unfurnished and furnished accommodation, but the Housing Act 1980 provided for a new form of tenancy – *protected shorthold tenancies*. These are lettings of not less than one year and not more than five years. Shortholds apply only to the letting of dwellings to new tenants and may be subject to fair rents. During the period of a protected shorthold tenancy, the tenant is fully protected from eviction provided that he or she pays the rent and otherwise keeps his or her part of the agreement. On expiry of the term, the landlord can compel the tenant to vacate the property, subject to the giving of three months' written notice.

The Housing Act 1988 provides for *assured tenancies* which generally provide for market rents, without the rent officer system, but security of tenure except for *assured shorthold tenancies*.

For most personal investors, the owner-occupied house or flat has undoubtedly proved to be the most profitable long-term investment over the last two decades, for the following reasons:

(a) Owner-occupation has proved to be an excellent hedge against inflation. Over the long run, house prices have risen faster than the general rate of price inflation. House and flat prices are determined by the willingness and ability of persons to pay. They are closely linked to average earnings, and over the long term the average house price has been around $3\frac{1}{2}$ times average annual earnings – see fig. 20.2. With economic growth, earnings have risen faster then retail prices. The inflation in house and flat prices in recent times has increased as a result of social forces resulting in more single-person households and Government policy on matters such as public-sector housing and local authority financing.

(b) House prices are much more stable than equity prices. A downturn in

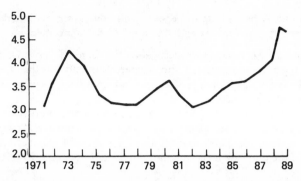

Fig. 20.2   House prices as a multiple of average earnings. For example, an average house price of £80 000 divided by average earnings of £20 000 equals a ratio of 4.0.

the market is generally reflected much more in a fall off in purchases and sales than in a drop in prices. 1989/90 was the first time since the early 1950s that house prices had fallen significantly in money as well as 'real' terms.

(c) Houses and flats are among the few assets for which it is possible to borrow up to 100 per cent of the purchase price. A high level of personal gearing means that any capital gains on the property are magnified in their impact on the investor's equity.

(d) Housing finance is probably the cheapest money available to the investor. One reason is that most of the funds raised are very short-term, although lent by the lenders for long periods. Another is the effect of Government policy. Mortgage interest rates are a political hot potato, particularly around election times, and it is almost inevitable that from time to time formal or informal pressure is put upon lenders to hold rates below the free-market level. With the entry of banks and wholesale lenders into this market in recent years, lending rates have become very competitive.

(e) Mortgages for home purchase are one of the very few forms of personal borrowing where tax relief is available. This applies to borrowings up to £30 000, at the time of writing. The higher the investor's marginal tax rate, the greater the tax relief and the lower the net cost of the mortgage.

(f) Any capital gain on the owner-occupied house or flat is entirely free from capital gains tax, provided that it is the nominated principal private residence when more than one property is owned.

(g) Also free from tax is the *imputed rent* from the owner-occupied house or flat – what the investor could have received if he or she had let the house rather than living in it personally. Until 1963 this was taxed under Schedule A – the tax schedule that applies to rental income – and tax relief on mortgage interest was restricted to this income. After 1963,

Schedule A liability on owner-occupied houses was abolished and the interest tax relief was extended to other forms of income.

It is not surprising that owner-occupation has been such a good investment – borrowing at a tax-subsidized rate of interest, usually less than the rate of price inflation, to invest in a tax-free asset which is likely to grow at a faster rate than prices generally.

The direct costs of buying and selling owner-occupied property are stamp duty and the expenses of estate agents, solicitors, and removal. Stamp duty is charged in England, Wales, and Scotland at a rate of 1 per cent on the full amount of the purchase consideration, provided this exceeds £30 000.

20.5 Types of mortgage

There is a wide variety of types of mortgage available to the house- or flat-buyer. The traditional mortgage is the *repayment* one, which involves repayment of capital and interest over its term. In the early years, repayments are virtually all repayment of interest, but in the later years the capital repayment element increases significantly. Only the interest repayment attracts tax relief at the investor's marginal rate of tax, on sums up to £30 000. Basic-rate tax relief is normally granted at source by the borrower paying the interest net of basic-rate tax under Mortgage Interest Relief At Source (MIRAS). The borrower should normally also take out a mortgage protection term assurance policy to provide security of repayment in the event of death during the term of the mortgage.

The advantage of the traditional repayment mortgage is its flexibility in varying the repayment amounts, or the term of the mortgage, or the sum borrowed, particularly when moving house. This is significant when one considers that households move on average approximately every seven years.

In recent years, banks and building societies – the primary mortgage lenders – and chains of estate agents have developed strong ties with insurance companies, and have attempted to increase their total remuneration by selling insurance services to homebuyers. The main method has been through selling *endowment mortgages*, instead of repayment ones. With an endowment mortgage, the sum assured plus bonuses, if 'with profits', are used to pay off the original sum borrowed at the end of the mortgage term. During the life of the mortgage, only the interest is repaid, and this attracts tax relief at the investor's marginal rate. One advantage claimed for the endowment mortgage is that the tax relief is maximized, and does not decline in the later years as is the case with a repayment mortgage. However, an undoubted attraction to the institutions involved is the high rates of commission that can be earned from customers usually more concerned with securing their borrowings than with the merits of a particular insurance policy.

'*Low-cost*' *endowment mortgages* are designed to minimize the outgoings of the borrower. The sum assured is significantly less than the mortgage, and greater reliance is placed on the reversionary and terminal bonuses being of a sufficient amount to cover the shortfall. There are obvious dangers of excessive optimism, particularly when recent past performance has been exceptionally good.

The most tax-efficient mortgage is a *pension mortgage*. Not only does the borrower receive the tax relief on the interest, but the pension contributions into an approved scheme also receive tax relief, and the fund itself and the lump sum used to pay off the mortgage are also tax-free. Since the introduction of personal pensions, pension mortgages have become much more common, and some insurance companies are also prepared to arrange them on occupational pensions. The investor should, however, be aware that, if the pension lump sum is used to pay off the mortgage, additional investment may be required elsewhere in order to make adequate provision for retirement income.

A relatively recent innovation is the *PEP mortgage*. This is similar to an endowment or pension mortgage in that a sum is accumulated to repay the capital sum borrowed, while the interest is paid annually. It is more tax-efficient than an endowment mortgage, because the income earned is free of income and capital gains tax, but it suffers in comparison with a pension mortgage because there is no tax relief on contributions into a PEP. Also, the expenses involved may be high – outweighing the income benefits in the early years at least.

Unit trust and *investment trust* mortgages are also available. As mentioned in chapter 17, they are likely to be better investments than life assurance, but they do not have the tax advantages of PEP or pension mortgages. Unit-linked life assurance mortgages seem to have little to commend them, as they share the uncertainty of performance with other unit-based investments, and have the high expenses and tax regime of life assurance.

At times of high interest rates, borrowers may be attracted to '*low-start*' or *deferred-interest* mortgages and *foreign-currency* mortgages. Deferred-interest mortgages usually simply roll-up the whole or part of the interest for a specified period. Invariably this results in higher future payments, although this fact is often not apparent in the advertising.

Foreign-currency mortgages usually involve borrowing in a 'strong' currency or mixture of currencies. Borrowing at low rates of interest in German marks, Swiss francs, or Japanese yen may appear superficially attractive, but the borrower should realize that such currencies have, in past years, invariably appreciated over the longer term against the pound sterling. Consequently, the apparent saving in interest may be counterbalanced by a rising interest cost and a larger repayment of capital in sterling terms at some future date. The borrower will not receive tax relief on such exchange-rate losses. There is usually a 'trigger point' when a foreign-currency loss will result in a switch back into a sterling-based mortgage.

20.6 Early repayment of a mortgage

Sometimes a person receives a lump sum, often at retirement, and has to determine whether to use part or the whole of the sum to pay off the balance of an outstanding mortgage.

Paying off the mortgage early may result in 'psychological income' – the investor may feel more content knowing that he or she has no debt. In retirement, an investor may feel it is safer to pay off the mortgage rather than risk investing the capital elsewhere. Paying off a liability rather than holding financial assets might entitle the investor to claim social security benefits that might not otherwise be available.

The decision should rest primarily upon whether the investor can earn a higher net-of-tax return on the capital than the net-of-tax cost of servicing the mortgage. For basic-rate taxpayers the difference is normally not likely to be significant. However, with certain types of mortgage it may be beneficial to pay off early. This is the case with a repayment mortgage where the interest is calculated on the opening balance at the beginning of each year, rather than on the average loan outstanding during the year. The greater the difference between the opening and average balances, the larger the difference between the quoted and true rates of interest. In the early years of a repayment mortgage using this method, the difference is not likely to be significant. But in the year before maturity the true rate will be twice the quoted rate because the average balance outstanding during the year, on which the true rate is based, will be half the opening balance, as the outstanding mortgage reduces to zero by the end of the year. Early repayment may be advisable in the last years of a mortgage, particularly for basic-rate taxpayers who are unlikely to be able to invest at such high returns as the true cost of the mortgage.

Apart from the special circumstances mentioned above, higher-rate taxpayers in particular will generally find it beneficial to retain the mortgage and invest the equivalent sum in tax-efficient assets. Another argument for retaining the mortgage is liquidity. If necessary, all or part of the investments may be turned into spending power and thereby avoid incurring high borrowing costs. If the mortgage is repaid early, an early redemption fee may be incurred; and, once the mortgage is repaid, the customer may have to pay for safekeeping of the house deeds.

20.7 Home-income, home-reversion, and roll-up schemes

Most people, when questioned about the gains made from house purchase, say that they are no better off because they cannot sell one house without buying another. Nevertheless, owner-occupied houses or flats provide appreciable assets that can be passed on to one's heirs. Alternatively, on retirement the owner can move into a smaller property or rented accommodation, and so be able to consume part or all of the capital. Home-income schemes are also available from insurance companies or building societies whereby the property can be remortgaged in return for an annuity income.

Home-income schemes – formally known as 'mortgage annuities' – involve taking a loan on the value of the property and using the money to buy an annuity and thereby increase income. Any loan is limited to £30 000, or 80 per cent of the value of the property if this is less. The 'income' arises from the difference between the annuity income and the mortgage interest. Tax relief is granted on the mortgage interest if the borrower is 65 or more. Also, the capital repayment element of the annuity income will be tax-free. Normally, only the interest is repaid on the mortgage during the lifetime of the borrower. On death, the capital is repaid from the estate. In practice, the schemes are generally not regarded as worthwhile until houseowners are in their seventies – minimum around 70 for a single man, 73 for a single woman, and combined ages of around 150 for joint lives.

Although any capital gain accruing on the property after the loan is taken out still belongs to the borrower and his or her beneficiaries, such plans are not popular. The idea of incurring fresh debts obviously deters many people in this age range. The expenses charged can be quite high, and the borrowing limit of £30 000 is no longer substantial.

A variant of the home-income scheme is the *home-reversion scheme*. Under this scheme the property is sold rather than mortgaged to an institution. The occupier remains a sitting tenant for the rest of his or her life. This is even less popular than the home-income plan, for obvious reasons, particularly as the capital sum raised is usually at a substantial discount to the open-market value of the property because of the sitting tenant. However, it might appeal to an individual without family who simply wished to remain in his or her home until death but needed additional spending power.

Some lenders offer special *interest roll-up mortgages* for the elderly, where the interest is rolled up and the full capital and interest are repayable only on death. They can provide a higher cash sum than home-income plans and be used by persons in their sixties, but there is no tax relief. Usually the loan can be drawn down in portions over a number of years to provide the income. Borrowers should generally avoid schemes which require the whole sum to be borrowed at the outset and invested in a single-premium investment bond from which an income is drawn. The disadvantage of 'roll-up' schemes is that, when property prices are stagnant and interest rates high, the loan will appreciate at a faster rate than the property. In extreme cases, the property might have to be sold during the borrower's lifetime in order to repay the loan.

In every case, the potential borrower should fully consider all factors before entering any commitment. The tax situation needs to be reviewed, and also the possible loss of social security benefits. A particularly good source of specialist impartial advice is Age Concern.

20.8 Time-share and holiday homes

Time-share entitles the purchaser to use a particular property during specified weeks of the year, usually for a specified number of years. While having attractions to persons wishing to visit a particularly exclusive part of a country on a regular basis, many time-share schemes, particularly abroad, are sold on specious claims. Time-share has become infamous for its 'hard-sell' techniques, usually involving some form of free gift if a person attends a presentation of the scheme. The claims made when comparing the costs of time-share with normal hotels or apartments are often spurious because they ignore travel costs, maintenance charges, and the income return forgone on any investment made. Swap and resale arrangements often prove to be more troublesome and expensive than originally outlined.

Time-share and other property agreements do not come within the Financial Services Act, and so the investor does not have the same statutory 'cooling-off' and 'cancellation' rights as investors in many other investments. Investors should never sign any agreement under duress – least of all when in a foreign country.

The merits of a holiday home very much depend upon the personal circumstances of the purchaser, and often depend upon ease of access to and from the main residence. When not used by the owner, a holiday home can be let, and is exempt from Rent Act protection. If it is not the investor's main residence it will not be exempt from capital gains tax, but interest on money borrowed can be charged against rental income. As with time-share, specialist advice should be sought when buying holiday homes abroad, preferably involving a UK agent with an established reputation.

20.9 Indirect investment in property

There are a number of ways of investing indirectly in property. The two traditional ways have been by means of *property shares* and *property bonds*. In recent times there have been two innovations: authorized property unit trusts and BES 'assured tenancy' schemes.

20.9.1 Property shares

Shares in the larger property companies provide a means of participating in a well-diversified portfolio of prime properties, both in the United Kingdom and in Europe as a whole, for a relatively small outlay and without the need for skilled knowledge. Besides the properties themselves, an investor is buying property expertise in the areas of management, development, and trading.

The particular attraction of property shares to many investors is their gearing. This means that any increase in the value of the company's assets leads to a more than proportionate change at the equity level. But such a practice may have its drawbacks. High interest rates paid on borrowings used to finance property investment which itself has an initially low yield mean that property shares have very low earnings and dividends relative to their assets. Current income is sacrificed for greater future capital growth. The gearing effect is also a contributory factor in the extreme volatility of property shares relative to other share prices, because it makes shareholders' net assets more variable. In addition, as with investment trusts, the share price can change independently of the net asset value, depending on the forces of supply and demand for the shares.

20.9.2 Property bonds

Property bonds have no gearing, so they have no interest payments to offset against income before corporation tax is calculated. Although they pay no dividends, the withdrawal schemes available with property bonds provide a higher potential income stream to a bondholder than would dividends from a comparable investment in property shares. As with other single-premium bonds, it is possible to defer or avoid higher-rate tax by means of the 'top-slicing' arrangements.

Bond values are also more stable than property share prices. This reflects the absence of gearing, and the valuation of the bond on a unit basis, as with a unit trust. It is also due to the fact that the funds are never fully invested in property: liquid assets are also held, because of the 'lumpy' nature of property investment, because prospects in the property market may be unfavourable, and in order to meet possible bond redemptions.

Valuation methods are not subject to such strict regulation as with unit trusts. Unlike a share, an individual property is not dealt in daily, so any method of valuation must inevitably be arbitrary, particularly at those times when the market has 'dried up'. Fund valuations are undertaken by independent valuers, but there is a suspicion that prices are 'smoothed' to disguise wide variations in price.

Most property funds are considerably smaller than the leading property companies and therefore lack the latter's diversification. Although maintaining a margin of liquidity, a bond fund may exercise its right to delay repayment in the event of a large number of net redemptions. In these circumstances, property bonds are more illiquid than shares, which are dealt in through the stock market independently of the company. On the other hand, the specialist nature of some bond funds, such as those investing solely in agricultural land, appeals to certain investors.

20.9.3 Authorized property unit trusts

Until late 1990 the only property unit trusts available were either authorized trusts which invested in property company shares, rather than property directly, or special funds designed for tax-exempt investors such as pension funds or charities. The latter were designed for institutions which are not large enough to buy a diversified portfolio of properties themselves.

However, the wider range of unit trusts permitted under the Financial Services Act includes authorized property unit trusts, which have become available to the general public from late 1990. For the small investor, they are likely to be an attractive alternative to property bonds.

20.9.4 BES 'assured tenancy' schemes

As outlined in chapter 12, the Finance Act 1988 extended the Business

Expansion Scheme to companies raising funds to provide properties on
'assured tenancies' under the Housing Act 1988. The attraction of these
schemes is based on their tax-efficiency – income tax relief on investment of
up to £40 000 per year, and freedom from capital gains tax on the first
disposal after five years – allied to the underlying property investment. The
schemes permit the companies to charge a market rent to occupants who
have security of tenure.

20.10 Investment in chattels

The other type of investment in real assets is *chattels*, or personal possessions. Examples of investments in this field which may appeal to the investor
are:

Precious stones and jewellery	Books and manuscripts
Antique silver	Postage stamps
Antique furniture	Coins and notes
Pictures	Clocks and watches
Sculpture	*Objets d'art* of many kinds
Porcelain, china, and glass	

New areas to have developed rapidly in recent years have been:

Wine	Old photographs
Tribal art	Old share and bond certificates
Musical instruments	

The collecting of old bond and share certificates is known as 'scripophily'.
Those with little or no possibility of redemption are known as 'busted' bonds,
which are collected primarily for their artistic appeal (see fig. 20.3). However, in recent years major settlements have been agreed with the Soviet
Union, China, and Bulgaria, covering pre-revolutionary debts.

The common feature of all chattels is that they provide no income – they
are essentially a hedge against inflation. They have attracted interest at times
when other investment markets have been depressed. They provide additional diversification to a portfolio.

'Alternative investments', as they are commonly called, have at times
attracted the interest of the institutions. In the early 1970s, for example,
British Rail's pension fund invested in paintings, porcelain, tapestries, glass,
rare coins, and even a score by Wagner! The accumulation of works of art by
the pension funds attracted considerable criticism from the art world. British
Rail eventually decided to sell off its investments. Its reasons were the high
insurance and security expenses, particularly when the items were displayed,
and also the tax-inefficiency of a pension fund – a gross fund – investing in
assets that yield no income.

The position of pension funds is in complete contrast to that of the
higher-rate taxpayer, for whom returns in the form of capital gain are
attractive.

Source: Hertzog Hollander Phillips & Co.

Fig. 20.3   A 'busted' bond

Besides the general concessions on capital gains – exemption on gains accrued before March 1982, indexation, and annual exemption – certain types of chattel and transactions are completely exempted from capital gains tax. These are 'wasting' chattels, such as wine; private motor cars; small-

'How much would a first issue Access card, unused, fetch?'

value chattels, with a disposal value of £6000 or less; and British money, including gold sovereigns minted after 1836 and gold Britannia coins.

While each type of investment has its own characteristics, and each requires specialist knowledge, there are several common factors that the potential investor should understand:

(a) Since they yield no income, there is no rational method of valuation. In any market, price depends on the balance of supply and demand. These in turn are influenced by rational expectations of the future, speculation, and fashion. Fashion is a factor in investment in shares, with certain sectors of the market being in and out of favour with investors from time to time. Here, though, there is a limit below which prices cannot fall on grounds of fashion alone. The assets, earnings, and dividends of a company exist and have value outside the stock market. Dividend and earnings yields therefore never get too far away from the general market levels. But this is not true of personal possessions. In many areas demand has been constant for years, but in others changes in fashion have markedly affected the demand from collectors, with a consequent effect on prices.

(b) There is the risk of buying forged, faked, doctored, or stolen items.

(c) Storage presents a problem, in terms of space and conditions of light and temperature, particularly for items such as furniture, books, and wine.

(d) Valuables need to be insured against hazards such as theft and fire. Extra expense may also be involved in fitting special locks, burglar alarms, floodlighting, and so forth. One way of overcoming this and the preceding problem is to pay for the asset to be stored with a dealer, but of course the investor is then denied any immediate enjoyment of his or her possession.

(e) Valuation presents a problem, as generally no two items are identical and prices may well vary considerably between dealers.

(f) Dealers' margins and expenses are usually much greater than is the case with financial assets – sometimes as much as 50 per cent, or even more. For this reason alone the investor should be wary of promises of quick returns. He or she should also be sceptical of promises to buy back at a significantly higher price after a fixed period. These guarantees are only as good as the credit-worthiness of the dealers who make them.

The performance of 'alternative investments' tends to be negatively correlated with that of financial assets. In other words, these investments tend to attract funds when alternative outlets are unattractive. Their performance during the 1970s was impressive, but during the 1980s they found it difficult to attract funds when equity markets were buoyant and interest rates rising.

The investor should be cautious when venturing into these unfamiliar fields. Investment in chattels should perhaps be restricted to items which not only appreciate in value but also give pleasure to the owner, because of either their beauty or their 'hobby' appeal.

20.11 Commodities

Commodities, for investment purposes, are essentially raw materials which can be bought and sold easily in large quantities on organized markets, usually based in the City of London. They fall into two groups: 'hard' and 'soft'. Hard commodities are almost all metals (such as copper, lead, gold, silver, tin, and zinc) together with diamonds; while soft commodities are mostly foodstuffs (such as barley, cocoa, coffee, palm oil, soyabean meal, sugar, and wheat) together with rubber and wool.

Investors can buy and sell commodities either for delivery straight away or for delivery at an agreed date in the future. The former is known as buying and selling 'physicals' or 'actuals', and the price paid is called the *spot* price. Payment has to be made in full at the time of purchase, and charges are made for storage and insurance. Quite large minimum amounts must be bought or sold. Buying or selling for delivery on an agreed date in the future is known as dealing in 'futures', and the agreement is called a *'futures contract'*. There are specific rules applicable to each commodity as to how far in advance deals can be arranged. The main advantage of dealing in futures are the 'gearing' – payment is not required in full initially, only a deposit – and the absence of storage expenses.

The personal investor can buy and sell commodities directly through a commodity broker, or put money into a fund which has been specifically established to invest in commodities. Dealing directly in physical commodities is not a practical proposition for most personal investors. 'Futures' involve smaller initial stakes, and there are no worries about the commodity deteriorating in storage.

Some commodity brokers run syndicates for investors to pool their funds. Nevertheless, the risk of loss deters many persons from investing in commodity futures. Until recently, the choice for most investors was an offshore commodity fund. With the relaxation of controls on investments by authorized unit trusts under the Financial Services Act, it is now possible to have an authorized commodity unit trust, which invests directly in commodities, including futures contracts.

Gold has been an excellent investment over the centuries, and always performs well in times of currency turmoil and international crisis. Since the earliest times it has been a traditional investment for savers in the East, and also for Continental Europeans. Ironically, its price peaked in dollar terms in 1979, when the Soviet Union invaded Afghanistan, and it subsequently declined with the easing of the Cold War.

UK investors have a choice of gold coins or bullion. The major coins available are the British Britannia, the Canadian Maple-leaf, the American Eagle, the Australian Nugget, and the South African Krugerrand. The coins sell at a small premium to the underlying gold prices.

As regards bullion, many customers do not want to take delivery of the gold personally, and London dealers are happy to hold it in *unallocated accounts*, the cheapest and normal method of storage. So many ounces of gold are simply credited to the customer's account, and the question of price fluctuations, as well as the eventual sale, is no more than a book-keeping exercise.

One disadvantage of buying bullion and coins is that they are subject to value added tax. Unless the purchaser is registered with the Customs and Excise for VAT purposes, he or she cannot reclaim VAT when the gold is sold. Investors can avoid the problem by channelling their gold purchases offshore where no sales tax is applied.

Methods of investing indirectly in gold include authorized unit trusts which invest either in gold itself or in gold-mining shares.

20.12 Questions

1. (a) The most important factor influencing house prices in the long term is usually held to be:

   A the earnings of borrowers.
   B general price inflation.
   C interest rates.
   D mortgage interest relief.

   (b) The most tax-effective form of house purchase in the UK is by means of a:

   A full endowment mortgage.

   B low-cost endowment mortgage.
   C repayment mortgage.
   D pension mortgage.

(c) Give four differences between property bonds and property shares.
(d) Which of the following could be a 'real' in contrast to a 'financial' investment?

   A Gold certificates.
   B Unit trusts.
   C Chinese 1898 bonds.
   D Premium Bonds.

2. What are the advantages and disadvantages for the private investor of the purchase of:

(a) residential freehold property for owner-occupation;
(b) freehold shop property to provide a regular income?

(CIB 4/87)

3. A customer, aged 45, has a mortgage of £15 000 outstanding on his house, which is worth £75 000. He has just received a legacy of £32 000 and seeks your advice as to whether he should invest the whole legacy or pay off his mortgage and invest the balance. He wishes to maximize his capital by the time he retires at age 60. Set out the advice you would give him in the following alternative sets of circumstances:

(a) The outstanding mortgage will be paid off from the proceeds of an endowment policy maturing when he is 60. Meanwhile he pays interest on the mortgage at current rates.
(b) There is no insurance cover on the mortgage and the mortgage is being reduced by instalments. The final instalment is due to be paid when he retires at 60.

(CIB 4/85)

4. What are 'alternative investments' (chattels)? What are the special risks and problems associated with investment in them?

(CIB 5/88)

21 Personal portfolio planning

21.1 'Know your customer'

No one investment policy is right for every investor in every circumstance. Investment strategies of institutional investors, for example, are to a large extent dictated by the nature of their liabilities and the restrictions of law or trust deed. Institutional investors nevertheless retain some discretion to decide on the relative weightings of assets in their portfolios, and to adjust them when their 'reading' of economic trends deems this to be necessary. However, for a large insurance company or pension fund to try suddenly to switch all its investments out of one area and into another is rather like asking a huge oil tanker, travelling at full speed, to turn about on the spot! It cannot be done. It is usual to adopt a gradualist approach by redirecting the new moneys coming in, rather than turning over the fund itself. This makes it all the more imperative that the correct long-term strategy is adopted, and that it is not influenced too strongly by short-term events and trends in performance.

The personal investor is obviously much more flexible in portfolio planning, but in many ways the task is more complicated because of the need to take account of so many factors relevant to the individual. No two people are the same; nor are their investment needs. An investment adviser needs to know certain personal details before beginning to give advice on particular investments. These details fall under three headings:

(a) financial situation,
(b) family circumstances,
(c) personal preferences.

21.2 Financial situation

Income available and spending needs vary over a lifetime. In the case of 'white-collar' workers, income, in real terms, may be at its lowest level when they are students or pensioners, and at its peak somewhere between middle age and retirement. The income of manual workers is more evenly spread.

The demands on income for spending needs are usually greatest when one is still fairly young, having invested in a house and started a family. The surplus of income over spending needs is probably greatest when, in the typical family, the children have grown up and perhaps left home, while the husband is reaching the peak of his earning power and the wife is back at work.

The size of income, relative to spending needs, determines how much an individual can afford to invest. It also determines his or her tax position, and therefore the type of investments most suitable. Higher-rate taxpayers generally prefer capital growth to income. Capital growth can be guaranteed with some investments; with others, such as equities, it is more suspect and the investor obviously should not rely on it as an important source of funds for day-to-day living expenses. The greater the stability and certainty of income and spending, the larger the proportion that can be invested in a regular or long-term form.

To make such judgements, the sort of questions the investor or adviser should bear in mind are as follows:

(a) *Earnings*

- What are net earnings after tax?
- How secure is that level of earnings?
- How would illness or injury affect them in the short term?
- How secure is the investor's employment?

(b) *Pension*

- How long is it to retirement?
- What level of pension is likely to be received? Is the type of pension the most suitable?

(c) *Assets and liabilities*

- What is the investor's overall 'net worth' position?
- Is net income being received or do expenses exceed income?
- Is the investor a beneficiary of a trust fund?
- Is the investor a member of a Lloyd's syndicate?
- Is there any other factor likely to cause a major change at some stage in the investor's life, such as an inheritance?

The amount of an investor's net capital will determine the type of investment service that can be provided by the adviser.

(d) *The investor's tax position*

- Is the investor resident, ordinarily resident, and domiciled in the UK?
- What is the investor's marginal rate of income tax?
- What is the investor's capital gains tax position? Is CGT likely to be paid?
- Is the investor's wealth such that consideration should be given to avoidance of inheritance tax?

21.3 Family circumstances

Spending needs have already been touched upon, and these reflect the responsibilities and commitments of the investor at different stages of his or her life.

(a) *Age*   At fifty, for example, the investor is more likely to be concerned with building a nest-egg for retirement than with saving up for the deposit for a first home. Certain investments impose minimum and maximum ages. Personal pension contribution limits depend upon age.

(b) *Dependent spouse and children*

- What is the investor's state of health? Is there likely to be any difficulty obtaining the right sort and amount of life assurance?
- Are dependants adequately provided for in the event of the investor's early death? Has the investor made a will?
- Have precautions been taken to reduce the liability for inheritance tax on death?
- Does the investor want to leave money for the family to inherit?
- Is money required, or likely to be required, in order to send children to fee-paying schools, or to provide assistance in further or higher education?

(c) *Housing*

- Is cash likely to be required in the foreseeable future to buy a house, or a different house?
- Is the mortgage of the appropriate type and size?
- Is the mortgage covered by life assurance?

(d) *Other commitments*

- Is the investor likely to have to assist any other relatives?
- Is cash likely to be required for any other specific purpose in the foreseeable future (house repairs, for example, or buying new furniture or a washing-machine, or going on holiday)?

These questions should naturally lead to the question of sickness, accident, and life assurance cover. Special insurance schemes are also available to assist in such matters as school fees.

The primary purpose of life assurance should be to provide *protection* against the financial consequences of early death, rather than investment.

21.4 Personal preferences

(a) *Risk aversion*   Some investors are inherently nervous; they cannot help worrying about their investments. There are people who are frightened by equity investment, since they feel that, unless their money is invested in something where the value cannot fall (in money terms), they are likely to lose their wealth. Diversification can reduce risk, but, at the end of the day, the question must be asked: 'Are you prepared to risk losing some money for the chance of a greater gain?' This inevitable trade-off between risk and return must be clearly understood.

Very risk-averse investors are likely to hold a disproportionately large amount of 'cash' and National Savings investments. Although their investments are secure in money terms, many such investors have subsequently realized that the real value of their capital has been eroded over time. Index-linked National Savings Certificates and index-linked gilts are secure from default risk and provide more than just a guaranteed protection against inflation.

(b) *Ethics*   Certain investors will not purchase shares in particular sectors of the market, such as breweries, tobacco companies, distilleries or gaming organizations. Other investors find a company objectionable if it operates in a country whose Government they see as politically unacceptable.

Others will wish to hold shares in certain companies irrespective of investment merit in the usual sense, often because of the gifts or special concessions offered to holders of a stipulated number of shares, such as Sketchley's concession of reduced charges for dry-cleaning.

(c) *Control*   Is advice sought or simply an 'execution-only' service? Does the investor wish to manage his or her own portfolio or delegate responsibility to an investment adviser?

21.5 Time-horizon

The investor's time-horizon depends partly on age and partly on the circumstances regarding finances and family. The time-horizon should reflect a period over which the investment strategy is not likely to be changed. For example, someone aged 50 who intended to retire at 60, and whose income/expenditure pattern is reasonably stable, should have a ten-year time-horizon. At that point the investment strategy might be revised to take account of the differing income and tax circumstances.

On the other hand, a young person with an income and life-style which could be subject to sudden change should have a short investment time-horizon, in order to maintain maximum flexibility.

21.6 Liquidity

Part of any investment fund should be in liquid form – that is, as 'cash' or 'near-cash' investments. The rule of thumb is around 10 per cent of capital, or six months' income, but these proportions are not rigid and depend on the investor's security of income and employment, time-horizon, immediate commitments, and view of the state of the markets for different types of longer-term asset.

At certain times, when the yield curve is downward-sloping, cash investments provide a high return compared with other assets. If neither the equity nor the fixed-interest market appears attractive, the personal investor might seriously consider 'going liquid' to a large degree. The danger of such a policy is that income is uncertain, and it is difficult to predict when interest rates have reached a peak or the share market has 'bottomed-out'.

21.7 Diversification

The old adage about avoiding putting all your eggs in one basket is highly relevant to investment theory. The investor's objective is to obtain the highest return for a given level of risk, and the lowest level of risk for a given return.

Much risk is unnecessary and easily avoidable. This is *independent* (or *unsystematic*) risk, which can be eliminated by holding a reasonably diversified portfolio. An extreme example will illustrate the principle.

Suppose two shares, A and B, each offer a 50 : 50 chance in a particular year of earning either 20 per cent or nothing, the outcome depending on certain unpredictable economic events. These are obviously risky investments, each with a mean expected return of 10 per cent. But what if they were shares in an ice-cream company and an umbrella manufacturer? When one prospers, the other does badly. When one earns 20 per cent, the other earns zero. In this case, although both securities are risky if held independently, if held together they are risk-free because they always yield 10 per cent (20 per cent + 0 per cent, or 0 per cent + 20 per cent).

This is admittedly an idealized example, but the principle is nevertheless sound. Provided the returns on any two securities are not perfectly correlated (that is, they do not move perfectly together in the same direction), their combined risk is less than a weighted average of their individual risks. In fact, the riskiness of a portfolio depends on three factors: the riskiness of the individual assets, the proportion of the portfolio invested in each asset, and the correlation of returns between assets. The smaller the positive correlation of returns, or the greater the negative correlation, the greater the risk reduction through diversification.

The scope of diversification within a fairly homogenous sector of the market – such as banking, insurance, or brewing – is strictly limited, because most shares within these sectors move up and down very much in line with the sector as a whole. Research has shown, however, that by far the greater part of independent risk can be eliminated by holding about fifteen to twenty shares selected fairly randomly. This gives a level of risk broadly similar to that of the stock market as a whole.

The advantages of international diversification were commented upon in chapter 19.

A personal investor does not need to worry about adequate diversification if he or she opts for indirect investment via a broad-based unit trust, investment trust, or insurance scheme. Specialist unit trusts, concentrating on certain sectors of the market or geographical areas, should not dominate a portfolio, and should be purchased only after adequate diversification has been achieved. Many of these specialist funds have a far more volatile performance record than that of the general trusts, but much of this risk can be diversified away if they are held in conjunction with the latter. Held in isolation, their risk/reward ratio tends to be poor.

The degree of diversification in an insurance policy depends on the policy itself. The funds of traditional 'with-profits' endowment policies, for example, are spread across equities, gilts, property, and cash. Unit-linked policies are more risky, being far more dependent on capital values at the time the policy is encashed and the degree of diversification in the chosen unit fund.

21.8 Stability

In a fairly straightforward portfolio consisting primarily of equities and gilts, gilts provide the stability. Over the long term, equities should outperform gilts, but this superior performance cannot be guaranteed over relatively short time-periods. Gilt interest and capital change is guaranteed, either in money or in 'real' terms depending on whether they are conventional or index-linked gilts. Thus an investor would buy equities for performance but gilts for security.

A portfolio for a wealthier investor might be along the lines of

Liquid investments	10%
Gilts	40%
Equities	50%
	100%

In any portfolio, the investor should always ensure that attention has been paid to liquidity, protection, diversification, and stability.

21.9 Range of investments

When constructing a portfolio, there is a wide range of assets to choose from. Among those considered in this book have been:

(a) *Bank and building society and related accounts*

- 'Instant-access'
- Seven-day/one-month
- Term
- Notice
- High-interest cheque-book
- Offshore
- Fixed-rate
- SAYE
- Subscription
- TESSA

- Money-market
- Finance houses

(b) *Local authority investments*

- Temporary loans
- Town-hall bonds
- Yearling bonds
- Quoted stocks

(c) *National Savings investments*

- Ordinary Account
- Investment Account
- National Savings Certificates (fixed-interest and index-linked)
- Income Bonds
- Capital Bonds
- Yearly Plan
- Premium Bonds

(d) *Gilt-edged and related securities*

- Shorts, mediums, longs, undated
- High-coupon/low-coupon
- Index-linked
- Public boards
- Commonwealth and foreign Governments

(e) *Company loan stocks*

- Fixed charge
- Floating charge
- Unsecured loan stock
- Subordinated unsecured loan stock
- Convertibles

(f) *Company shares*

- Preference
- Equities

(g) *Business Expansion Schemes*

(h) *Options*

- Traditional
- Traded
- Employee schemes
- Warrants

(i) *Unit trusts*

- Authorized mainland

- Authorized offshore
- Equity income
- Growth
- General
- Overseas
- Index (tracking)
- Other specialist
- Accumulation
- Unauthorized

(j) *Investment trusts*

- Balanced
- Specialist
- Income shares
- Capital shares

(k) *Personal Equity Plans*

- Self-select
- Managed
- Corporate
- Unit and investment trusts

(l) *Life assurance*

- Term
- Whole-life
- Endowment
- Traditional 'with-profits' or 'without-profits'
- Unit-linked
- Guaranteed income and growth bonds
- Annuities
- Friendly societies

(m) *Pensions*

- SERPS
- Occupational, AVCs
- Personal, 'with-profits', unit-linked

(n) *Property*

- Freehold
- Leasehold
- Owner-occupation
- Home-income and similar plans
- Property shares and bonds
- Holiday homes, time-share
- Chattels
- Gold and other commodities

21.10 Investing for income

A high yield is provided by all of the following investments, and in all cases any tax deducted at source can be reclaimed by non-taxpayers from 1991/2, following the abolition of composite rate tax.

(a) Bank and building society accounts
(b) National Savings Investment Account
(c) National Savings Income Bonds
(d) High-coupon gilts and local authority stocks
(e) Yearling bonds
(f) Town-hall bonds
(g) High-coupon company loan stocks
(h) Preference shares
(i) High-income unit trusts – particularly gilt and money-market trusts
(j) Income shares of a split-level investment trust
(k) Retirement annuities

Guaranteed income bonds also pay a competitive fixed rate of interest, but basic-rate tax deducted at source by the life assurance company is not recoverable by non-taxpayers.

Provided the investment is of at least a minimum size, many of the above offer monthly income facilities – in particular, National Savings Income Bonds and certain investments with banks, building societies, and life assurance and unit trust groups. In other cases, as with direct holdings of gilts, it is possible to manufacture a 'home-made' income plan by holding at least six gilts with different monthly payment dates. However, this may be unduly restrictive in terms of stock selection, so a simpler solution would be simply to have the interest paid into a 'liquid' account and make regular drawings.

Equities should not be bought for their immediate income, as their initial yields are generally low compared with those obtainable on fixed-interest securities – the 'reverse yield gap' – and cash investments. Nevertheless they do provide a growing income stream which is attractive for someone wishing to maintain at least a constant level of purchasing power. Some individual equities or equity unit trusts offer relatively high yields, but these are only commensurate with their higher levels of risk and poorer long-term growth prospects. An alternative might be *income shares of a split-level investment trust*. These provide a growing stream of income until their redemption date.

For investors of beyond retirement age, *annuities* provide a high level of income per pound invested – more than could be obtained on a fixed-interest security. This is because the interest is boosted by an annual return of capital. The initial return is less if a growth rate is built into the return, or if the annuity is on joint rather than single lives. The annuity might be financed by a mortgage in the form of a home-income plan.

Corporate debt offers higher yields than Government borrowing but also a higher risk and no facility for purchase through the Post Office (National

Savings Stock Register). Moreover, it is harder to find a stock with adequate interest and asset cover and a redemption date coinciding with that at which the investor is looking for full and certain recovery of capital. Local authority debt offers higher returns than British funds, with very little additional risk. Preference shares are relatively unattractive to the personal investor.

It has usually been more tax-efficient for a higher-rate taxpayer to generate income by regular realization of capital profits than by receiving income directly. However, in 1990/91 such an investor pays tax at 40 per cent on both income and capital gains. Capital gains still receive more lenient treatment than income, because of the range of exemptions, the 'indexation' rules, and the annual exemption, but the distinction between income and capital gain is less critical. Single-premium investment bonds, in particular, are investments which provide a higher-rate taxpayer with a withdrawal facility (5 per cent) and the opportunity to postpone the tax liability until a more advantageous time, such as retirement.

21.11 Tax-efficient investments

There is a wide range of investments which are tax-efficient for higher-rate taxpayers, with the emphasis being on capital gain rather than income. Their tax-efficiency in terms of income and capital gains tax can be categorized as follows:

(a) *Completely tax-free*

- National Savings Bank Ordinary Account – first £70 of interest per person per year tax-free
- National Savings Certificates (fixed-interest and index-linked)
- National Savings Yearly Plan
- National Savings Premium Bond prizes
- Bank or building society Save-As-You-Earn contracts
- Bank or building society TESSA account – five years
- Personal Equity Plan
- Business Expansion Scheme – on first disposal after five years
- Proceeds of a 'qualifying' life assurance policy (but the fund itself is subject to tax)
- Friendly-society policy
- Approved pension plans
- Principal place of residence
- 'Wasting' chattels
- Private motor cars
- 'Small-value' chattels – disposal proceeds £6000 or less
- Post-1836 gold sovereigns and Britannia coins
- Betting winnings – including betting on the movement of share indices

(b) *Investments with no income, and subject only to capital gains tax*

- Traditional and traded options

- Warrants
- Capital shares of a split-level investment trust
- Most chattels

(c) *Investments with little taxable income and gains tax-free*

- Low-coupon short-dated gilts
- Index-linked gilts

(d) *Investments with little taxable income and gains subject to CGT*

- Growth-orientated equities
- Growth-orientated unit trusts and investment trusts
- Property for letting

(e) *Investments where tax liability can be deferred*

- Single-premium investment bonds, including guaranteed growth bonds
- Offshore 'roll-up' funds

(f) *Investments which receive tax relief*

- Approved pension plans
- Business Expansion Scheme
- Owner-occupied property – mortgage interest tax relief on loans up to £30 000

21.12 Regular-savings schemes

An investor who wishes to save on a regular basis has the choice of either contributing to a scheme which especially provides for regular savings or simply investing regular sums on an *ad hoc* basis. Examples of the former include:

(a) National Savings Yearly Plan
(b) Bank or building society SAYE
(c) Bank or building society TESSA account
(d) Other bank or building society regular-savings schemes
(e) Unit or investment trusts
(f) Personal Equity Plan
(g) Regular-premium life assurance
(h) Friendly society
(i) Pension scheme.

21.13 Investing for children

Let us consider Mr D, a higher-rate taxpayer, who proposes to give his eight-year-old son, Paul, £1000 per annum. He asks for advice on the best method of doing this and on the most suitable ways of investing this money for Paul, who has no other assets or sources of income. As an alternative, it is suggested that Paul's grandfather, who is a basic-rate taxpayer, could give Paul £1000 per annum for investment.

Tax-efficiency is one consideration when gifting money to children and possibly investing it on their behalf. If a parent gives money or investments to his or her child, any income earned is normally aggregated with the parent's income for income tax purposes, until the child reaches the age of eighteen, or marries if earlier. However, from 1991/92 aggregation will apply only if the income exceeds £100 per year. If the gift came from a grandparent or remoter relative or friend, the child's investment income would be taxed in the child's own name and the child would have the single person's allowance. In both circumstances there would be an immediate liability for capital gains tax on the accrued gains of any chargeable assets gifted.

At first sight it would appear, therefore, that, since Paul's father is a higher-rate taxpayer, the appropriate investments would be ones suitable for a higher-rate taxpayer and also appropriate to the amount involved and the likely time-horizon, around ten years, at which date Paul will be eighteen. A regular-saving facility would be useful. Possible investments could include:

(a) National Savings Yearly Plan,
(b) growth-orientated unit trusts or investment trusts,
(c) 'qualifying' life assurance.

Many of the other tax-efficient regular-saving schemes generally available – such as SAYE, TESSA, PEPs, and friendly societies – stipulate a minimum age, usually eighteen. However, Paul's father could use them personally and eventually make over the proceeds, either by means of a simple gift, a deed of assignment, or, in the case of life assurance, by completing a standard trust form produced by the life company at the time of taking out a policy. Regular payments could also be made into lump-sum investments such as NSCs. An offshore roll-up fund could be added to each year. The fund itself would be tax-free until encashment, which could be deferred until Paul reached eighteen, at which point he would be taxed in his own name.

Apart from investment below the £100 income threshold mentioned above, it is not normally possible for a parent to separate his or her income from that of a child, in order to use the child's personal allowance. However, in theory, use could be made of one particular type of trust fund, known as a 'bare' trust. (This and other types of trust are explained in detail in chapter 22). The Inland Revenue take the view that, for such trusts, the income belongs to the child, provided that all the income is accumulated, and no payments are made to the child before the age of eighteen or earlier marriage. However, in this particular case the annual sums are too modest to justify the creation of such a trust.

Independent taxation has created a further possibility, provided that one spouse does not work. If Paul's mother did not work, she could give him the £1000 per year and the investment income could be set-off against her single person's allowance. Provided that there was sufficient unused personal allowance from his mother, Paul could thereby receive income free of tax. He would also have his annual capital gains tax exemption. However, the Inland Revenue would dismiss the arrangement if there were evidence that Paul's father had transferred assets to his wife with the intention that they should be transferred to Paul.

The use of a 'bare' trust, the spouse's unused personal allowance, or the gift from the grandparent would in all cases result in Paul being able to use a single person's allowance and receive income free of tax. If such is the case, investments chosen should be ones which benefit from this tax advantage, such as, from 1991/2,

(a) Bank or building society schemes,
(b) Local authority bonds or quoted stocks,
(c) NSB Investment Account,
(d) National Savings Capital Bonds,
(e) Appropriate dated gilt-edged securities,
(f) High-income unit or investment trusts.

Gifts from both Paul's father and grandfather would be exempt from inheritance tax, if the £3000 annual exemption had not already been used. Larger gifts would be classified as potentially exempt transfers (PETs). It can be particularly tax-efficient for inheritance tax purposes for capital to skip a generation – to pass directly from grandparent to grandchild – and trusts, particularly accumulation and maintenance trusts, are often used for this purpose if the capital is substantial.

21.14 Young persons

Mr A is a young man aged twenty. He is unmarried and lives with his parents. He earns £10 000 gross per annum and plans to save £100 monthly. He has no assets at present and wishes to build up a reserve for the future, although he has no specific plans.

For young persons of around this age, the main considerations in constructing a portfolio will normally be

(a) liquidity,
(b) flexibility,
(c) future house purchase.

Most young persons have relatively modest net financial assets and may, in fact, need to borrow in order to finance courses in further or higher education. They may decide to travel abroad, change jobs, get married, or all three! Given these uncertainties surrounding income and expenditure, and the general lack of opportunity to have accumulated capital other than through inheritance, emphasis should be placed on 'cash' and 'near-cash' investments, and investments generally which are readily realizable.

In general, unmarried young persons should avoid becoming 'locked-in' to long-term, illiquid investments, such as regular-premium life assurance contracts or term deposits.

Life-assurance-related products are usually unattractive to such persons, as they may need to be encashed if circumstances change. As outlined in chapter 17, life assurance is subject to a taxation and commission structure which to a basic-rate taxpayer generally makes it unattractive as an investment when compared with alternative investments such as unit trusts, investment trusts, PEPs, and personal pensions.

At this age, single individuals should have little need for life assurance either as an investment or for protection. Term cover can easily be arranged if they should take on marital or family responsibilities, provided that there is no problem of ill health. Personal pensions are not normally payable until 50, and therefore represent a form of locked-up savings.

The young person would probably be better advised to channel savings into areas which are readily accessible, and which can be used to purchase property.

Mr A should first of all accumulate the necessary amount of liquidity through a bank or building society account offering instant access, or possibly use a high-interest cheque-book account. This could hold of the order of £5000 – that is, six months' salary.

Further savings could be invested in regular-savings schemes which allow for flexibility, and possibly establish a basis for future house purchase. The £100 per month could be invested as follows:

		£ per month
(a)	Building society subscription shares	25
(b)	National Savings Yearly Plan	25
(c)	General-type unit trust regular-savings scheme	25
(d)	General-type investment trust regular-savings scheme	25
		100

Equity investment via a unit or investment trust should provide protection against inflation over the longer term. Over the shorter term, however, there is no guarantee that such investments will not fall in value. As an alternative, some of the savings could be invested in index-linked NSCs or index-linked gilts, although they do not have explicit regular-savings schemes – they would have to be bought on an *ad hoc* basis.

21.15 Married persons with children

The transition from 'dinkies' – dual incomes, no kids – to 'oiks' – one income, kids – can have painful effects on family finances! There is likely to be a significant drop in income, at least temporarily, and a rise in expenditure. If the wife does not intend to return to work as soon as possible, any portfolio should be structured so as to use as fully as possible her personal allowance.

At a time of pressure on savings, and the necessity of increased-protection insurance, 'term' assurance will often be the most appropriate additional life policy for the investor to purchase.

Parents may wish to have the children privately educated, and make provision for the costs involved in further and higher education. There is a wide range of schemes available for school-fees planning. The most basic form of investment is a straightforward discount on future fees. Alternatively, a lump sum can be invested with a school in advance to purchase a deferred annuity. The annuity is not liable to either income or capital gains tax if the school is a charitable trust. The disadvantage of these two schemes is their inflexibility: they commit the parents to one specific school, and problems might be encountered if parents decided not to use the school or if 'little Johnny' failed the entrance exam!

A more flexible scheme is an investment with an educational trust. The trustees, rather than the school, purchase the requisite annuity from an insurance company. By this method, the parents retain the full benefits of the tax-free status of a charitable trust, but they can transfer the annuity to any school. A number of well-known life assurance companies operate educational trusts. These come in various forms, including 'with-profits' policies.

Accumulation and maintenance trusts (discussed in chapter 22) are another form of trust used for educational needs, particularly when they are paid for by grandparents.

The advantage of charitable trusts, including educational trusts, is their tax-free status. But it may be simpler for the investor to use other tax-efficient savings schemes to accumulate capital, such as PEPs, SAYE, TESSA, friendly-society bonds, BES, and personal pensions. Endowment policies have been a traditional means of accumulating capital, because regular-premium policies are tax-free on maturity; but the funds themselves have borne tax. Alternatives could be a regular-saving scheme with a unit or investment trust, perhaps via a 'qualifying' PEP.

21.16   Widows and widowers

The recently widowed are in a particularly vulnerable financial position if they have not recently worked and have children to support. Unless they are particularly wealthy, such investors have a number of common characteristics. Firstly, the need for protection insurance, particularly 'term' insurance. Secondly, the need to maintain a home for themselves and the children. If they were already living in owner-occupied property, the mortgage will probably have been discharged by an insurance company, as is the case with a mortgage protection policy. Thirdly, they should avoid high-risk investments, such as options – not for 'widows and orphans'! The emphasis should be on bank and building society accounts, National Savings, gilts, and equities via well-diversified media such as general-type unit or investment trusts. Index-linked investments may be particularly attractive. Generally there will be a requirement for income, but some capital growth will be required to compensate for inflation.

For income tax purposes, the year of death is divided into two parts: one before and one after the death. In the first period, both partners receive a personal allowance, and the husband receives the married couple's allowance. For income received after the husband's death, the widow can claim the rest of her personal allowance and the rest of the married couple's allowance, if not already fully used, plus the full additional personal allowance if she is caring for children, plus the widow's bereavement allowance. The last item is available in the year of bereavement and the subsequent year if she has not remarried before the start of that year. In 1990/91 the additional personal allowance and the widow's bereavement allowance were both £1720. Social security cash benefits are also available in the form of 'widowed mother's allowance' and 'widow's pension', both of which are taxable. There may be also an entitlement to a one-off 'widow's payment'. There is also an enhanced child benefit for one-parent families.

Example Mrs Y, whose husband died in March 1990, requires investment advice. She is about 40 years old, and has two children aged eight and twelve, attending non-fee-paying schools. She rents the family house, has no income except for State benefits of £3500, of which £2400 is taxable, and has no capital resources except for the sum of £60 000 which she has received from insurance policies on the life of her late husband. She can buy the house at a discounted price from the local authority for £30 000. She would like to have a net income of at least £7500 in 1990/91, and also be able to purchase the house.

Her tax allowances are as follows:

	£
Tax-free benefits	1100
Personal allowance	3005
Additional personal allowance	1720
Widow's bereavement allowance	1720
	7545

Thus the total required income of £7500 is achievable free of income tax.

The required yield is

$$\frac{£7500 - £3500}{£60\,000 - £30\,000} \times 100\% = \frac{£4000}{£30\,000} \times 100\%$$

$$= 13.33\%$$

At the time of writing in 1990 a yield of 13.33 per cent could be obtained from investments such as offshore bank and building society accounts, National Savings Income Bonds, and high-coupon short-dated gilts. But there would be no growth element apart from the property. In 1991/92 the widow's bereavement allowance would no longer apply. Also it is crucial that Mrs Y takes out term assurance to provide adequate financial protection for the children in the event of her own death.

One important factor to be considered is whether or not Mrs Y intends to seek full- or part-time employment. If so, it would not be so critical that the investment income was not sustainable in real terms.

Another factor to consider would be the loss of all or part of the social security benefits, including benefits in kind, and to what extent these depend on the level of her financial assets.

Widowers do not receive the widowed mother's allowance, nor the widow's pension before retirement age, nor the widow's bereavement allowance. In the year of the wife's death they can claim their own personal allowance and the married couple's allowance, plus the additional personal allowance for any children. In subsequent years they lose the married couple's allowance.

21.17 Planning for retirement

Example Mr X is a married man aged 49. His wife is 47. They have two children, aged 24 and 22, both of whom have left home and are self-supporting. Mr X's salary is £50 000 per annum. He is a member of his employer's pension scheme and has a company car. Mrs X has no earned income. The X's house is worth £175 000 and there is an outstanding mortgage of £12 000. They have no other financial assets. Mr X has recently inherited £200 000. He has consulted two investment advisers, who have put forward schemes for the investment of £200 000 as summarized below.

Scheme 1	£
National Savings Certificates (fixed-interest)	2 000
Index-linked National Savings Certificates	10 000
Treasury 13½% 1994	38 000
Single-premium investment bonds:	
A Life Assurance Co. capital growth bond	40 000
B Life Assurance Co. equity bond	40 000
C Life Assurance Co. managed bond	40 000
Authorized unit trusts:	
D Unit Trust Group dollar fund	10 000
E Unit Trust Group Far East fund	10 000
F Unit Trust Group technology fund	10 000
	200 000

Scheme 2	
Building Society one-month-notice account	7 200
National Savings Bank Ordinary Account	2 800
National Savings Certificates	2 000
Building Society SAYE scheme	
(to be financed from income)	

2% Treasury Index-linked Stock 1996	10 000
Exchequer 3% Gas 1990–95	7 000
Funding 6% 1993	6 000
A selection of UK ordinary shares	145 000
Authorized unit trusts:	
G Unit Trust Group American growth fund	10 000
H Unit Trust Group Pacific fund	10 000
	200 000

Adviser 2 has offered to manage the gilts and ordinary shares.

Mr X is a 40 per cent taxpayer. His salary is £50 000 per year, but he would be able to claim the personal allowance of £3005 plus the married couple's allowance of £1720 (1990/91) – that is total allowances of £4725. The gross cost of his mortgage would also be offsettable against taxable income, but he clearly still remains a higher-rate taxpayer, since the higher-rate tax threshold is £20 700 (1990/91). Mr X will also have to pay tax on the company car – a 'benefit in kind'. For example, for 1990/91, a car under four years old in the 1400–2000 c.c. range would constitute a benefit in kind of £2200, assuming business mileage was between 2500 and 18 000 miles.

The first portfolio, Scheme 1, appears to have been put together by a financial intermediary. The emphasis is on indirect investments in life assurance and unit trusts. Mr X presumably wishes to accumulate capital until retirement. Single-premium investment bonds are often sold on the basis of their supposed tax-efficiency for higher-rate taxpayers, particularly in respect of the 5 per cent withdrawal facility. The unit trusts are all specialist funds, which are likely to have low dividend yields, which suits Mr X's requirements. The bonds and the unit trusts provide diversification indirectly. But Mr X is unlikely to require the 5 per cent withdrawal facility, and a better performance is likely to be obtained from a mixture of investment trusts and unit trusts.

The main deficiencies of the first portfolio are the absence of liquidity and the probable lack of adequate protection insurance. Single-premium investment bonds normally provide only the minimum possible life assurance cover.

Scheme 2 was probably constructed by a stockbroker, since the emphasis is on direct holdings of gilts and equities. The gilts are appropriately short-dated and index-linked, thus providing mainly tax-free capital growth rather than income.

£145 000 is sufficient to put together an adequately diversified equity portfolio, consisting of a minimum of ten to fifteen different companies. The suggested unit trusts are overseas-orientated, and thus provide a straightforward means of including overseas diversification within the overall equity portfolio.

The gilts provide the guaranteed income and capital growth, plus some inflation-proofing. The capital value of the equity element of the portfolio will be more volatile, but over the long run equities should outperform gilts.

Scheme 2 also suffers from inadequate liquidity – an 'instant-access' or high-interest cheque-book account would be more appropriate than a one-month-notice account. The SAYE contract provides a poor return if encashed within five years. The NSB Ordinary Account is superficially attractive to a higher-rate taxpayer because the first £70 of interest per person per year is completely tax-free, but at the time of writing the fixed rate of 5 per cent is uncompetitive. There is also no mention of protection insurance with Scheme 2.

Scheme 1 would involve considerable expense in terms of front-end charges on the life assurance bonds and unit trusts. Mr X would be safer investing in a spread of management companies rather than buying them all from a single management company through a tied intermediary.

In the case of Scheme 2, it would be important to establish the type of service to be provided by the stockbroker – advisory, non-discretionary management, or discretionary management – and the tariff of charges. The performance of the portfolio might be dependent on the expertise of a single investment adviser.

As Mrs X has no earned income, tax could be saved by transferring sufficient assets into her name to use all of her own personal allowance of £3005 (1990/91), available since the introduction of independent taxation. The taxable income generated by Scheme 1 would come primarily from Treasury $13\frac{1}{2}$% 1994. A high-coupon gilt would not normally be recommended for a higher-rate taxpayer, but in this instance some of the stock could be retained in Mrs X's name to provide the income to use her personal allowance.

Other investments that could be appropriate for Mr and Mrs X are

(a) a bank or building society TESSA account,
(b) a PEP,
(c) capital shares of a split-level investment trust,
(d) chattels.

Mr X would be well-advised to consider the relative merits of his employer's pension scheme and a personal pension. Given his age and status, he would probably find that he is better off staying in the employer's scheme – particularly if it is a defined-benefit scheme. However, he could supplement his pension contributions with AVCs, if he would not otherwise draw the full pension entitlement on retirement. As a higher-rate taxpayer, Mr X would usually be advised to retain the outstanding mortgage.

On retirement, Mr and Mrs X should reconsider their portfolio, bearing in mind the change in financial circumstances. The expected retirement date will be critical in determining the required maturity date for many of the investments.

21.18 Retirement

On retirement, it often happens that persons come into possession of large sums of capital, either from pension commutation, maturing endowment policies, or from the sale of a business. This represents considerable opportunities – to move house; to extend, alter, or refurbish the existing home; to take a long holiday; and to seek out investments providing the best combination of income and capital growth.

The disadvantages of receiving a large sum of money on retirement centre around knowing what to do with it. The person concerned may worry how best to invest a sum probably larger than he or she has ever previously handled. There may be a considerable degree of ignorance of the investment alternatives and sources of investment advice. Investors may be faced with the choice between investing the money themselves, without being fully aware of the situation, or entrusting the money to an adviser with whom they have had little or no previous contact. This book is designed to overcome some of the problems of the first option. The Financial Services Act provides some protection against unscrupulous investment advisers – the fraudulent rather than the incompetent.

When deciding on how to invest a relatively large capital sum, the investor should consider matters commented upon earlier in this chapter – time-horizon, tax-efficiency, inflation, diversification, liquidity, etc. – and be aware of the level of commissions which advisers are likely to receive when recommending certain types of investment.

An investment strategy for retired persons should incorporate the following points:

(a) *Risk-aversion*   High-risk investments should generally be avoided, since there is likely to be little opportunity to rebuild lost savings.
(b) *Income*   Retired persons normally look to an investment portfolio to supplement pension income. Income can be provided directly – perhaps through a monthly income facility – or indirectly through encashment of investments.
(c) *Inflation protection*   The portfolio should be protected as far as possible from the effect of inflation. Index-linked NSCs and index-linked gilts provide guaranteed protection against inflation if held to maturity. Equities and property should more than keep pace with inflation over the longer term.
(d) *Liquidity*   There should be an adequate liquid reserve for emergencies and to smooth irregular income receipts and payments.
(e) *Efficiency*   The portfolio should take into account the implications of tax and social security. In particular, attention should be paid to inheritance tax, and the clawback of age allowance and any social security benefits.
(f) *Inheritance*   The investor should determine whether capital is to be consumed, in whole or part, before death, or whether it is intended to bequeath assets to other members of the family or other beneficiaries.

Wills should be written, to avoid the problems of dying intestate. Annuities provide the simplest means by which an investor can consume capital until death, but investors should be reminded of the diminution in the purchasing power of an immediate level annuity over an extended period of time.

(g) *Understandability*   For most ordinary personal investors there is no necessity to engage in complicated schemes to minimize tax. Generally, investments should be relatively easy to understand and not likely to cause the investor unnecessary unease. For larger portfolios, complications may arise with the use of trust funds (see chapter 22) to preserve capital and minimize inheritance tax liability.

Example   Mr C and his wife are both aged 65. Mrs C receives a retirement pension of £4000. Mr C has just retired and will receive pensions of £15 000 per annum, together with a lump sum of £30 000. In addition he has bank and building society accounts amounting to £20 000. His house is paid for, and the children are independent. He estimates that he and his wife will need a net income of approximately £400 per week. Is this feasible, without consuming capital?

Total net income required = £400×52		= 20 800.00
Using 1990/91 tax rates and allowances,		
Mr C	£	
Pensions	15 000	
less Personal allowance	3 005*	
less Married couple's allowance	1 720*	
Taxable income	10 275	
Tax = 25%×£10 275	= 2 568.75	
Income after tax		
= £15 000−£2568.75	= 12 431.25	= (12 431.25)
Mrs C		
Pensions	= 4 000.00	
less Personal allowance		
(age 65–74)	= 3 670.00	
Taxable income	= 330.00	
Tax = 25%×£330	= 82.50	
Income after tax		
= £4000−£82.50	= 3 917.50	= (3 917.50)
Income shortfall		= 4 451.25

*Because Mr C's income is in excess of £14 479, the additional age allowance reliefs available for both the personal allowance and the married couple's allowance are clawed back to the basic allowances.

Capital available for investment:

	£
Lump sum pension	= 30 000
Bank and building society accounts	= 20 000
	50 000

$$\text{Net return required} = \frac{£4451.25}{£50\,000} \times 100\%$$

$$= 8.90\%$$

$$\text{Gross equivalent required} = \frac{8.90\%}{0.75} = 11.9\%$$

It should be indicated to Mr and Mrs C that the required return is feasible initially. In 1990 such a yield could have been obtained with a portfolio consisting primarily of bank and building society accounts, and medium- to high-coupon gilt-edged securities. But over the longer term the purchasing power of the income from the portfolio will diminish because the investments cited provide no inflation protection. The problem will be even more acute if the pensions are not fully index-linked. Equities and index-linked gilts would only provide an intial gross yield of 4–5 per cent. An index-linked annuity would also have a low initial yield and would, of course, involve loss of capital, although ownership of the house would still remain intact.

21.19 Questions

1. (a) A critical factor for all portfolios should be:

   A capital gains.
   B absence of risk.
   C freedom from tax.
   D liquidity.

   (b) List six types of UK investments which will bring in a regular high annual income for the personal investor. Explain concisely the advantages and disadvantages of each of these types of investment. For each type indicate the approximate net yield currently obtainable by a UK basic-rate taxpayer and explain the income tax implications for a higher-rate taxpayer and for an investor not liable to tax.

   (CIB 4/87)

   (c) Your customer, Eric Smart, a bachelor aged 56, is a higher-rate taxpayer. He asks you for details of investments (both direct and indirect) where the income, capital gains, or sale proceeds are tax-free in the hands of the investor.

   Required:
   Prepare *two* lists of investments in tabular format as indicated below:

A Investments which are **absolutely** free of both income tax and capital gains tax.

Name/type of investment	Limit (£) (if any)
1.	
2.	
3. etc.	

B Investments with **some** limitations on freedom from tax in the hands of the personal investor.

Name/type of investment	Limit (£) (if any)	Degree of tax freedom
1.		
2.		
3. etc.		

(Under the heading 'Limit (£)' you should indicate (where appropriate) whether this limit is per month, per annum, for the fiscal year 1990/91, or for some other period. In the case of the second group (B) you should indicate also the extent of the tax benefit, e.g. 'free of CGT only'.)

(CIB 5/90)

(d) Gerald Hopkins is the principal shareholder and managing director of a local trading company. Up to this time the shares he holds in the company have been his only investment, and his salary and the dividends are his only sources of income. His marginal rate of tax is 40 per cent. After discussion, his accountant suggests to Mr Hopkins that he makes certain investments. The investments and the amounts suggested are as follows:

National Savings Certificates – the maximum amount possible;
£30 000 in Exchequer 3% Gas 1990/95 – price 76½;
Business Expansion Scheme – an amount such that he will obtain the maximum annual tax saving;
£10 000 in a Guaranteed Growth Bond – provides a net return of 11 per cent per annum compound over five years;
Japan Unit Trust – a sum which, based on a yield of 0.9 per cent, will provide a gross income of £250 per annum;
Equity Growth Bond – a sum such that he will be able to draw £1000 per annum without immediate tax consequences;
Building society paid-up share account – £5000 at a net rate of 11.5 per cent per annum (variable).
Required:

(i) Set out all the suggested investments *under three headings* in the form of a table, as follows:

Investment	Cost (£)	Cash receivable (£)

Note: (1) Investment – State nominal value also if different from actual cost.
(2) Cost (£) – Ignore dealing costs.
(3) Cash receivable (£) – State cash receivable, if any, and only for first year, based on information given above.

(ii) Which of the annual cash receipts shown in your answer to part (i) would be subject to further tax for the current year? Calculate the amount of the additional tax payable.
(iii) Do you consider any of the suggested investments unsuitable for Mr Hopkins? Give reasons for your answer.
(iv) Comment on the attractions of those suggested investments which may be suitable for Mr Hopkins but do not provide any cash receipt in the current year.

(CIB 5/88)

(e) State which of the following investments you consider would *not, in any circumstances*, be suitable for Mr C, a higher-rate taxpayer:

(i) National Savings Certificates,
(ii) unit trusts,
(iii) deferred dividend shares,
(iv) 'A' ordinary shares – yield 6 per cent gross,
(v) convertible loan stocks,
(vi) National Savings Income Bonds,
(vii) equities with low P/E ratios,
(viii) split-capital investment trust shares,
(ix) warrants,
(x) National Savings Bank,
(xi) guaranteed growth bonds.

State *with reasons* why each of the remaining investments could be suitable for Mr C.

(CIB 9/87)

2. Robert James is on the staff of a bank which elected to operate as an independent intermediary under the rules formulated under the Financial Services Act 1986. The bank obtains full particulars of each of its clients seeking investment advice under the SIB's 'know your customer' rule.

On the basis of the limited information provided and on the SIB principle of 'best advice', state, *with reasons*, which financial product(s) Robert is likely to recommend in each of the following cases:

(a) Adam Long is aged 35 and his third child was born recently. How can he set money aside on a regular basis so that a guaranteed lump sum will be payable if he dies before this child becomes eighteen?

(b) Belinda Harcourt is a single woman, aged 28. She has been working for her present employer for nine years, during which period she has contributed to SERPS. She has recently discovered that she can withdraw from the scheme under the Social Security Act 1986. Should she do so?

    Would the answer differ if Miss Harcourt were aged 50 and had been working with the same firm ever since she left school?

(c) Clive Harrison, aged 54, is a teacher in the public sector. He worked in industry until he was 39 but his only pension entitlement, apart from the basic State pension, relates to his years in teaching. Thus, if he retires at 65, he will be entitled to a pension of less than a third of his final salary. How can he improve on this?

(d) Diana Raine is a single parent aged 27 who wishes to buy a house. The mortgage required (25 years) will have to be a high multiple of her £15 000 p.a. income and must be the least expensive mortgage in terms of immediate outgoings.

(CIB 5/89)

3. Matthew and Christine Blake are a recently married couple in their mid-twenties. After university Matthew obtained a job in advertising where he made rapid progress. He now earns about £30 000 per annum as a consultant on a self-employed basis. His wife, a university lecturer, earns £15 000 per annum. She contributes 6 per cent of her salary towards a pension. The couple rent a flat in Chelsea (£950 a month) and are managing to live on Matthew's salary and save Christine's.

   Their only investment, apart from a small holding in the privatized Rolls-Royce Plc (manufacturers of civil and military aero-engines), is £12 000 in a standard building society share account. The savings are intended to provide a 'nest egg' for the purchase of their own home in five years' time.

   Required:

(a) Specify and comment upon *three* items of information which are *not* included (explicitly or implicitly) in the facts given above and which you consider necessary to know in order to give the Blakes useful general investment advice.

(b) Name *four* types of investment which would be more appropriate for their regular savings than the building society account mentioned.

(c) In a discussion with them, you ask why they continue to rent a flat when it ought to be possible to buy instead. They point out that a flat similar to the one they currently rent would cost around £100 000.

'We did ask a building society for a loan about two years ago, but they wouldn't lend as much money as we needed. We'll never be able to borrow enough the way prices are moving in London.'

(i) What financial arguments would you advance in favour of the purchase of property?
(ii) What type of mortgage do you consider most suitable for the Blakes? Give reasons for your answer.

(CIB 5/88)

4. Cuthbert and Anne Goode are a married couple, aged 74 and 72 respectively, and in good health. They live in a comfortable cottage which Anne inherited when her mother died five years ago. They have no children.

Cuthbert receives a pension of £1500 per annum from his former employer, and the Goodes receive the State pension of £75.10 per week. The greater part of their savings of £80 000 is with various building societies and the National Savings Bank. They say their income is adequate at present but they are concerned about inflation and they find frequent changes in interest rates confusing and worrying.

On the basis of the information provided above, discuss the Goodes' situation and the kinds of investment which could meet their needs.

(CIB 10/89)

22 Trusts

22.1 Introduction

A trust is a relationship between persons and assets, under which assets provided by one person – the *settlor* – are held by a group of persons – *trustees* – for the benefit of another group of persons – the *beneficiaries*. A trustee may also be a beneficiary. The various interests of the beneficiaries can be laid down in the formal document (if there is one) creating the trust, or they can be implied by trust law.

There is a similarity between the position of a trustee and that of a *personal representative* (PR) appointed to tidy up someone's affairs after his or her death. If the deceased had made a will the *executor*, or *executrix* (if a woman), will act as PR. If there is no will, the deceased is said to have died 'intestate', and the PR in this case is designated an '*administrator*'. Although technically executors and administrators may be regarded as being trustees for the beneficiaries under the will, they act in true trusteeship capacity only once probate has been granted and where a trust has been created, either expressly or implicitly, by a will or through intestacy. The PR is entitled to appoint new trustees to execute the trusts; otherwise the PR becomes a trustee in the full sense.

22.2 Creation of a trust

The principal reasons for creating a trust are as follows:

(a) To ensure the succession of property. For example, a '*life-tenant*' may be entitled to income from, or use of, assets – an 'interest-in-possession' – for a number of years, or until death, whereupon the assets pass to another beneficiary known as the '*remainderman*'.
(b) To enable the assets to be held for a person who is not capable of dealing with such assets, such as a young child or someone who is mentally handicapped. In law, land cannot be held directly by a minor, but with the creation of a trust a minor becomes the beneficial owner, with the rights of occupation or receipt of income from the land.
(c) To protect the property from spendthrifts, by setting up a 'protective' trust. As a general rule such a trust lasts for the lifetime of the benficiary unless a specified event, such as a criminal conviction, occurs which has

the effect of depriving the beneficiary of his or her automatic right to an 'interest-in-possession'. In this event, a 'discretionary' trust (discussed later) is created in favour of the beneficiary or immediate family.

(d) To make a confidential disposal of property and enable the beneficial ownership of property to be kept secret. For instance, when an executor is granted probate, the will becomes available for public inspection at the probate registry. To avoid the identity of the recipient of a gift after death becoming public knowledge, it is possible to place someone else under an obligation to make the gift – with that person's prior agreement – and that person becomes a trustee of the subject matter of the gift. This is known as a *'secret'* trust – a form of *'bare'* trust (see section 22.3.1).

(e) To make gifts which can effectively deal flexibly with a range of possible future circumstances. The trustees of a *'discretionary'* trust are given freedom of action in regard to disposal of income and capital between a 'class' of beneficiaries.

(f) To minimize the incidence of tax. Trusts are an important tool in tax planning, particularly in respect of inheritance tax.

(g) To benefit charitable objectives. Charitable trusts can be established in order to meet certain charitable objectives, specifically

- the relief of poverty,
- the advancement of religion,
- the advancement of education,
- 'any other purpose beneficial to the community'.

These four rules determining charitable status were laid down by Lord Macnaghten in 1891. Gifts to charitable trusts are completely exempted from capital gains tax and inheritance tax; the funds themselves are tax-free, and may continue into perpetuity.

Trusts are also the legal form used to create unit trusts, pension schemes, and employee share-ownership schemes.

Every trust must possess the 'three certainties' which were laid down by Lord Langdale in *Knight* v. *Knight* (1840):

(i) certainty of *intention* – the words must show clearly the intention to create a trust;

(ii) certainty of *subject matter* – the trust property must be clearly set out;

(iii) certainty of *objects* – the beneficiaries must be clearly ascertained or ascertainable.

If any one of these certainties is not fulfilled, the trust is invalid:

(a) if the trust fails under (i), the beneficiary will take possession of the assets absolutely;

(b) if failure is under (ii) or (iii), the gift lapses.

22.3 Family trusts

There are four different types of family trust, discussed below. These are 'bare', 'interest-in-possession', 'discretionary', and 'accumulation and maintenance' trusts.

A 'disposal', for capital gains tax purposes, is treated as taking place when there are transfers of assets into family trusts and when these assets are transferred out of the trust, other than on the death of a life-tenant. Only in the case of transfers into a discretionary trust can the gain be 'held over'. But, although the most flexible type of trust, a discretionary trust is the most penally treated for inheritance tax. Unlike other forms of trust, transfers into a discretionary trust are not 'potentially exempt transfers' (PETs).

22.3.1 Bare trusts

A *bare* trust is the simplest form of trust – the trustee normally holds the assets for a single beneficiary. The beneficiary must be a named and living individual, and no conditions other than age remain to be fulfilled before the individual can give a valid receipt for the trust funds. The trustee's only duty in relation to the trust is to carry out the beneficiary's instructions, and to transfer the assets to the beneficiary when so requested. Uses of a bare trust – 'nomineeship' – include secrecy, convenience, and for minors who are too young to deal with investments.

The general rule for tax purposes is that 'a bare trust is no trusteeship' – the trustee is ignored and the beneficial owner is taxed as if he or she owned the assets directly. But, provided that income is entirely accumulated during the infancy of a child, an Inland Revenue concession has been that no income tax is paid, up to a single person's allowance, irrespective of the settlor. If income is distributed, it will be aggregated with the parent's income for income tax purposes if the parent is the settlor. For capital gains tax purposes, any gains on assets within the trust are treated as belonging to the beneficiary, who is entitled to a full annual exemption. A transfer into a bare trust is a PET for inheritance tax purposes.

22.3.2 Interest-in-possession trusts

These give a beneficiary the right to claim the income of the trust fund, or to use the property comprised in it, such as the right to live in a house rent-free. Usually the beneficiary having this right will be different from the person or persons who may ultimately inherit the capital. Alternatively, it may be a provision that the beneficiary may have only the income until he or she reaches a specified age, when he or she will also receive the capital.

The income arising is taxed as the beneficiary's income. When the trustees dispose of any chargeable assets they are liable to capital gains tax at a fixed rate of 25 per cent (1990/91), subject to an annual exemption (£2500 in 1990/91). If a beneficiary becomes absolutely entitled to trust property following a life-tenant's death, no capital gains tax liability arises; if benefit passes in other circumstances, there will be a liability. The capital underlying the beneficiary's interest in possession is deemed to belong to the beneficiary, and is subject to inheritance tax on the death of the beneficiary, or if the beneficial interest ceases within seven years of death; but, if the interest of the beneficiary ceases more than seven years before that beneficiary's death, the funds transferred will be exempt from inheritance tax.

Many of these trusts are *will trusts*, where the testator has given a life interest to a surviving widow or widower, with the capital passing on the later death to children or other relatives. This may be particularly important if there are children from previous marriages. Sometimes, too, a life interest is given so as to preserve the capital of the trust for the testator's immediate family or remoter issue, while in the meantime benefiting persons to whom the testator feels an obligation.

22.3.3 Discretionary trusts
When a discretionary trust is established, it is left to the discretion of the trustees which of the possible beneficiaries will benefit from the trust assets. Appropriate trust powers may enable income to be accumulated or paid out, or enable trust capital to be advanced to any of the beneficiaries. None of the beneficiaries has any predetermined right to claim any of the income arising, and normally they will have no right to the capital either. Discretionary trusts enable assets to be held in suspense for a wide class of beneficiaries, some of whom may not yet be born. Different beneficiaries may receive benefits from the fund, but for tax purposes the fund is not treated as belonging to any of them.

If the settlor cannot benefit under the fund, or if the settlor is deceased, any income which is accumulated is taxed at a fixed rate of basic-rate plus 10 per cent – that is, 35 per cent (1990/91). Income which is distributed is taxed at the marginal income tax rate of the beneficiary, and tax can be reclaimed by non-taxpayers and basic-rate taxpayers.

Since the assets are held in suspense and cannot be taxed as belonging to any of the beneficiaries, special rules apply to capital taxes – that is, inheritance and capital gains tax. The assets of the trust are subject to inheritance tax in three separate ways. Firstly, when they are transferred into the trust – transfers are not PETs. Secondly, every ten years thereafter. Thirdly, when funds leave the trust – an 'exit' charge. Transfers into a discretionary trust are subject to the lifetime rate of IHT, which is half the normal rate applied at death – that is, 20 per cent (1990/91). The ten-year and exit charges are, however, only 15 per cent of the death scale rates – that is, 6 per cent (1990/91).

Capital gains tax is payable on a disposal of chargeable assets by the trustees, subject to an annual exemption – £2500 (1990/91). The rate of tax is fixed at 35 per cent (1990/91). When a beneficiary becomes absolutely entitled to any chargeable assets of the trust, capital gains tax is payable.

22.3.4 Accumulation and maintenance trusts
These are a special form of discretionary trust for the benefit of minor

children. They can be useful where an individual wishes to provide for his or her children or grandchildren. This type of trust can include both existing and unborn beneficiaries, and so is very flexible. It is a condition of accumulation and maintenance trusts that beneficiaries must become entitled to their share in the assets of the trust, or an interest-in-possession in them, by the age of 25. Additionally, in order to qualify, the life of the trust must be limited to 25 years, *or* all of the beneficiaries must be grandchildren of a common grandparent or, if such persons died before receiving their entitlement, their widows, widowers, or children.

Income can be accumulated for up to 21 years from the date of the settlement, under the Perpetuities and Accumulation Act 1964. If this power of accumulation runs out before a beneficiary reaches the age of 25, the beneficiary will receive any entitlement to income early. The maximum life of the trust is often 80 years, but it could be based on a 'life or lives in being' plus 21 years. Any income accumulated is taxed at basic-rate plus 10 per cent – that is, 35 per cent (1990/91).

Income can be paid out for the 'maintenance, education, or advancement' of the beneficiaries; so, for example, the trust can be used for school-fees planning. If the beneficiary is a non-taxpayer or a basic-rate taxpayer, tax can be reclaimed on distributions, but distributions will be aggregated with a parent's income for income tax purposes if a parent is the settlor.

Accumulation and maintenance trusts have important inheritance tax advantages over other discretionary trusts. Gifts to them are PETs – there is no lifetime inheritance tax charge when assets are transferred into the trust; the ten-yearly lifetime inheritance tax charge is not applicable; and there is no exit charge when a beneficiary becomes entitled to an interest-in-possession or absolute entitlement to assets. Trusts for the benefit of grandchildren are particularly advantageous, because they can exist for a longer period of time than if the trust was set up for children, and the settled assets will not be subject to inheritance tax on the death of the settlor's children. The tax treatment of capital gains within the trust is the same as for other discretionary trusts.

22.4 Duties of trustees

There are a number of duties and responsibilities imposed upon trustees, as follows:

(a) Trustees must preserve the trust's assets and, in doing so, must exercise the same care as a business person would give to his or her affairs. If trustees are paid, the expected standard is higher in accordance with their professional skills.
(b) Trustees must not profit from their position. Trustees are entitled to recover trust expenses, and the trust deed or the Court may allow remuneration for their work.
(c) Trustees must not purchase property for their own use.

(d) Trustees must keep proper accounts and other records and allow the beneficiaries to examine them.

(e) Trustees must act personally, and not delegate duties except as allowed by the trust deed, or the Trustee Act 1925.

(f) A trustee must act jointly with the co-trustees. This involves unanimous decisions, and joint cheque-signing.

(g) Trustees must act strictly in accordance with the trust deed, unless the Court has varied the terms.

(h) Trustees must pay the proper amounts, of capital and income, to the beneficiaries, and will be personally liable if funds go to the wrong person.

(i) Trustees must invest the trust funds as authorized by the trust deed or the Trustee Investments Act 1961, and hold a balance between the interests of a life-tenant and a remainderman.

(j) Trustee shall have regard to

- the suitability to the trust of the investments;
- the need for diversification;
- the need to review and reconsider the trust portfolio at regular intervals.

These requirements apply to all trustees, whatever their powers of investment, not just those governed by the Trustee Investments Act 1961 or some other statutory power.

22.5 Rights of beneficiaries

If they are all over eighteen years of age and of sound mind, the current and potential beneficiaries can unanimously bring the trust to an end, or vary its provisions, or force the trustees to deal with the trust's assets in accordance with their wishes.

Any beneficiary can procure the proper administration of the trust, or seek through the Court a remedy for a breach of trust, or, exceptionally, secure the removal of a trustee by application to the Court.

Furthermore, any beneficiary can demand information about the trust, and has the right to inspect the trust documents.

22.6 The investment powers of trustees

Powers of investment are given to trustees in two ways: by the trust instrument and by statute. The investment powers, if any, contained in the deed (or will) setting up the trust override the powers given to trustees by law. The statutory powers come into effect in cases where the trust instrument is silent or gives powers less wide than those contained in the relevant Act of Parliament, and in cases of intestacy.

In modern wills and settlements and in the trust deeds of charitable trusts and pension funds, a clause is customarily included giving the trustees the

widest powers of investment. This does not necessarily mean that the trustees
will use these powers, but it increases their flexibility of investment. The
wording of clauses varies, but most often they include a power for the
trustees to invest 'in all respects as though they were the beneficial
owners . . .' of the trust property. Such clauses are therefore commonly
known as *beneficial owner clauses*.

In older trust deeds, beneficial owner clauses are less usual. Some deeds
contain lengthy clauses specifying the type of investment that can be
purchased. Others include a power to retain the investments originally
settled, but limit any reinvestment of the proceeds of their sale. Wills often
direct that the property settled shall be sold, but give the trustees power to
postpone that sale for as long as they think fit. Some deeds and wills have
clauses authorizing the retention of, or the investment in, specific companies
– often family companies. All these clauses are known as *special powers of
investment*, and override the statutory powers.

Some trust deeds or wills authorize investment according to the law for the
time being in force, while others are completely silent on investment powers.
Then there are cases of statutory trusts in favour of dependants which arise
on an intestacy. In all these situations the statutory powers have full effect. It
is possible – though rare – for the investment powers of trustees to be limited
by clauses naming certain types of investment or certain companies which the
trustees may not invest in, notwithstanding any statutory power to the
contrary. It is also possible – though even rarer – for the powers of
investment to be limited to a specific investment or type of investment,
overriding the statutory powers in the opposite way to a beneficial owner
clause.

The statutory powers of investment are contained principally in the
Trustee Investments Act 1961.

22.7 The Trustee Investments Act 1961

Before this Act, trustees restricted to statutory powers of investment could
generally purchase only investments specified in the Trustee Act 1925 or the
Trusts (Scotland) Act 1921 – principally gilt-edged securities. The main
exception to this restriction was the Settled Land Act 1925, which gave
additional powers to trustees of settled land to purchase land and buildings,
and to invest capital moneys in carrying out certain alterations and improve-
ments to land and buildings owned.

There was a prolonged period after the passing of the Trustee Act 1925
during which prices were falling, but inflation was substantial during the
Second World War and apparently endemic thereafter. There was thus an
urgent need to give trustees powers to make realistic investments – particularly in equities – during periods of inflation. The Trustee Investments Act
1961 was passed to meet this requirement. It is significant that it was passed
not long after the reverse yield gap appeared, but the Act itself is only one of
several factors contributing to the extent of yield differentials today. The

proportion of the fund permitted to be invested in equities is limited, and the equities purchased must fulfil certain requirements. The Act also for the first time permitted investment in certain industrial debenture and unsecured loan stocks.

Trustees do not have to invoke the Act but, unless they do so, their investment powers are limited in the same way that they were before the Act was passed. Use of the investment powers granted by the Act involves the division of the trust fund initially into two equal parts: *narrower-range* investments and *wider-range* investments. In certain circumstances a third category of investment – *special-range* – may also be held.

22.8 Investments authorized by the 1961 Act

The First Schedule of the Trustee Investments Act 1961 authorizes the following investments in the narrower-range and wider-range parts of trust funds:

22.8.1 Narrower-range investments
Without advice, a trustee may hold or invest only in National Savings, with the exception of Premium Bonds, and the National Savings Bank.

With advice, a trustee may invest in

(a) other fixed-interest securities issued by the Governments of the United Kingdom or the Isle of Man, and Treasury bills;
(b) securities, the interest on which is guaranteed by the Government of the United Kingdom;
(c) fixed-interest securities issued in the United Kingdom by public authorities;
(d) fixed-interest securities issued in the United Kingdom by the Government of an overseas Commonwealth territory, or by any public or local authority within such territory, and registered in the United Kingdom;
(e) fixed-interest securities issued in the United Kingdom by the International Bank for Reconstruction and Development and the Inter-American Development Bank and registered in the United Kingdom;
(f) debentures registered in the United Kingdom and issued in the United Kingdom by a company incorporated in the United Kingdom (debentures include, for this purpose, debenture stocks, whether charged on specific assets or not, and loan stocks);
(g) stock of the Bank of Ireland;
(h) debentures issued by the Agricultural Mortgage Corporation PLC and its Scottish equivalent;
(i) loans to local authorities in the United Kingdom and certain other authorities;
(j) debentures and guaranteed and preference stocks of water boards which have paid a dividend on their ordinary shares of at least 5 per cent per annum in each of the ten years preceding the investment;

(k) building society deposit accounts (the societies must be designated under section 1 of the House Purchase and Housing Act 1959, generally referred to as having *trustee status*);
(l) mortgages of property in England, Wales, or Northern Ireland which is freehold or leasehold with sixty years or more unexpired, and loans on hereditable security in Scotland;
(m) perpetual rent-charges on land in England, Wales, or Northern Ireland, fee-farm rents issuing out of such land, and feu duties or ground annuals in Scotland.

22.8.2 Wider-range investments
With advice, a trustee may invest in:

(a) any securities issued in the United Kingdom not being narrower-range investments, by a company incorporated in the United Kingdom, and which are registered in the United Kingdom;
(b) shares in building societies of which the deposits qualify as narrower-range investments;
(c) authorized unit trusts.

Securities of companies – both shares and debentures – must meet six criteria to qualify as investments under the Act:

(a) securities must be quoted on the International Stock Exchange, or another recognized stock exchange;
(b) any shares must be fully paid, except for new issues to be paid up within nine months;
(c) the company must have a paid-up share capital of at least £1 million;
(d) the company must have paid a dividend on all clauses of share capital entitled to dividends in each of the five years preceding the investment;
(e) the company must be UK-registered;
(f) the securities must be denominated in sterling.

Two criticisms may be levelled at these criteria. The capital requirement of £1 million – adequate in 1961 – represents quite a small company today and trustees, especially professional trustees, may well set themselves a more stringent requirement. Secondly, the Act requires only that a dividend is paid in each of the last five years. Therefore a company does not lose its trustee status even if its dividend falls in five or more successive years.

While the securities must usually be registered in the United Kingdom, the Trustee Act 1925 authorizes the purchase and retention of bearer securities if the issuing body meets the requirements for authorized registered securities.

Although at first sight the list of investments may appear quite comprehensive, there are several important omissions. There is no mention of freehold or leasehold land and buildings – the most outstanding major investment by far since 1961 – nor are trustees permitted to invest without specific power in any of the many insurance-based investments. Furthermore, while the

National Savings Bank and building society deposits and share accounts are specifically mentioned, commercial bank accounts are not.

22.9 Division of the fund

22.9.1 Narrower-range and wider-range property

The Trustee Investments Act 1961 requires trustees wishing to invoke the powers contained in it to divide the trust fund into two or three parts: the narrower range; the wider range; and, if applicable, the special range. The narrower-range and wider-range parts of the fund must be equal in value at the time when the division is made, and the division, once made, is final. The original allocation of securities between the two ranges can be made in any way the trustees think fit, as long as the ranges are equal in value at that time. After the fund is divided, only investments authorized as narrower-range investments under the First Schedule to the Act may be held in the narrower-range part of the fund. Any other investments in that range must be disposed of for reinvestment in narrower-range investments. Narrower-range investments may be held in the wider-range part of the fund in addition to authorized wider-range investments. Any investment in the wider range not authorized as either a narrower-range investment or a wider-range investment must be disposed of for reinvestment in authorized investments.

Let us consider the example in Table 22.1. Three of the holdings would

Table 22.1 Division of a trust fund under the Trustee Investments Act 1961

Amount (£)	Stock		Xd	Pay	Current value (£)
25 000	Exchequer Stock 12¼% 1992		19 Jan.	25 Feb.	26 344
20 500	Treasury Stock 8½% 1994		28 Dec.	3 Feb.	19 219
2 000	Imperial Chemical Industries (£1)	α	15 Aug.	3 Oct.	24 000
500	Jones Stroud		5 Sep.	14 Oct.	1 295
1 000	Amstrad	α	17 Oct.	29 Nov.	1 725
1 000	RTZ bearer stock 10p	α	19 Sep.	14 Dec.	5 140
1 500	De la Rue	β	28 Nov.	4 Jan.	6 727
2 500	P & O (£1)	α	5 Sep.	3 Oct.	16 255
1 500	Pacific Assets warrants	γ	—	—	1 200
7 000	J. Sainsbury	α	28 Nov.	13 Jan.	16 380
5 000	Downiebrae 10p	γ	Oct. 86	—	2 125
100	Union Carbide $1		2 Feb.	1 Mar.	1 525
1 000	British Airways	α	28 Nov.	13 Jan.	1 880
250	Armstrong Equipment	β	19 Sep.	18 Nov.	371
3 000	Barclays Unicorn American unit trust				2 366
4 000	Legal and General Gilt unit trust				3 345
10 000	Halifax Building Society Share Account				10 000

have to be sold under the Trustee Investments Act 1961. These are:

(a) Pacific Assets warrants. Strictly speaking, warrants are not outlawed by the 1961 Act, but in the cases of Power (1947) and Peczenik (1964) it was established that an 'investment' means an income-producing asset.
(b) Downiebrae, because the company has not paid a dividend in each of the last five years.
(c) Union Carbide, because it is not a UK-registered company, and its shares are not denominated in sterling.

While not strictly allowable under the 1961 Act, the bearer stock of RTZ could be retained under the Trustee Act 1925, since RTZ's registered stocks meet the requirements of section 7 of the Act (see section 22.12).

The two narrower-range investments are the Exchequer Stock $12\frac{1}{4}\%$ 1992 and the Treasury Stock $8\frac{1}{2}\%$ 1994. The Pacific Asset warrants, Downiebrae, and Union Carbide securities could also be initially allocated to the narrower range. Altogether they would have a total value of £50 413. The remaining investments would have a value of £89 454. In order initially to equalize the narrower- and wider-range parts of the fund, £19 521 of wider-range securities must be transferred to the narrower-range. Unless there are special powers of investment to retain or postpone sales, the three ineligible investments, with a valuation of £4850, and the excess wider-range investments, with a valuation of £19 521, must be sold as soon as possible. The proceeds should be invested in further narrower-range investments.

22.9.2 Special-range property

The trust instrument may give no general powers but it may give the trustees specific power to retain or acquire investments that would not be allowed under the Act, such as unquoted shares. Any such investments must be allocated to the special-range part of the fund. Sometimes the trust deed specifies investment in certain assets which do not come within the Act. If they come within the definition of narrower-range investment, they can be included either in the narrower-range or the wider-range part of the fund; but any investment coming within the definition of wider-range investment must, notwithstanding, be placed in the special-range part of the fund.

If a special power to invest is contained in the trust instrument, the proceeds of either narrower-range or wider-range investments may be used to buy investments authorized by that special power, and the investments so purchased will be transferred to the special-range part of the fund. This would immediately make the narrower and wider ranges of the fund unequal, but no compensating transfer is required. When special-range investments are sold, the proceeds may be used to purchase other special-range investments if a power to do so exists in the trust instrument. Otherwise the proceeds must be divided equally between the narrower- and wider-range parts of the fund for investment accordingly.

22.10 Transfers, additions, and withdrawals

Once a trust fund has been divided, transfers from the narrower range to the wider range can be made only by making compensating transfers of equal amounts from the wider range to the narrower range, and vice versa.

If any investments are added to the fund, they must be divided in the same way as if they comprised the fund at the date of the division. Thus if the settlor were to add equities to the value of £10 000, this would involve a compensating transfer of £5000 from the wider-range to the narrower-range part of the fund. Any additions such as a bonus issue or a rights issue will accrue to that part of the fund that includes the underlying holding. Any capital moneys that need to be paid out of the fund may be taken from any part of it and no compensating transfer will be necessary.

22.11 Expert advice

Apart from the few narrower-range investments which can be purchased or retained without advice, all investments coming within the ambit of the Trustee Investments Act require the attention of an 'expert'. An investment expert is defined in the Act as one 'who is reasonably believed by the trustee to be qualified by his ability in and practical experience of financial matters'. This is almost unbelievably vague in a statute, and it has been said that the investment expert should be 'something of an actuary, an accountant, an economist, a stockbroker, a man of affairs. . . . Above all he must have the ability to make up his mind quickly on the merits and demerits of an investment, then to act quickly'. The requirement to obtain advice always applies. If the sole trustee is a stockbroker/dealer or a trust corporation, the advice can be given by an employee of that person or corporation. The expert must be made fully aware of the objects of the trust and must make or confirm his or her recommendations in writing.

Trustees who make an investment without seeking appropriate advice must make good any loss arising from it, even if they make a profit on all the other investments. They will therefore ignore expert advice at their peril. Trustees in doubt as to their powers should consult the Act itself and take legal advice if necessary.

22.12 The Trustee Act 1925

The Trustee Investments Act 1961 repealed section 1 of the Trustee Act 1925 entirely, as well as portions of sections 2 and 5. Certain important statutory powers of investment given to trustees by the 1925 Act remain in force, however. Section 7 authorizes the purchase and retention of bearer securities, providing that the company also has registered securities which are authorized investments. Sections 8, 9, and 10 of the Trustee Act 1925 contain powers and duties of trustees in lending money on mortgages in exercise of the power contained in the Trustee Investments Act. They provide, among other things, that no more than two-thirds of the value placed on a property by an independent valuer ought to be advanced by a trustee, and that, if a property owned by the trust is being sold, two-thirds of the proceeds may be left on a mortgage of the property without an independent valuation being made. Like the Trustee Investments Act 1961, the 1925 Act is highly complex, and a trustee wishing to invest in a mortgage ought to be legally advised as to his or her powers.

Section 10 of the 1925 Act also concerns powers relating to stock and share investments. Section 10(3) authorizes trustees to concur in any scheme or arrangement for the reconstruction, amalgamation or take-over of a company in which the trust holds authorized investments and for the release or modification of any rights attaching to any authorized securities held. Section 10(4) authorizes trustees to exercise any conditional or preferential right to subscribe for any securities which may be offered to them by reason of the trust having any authorized holding. Any proceeds of sale of any such right accrue to the capital of the trust. Retention of securities received under this clause was specifically authorized by an amendment contained in the 1961 Act.

Section 11 permits trustees to pay any trust funds into a bank account while awaiting investment, and the interest earned is applied as income.

22.13 Investment policy of trustees

During the passage of the Trustee Investments Act 1961 through Parliament, it was described as 'nearly as incomprehensible to a layman as an Act of Parliament can be'. The need to maintain the division of funds certainly makes it complex to administer, and it is highly desirable that, where at all possible, trustees are given the widest possible powers.

Despite the insistence in the Act on maintaining the division of trust assets, once the division has taken place the two funds invariably cease to have the same value because (among other reasons):

(a) market forces affect fixed-interest stocks and equities differently;
(b) if there are special powers to invest, then either of the two statutory funds can be used;
(c) payments to beneficiaries or expenses can be made from any part of the fund without compensating transfers.

The great majority of modern wills and trust deeds incorporate beneficial owner powers which make the complex and cumbersome procedures and anomalies of the 1961 Act appear increasingly irrelevant.

A further problem is that the interests of the persons entitled to the trust assets may conflict, and in his or her investment policy the trustee must give consideration to the interests of all the parties concerned.

The choice of investments and the interests of the beneficiaries of the trust will vary considerably, depending on the nature of the trust and the persons entitled to benefit. The circumstances of a large pension fund or charitable trust are clearly different from those of a small family trust; the investment policies to be followed by each will also differ.

For example, in the case of an interest-in-possession trust, the trustee may have a duty to balance the interest of the *life-tenant*, entitled to the income of the trust for life, against that of the *remaindermen*, entitled to the capital of the trust on the death of the life-tenant. Clearly the remaindermen wish to see the capital of the trust grow as much as possible, which might require a total commitment to equities. However, the life-tenant may wish to see the maximum income return from the trust's investments. Although equities should show a growing income over the medium term, it is often difficult to persuade a life-tenant to accept willingly a medium-term policy, especially where he or she needs a reasonably high income to maintain his or her standard of living. The life-tenant may not live to enjoy a reasonable return from the fund if a policy devoted to growth is vigorously pursued. The policy to follow in these cases is a compromise. The funds available should be invested in such a way as to produce a moderate income coupled with prospects of maintaining the 'real' value of the fund over the medium to long term. This could be achieved by investing part of the fund in fixed-interest stocks offering a high yield, and the balance in growth equities or, in the case of smaller estates, unit trusts.

The same conflict between income and capital growth may arise if a trust is established to prevent children squandering capital. Their interest may for a specified number of years be restricted to the income, so that the capital is preserved for their later benefit.

22.14 Questions

1. (a) A man dies leaving the bulk of his estate in trust for the benefit of his widow and after her death to their children absolutely. The widow is technically known as the 'life-tenant'. What collective term is used to define the children of the deceased?

   (b) Many companies regard it as important that their quoted securities maintain 'trustee status'. Which Act of Parliament defines 'trustee status'?

   A Trustee Act 1925.
   B Trustee Investments Act 1961.
   C Financial Services Act 1986.
   D Companies Act 1985.

   (c) Which of the following could be held in either the narrower-range or the wider-range of a trust fund subject to the Trustee Investments Act 1961?

   A Building society share account.
   B Preference shares.
   C Convertible loan stocks.
   D Units in an authorized gilt-edged unit trust.

(d) Which (one or more) of the following investments requires advice under the Trustee Investments Act 1961: National Savings Certificates, building society shares, gilts, deposits with the National Savings Bank?

(e) What investments, apart from company securities, satisfy the requirements of the Trustee Investments Act 1961 as wider-range investments?

(f) Name four conditions that must be satisfied by company shares and debentures to be acceptable as trustee investments under the Trustee Investment Act 1961.   (SIE)

(g) Under the rules determining charitable status laid down by Lord Macnaghten in 1891, charities can be approved for various purposes. Name these purposes.

2. The assets of a settlement set up exactly four years ago for a grandchild of the settlor now consist of £40 000 cash following the repayment of a British Government stock. Under the terms of the settlement, income may be applied by the trustees for the maintenance, education, and benefit of the beneficiary but, subject to this provision, is to be accumulated. The trust will terminate when the grandchild attains age eighteen in May 2004. The trustees are restricted to investments authorized by law.

Required:

(a) What is the tax position in respect of income arising from the trust?

(b) If the original fund had amounted to £28 000, calculate the annual compound rate of growth over the past four years.

(c) Indicate the investment policy you would recommend to the trustees, and suggest the types of investment which would be appropriate.

(CIB 5/88)

3. Edna Collins, the life-tenant of a will trust, is a widow aged 63, the remaindermen being her children, Bill aged 36 and Carol aged 32. Bill is married with two children and Carol is unmarried. The trustees are restricted to investments authorized by law, with power to retain any investments held by the testator at the date of his death. The portfolio consists of the following securities:

Narrower range		Price £	Value £	Gross redemption yield %
£10 000	Treasury 10% 1994	98⅜	9 862	10.30
£12 000	Treasury 10% 2001	100⁵⁄₁₆	12 037	9.95
£11 500	Treasury 2% Index-linked 2001	128⁵⁄₁₆	14 756	3.57*

*(The real gross redemption yield based on an assumed inflation rate of 5% p.a.)

		Price	Value	Gross redemption yield
			£	%
Wider range				
2 500	Sainsbury J.	267p	6 675	2.5
1 000	Kingfisher	342p	3 420	4.1
1 500	ICI	1253p	18 795	5.3
5 000	Lloyds Bank	349p	17 450	6.4
5 000	Tesco	192p	9 600	2.4
1 000	Thorn EMI	792p	7 920	4.5
Special range				
400	Guinness	527p	2 108	2.9
1 000	Wyjes	100p	1 000	7.1

N.B. Wyjes Plc is an unquoted company. The valuation of 100p is based on a recent deal under Stock Exchange Rule 535(2).

Required:

(a) On what matters must the trustees obtain advice under the Trustee Investments Act 1961?

(b) State briefly, with reasons, any changes you would suggest in the *structure* of the portfolio. (Do not discuss individual shares.)

(c) Within the limitations of the Act, how could the trustees:

 (i) increase the equity content of the portfolio?

 (ii) introduce an overseas element into the portfolio?

(d) In the case of the Guinness holding, assume that the company makes a one-for-five rights issue at 410p. Explain the various effects this could have on the structure of the portfolio. (N.B. No calculations are required.)

(CIB 5/90)

4. The life-tenant of a will trust is a widow, aged 63, the remaindermen being her two children, aged 31 and 33 respectively. The portfolio consists of the following securities:

		Price	Value	Gross income	Yield
			£	£	%
Narrower range					
£20 000	Exchequer 10½% 1997	101½	20 300	2100	10.34
£15 000	Conversion 9¾% 2001	97¾	14 662	1462	9.97
£10 000	Treasury 10% 2003	99¼	9 925	1000	10.08
Wider range					
400	Barclays Bank (£1)	535	2 140	105	4.91
900	J. Sainsbury (25p)	440	3 960	71	1.79

2 000	Hill Samuel Group (25p)	580	11 600	429	3.70
500	British Telecom (25p)	219	1 095	52	4.75
1 800	Tesco (5p)	439	7 902	150	1.90
2 000	British Petroleum (25p)	768	15 360	952	6.20

Special range

500	George Wimpey (25p)	209	1 045	26	2.49
1 000	Cadbury Schweppes (25p)	215	2 150	84	3.91
			£90 139	£6 431	

(a) Suggest reasons for the establishment of the Special Range part of the fund.

(b) How could the trustees increase the 'equity' content of the portfolio within the limitations imposed by the Trustee Investments Act 1961?

(c) Is there any way the trustees could introduce a property element into the portfolio?

(d) Barclays Bank announces a rights issue of one new 25p share at 228p for every five existing shares. Suggest two ways, using the existing portfolio, in which the moneys could be provided to take up the rights issue.

(e) George Wimpey announces a 'bonus' issue of one new share for every three now held. What action should the trustees take?

(f) Cash of £20 000 is added to the trust fund following the termination of a reversionary interest. How should the trustees deal with this cash?

(g) From which parts of the fund could moneys be provided to raise cash to build up a working balance on capital account?

(h) State briefly what changes you would like to see made to the *structure* of the portfolio.

(CIB 9/87)

23 The successful investor

23.1 A sensible approach

Success in investment can never be guaranteed: too many factors lying outside the investor's control can influence the value of his or her investment. Inflation is one of these; yet it is essential that every investor has part of his or her capital in a cash investment which, by definition, is not inflation-proof. Because market forces can bring down the price of ordinary shares in the short term, even while inflation is rampant, to depend on ordinary shares for additional cash in emergencies is foolhardy.

But the investor can be relatively successful if he or she sets out with a sensible approach, and if he or she is prepared to spend some time and trouble on the selection of investments and the taking of decisions concerning existing holdings. A summary of the requirements for a successful investment policy might be as follows:

(a) *Suitability* Every investment, of whatever type, must be *suitable* for the investor and for inclusion in the investment portfolio. This presupposes that each investor is aware of the nature of a proposed investment, as only then can suitability be judged. Strangely enough, whereas hardly anyone buys an overcoat for protection against the weather without trying it on to see if it fits, many people buy an investment to protect them against inflation without the slightest idea whether it fits their requirements or not.

(b) *Crisis-proofing* An investment portfolio should be free from the effects of *personal crises*. No foreseeable situation should ever cause the sale of an investment at a loss. Before setting out on a policy of investment in risk situations – and every ordinary share involves a risk – there should be enough provision for unforeseen circumstances. Thus the investor should have guarantees against loss of income through sickness or accident and also life assurance cover to protect his or her dependants and to meet inheritance tax liabilities. And he or she needs cash investments so that the need for a new car or household appliance, redundancy, or unemployment does not cause financial embarrassment.

(c) *Diversification* An investment portfolio needs to be *diversified*. Concentration of interest can, of course, produce greater profits. Obviously having all one's capital in the company which is going to be the best market performer over the coming year will yield maximum profits. So will putting all one's possessions at long odds on the horse that is going to win the next race. Diversification will never make millionaires out of most people, but it does help them to sleep at night.

(d) *Flexibility*   The investment portfolio must be *flexible*. This means that holdings must generally be readily realizable, and the investor must be prepared to dispose of any holding if necessary. Holdings where he or she is 'locked-in' for any reason should be avoided.

(e) *Timing*   The greatest art in investment is probably *timing*. Few investors know, except on rare occasions, just when to buy and when to sell individual equities, let alone when to back the market as a whole. The stockbroker/dealers BZW, for example, showed that between 1946 and 1981 £1000 invested in a building society would have grown steadily with net income reinvested to £4677 and the same sum in equities would have amassed £16 480, but that a theoretical 'best performance' fund, in which every year the correct choice was made, would have grown to nearly £218 000!

(f) *A balanced view*   The most inhibiting factor in the making of investment decisions is taxation. A successful investor will try to take a balanced view of the taxation and investment merits of a decision. If it is right to sell a share because it is overpriced, then the fact that capital gains tax is payable on a profit should not prevent the sale. A profit after tax is still a profit.

A balanced view should also be taken generally. The successful investor sees fashion trends for what they are and refuses to follow the herd, willy-nilly, or to let the enthusiasm of others outweigh his or her own judgement. He or she is not to be persuaded by salespeople or advertisements to enter into a scheme which is not exactly what is required. He or she realizes that no one is *always* right. And above all he or she knows that there is no guaranteed road to fortune.

23.2 Conclusion

To end this book on a reflective note, there are three facts which you, as an investor, should never forget:

(a) A free market requires a balance of buyers and sellers. Therefore every time someone sells a holding of ordinary shares because he or she thinks the price is too high, someone else is buying those same shares believing them to be cheap.

(b) The vast majority of investment decisions which result in purchases or sales on the market are made by professional investment managers and advisers. Therefore every time a professional investment manager sells a holding, the chances are that another professional is buying those same shares.

(c) Anyone who had the key to a fortune would not be advising others for a living. And that applies not only to investment managers and advisers, but also to authors of books on investment!

23.3 Questions

1. (a) Which of the following companies is most highly geared?

	Issued capital	Reserves	Preference shares	Loan stock
A	50	50	50	50
B	100	100	50	75
C	400	100	100	300
D	500	900	200	700

(b) Which of these is not true about unit trusts?

   A Units reflect the value of the underlying investments.
   B Unit trusts are allowed to have gearing.
   C Unit trusts have the legal status of trusts.
   D Unit trusts are predominantly held by individuals.

(c) Form Y on a provisional allotment letter needs to be completed by:

   A the seller of rights.
   B the buyer of rights.
   C neither of them.
   D both of them.

(d) Define each of the following: (i) interest yield, (ii) gross redemption yield, (iii) net asset value per share, (iv) 'nil-paid' shares.
(e) Explain what are: (i) 'index' or 'tracker' funds; (ii) beta coefficients.
(f) In respect of the investment powers of trustees, what are meant by: (i) beneficial owner clauses; (ii) special powers of investment?

2. The issued capital of a previously unquoted public limited company consists of 4 million fully paid ordinary shares of 25p each. Three million new 25p ordinary shares are being offered for sale by tender at a minimum tender price of 125p per share. This will increase the issued capital of the company to £1.75 million. The proceeds of the offer for sale will be used to provide additional working capital and to finance expansion. Application is being made for a Stock Exchange quotation. The following figures have been extracted from the prospectus:

Year ended 31 August	1988 £000s	1989 £000s	1990 £000s
Issued capital	1 000	1 000	1 000
Sales	17 000	21 000	22 500
Profit before tax	1 110	2 050	2 650
Profit after tax	720	1 330	1 720
Net tangible assets	1 800	3 000	4 580
Net dividend	120	130	140
Reserves	800	2 000	3 580

On the assumption that the offer for sale is fully subscribed at the minimum tender price of 125p, the directors forecast that the profits before tax for the year ending 31 August 1991 will be not less than £4.65 million, and they expect to recommend a dividend of 5.5p per share on the increased capital.

Show how an investor who wishes to make an application for some of the shares could assess the recent performance and future prospects of the company, and how he could decide upon a reasonable price to tender.

What general conclusions might he or she draw about the company's performance? Your answer should be supported by calculations based upon the information provided.

Note: Assume that the applicable rate of corporation tax is 35 per cent, advance corporation tax is $\frac{25}{75}$ths, and basic-rate income tax is 25 per cent. Ignore the expenses of the share issue.

(CIB 9/84)

3. Jane Seymour, a single woman of 33, earns £20 000 p.a. as a graphic designer. Her employers do not yet provide any pension scheme. She has approximately £15 000 in savings and indirect investments. She informs you that she has become increasingly attracted to the idea of ethical investment. She says she is definitely against investing in alcohol and tobacco and in companies operating in countries whose Governments she disapproves of, but is keen to invest in companies whose policies she finds attractive for ethical reasons. She adds that 'One of the problems is that, except in a few obvious cases like Guinness and Rolls-Royce, it is difficult to know from a company's name what its business really is.'

She also expresses an interest in, and apparently some awareness of, three of the newer forms of investment – index funds, National Savings Capital Bonds, and deposit-based personal pensions.

Required:

(a) *List* further matters that concern, and interest, ethical investors. Explain to Miss Seymour what investment vehicles are available to ethical investors.

(b) *List* the main attributes of *two* of the newer forms of investment mentioned by Miss Seymour and in each case state, with reasons, whether they would be suitable for her.

(CIB 5/90)

4. You have been asked by your banking colleague to visit his office to interview four customers about their investment problems. Background information about each of the four customers is as follows:

(a) Customer A is a farmer, a widower aged 66 in good health, who has handed his business over to his two sons. He lives in a cottage, which he owns, and receives the State pension of £46.90 per week (before tax). He has £175 000 in various building society higher interest accounts. He requires a spending income of £200 per week and wishes to keep his tax liabilities to a minimum.

(b) Mr and Mrs B, aged 45 and 42 years respectively, are trustees of Mr B's late mother's estate. The following investments have been settled under her will in trust for their daughter, who is fifteen years of age and will inherit the capital when she attains 21. The will contains wide powers of investment and power to retain existing investments. Mr and Mrs B need your advice on the suitability of the following investments and whether any changes should be made:

	Price	Gross income yield %
£5000 Exchequer 3% Gas 1990–95	76½	3.92
1000 British Telecom 25p shares	291½	5.5
2000 TSB Group shares (50p paid)	144½	5.4
5000 Marks & Spencer 25p shares	227½	3.8
5000 J. Sainsbury 25p shares	287½	2.8
£2000 capital in cash		

(c) Customer C and his wife are both aged 60. He has just retired and has received a lump sum of £50 000 plus an index-linked pension of £15 000 per annum before tax. His house is paid for and both children are independent. He has bank accounts with balances totalling £5500. He requires an income of £300 per week (after tax). He wishes you to prepare a scheme showing types of investment and expected annual income, for discussion at the meeting. He wants you to manage the investments for him and would like an indication of the annual costs.

(d) Customer D is a widow aged 77 with her own house worth £70 000. She receives pensions of £46.90 per week before tax. She has no relatives and intends to leave her estate to a charity. She has £2000 on deposit with the bank. She wishes to increase her income. She is not anxious to move if this can be avoided.

Required:

In anticipation of your visit to your colleague's office, prepare detailed notes showing the courses of action that you propose for each of the four customers. Give reasons for your proposals, and indicate any further information that you may need to ascertain.

(CIB 4/87)

Appendix 1
Selected further reading

Books

- Williams S., and Willman, J., *Lloyds Bank Tax Guide* (Penguin, annually)
- Homer, A., and Burrows, R., *Tolley's Tax Guide* (Tolley Publishing, annually)
- Sinclair, W. I., *Allied Dunbar Tax Guide* (Longman, annually)
- *The Investment Trust Yearbook* (FT Business Publishing, annually)
- *The Unit Trust Yearbook* (FT Business Publishing, annually)
- *The Hambro Company Guide* (Hambro Publishing)
- Holmes, G., and Sugden, A., *Interpreting Company Reports and Accounts* (Woodhead-Faulkner, 4th edn, 1990)
- *Extel Cards – A User's Guide* (Extel Financial Services Ltd)
- Lorie, J. H., Dodd, P., and Kimpton, M. H., *The Stock Market: Theories and Evidence* (Irwin, 2nd edn, 1985)
- Malkiel, B., *A Random Walk down Wall Street* (Norton, 5th edn, 1990)

Magazines, journals, and newspapers

The *Financial Times* and the business pages of *The Times*, the *Daily Telegraph*, the *Independent*, and the *Guardian* contain much that is of interest to the student of investment. Articles concerning the personal investor generally appear on a Saturday. The business sections of the 'quality' Sunday papers, include similar material. More specialized publications include the weekly journals *The Economist* and *Investors' Chronicle*; the monthly *Money Management*, *Planned Savings* and *What Investment?*; and the quarterly *Money Which?*

There are also regular investment articles in *Banking World*, and in the accountancy journals – particularly *Accountancy*. Television and radio programmes concerned with money matters are broadcast regularly – for example, the excellent 'Money Box' on Radio 4, 'Business Daily' on Channel 4, and 'The Money Programme' on BBC2. British Telecom's viewdata system, Prestel, supplies answers to innumerable questions on financial and business affairs. The teletext services, ORACLE (ITV) and CEEFAX (BBC), also cover news bulletins, financial reports, and topical information.

Appendix 2
Some useful addresses and telephone numbers

Investor protection

- **The Securities and Investments Board [SIB]**
  3 Royal Exchange Buildings
  London EC3V 3NL

  Tel. 071–283 2474
  Register enquiries 071–929 3652
  Complaints unit 071–283 2474

- **The Securities Association [TSA]**
  The International Stock Exchange
  Old Broad Street
  London EC2N 1HP

  Tel. 071–256 9000
  Complaints and Conciliation Bureau – same telephone number

- **Association of Futures Brokers and Dealers [AFBD]**
  B Section, 5th floor
  Plantation House
  5–8 Mincing Lane
  London EC3M 3DX

  Tel. 071–626 9763

- **Financial Intermediaries, Managers and Brokers Regulatory Association [FIMBRA]**
  Hertsmere House
  Hertsmere Road
  London E14 4AB

  Tel. 071–538 8860

- **The Investment Management Regulatory Organization** [IMRO]
  Broadwalk House
  5 Appold Street
  London EC2A 2LL

  Tel. 071–628 6022

- **The Office of the Investment Referee** [FIMBRA, IMRO]
  6 Frederick's Place
  London EC2R 8BT

  Tel. 071–796 3065

- **The Life Assurance and Unit Trust Regulatory Organization** [LAUTRO]
  Centre Point
  103 New Oxford Street
  London WC1A 1QH

  Tel. 071–379 0444

- **Office of Banking Ombudsman**
  Citadel House
  5–11 Fetter Lane
  London EC4A 1BR

  Tel. 071–583 1395

- **Building Society Ombudsman**
  Grosvenor Gardens House
  35–37 Grosvenor Gardens
  London SW1X 7AW

  Tel. 071–931 0044

- **Insurance Ombudsman Bureau/Unit Trust Ombudsman**
  31 Southampton Row
  London WC1B 5HJ

  Tel. 071–242 8613

- **Personal Insurance Arbitration Service** [PIAS]
  75 Cannon Street
  London EC4N 5BH

  Tel. 071–236 8761

- **Insurance Brokers' Registration Council**
  13 St Helens Place
  London EC3A 6DS

  Tel. 071–588 4387

- **Panel on Take-overs and Mergers**
  20th floor
  Stock Exchange Building
  PO Box 226
  London EC2P 2JX

  Tel. 071–382 9026

National Savings

- Freephone Hotline 0800 868700

Shares

- **Investor Research and Education**
  The International Stock Exchange
  Old Broad Street
  London EC2N 1HP

  Tel. 071–588 2355 ext. 29050

'No frills' dealing services:

- **Sharelink Ltd**
  PO Box 1063
  Birmingham B3 3ET

  Tel. 021–200 2242

- **Barclayshare Centre**
  PO Box 205
  Watford WD1 1BP

  Tel. 0923 51212

Building societies

- **Building Society Association**
  3 Savile Row
  London W1X 1AF

  Tel. 071–437 0655

Unit trusts

- **The Unit Trust Association**
  65 Kingsway
  London WC2B 6TD

  Tel. 071–831 0898

Investment trusts

- **The Association of Investment Trusts**
  Park House
  6th floor
  16 Finsbury Circus
  London EC2M 7JJ

  Tel. 071–588 5347

Ethical investments

- **The Ethical Investment Research Information Service [EIRIS]**
  401 Bondway Business Centre
  71 Bondway
  London SW8 1SQ

  Tel. 071–735 1351

Purchase and sale of secondhand life assurance policies

- **Foster and Cranfield**
  20 Britton Street
  London EC1M 5NQ

  Tel. 071–608 1941

- **Policy Network**
  68 Chandos Place
  London WC2N 4HG

  Tel. 071–929 2971

- **Beale Dobie**
  3 The Friars
  Friars Lane
  Moldon
  Essex CM9 6AG

  Tel. 0621 851133

- **Policy Portfolio**
  Wellington House
  270 Watford Way
  London NW4 4UJ

  Tel. 081–203 7221

Pensions/retirement

- **Age Concern**
  Astral House
  1268 London Road
  London SW16 4EJ

  Tel. 081–679 8000

- **Information on State pensions**
  Freephone Social Security 0800 666555

- **Occupational Pensions Advisory Service [OPAS]**
  8A Bloomsbury Square
  London WC1A 2LP

  Tel. 071–831 5511

RPI figures

- Department of Employment, Tel. 0923 815 377

Appendix 3
Retail Prices Index figures

79.4	Mar 1982	90.1	Sep
81.0	Apr	90.7	Oct
81.6	May	91.0	Nov
81.9	Jun	90.9	Dec
81.9	Jul	91.2	Jan 1985
81.9	Aug	91.9	Feb
81.9	Sep	92.8	Mar
82.3	Oct	94.8	Apr
82.7	Nov	95.2	May
82.5	Dec	95.4	Jun
82.6	Jan 1983	95.2	Jul
83.0	Feb	95.5	Aug
83.1	Mar	95.4	Sep
84.3	Apr	95.6	Oct
84.6	May	95.9	Nov
84.8	Jun	96.0	Dec
85.3	Jul	96.2	Jan 1986
85.7	Aug	96.6	Feb
86.1	Sep	96.7	Mar
86.4	Oct	97.7	Apr
86.7	Nov	97.8	May
86.9	Dec	97.8	Jun
86.8	Jan 1984	97.5	Jul
87.2	Feb	97.8	Aug
87.5	Mar	98.3	Sep
88.6	Apr	98.5	Oct
89.0	May	99.3	Nov
89.2	Jun	99.6	Dec
89.1	Jul	100.0	Jan 1987
89.9	Aug	100.4	Feb

100.6	Mar	111.0	Jan 1989
101.8	Apr	111.8	Feb
101.9	May	112.3	Mar
101.9	Jun	114.3	Apr
101.8	Jul	115.0	May
102.1	Aug	115.4	Jun
102.4	Sep	115.5	Jul
102.9	Oct	115.8	Aug
103.4	Nov	116.6	Sep
103.3	Dec	117.5	Oct
103.3	Jan 1988	118.5	Nov
103.7	Feb	118.8	Dec
104.1	Mar	119.5	Jan 1990
105.8	Apr	120.2	Feb
106.2	May	121.4	Mar
106.6	Jun	125.1	Apr
106.7	Jul	126.2	May
107.9	Aug	126.7	Jun
108.4	Sep	126.8	Jul
109.5	Oct	128.1	Aug
110.0	Nov	129.3	Sep
110.3	Dec	130.3	Oct

Index